The Psychedelic Safety Wheel

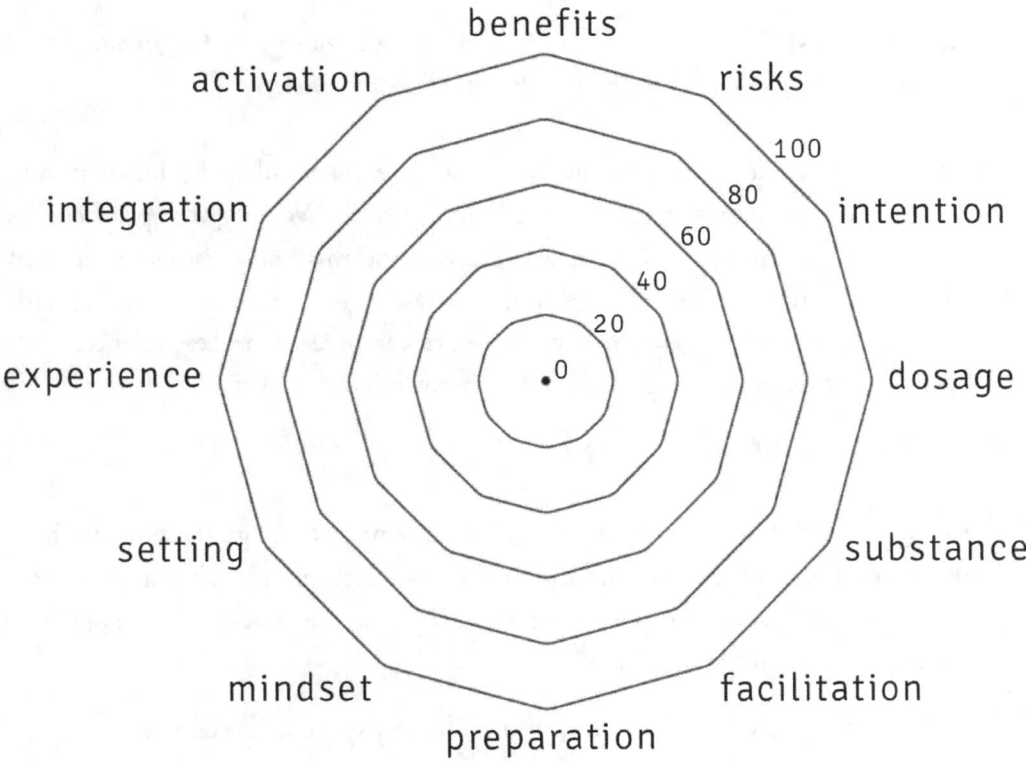

Praise

"*Healing with Psychedelics* provides invaluable guidance for the experiencer about the choices they can make during preparation, the psychedelic session itself, and the integration period. This is the first book I've seen that is totally dedicated to educating and empowering the psychedelic consumer, and is a must-read for anyone who contemplates embarking on the psychedelic journey."

—Kylea Taylor, LMFT, founder of InnerEthics® and author of *Peer Consultation Groups and Ethical Awareness Tools for Psychedelic Practitioners*

"After decades of pushing to achieve more, to be a more impactful leader, husband, and father, years of compounding stress took a toll on my health. Working with psychedelics transformed how I approached healing and growth, and this book distills so much of what I learned during that time into one invaluable resource. It offers exactly what I wish I had known at the start of my journey: grounded research, real-world experience, and a step-by-step approach to healing, all shared with raw honesty and care."

—Derek Weber, entrepreneur and seeker

"In *Healing with Psychedelics*, Gv Freeman offers an empowering guide to using these remarkable tools as both entheogens and medicines. His seamless integration of tradition, research, and personal experience creates a healing framework that deeply honors both the seeker and the medicine."

—Matt Zemon, MSc, educator, author, and leader in psychedelic wellness

"*Healing with Psychedelics* is a thoughtful and comprehensive guide for anyone seeking deeper transformation through these powerful tools. Gv Freeman masterfully combines science, personal insight, and ancient wisdom to create a grounded approach to healing. This book not only emphasizes safety and integrity, but also invites readers into a more relational and intentional way of working with psychedelics. It's a must-read for anyone ready to explore the profound potential of these substances with courage and care."

—Ashley Carmen, LMFT, psychedelic psychotherapist, founder of Psychedelic Guide Network, and mentor to licensed providers

"*Healing with Psychedelics* is the essential guide I wish I had had before I embarked on my first psychedelic retreat in Mexico. As a primary care nurse practitioner, my top priority is safety, and this book fills a critical gap in preparing individuals for these transformative experiences. This book provides thoughtful, individualized insights, offering the knowledge and tools necessary to make informed decisions. For patients exploring alternative methods for enhancing mental health and wellness, *Healing with Psychedelics* empowers readers to approach their journey with clarity, understanding, and confidence, ensuring safety and meaningful growth. This book is a must-have for anyone considering or supporting others in psychedelic healing."

—Andy Gucciardo, NP, AGPCNP-BCE, primary care nurse practitioner,
    and seeker

"I highly recommend this book! It's holistic, actionable, and realistic; offers a grounded, no-nonsense, deeply insightful framework for using psychedelics; and fuses Indigenous wisdom, scientific research, and lived experience in practical ways, so that people whose deepest desire is to take personal responsibility for their healing can do so. A touchstone for our age!"

—Bill Protzmann, founder of Musimorphic™, psychedelic preparation
    and integration coach

"*Healing with Psychedelics* is a compass for those brave enough to navigate the uncharted territories of the self. Gv Freeman lifts readers out of their cognitive Kansas and into the boundless realms of possibility, offering not just a map but a philosophy. Drawing on ancient wisdom and modern insight, he reminds us of a truth the Stoics knew well: it is not external events but our perception of them that shapes reality. Psychedelics, Freeman argues, are tools for unearthing this deeper truth—for shattering illusions, tempering the soul, and aligning with what truly matters. This book is a call to courage: to embrace discomfort, confront chaos, and emerge, like the sage, with clarity and purpose. For anyone ready to dismantle the ordinary and rebuild the extraordinary, *Healing with Psychedelics* is the guide you've been waiting for."

—George Monty, host of the podcast TrueLife

Healing
WITH
Psychedelics

A STEP-BY-STEP HANDBOOK TO
SAFE & SUSTAINABLE TRANSFORMATION

GV FREEMAN

Healing with Psychedelics
A Step-by-Step Handbook to Safe and Sustainable Transformation
Gv Freeman

Published by PsychedelicIQ Press, St. Louis, MO

Cover Design and Illustrations: Timothy David Cooper
Managing Editor: Ashten Luna Evans
Interior Design: Davis Creative, LLC, dba: DavisCreativePublishing.com

Publisher's Cataloging-in-Publication
Names: Freeman, Gv, author.
Title: Healing with psychedelics : a step-by-step handbook to safe and sustainable transformation / Gv Freeman.
Description: St. Louis, MO : PsychedelicIQ Press, [2025] | Includes bibliographical references.
Identifiers: ISBN: 979-8-9924661-0-2 (paperback) | 979-8-9924661-1-9 (ebook) | LCCN: 2025901103
Subjects: LCSH: Hallucinogenic drugs--Therapeutic use. | Hallucinogenic drugs--Psychological aspects. | Mental health. | Self-realization. | Change (Psychology) | LCGFT: Self-help publications. | BISAC: BODY, MIND & SPIRIT / Psychedelics. | SELF-HELP / Personal Growth / Happiness. | PSYCHOLOGY / Psychotherapy / Counseling.
Classification: LCC: RC483.5.H3 F74 2025 | DDC: 615.7883--dc23

ATTENTION CORPORATIONS, UNIVERSITIES, COLLEGES, AND PROFESSIONAL ORGANIZATIONS: Quantity discounts are available on bulk purchases of this book for educational, gift purposes, or as premiums for increasing magazine subscriptions or renewals. Special books or book excerpts can also be created to fit specific needs. For information, please contact PsychedelicIQ Press by emailing press@psychedeliciq.com.

A mi maestro y los hermanos, Roberto y René Flores Solís,
y a los "doctores," cuyas sanaciones y bendiciones
trascienden la comprensión humana.

Su amor y enseñanzas son sin igual.
Mi gratitud y amor por cada uno de ustedes es infinito.

To my maestro and brothers, Roberto and René Flores Solís,
and to the "doctors," whose healing and gifts transcend human understanding.

Your love and teachings are unlike anything I have ever known.
My gratitude and love for each of you are boundless.

Table of Contents

Foreword   xi
Author's Note: Sacred Reciprocity and Financial Considerations   xiii
What Is PsychedelicIQ?   xvii
Preface   xix

PART I: JOURNEY INTO PSYCHEDELIC HEALING   1

Chapter 1   An Introduction to the Psychedelic Landscape   3
Chapter 2   How and Why Psychedelics Heal   17
Chapter 3   A Map to Guide Your Journey   39
Chapter 4   A New Psychedelic Framework for the Modern Era   55
Chapter 5   An Ideal (and Realistic) Healing Journey   63

PART II: THE PSYCHEDELIC SAFETY WHEEL   71

Chapter 6   Benefits   73
Chapter 7   Risks   83
Chapter 8   Preparation   105
Chapter 9   Substances   135
Chapter 10   Facilitation   163
Chapter 11   Intention   191
Chapter 12   Dosing   199
Chapter 13   Setting   213
Chapter 14   Mindset   227
Chapter 15   Experience   243
Chapter 16   Integration   263
Chapter 17   Activation   283

Conclusion   297
Acknowledgments   303
About the Author   307
Appendix   309
Notes   329

Foreword

As someone who has been at the forefront of integrating psychedelics into a medical practice, I've seen firsthand the transformative power these substances can have for people who are committed to living their most healthy lives. When I opened one of Chicago's first ketamine clinics, it was in response to a dire need—people were looking for new ways to manage chronic mental health conditions. Traditional methods weren't cutting it, and the health care system was failing to provide supportive interventions. Much like the structured approach we take at Innovative Psychedelics, my clinical practice in Chicago, the ideas cultivated and shared in this book by Gv Freeman provide a pathway toward healing.

Over time, we've learned that psychedelics, when used responsibly and with the support of experienced practitioners, can offer profound healing. But let's be clear: this is no "magic bullet." Psychedelics are a tool, not a cure. They unlock doors, but you still have to do the work of walking through them. As Aldous Huxley wrote in *The Doors of Perception*, "There are things known and there are things unknown, and in between are the doors of perception." Psychedelics provide a unique opportunity to open those doors and explore the unknown—but the journey beyond them is deeply personal and requires courage, reflection, and compassion.

This book, *Healing with Psychedelics*, serves as a valuable guide for those seeking to embark on this journey. The Psychedelic Safety Wheel, as laid out in the pages ahead, offers a comprehensive and thoughtful approach to psychedelic therapy. It's not just about "set and setting" anymore—though, trust me, those are still crucial. The framework recognizes that each person's path to healing is unique and requires more than just the ingestion of a substance. It's about preparation, mindset, and—most importantly—integration.

Healing with Psychedelics emphasizes the importance of a holistic and individualized process. Psychedelics aren't about escape—they are about deeper understanding. They help you confront your trauma, explore yourself in relation to the world, and ultimately transform your life. And yes, there will be moments that are downright uncomfortable. As Ram Dass said, "The most important aspect of love is not in giving or receiving: it's in being. When a person is just being, it is an act of love in itself." Psychedelics help us be, and in that space of being, we find healing.

The stories and strategies within this book offer practical wisdom for anyone curious about psychedelics—whether you're a health care provider like myself, a curious explorer, or someone struggling with their health and seeking new options. What I appreciate most about this work is its balanced tone. There is no evangelizing—just honest, grounded advice to help you make informed decisions.

We are on the cusp of a revolution in health care, and psychedelics will play a pivotal role. But like any powerful tool, they must be used responsibly and with clear intentions. This book doesn't shy away from discussing the risks and challenges, and that's part of what makes it such an essential read. It's your roadmap for navigating this brave new world, with all its promises and potential pitfalls.

So, as you embark on this journey, remember that the power of psychedelics lies not just in the experience itself, but in the preparation and the integration that follows. *Healing with Psychedelics* will guide you through that process. You won't find any shortcuts here—just thoughtful, practical guidance designed to help you find your own path to healing.

Dr. Rahul K. Khare, MD, MS
Founder, Innovative Care
Chicago, IL

Author's Note:
Sacred Reciprocity and
Financial Considerations

I n the Quechua language of Peru, *ayni* is a word that translates to "sacred reciprocity." In daily practice, sacred reciprocity means "today for you, tomorrow for me." So much of this book and the wisdom contained within its pages was freely given to me by my Peruvian teachers (and many others whom you can read about in the acknowledgments). In honor of these gifts, and in the spirit of *ayni*, 10 percent of the profits from this book will be donated to the lineage I have been initiated into, and to which I owe so much of my healing, experience, and wisdom. I wish to deeply honor all the ancestors—past, present, and emerging—who have handed down the gift of Sacred Medicine. May this book honor and support their wisdom, energy, legacy, and intention to heal.

Moving beyond the boundaries of this book, it is important to draw attention to the larger issues of equity and access present in today's psychedelic and healing landscapes. Unfortunately, there is very little overlap between the large sections of the global population struggling with the mental health and addiction crises, and those who have access to psychedelics covered by health insurance. For those people who have tried nearly every other option to heal, psychedelics may be their last hope, yet our current legal system and medical infrastructure do nothing to support these services.

For many who have abandoned modern medicine for their healing, there exists a belief that "spirituality should be free," or that if healers use their spiritual work as their primary source of income, it somehow diminishes their ethics and increases their willingness to manipulate their clients for their own financial gain. While this does happen on occasion, the truth is that many of the most qualified practitioners, be they aboveground or underground, still have bills to pay and groceries to buy.

Whereas most medical doctors rely on insurance to supplement their income, we are a very long way from psychedelics (and holistic healing in general) operating within this framework.

As you consider the healers you may meet on your path, please take a moment to evaluate the cost versus benefit of your work and the level of risk each of them carries. If you've been struggling for many years, you have likely paid doctors, therapists, and pharmaceutical companies thousands of dollars, perhaps with little to no lasting benefit. If you are working with a true psychedelic professional, I invite you to place them in this same category of care. Many have spent decades and tens of thousands of dollars in training or apprenticeships to safely do what they do—and largely at their own potential legal risk.

Ask yourself if you would want to spend $300 for a surgeon to perform your six-hour brain surgery. That's the length of time of a typical psychedelic experience (not counting any time spent on preparation and integration). At that rate, your facilitator is making roughly twenty dollars per hour. In 2024, the average hourly wage for a fast-food worker in the United States was $19.51.[1] It's hard for psychedelic professionals to pay for rent, let alone receive adequate training, at that kind of wage.

The issue I'm pointing toward is less about focus and more about ethics. Please remember that if you choose to take your healing into your own hands and step outside of a regulated industry, you—not a licensing body—will need to become responsible for your own decisions and safety. But working with an "alternative treatment" should not, in any way, devalue the service you receive or make the provider's training any less valid.

One viable way I foresee large numbers of people receiving the psychedelic treatments they need is through professionally facilitated group ceremonies and community-led preparation and integration support. This combination represents two of the most accessible options for increasing access and decreasing costs until enough laws and policies are changed to retrofit psychedelics into our industrial medical complex.

One often-discussed method of expanding access is through peer-to-peer facilitation—essentially, one community member holding space for another. While advantageous at first glance, a great number of challenges can arise when well-meaning, yet untrained community members begin holding the responsibility for the health and safety of their friends and family. Handing over the deeply personal work of serving psychedelics, and the responsibility of witnessing and holding decades of unprocessed trauma, is unfair (if not outright psychologically and energetically dangerous) to lay members of our communities. While experiences with small dosages may be fine, very few of your friends and family members are equipped to hold the space required for you to do your deepest work. In short, there is no "easy button" to press and quickly resolve these challenges.

What I hope to do in this book is give you, the seeker, enough information to make better decisions for your own health and well-being. The medical and political organizations that could make these treatments more accessible may be years away from substantial change, and many of you simply don't have that much time to waste. You may be desperately seeking a solution today, and will go to nearly any lengths to find it. I hope the information in these pages can help you, even when the appropriate laws and licenses are not yet in place.

Should you choose to move forward, please consider working with these substances in a relational versus transactional way. If you treat psychedelic substances like a slot machine, inserting a quarter and expecting a healing prize, you may eventually go broke. On the other hand, if you pair your psychedelic healing with other commonly used and financially accessible modalities, the potential for long-term, sustainable change becomes much higher.

If you are reading this message and have resources to spare, please reach out. The PsychedelicIQ website can help put your valuable resources to good use and help those less fortunate to get the healing they need. If you are financially struggling and are seeking to use psychedelics on your healing path, consider approaching a qualified facilitator for a scholarship or payment plan. The chances are high that they want to help you just as much as they need to pay their electricity bill. Many times, a middle ground can be achieved.

Until we can find a better and more cost-effective approach to true healing in this country, we will all need to work together to create equitable and accessible options for everyone. Please do not make your most important healing decisions based solely on finances. You must learn to practice discernment over desperation. As the saying goes, "Speed, quality, and price… you can only choose two."

What Is PsychedelicIQ?

The mission of PsychedelicIQ is to provide safe, grounded, and practical insights for responsibly using psychedelics as tools for healing, growth, and transformation. Throughout the book, I will refer you to www.psychedeliciq.com. This website is designed to be a jumping off point for additional resources, including the following:

	Resources Most of the resources mentioned in this book can be found on the resources page of PsychedelicIQ.
Psychedelic Safety Wheel Assessment Take the free assessment to gauge your level of confidence and preparedness for your upcoming psychedelic experience.	
	Community If you are looking to connect with others using psychedelics for healing, join our free online community to receive the support you need during your preparation and integration.
Education Enroll in the free PsychedelicIQ Academy for articles, online training, webinars, and workshops.	
	Calendar PsychedelicIQ hosts multiple events and experiences for seekers wanting to go deeper into their practice.

Preface

"Nervous Tension" by Lemon Jelly

After nearly fifteen years of ignoring my trauma and medicating with food, drugs, and alcohol, my healing journey started in 2007. After I was rather forcefully invited by a judge to stop consuming alcohol, I stumbled my way onto a court-mandated healing path. If one can appreciate that an addiction is just a numbing mechanism that prevents us from feeling uncomfortable feelings, then my story made perfect sense. Getting "outed" as a fourteen-year-old gay kid in a tiny Nebraska town in the mid-1990s was no walk in the park, and it's no surprise that I spent the better part of two decades engaging in all kinds of addictive behavior. After finding therapy and then completing my yoga teacher training, I was introduced to psychedelic healing in the jungles of Peru in 2015. Since then, the substances and practices I will introduce in this book have been an instrumental part of my healing journey. Mind you, psychedelics have never been the only tool in my toolbox. Throughout the last ten years, I have also relied on twelve-step recovery, exercise and personal training, different forms of psychotherapy, yoga, meditation, acupuncture, Reiki, massage, and many other healing modalities to get me to where I am today.

After writing a short book about psychedelics in 2020, I knew that there was something more important bubbling under the surface. With the intention to soon start another book, I found myself in Vilcabamba, Peru, on November 7, 2023. This trip was an opportunity to do my own deep healing work and spend time studying with my teachers, while also guiding my clients to Peru and creating an opportunity for them to experience the majesty of the country and its Indigenous medicine.

When I asked my teacher for permission to write this book, and to include the teachings he had been sharing with me for years, he gave me one simple instruction: "Ask the doctors." The "doctors" he spoke of were not the ones with white coats and stethoscopes, but rather the spirits that embody the plants we work with—in this

FIGURE 1. The sacred temple located in Vilcabamba, Peru.

case, Doctor Ayahuasca, Doctor Wachuma, Doctor Mushroom, and Doctor Tobacco. We call these spirits (and the plants, cacti, and fungi they inhabit) doctors because in our tradition, they are always healing. So, as I knelt at the foot of an amazing and powerful stone temple in Vilcabamba, I asked permission to write this book from Doctor Wachuma, the cactus known as "San Pedro" in the Global North, and was granted the go-ahead with one condition: I must write the book with love and in service to God.

A few months after I began writing, I was thrown off course by one of the most harrowing psychedelic journeys of my life (more on that in chapter 10, "Facilitation"). Yet a few months after that, I was then gifted the most profound experience of my life when Doctor Ayahuasca helped me experience my true nature for the very first time. (The gift of realizing who you truly are when you take off all the modern costumes of society is a gift I hope each of you can eventually receive.) Yet even after that, my writing was still stuck, and the words would not flow.

Then, only three short months later, once again on a divine date with Doctor Wachuma, I experienced the most healing journey I could have imagined. On August 4, 2024, the doctors performed an "emergency surgery" which gifted me with a new "heart." While fully conscious and with my eyes open, having only ingested one-third of a typical dose of cactus, my spiritual heart was replaced with something new. Why?

What for? Only the doctors know. I can only tell you that before this experience, anger, judgment, and frustration were frequent guests in my mind. Since then, they only rarely drop in for tea. You may not believe it (and I still can't fully explain it), but I know my life has never been the same. Not a single human physically touched my body that night, yet for a week, my chest was sore to the touch where the doctors did their work. The healing technology these doctors have is far beyond what modern medical science understands. What happened to me that night remains beyond words—genuinely ineffable.

It was this mystery, this energy, and my new heart that finally allowed the words to start flowing again. Today, I feel like I am a completely different person than I was that November afternoon in the high jungle of Peru. The magic that has occurred in my life since I began using these substances in 2015 is truly immeasurable.

Despite my healing progress, I tell you this story with caution. Every person has their own unique process, and I can assure you that your process will look nothing like mine. Attempting to compare your experiences with mine will only result in discomfort and suffering. And if there's one thing I've learned throughout my journey, it's that comparison is the thief of joy. While I may reference the occasional mystical experience throughout this book, I will also go out of my way to weave together elements of science and psychology in an effort to keep you and the content grounded and accessible.

This book attempts to share what I've learned, especially about the substances we'll discuss and some best practices for using them. Many call them "medicines" because, in many ways, they are some of the most powerful healing tools humans have ever encountered. Not powerful in a destructive, atom-bomb sort of way, but more like a deep-cleaning kind of way—scrubbing and filtering away the layers and debris that prevent us from clearly seeing our true Selves. Their transformative potential is profound, offering hope to those who have yet to find healing through modern allopathic medicine—the conventional, science-based system that primarily treats symptoms and disease with drugs, surgery, and similar interventions.

But remember, with great power comes great responsibility. As Yogananda wrote in *Autobiography of a Yogi*, "A man who has reformed himself will reform thousands." My reformation journey has spanned nearly two decades, and most days, I still feel like a toddler in the ways of these medicines. The approach I will offer comes from my experience, but your experience will undoubtedly be unique to you.

This book is a reflection of my healing journey, viewed through the lens of psychedelics. The left eye looks through the sacred lens, and the right eye looks through the secular. The demand for healing with these substances is exploding faster than we can build the policies, education, experience, culture, or community to support them. Many people come to psychedelics with only the 1960s counterculture idiom of "set and setting." This turn of phrase formally entered the psychedelic lexicon when Timothy Leary presented a paper at the American Psychological Association annual meeting in 1961. In his presentation, Leary suggested that these two variables represented the most critical determinants of the contents of a psychedelic experience. While it was definitely a good start, now, over sixty years later, these two variables are desperately insufficient to ensure safety and effectiveness in a modern context. This book offers an upgrade to Leary's "set and setting" and an integral theory of how and why psychedelics heal.

Remember, there is no one right way to psychedelic, and I'm not here to convince you I'm an expert. Instead, I'll offer twelve variables—buckets, if you will—that educators, practitioners, researchers, and seekers can fill with whatever content best fits their needs. These variables will cover aspects such as risks, benefits, preparation, integration, and activation. The entire framework has been designed as a bottom-up approach to harm reduction, providing a comprehensive guide to these powerful substances.

Over the past decade, I've learned much from my own personal work and helping others on their journeys. I'm sharing my experience, strength, and hope, but you're not obligated to believe a single word. Like the best spiritual traditions, direct experience should always supersede belief. Take what you want and leave the rest. Working with clients, I've witnessed countless miracles. But I've also learned that the moment you expect something to happen, it won't. Choosing this path requires time, dedication, courage, and—most challenging of all—trust and surrender. Psychedelics can change your life forever if you're willing to go slow, let go of your expectations, and work with pure intention.

So, if you're looking for an honest, safe, practical, and grounded approach to healing with psychedelics, this book is for you. I wrote it with three specific groups of people in mind, and each group may benefit from using this text in a different way:

- **Psychedelic Newcomers** — If you're just beginning your psychedelic journey, there's more ground to cover than you may think. Flip to chapter 3, "A Map to Guide Your Journey," then dive straight into the Psychedelic Safety Wheel in part II.
- **Recreational Users** — You have some experience using psychedelics in a more recreational fashion. For you, psychedelics may feel less daunting than for a beginner. If you are now turning to psychedelics to enhance your healing journey, my suggestion would be to focus on preparation, facilitation, integration,

and activation. These steps will begin to shift your relationship with these substance from recreation to healing.

- ◆ **Seekers with Challenging Experiences** — If you've already begun your healing journey with psychedelics, and you've hit a bump in the road or had a challenging experience, flip to the section you most need today, then read the rest when you're ready. Much of the content of this book builds upon itself, so address your core concern from the start. If you decide you'd like to continue using psychedelics in your healing practice, try incorporating the other steps into future experiences.

For any potential reader, it's important to know that the approach presented in this book prioritizes safety and responsible use. (Yes, these substances carry risks, and while many risks can be reduced, they can never be fully eliminated.)

If the medical–industrial complex has failed you, maybe it's time to try a new path, one where *you* take full responsibility for *your* safety. Push too hard or run too fast, and you might hurt yourself. But with the right approach and patience, your healing journey can be filled with joy and a sense of freedom, offering a more optimistic view of your entire life.

Even if you only read this preface, do yourself a favor: pull out your phone and take a picture of the table of contents. Use that as an outline to do your own research; I promise you'll be better off than when you started. And know this: these medicines are some of the most incredible healing tools the world has ever known. I know this because I, and the millions who have come before me, have felt their power firsthand. Scientists have tried and fail to fully understand them, but the ancient lineages that have been using them for centuries do understand them. In this book, I will offer wisdom from both modern and ancient interpretations.

So, go! Heal! Experience the peace, joy, and freedom that is your birthright. Your personal self-help manual is already written within you. All you must do is learn to read it. Once this connection with your inner truth begins to form, you will no longer need teachers, books, or courses, because you'll realize that all the answers you need reside within yourself. Eventually, you will realize this book isn't actually teaching you anything, it's only helping you remember what you already know.

As you embark on your journey, please take this mantra with you: Healing doesn't have to be hard; it can actually be sweet and easy.

With love,
Gv Freeman

PART I

Journey into Psychedelic Healing

"A Thought Is Just a Passing Train" by John Moreland

An Introduction to the Psychedelic Landscape

"No Shortcuts" by Heather Maloney & Darlingside

Considering that the title of this book is *Healing with Psychedelics*, I think it's essential to explain how I define the term "healing." Large corporations and governments control today's standard colonial and capitalist healing models. They serve as the gatekeepers to healing, regarding both modern allopathic medicine and our access (or lack thereof) to psychedelics.

In this standard model, you need a diagnosis to be "healed." Insurance companies require a code to determine what is treatable and how much money every participant in the revenue chain will receive at the end of each transaction. This is *not* healing. It is not even health care. It is a lot closer to *sick* care, and outside of acute issues, it rarely includes much sustainable healing at all. Very few traditional medical organizations are focused on your health. They are instead designed to return you to a baseline of "not sick."

I view healing on a continuum of emotions, or the average way you feel as you go throughout your day. As we'll discuss in detail in the next chapter, humans experience life through a broad spectrum of emotions. Looking at table 1 below, you can see how this spectrum starts with shame at the lowest level, peaks with enlightenment at the highest level, and has fifteen broad emotions sandwiched in between.

Name of Level	Energetic Log
Enlightenment	700–1000
Peace	600
Joy	540
Love	500
Reason	400
Acceptance	350
Willingness	310
Neutrality	250
Courage	200
Pride	175
Anger	150
Desire	125
Fear	100
Grief	75
Apathy	50
Guilt	30
Shame	20

TABLE 1. Map of Consciousness, by David R. Hawkins, in *Power vs. Force*, Hay House, 2014.

"Healing" can be defined as moving from a lower level on this continuum to a higher level. Starting from the lived experience of shame and growing to courage represents an increase of eight levels (or 180 units on the Energetic Log). This is healing. If your primary emotional way of seeing the world is through the lens of reason, and you step up three levels to peace (200 Energetic Log units), this is also healing.

If your average daily life resonates at 200 (courage) or above on the Energetic Log, you may already feel reasonably stable, secure, and happy. For some people who have already reached this level, it could be helpful to swap out the word "healing" for "growth." But no matter what you call it, healing with psychedelics is an ever-increasing path toward enlightenment and a sense of freedom in your daily life.

Healing, especially through the lens offered in this book, does not require you to have a diagnosis, a traumatic brain injury, or clinical depression. I propose that healing is simply a net reduction in suffering caused by an increase in your overall emotional well-being. Healing is progressively learning to live your life with more peace, joy, and freedom. You don't need a doctor's note to heal or improve your quality of life. You only need a desire to increase your level of consciousness and fully enjoy your life.

How Psychedelic Use Has Changed

In a spiritual context, a "container" is a person, place, or object that holds and sustains spiritual energy, intentions, or experiences. Think of it as a vessel supporting growth, healing, and transformation. If you attend a yoga class or a meditation session, the instructor is creating a container for your work. Expanding out from your individual class, yoga in the Global North is dramatically different from yoga in India. This is representative of how containers can differ.

If you choose to sit with psychedelics, your facilitator will create a container for your session. This container may include physical elements like the setting, the comfortable couch you're sitting on, or the music you're listening to. It can also contain elements not visible to the naked eye, like your ability to feel safe and seen—created by the invisible force of empathy, the groundedness of your facilitator, and the relationship you have built together.

In my estimation, psychedelics through the ages have been held by three primary containers. The first was built, and is still held, by Indigenous practitioners. These healers have employed the use of psychedelics for upward of 11,000 years and represent the first and oldest psychedelic container for the purposes of healing and connecting with the Divine. The second container began forming in 1938 when Albert Hoffman developed and released lysergic acid diethylamide (LSD) to the world. This discovery placed psychedelics into the hands of clinicians and researchers, and led to almost thirty years of significant research advancements. As the counterculture movement of the 1960s acquired access to these chemicals, the container began to degrade and then all but shattered in 1970 when the Controlled Substances Act was passed, severely restricting psychedelic use. Still, a small, dedicated group of underground guides carried on the work, quietly helping others heal and grow.

The third container emerged in the 1990s, as research resumed. Yet its crystallization truly occurred in 2018, when Michael Pollan's book *How to Change Your Mind* opened up the modern world's eyes to the incredible healing potential of psychedelics. The secret that was—depending on who you spoke to—both alive and dead for decades was no longer a secret. Schrödinger's cat was officially out of the bag. We can thank the true believers from the second container of psychedelic use for helping form the foundation for today's psychedelic understanding. Now psychedelics represent the possibility of profound healing and social taboo, scientific breakthroughs and recreational risk, cultural rivals and lingering stigmas.

For millennia, Indigenous healers often spent decades apprenticing under a teacher. The first container was built on generations of wisdom, tradition, practical application, and lived experience. Although very different from the base of scientists, psychotherapists, and explorers that formed the second container, both fostered a sense of community, authenticity, respect, and most importantly, accountability. But the third container holding today's psychedelic landscape feels different. It's mostly disconnected from the traditions, wisdom, and accountability that have guided this work for centuries. In many ways, this container feels like it's being held together with duct tape and bailing wire.

A recent tabulation showed over 150 psychedelic training programs available today across the globe, many more interested in profit than principles, doling out "authority to practice" under the guise of capitalism and colonialism. Some of these programs don't even require their graduates to have any personal experience with the medicines they are serving, let alone practical experience sitting for others.

This has created a significant challenge within the psychedelic landscape. The Pollan Effect,[2] and the funding and research that followed, have exploded demand for psychedelics and psychedelic facilitators. As with every revolution, first come the dreamers, then the bankers, the salesmen, the sharks, the desperate, and finally, the thieves. Where the psychedelic revolution stands today depends a lot on who you talk to.

We know these substances work (as we will discuss in chapter 6, "Benefits"), but in a late-stage capitalistic system, when demand rises quickly, so does supply. Now quality is suffering. We've created a recipe for disaster, with an uninformed consumer population and no approved certification, standardization, or oversight governing the use of psychedelics. Throughout history, trust has served as the cornerstone of psychedelics, and clients depended on their guides to ensure their safety. Today, that foundation of trust is eroding before our very eyes.

An Indigenous healer, or *curandero*, was once trusted among the village to heal your spirit. A scientist or therapist was trusted to have the training to handle these substances (and your mind) with safety and care. But today, thousands of untrained and unqualified individuals call themselves "guides," having little to no experience doing their own work, let alone being qualified to help you with yours.

Unfortunately, many of those suffering will seek healing in locations where legal and qualified practitioners are in short supply. In their stead, charlatans, false prophets, cult leaders, egomaniacs, and neophytes (just to name a few) make mistakes and cause harm—some intentional, some accidental. Trust is essential in this work, and being hurt by an unprofessional or unethical facilitator in the pursuit of healing is incredibly difficult and may cause damage that could take months or years to heal.

Throughout the past six decades, the essential principle of psychedelic use has been "set and setting," referring to the mindset of the person taking psychedelics (the set), and the location where that person is taking psychedelics (the setting). These variables have long been heralded as the most important elements of a psychedelic experience. However, because the modern psychedelic container is not as stable as its predecessors, it's high time (no pun intended) for a serious update.

The Psychedelic Safety Wheel (PSW), which I introduce in part II, updates the "set and setting" concept for the twenty-first century. Whether your path is clinical, therapeutic, or spiritual, the PSW adds ten additional variables to help you become a more informed consumer and make better choices about how—and with whom—you embark on your journey. Much of the psychedelic landscape, and many of those working within it, feels shrouded by mystery and illusion. The PSW helps you peek behind the curtain and clears away just enough of the mystery to keep you safe, while continuing to honor the ineffable. While we can never fully account for the unpredictable nature of these potent molecules, the PSW aims to reduce harm and increase your chances of sustainable, safe, and meaningful transformation.

Residual Trauma and the Mind-Body Connection

We are currently experiencing a mental health crisis like our world has never before experienced. Studies suggest that one in two people globally will face a mental health disorder during their lifetime.[3] On top of that, we understand the connection between the mind and body much more deeply than ever before. Modern research shows that the connection between our gut and our brain is both complex and bidirectional. Signals pass both ways between our digestive system and central nervous system, and health or disease in one can affect the other.[4] Further studies have clearly shown that meditation can help manage physical symptoms associated with asthma, cancer, chronic pain, heart disease, high blood pressure, irritable bowel syndrome, and tension headaches. More than ever, we realize the significant influence our mental state has on our body. Prolonged mental dysregulation adversely affects the body, leading to disease and chronic illness.

Gabor Maté, a renowned addiction expert and bestselling author, says, "Trauma, from the Greek for 'wound,' is not what happens to you; it is what happens inside you as a result of what happens to you. Trauma is the invisible force that shapes our lives. It shapes the way we live, the way we love, and the way we make sense of the world."[5] I like to think of trauma as "what's left over." It is the residue that remains after an injury to our body, mind, or spirit.

Whether or not you believe it, if your condition can be linked to that residue, the only way to cure the condition is to first heal the trauma—and then purge your system of the residue. Today, psychotherapy remains our top remedy for trauma despite it being slow, expensive, and frequently uncomfortable. Many have claimed that using psychedelics is like "ten years of therapy in a day." I don't want to set an unreasonable expectation, but I can say without an inkling of doubt that this can be an accurate description of *some* psychedelic experiences.

If you've chosen to rely on pharmaceuticals to heal your trauma, you may feel like someone has abandoned you at the altar. For some, antidepressants might feel like a lifesaver in an ocean of misery. But what Big Pharma isn't telling you is those pills aren't healing trauma any more than NyQuil heals a cold virus. Until you eliminate the underlying issue, both only mask the symptoms. With a healthy immune system, most viruses resolve on their own. Trauma does not. In fact, without addressing it, it continues to deepen, burrowing its roots farther into our bodies and psyche. Sometimes, the side effects of antidepressant drugs can be more harmful than the conditions they were designed to treat. Some actually cause the suicides they are intended to thwart. (For more information addressing the link between antidepressants and suicidality, see the appendix).

We store the traumatic residue we collect throughout our lives in our body, mind, and spirit. Like plaque buildup in our arteries, trauma is a slow, progressive disease that eventually causes serious health problems. This residue accumulates with each challenging experience in our lives.

Have you lived through a childhood filled with abuse or neglect? Add a layer of residue. Have you experienced bullying or domestic violence? Add a layer. How about racism, sexism, homophobia, or transphobia? Add a layer. Have you lost a parent or a child? Add a layer. Put on a uniform to fight for your country? A layer. Have you experienced a breakup or a challenging end to a marriage? Another layer. Have a stressful job or financial insecurity? Layer. I think you get the point.

Because trauma is invisible and presents differently in every individual, it is more insidious and complex than physical ailments. We don't have an angiogram for trauma. Even more challenging is that an event that creates trauma for one person may have little to no effect on another. Humans are quite unique, and the most effective treatment for those hidden wounds may differ for each of us.

Today, the closest thing we have to treating trauma is evaluating the symptoms and offering a diagnosis. Built more for modern medicine and insurance companies, the *Diagnostic and Statistical Manual of Mental Disorders* (DSM) is the primary "objective" tool our mental health system relies on for diagnosis. After giving a diagnosis, doctors and psychiatrists prescribe pills and advise regular therapy sessions, sometimes for decades. As evidenced by the nearly seventeen veterans who died every day from suicide in 2021 (6,392 in total, with a rate continuing to rise), our current approach is simply not working.

The latest surge in psychedelic healing did not spring forth because of psychonauts exploring consciousness or "burners" enjoying one week a year tripping on the playa. Trippers have been tripping for over sixty years. The genesis of this newfound love affair with all things psychedelic is that our modern medical and mental health care systems are failing us.

Challenging Today's Scientific Materialism

Scientific materialism is a philosophical viewpoint that asserts that everything in existence (including all phenomena and processes) can be explained solely by physical matter and its interactions, as understood by the principles and laws of science, particularly physics and chemistry. This perspective holds that all aspects of reality—consciousness, thoughts, emotions, and complex social and cultural phenomena—ultimately arise from material processes.

Everything we know within our modern health care framework is based on scientific materialism. Yet, here's the rub: if we asked the world's most talented physicists to derive a formula to measure grief, courage, or love, they couldn't do it. Despite this, a search on Google Scholar for "science explaining consciousness" offers nearly four million results—over 17,000 from 2024 alone. Not a week goes by that I don't see another scientist attempting to define, measure, or pinpoint the origin of consciousness. But scientists will always fail at accomplishing this task because consciousness is the origin and foundation of science, not the other way around. This is as fundamentally impossible as asking a child to give birth to their parents.

Conversely, spiritual traditions and healers have offered their wisdom and services to the sick and weary for thousands of years. Spiritual philosophy has long been a means to reduce suffering and increase cognitive freedom. Yet today, because our modern society has grossly confused spirituality with religion and depends on medicine that ignores any solution it cannot measure, we deem these modalities as "woo-woo" and brush them into the dustbin of make-believe.

Even attempting to color slightly outside the lines of traditional medicine by using disciplines such as functional medicine, acupuncture, homeopathy, hypnosis, Reiki, or meditation often comes with enormous out-of-pocket costs not covered by insurance. Your doctor is unlikely to recommend it if they cannot measure it, and even if they did recommend it, there is every likelihood you could not afford it.

Unraveling this complicated set of dynamics will take decades. Our materially oriented system, hundreds of years in the making and operating on the fuel of late-stage capitalism, is so profoundly intertwined with so many other systems that any meaningful top-down change would require a serious overhaul. We would need to raise our level of collective consciousness, adopt a new worldview, and address the misalignments present in everything from the education and justice systems to modern medicine and insurance, religion and spirituality, and even the ways we parent and raise our children. We would have to abandon our worldly ways and reawaken to a culture of animism, the belief that all things have a spiritual essence and contain consciousness.

One suggestion I will offer from my own healing journey is that the less I know and the more I've forgotten about modern life, the better I feel. My life today doesn't look like it did twenty years ago. It has been a slow, step-by-step process to untangle many of my old beliefs, but this process can and does work. If you're unwilling to wait for a full societal reconstruction, you are reading the right book.

Threading the Needle of the Sacred and Secular

Ramana Maharshi, a Hindu sage and enlightened being, once said, "Wanting to reform the world without discovering one's true self is like trying to cover the world with leather to avoid the pain of walking on stones and thorns. It is much simpler to wear shoes." Since the rise and continued prominence of "litigation culture" in the US, much of society relies less on personal responsibility and self-governance, and more on attributing the way we feel to external sources. The materialistic and litigious world we live in today tries very hard to cover the world in leather, forcing others to conform to its needs rather than simply buying a pair of shoes.

When I imagine the pathways for healing, I tend to see two broad trails with hundreds of side-trails. Those two trails are labeled as "sacred" and "secular." On the sacred path, the side- trails include many spiritual philosophies such as shamanism, Advaita Vedanta, Taoism, Kabballah, Sufism, Buddhism, and yoga. Within each of those philosophies lies an infinite number of even smaller trails represented by the sects, methods, practices, and teachings that have been passed down through the ages. Most of these trails can be traced back to their origins through various lineages and enlightened beings. Amazingly, much of this wisdom does not have a "half-life." The teachings that worked thousands of years ago are still just as relevant today.

In today's culture, many people automatically equate the term "sacred" with religion. While that can be true, religion is not required to indulge in the sacred. As we'll discuss later in the book, separating religion from spirituality can be a very helpful endeavor for many readers. The one commonality of all the sacred paths is that they deal with Spirit—God, Universe, Source, a power greater than ourselves, or any number of terms one might use to describe the ineffable. Anyone may participate in a sacred tradition or experience, regardless of their affiliation (or lack thereof) with any organized religion or spiritual philosophy. In fact, it is highly likely you've already had a sacred experience of some kind without even realizing it. It could have been caused by seeing the ocean for the first time, taking a walk through Yellowstone National Park, or looking into the eyes of your first-born child. Each and every moment of our lives is filled with the sacred, if we choose to acknowledge it.

Now, turning our attention to the secular path, let's look at the way many modern societies approach healing. Secular healing orients toward the mind and the body, and tends to ignore the spirit—or anything that it cannot understand or measure. Driven primarily by science, secular healers tend to be licensed, certified, and have letters after their names. Most often, these healers are first trained in classrooms, and their initiation into the healing arts frequently commences with writing and successfully defending their personal healing thesis. These healers then enter the capitalistic healing market with human-made credentials.

Sacred methods of healing, while more difficult to quantitatively measure, have been successfully used for thousands of years. Energy, rituals, plants, and all things contained in the natural world have been the tools of the trade for millennia. Still widely practiced across the globe, many sacred methods of healing are incredibly powerful and very effective. Unfortunately, through the lens of scientific materialism, they remain opaque in their exact action of operation, and therefore remain uninsurable. On the other hand, more allopathic methods of healing (at least for non-acute conditions) are often less effective, never address root causes, and leave clients in a chronic state of maladaptation and symptom management. The advantage is these methods are measurable, which allows them to be productized and monetized.

Considering significant global structural change is unlikely to occur quickly, to truly move toward health and wholeness, we must personally step out of our secular ways. In this case, our healing demands regression rather than progression, and truly addressing the root cause of our ailments will require us to unlearn much of what we've been taught. Bluntly, this will require self-education, a comprehensive understanding of the risks, and a full-throated acceptance of responsibility. For us to truly feel happy and free, we can no longer shift the blame for our maladaptation to life on outward sources or project our discomfort onto others when we perceive their behavior is responsible for causing our discomfort. True healing requires making powerful choices, experiencing a reasonable amount of discomfort, and not suing the sacred healers holding space for us while we sit in that discomfort. Our long-term mission must be taking 100 percent responsibility for our own lived experience. Yes, you read that correctly—100 percent!

Because most human societies set up rules, customs, and habits to develop systems that work for *most* people *most* of the time, these systems will not offer the treatment and healing you're seeking. Yet, when choosing to live your life your way, you will inevitably encounter conflict with someone else's behaviors and expectations. Since you can't control the thoughts or actions of others, all you can do is learn to accept what is out of your control—and live your life in a way that most authentically honors your life choices and the life choices of others simultaneously.

Accepting this new paradigm, you now embark on a quest to find and follow your true path, guided by your true Self, and with the sense that everyone is connected at the deepest level. Your new mission is to figure out what life you are meant to lead, what inspiration calls to you, what forms of creativity appear to you—and then live that life, follow that inspiration, and express that creativity that is the unique manifestation of your being.

It is time to take your healing into your own hands and embrace a completely different model and mindset in order to educate yourself on new, unquantifiable, and unmeasurable alternative treatments and outcomes. Scientific materialism says, "You must see it to believe it," but the holistic shift I am proposing comes from an animistic worldview and says, "You have to believe it to see it."

An initiation into the secular path of the healing arts is usually granted by a group of humans, afforded the power by a government or private institution, who decide whether you're qualified as a healer. An initiation into the sacred path of the healing arts is granted by Spirit. The secular originates in the mind, the sacred in the heart.

If your mind has been trained more to rely on rational arguments and data, have no fear. This book still includes plenty of data and citations that demonstrate how psychedelics work in the body and brain, quantifiably showing their power to heal. If you're already more spiritually minded, there are personal accounts and plenty of methods and practices that will support your journey into this unconventional world of healing. Keeping today's porous and unregulated psychedelic container in mind, remember that relying too heavily on either the sacred or the secular can cause suffering. Without a trained sense of discernment, relying on facts and observable behavior may be the best method for embarking on your journey. Later on, some of these rubrics will fall away as you learn to trust your heart and your intuition.

My question to you is: are you willing to consider that your IBS, autoimmune disorder, inflammation, allergies, or memories (conscious and unconscious) are the residue of trauma? If so, keep reading. I have witnessed psychedelics heal every one of these conditions, each within a unique human and all within forty-eight hours, with absolutely no allopathic intervention. It is said that the longest journey any human must make is eighteen inches—the distance from your head to your heart. *Healing with Psychedelics* attempts to bridge that gap. With any luck, it will help you take the first steps on your journey safely and promote sustainable results.

Will You Choose the Red Pill or Blue Pill?

The psychedelic landscape is exploding. The laws, characters, roles, and opportunities for participation are constantly evolving, and for the uninitiated neophyte, stepping into this unfamiliar landscape can feel overwhelming and confusing, especially if you're already in distress.

I hope this book will assist you in bridging the gap between what you've been led to believe about psychedelics and what is relatively true. I say "relatively true" because any semblance of "absolute truth" is nonexistent in this highly subjective work. What is true for you may never be true for someone else. Unlike taking an aspirin or antibiotic prescribed by your doctor, two people could ingest the exact same type and amount of a psychedelic substance, at the exact same time, and have two completely different experiences. No two journeys will ever be the same because no two people on earth are exactly the same. Furthermore, what is true for you in one psychedelic session may not be true for you in the next. As the Greek philosopher Heraclitus put it, "You can never put your hand in the same river twice." As nonspecific amplifiers, these substances show what resides within you—something that changes every moment of every day. The only "truth" you will experience is relative to you and no one else. Uncertainty may be the only absolute truth of doing this work. You must accept that an "X factor" will always exist when working with psychedelics, making them unmeasurable and unpredictable. It is impossible to predetermine the exact nature or outcome of a psychedelic experience, so if certainty is what you seek, you may be better off returning to a medical doctor or psychiatrist.

Fortunately, scientific research around the use of psychedelics is growing. Much of the ancestral and anecdotal wisdom known for thousands of years in the jungles of the Amazon and cached in the minds of underground guides is finally bubbling to the surface and becoming increasingly quantifiable.

Rather than relying solely on quantifiable facts, this book also offers practical information from a decade's worth of my experience sitting, serving, and teaching about these substances. I include Indigenous wisdom, psychological conjecture, scientific data, storytelling, anecdotal evidence, and opinion. I'm calling on you to develop your own sense of discernment. I will offer many opportunities to believe, but belief will only get you so far. It is direct, lived experience that changes us forever.

If you come across something that doesn't sit well with you, I encourage you to do your own research. The psychedelic renaissance has no shortage of consumable content. There are many wonderful books, blogs, podcasts, videos, and research papers that will offer many different perspectives on these topics. I also offer many additional links on the resources page of PsychedelicIQ.com. If you find any content in this book lacking, shortsighted, or downright wrong, please join our online community to further this work safely, effectively, and responsibly.

One constant that I have found in my practice is that we only change when our pain exceeds our pleasure. You may decide you're not yet ready for true change, and that is absolutely okay. It is better to proceed with a "hell yeah" rather than a "maybe"— because the bell of healing can never be unrung. Once you step onto the path, there is no getting back off. Never choose to dive into psychedelics just because someone else convinced you it is the right path for you. It should be *you* and *only you* who is 100 percent onboard and ready to embark on a journey of transformation.

Like the decision facing Neo in the *Matrix* movies, indulging in the healing path of psychedelics is a choice not to be taken lightly. You can choose to swallow the red pill and potentially confront some of the most profound, difficult, and revelatory truths of your life and existence. Or you can choose the blue pill and remain blissfully unaware of your own consciousness and true nature. Which pill you choose comes down to two things: how much you are currently suffering and how much peace, joy, and freedom you would like to experience in this lifetime. The choice is yours and yours alone.

Just because our current scientific tools can't measure everything that happens during a psychedelic experience doesn't mean they don't work. Psychedelics are not, nor will they ever be, a purely factual or scientific endeavor. We cannot ever prove or completely understand what's happening in the spirit world any more than we can the psychological world. There is so much humans don't understand about psychedelics, and likely never will. While reading this book and navigating your own healing journey, I encourage you to always save a little room for Spirit.

How and Why
Psychedelics Heal

"Canyonlands (Return to Wichita)" by SUSS

As children, many of us heard fairy tales that tendered some of life's simplest yet most profound lessons. While less prevalent in most modern societies, storytelling as a tool for handing down wisdom to future generations is still a rich and valuable tradition in many cultures. "The Tortoise and the Hare" teaches us that slow and steady wins the race. (If you have a moment, go back and read that one again. It's just as relevant for psychedelic healing as it was for doing your math homework.) "The Ugly Duckling" teaches us that true beauty lies within, and that self-acceptance is essential. (Wait. Maybe you should read that one again, too.) "Little Red Riding Hood" instructs us to be cautious of strangers. "The Boy Who Cried Wolf" teaches us that our actions have consequences, and "The Three Little Pigs" demonstrates that hard work and preparation leads to safety and security. (Come to think of it, maybe you should set this book aside, pick up a copy of *The Complete Grimms' Fairy Tales* or *Aesop's Fables*, and start your healing there.)

Some of my personal favorite tales are those told about a man named Nasruddin. Nasruddin is a legendary Sufi mystic—one who practices a mystical form of Islam that emphasizes introspection and closeness with God—a folk character and a wise fool known across the Middle East, Central Asia, and parts of Europe. Nasruddin has the unfortunate ethos of teaching us that one can be foolish and wise at the same time. This is surprisingly similar to what we might refer to today as "dialectical thinking," which involves examining and reconciling seemingly contradictory ideas or perspectives. Nasruddin recognizes that reality is complex and often contains inherent tensions between opposing forces. Growing your skills as a dialectical thinker allows you to consider multiple viewpoints and find a synthesis between them; essentially, it's the ability to see both sides of an issue and understand how seemingly opposite ideas can coexist. How about an example?

One evening, Nasruddin was crawling on his hands and knees near the sidewalk, frantically looking through the grass under the light of a lamppost. A friend walked by and asked what he was up to.

"I'm searching for my house keys," said Nasruddin.

The friend offered to help, and the two spent considerable time searching under the light of the lamppost.

Finally, the friend asked, "Where did you last have your keys?"

"Oh, back at the house," replied Nasruddin.

Exasperated, the friend shouted, "Then why are we looking here?!"

Nasruddin dryly stated, "Because this is where the light is."

As with most tales describing Nasruddin's antics, this one is illogical yet logical, rational yet irrational, bizarre yet normal, and simple yet profoundly wise. Filled with paradox, we chuckle but also feel a sense of understanding when we realize Nasruddin is both right and wrong at the same time.

This is how much of the modern world perceives psychedelics. So much of what's being done and studied is both right and wrong at the same time. When I started my journey over a decade ago, I was confused by the available information. It was not until I began studying with an Indigenous maestro, or teacher, that I was fortunate enough to begin receiving wisdom from him and directly from the medicine.

Today, most scientists look to the brain to explain how psychedelics heal. Through functional magnetic resonance imaging (fMRI) scans, we have a better understanding of the brain's default mode network (DMN) and the responsibility the amygdala has for processing emotions, such as fear and anxiety, and tagging memories with those emotions.

Therapists often shift their focus away from the brain and look toward the mind/body complex for the source of trauma. In his bestselling book *The Body Keeps the Score*, Dr. Bessel van der Kolk delves into how trauma affects the brain and becomes imprinted on the body. This concept suggests that the body's tissues, muscles, and nervous system store traumatic experiences as memories. This explains why people with a history of trauma often experience chronic physical symptoms, such as IBS, fibromyalgia, lupus, or multiple sclerosis—even in the absence of a physical cause.

When we examine consciousness and healing from a spiritual perspective, we must look through a more subtle and esoteric lens. In Advaita Vedanta (the nondual philosophy that underpins Hinduism), *samskara* refers to mental impressions, psychological imprints, or habitual tendencies formed by past experiences, actions, or thoughts. Less regarded as "trauma," samskaras are the seeds of future actions and behavior stored in the subconscious mind, and are deeply rooted imprints left by past karmas, or actions. They become influential in shaping our personality, desires, and actions. These imprints are said to be stored in the *sukshma sharira,* or "subtle body," which is transferred from one physical body to another during reincarnation.

In summary, many domains—scientific and spiritual—are looking for the keys to healing under different streetlamps, because that's where their light is. None are inherently wrong, but in reality, their keys still haven't moved from the house.

Modern Meets Ancient: The Increasing Subtlety of Science

Gravity is a fundamental force in nature. Scientific understanding of gravity started with Aristotle's fourth century BCE belief that an object's natural place was "down."

In the sixteenth century, Galileo showed that gravity causes all objects to fall to Earth at the same rate. And it was Isaac Newton's 1687 development of the law of universal gravitation that formed the modern understanding of gravity. Science can tell you *how* gravity works, but it still doesn't know *why* it works.

A similar difficulty exists with the concept of matter. As early as the fifth century BCE, Democritus suggested that matter consists of small, indivisible particles called *atomos*. Fast forward to the nineteenth century, and John Dalton revived and formalized the concept of the atom, offering that all matter is comprised of these minuscule particles. In 1911, Ernest Rutherford discovered subatomic particles and showed that an atom has a nucleus surrounded by electrons. In the 1970s, quantum mechanics came to believe in even subtler fundamental particles like quarks, leptons, and bosons.

As quantum theory expands, our understanding of these fundamental entities is no longer described in terms of "particles," but of "strings." These strings are waves of energy that manifest as particles in the physical world. In layperson's terms, everything from humans to rocks to trees to the elements are composed of strings of energy so tightly braided together that they appear solid.

As time passes and technology increases, so does our knowledge of this phenomenon, allowing us to measure subtler forms of energy. One has to wonder when it will all end. What is more subtle than a string? The answer to that question actually lies in ancient India.

Over 3,000 years ago, a group of Indian mystics known as Rishis received and transmitted the Vedas, the foundational scriptures of Hinduism. These enlightened sages had insight into the deeper truths of existence and the cosmos. As part of these teachings, they received profound insights into a fundamental concept they referred to as *Brahman*. They defined Brahman as the ultimate, infinite, unchanging reality that underlies and permeates everything. Brahman is the substratum of the entire cosmos. Humans cannot comprehend it, and they cannot grasp it through the senses or intellect alone. Brahman is the Source from which all creation arises, the creator and sustainer of the cosmos, and the ultimate goal of spiritual realization.

The Rishis used three words, "*Sat-Chit-Ananda*," to describe Brahman's unmanifest version, which exists beyond time, space, and causality.

- **Sat** (meaning "existence") signifies Brahman as the eternal, unchanging reality.
- **Chit** (meaning "consciousness") indicates that Brahman is pure awareness, self-knowing, and the Source of all consciousness.
- **Ananda** (meaning "bliss") reveals that Brahman embodies supreme, infinite bliss and fulfillment.

Finally, the Rishis emphasized that Brahman is not a personal God, but an abstract, formless, and all-encompassing reality. To personalize this understanding, they gave us the concept of *Atman*. Atman refers to the individual Self or soul, while Brahman is the cosmic reality. The Rishis instructed that at the deepest level, Atman and Brahman are the same, encapsulated in the Vedantic dictum, "*Tat tvam asi*," or "I am that" meaning that the individual soul (Atman) is ultimately identical with the universal soul (Brahman).

Let's fast forward three thousand years. Stanislav Grof, a renowned Czech-born psychiatrist and one of the most influential pioneers in the field of transpersonal psychology and psychedelic therapy, along with the Multidisciplinary Association for Psychedelic Studies (MAPS, an organization seeking to legalize MDMA), began referring to an "inner healing intelligence," which I hypothesize the Rishis would have called Atman. This refers to our psyche, or soul. It represents the deepest, undamaged, and perfectly healed part of us, whose only role is to express pure existence, consciousness, and bliss. No matter what you want to call it—Atman, soul, or inner healing intelligence—it is this unseeable force that is our North Star and drives the deep and intrinsic sense of longing we all have to heal.

So, to connect all these dots, Brahman is the Source of everything we experience and has three fundamental attributes: universal existence, consciousness, and bliss. You and I, at our deepest level, are the same as Brahman, which also makes us universal existence, consciousness, and bliss.

What the Rishis described millennia ago as the substratum of everything is not very different from how quantum physicists describe their twenty-first century version of string theory. Both, in their own ways, name the energy that makes up all of existence. While Brahman and quantum physics come from entirely different traditions, one metaphysical and the other scientific, they are remarkably similar in the way they describe the nature of reality, consciousness, and the universe's interconnectedness.

We Are the Average of Our Emotions

Between 2000 and 2019, new diagnoses of autoimmune disorders such as multiple sclerosis, rheumatoid arthritis, ulcerative colitis, Crohn's disease, psoriasis, and idiopathic pulmonary fibrosis skyrocketed.[6] In his book *The Myth of Normal*, Gabor Maté shares, "Trauma is not what happens to you but what happens inside you," and continues with, "One of the things many diseases have in common is inflammation, acting as a kind of a fertilizer for the development of illness. We've discovered that when people feel threatened, insecure—especially over an extended period—our bodies are programmed to turn on inflammatory genes."[7]

In medicine, the term "conversion" refers to the psychological phenomenon where emotional distress or unresolved psychological issues manifest as physical symptoms. This can happen when a person experiences intense emotions or psychological conflict that their mind converts into psychosomatic manifestations in the body. These physical symptoms might include pain, paralysis, sensory disturbances, or other neurological issues with no underlying medical cause.

For example, someone might experience paralysis, seizures, or other physical symptoms with no identifiable neurological or physiological basis. These symptoms can be genuine and distressing for the individual experiencing them, but they rarely have an explainable origin. What we are learning is that psychological factors like stress, trauma, anxiety, or unresolved conflicts can cause inflammation in the body, and this inflammation is highly correlated with conversion symptoms.

So, how do we tie it all together?

In 2014, author, lecturer, clinician, physician, scientist, and pioneering researcher in the field of consciousness David Hawkins published *Power vs. Force*.[8] In this book, he proposed a model of human consciousness on a scale ranging from 1 to 1,000, correlating with emotional states and qualities of being. Hawkins and his team conducted millions of muscle tests (applied kinesiology) over twenty years to determine the truth or falsehood of various statements (e.g., love is the most powerful force in the universe vs. lying and deception create lasting success), political views, and even foods. During his seminars, Hawkins would frequently distribute randomized envelopes containing either sugar or vitamin C. Without fail, tested participants holding envelopes of vitamin C would demonstrate stronger muscle tests. Tests like these were also devised to measure the level of consciousness of different people, ideas, and even entire civilizations. The outcome of these tests is called the Map of Consciousness (MoC).

	Name of Level	Energetic Log	Predominant Emotional State	View of Life	God-View	Process
Spiritual Paradigm	Enlightenment	700–1000	Ineffable	Is	Self	Pure Consciousness
	Peace	600	Bliss	Perfect	All-Being	Illumination
	Joy	540	Serenity	Complete	One	Transfiguration
	Love	500	Reverence	Benign	Loving	Revelation
Reason & Integrity	Reason	400	Understanding	Meaningful	Wise	Abstraction
	Acceptance	350	Forgiveness	Harmonious	Merciful	Transcendence
	Willingness	310	Optimism	Hopeful	Inspiring	Intention
	Neutrality	250	Trust	Satisfactory	Enabling	Release
	Courage	200	Affirmation	Feasible	Permitting	Empowerment
Survival Paradigm	Pride	175	Scorn	Demanding	Indifference	Inflation
	Anger	150	Hate	Antagonistic	Vengeful	Aggression
	Desire	125	Craving	Disappointing	Denying	Enslavement
	Fear	100	Anxiety	Frightening	Punitive	Withdrawal
	Grief	75	Regret	Tragic	Disdainful	Despondency
	Apathy	50	Despair	Hopeless	Condemning	Abdication
	Guilt	30	Blame	Evil	Vindictive	Destruction
	Shame	20	Humiliation	Miserable	Despising	Elimination

TABLE 2. Map of Consciousness by David R. Hawkins, in *Power vs. Force*, Hay House, 2014.

The MoC ranges from shame at the lowest level (20) to enlightenment at the highest (700–1,000). Each level corresponds to a distinct emotional state, worldview, and life experience. Levels below courage (200) lie in what Hawkins refers to as the "Survival Paradigm." These levels are destructive and are associated with force, control, manipulation, and resistance. Individuals operating from a level of 200 or below are driven by fear, guilt, shame, anger, and pride. These states drain energy and create resistance, often resulting in conflict, suffering, and limitations in personal growth. Indicators of sub-200 levels are "survival mode," "victim mentality," and living in a state of fear and control.

Conversely, levels above 200 are constructive, life-affirming, and generate energy. These levels are characterized by emotions and attitudes such as courage, acceptance, love, and peace. Hawkins suggests that power at these levels is self-sustaining (Brahman), originates from a place of inner strength (Atman), and aligns with truth and integrity, rather than manipulation or control. Monikers of life lived in levels above 200 are empowerment, inner stability, connection, and contribution.

Returning to *The Myth of Normal*, Gabor Maté makes the connection that "chronic rage causes the body to release stress hormones for a longer duration than normal. Over the long term, such a hormonal surplus, whatever may have instigated it, can make us anxious or depressed; suppress immunity; promote inflammation; narrow blood vessels, promoting vascular disease throughout the body." While Maté's example focuses on the emotion of rage, I propose that any emotion below 200 on the MoC can produce the same outcome. The lower the vibration, the higher the potential for inflammation. Conversely, any emotion above 200 promotes greater health and well-being, and decreases conversion symptoms.

So, how is it that we can be the Brahman/Atman yet still vibrate at a level lower than Ultimate Reality? This is one of the many paradoxes of spiritual work. The deepest part of our soul, which is perfectly healed, always vibrates at the rate of Ultimate Reality. But our human personality (often referred to as the "ego" in psychedelic parlance) resonates at a much lower vibration. Because we have accumulated so much residue (e.g., karma, trauma, memories, etc.) throughout our lives, we cannot see through the film of delusion that prevents us from recognizing or remembering what we truly are, *sat-chit-ananda atma*. The Hindu tradition blames our lack of self-recognition on *maya*, the cosmic illusion that prevents us from seeing the truth. Spiritual practices are the antidote that allow us to remember who we are at our core.

Everything Is a Vibration

String theory proposes that all particles are tiny strings of energy, each with a distinct vibration. If all we are is energy vibrating at a frequency, how does this relate to our health? I propose that our cells, thoughts, memories, traumas, samskaras, or whatever word we'd like to use to encapsulate these low-vibrational strings are all vibrating at a measurable frequency.

In his book *Waking the Tiger*, Peter Levine, an American psychotraumatologist, biophysicist, psychologist, and developer of Somatic Experiencing®, approaches the concept from the position of somatic psychotherapy. He writes, "Sensations come from symptoms, and symptoms come from compressed energy; that energy is what we have to work within this process. Through sensation and the felt sense, this vast energy can gradually be decompressed and harnessed for the purpose of transforming trauma."[9]

Through the lens of Internal Family Systems, a popular therapeutic modality often used with psychedelic work, you can make the connection that each of our "parts" holds its own average vibration. From a more esoteric perspective, each imprint stored in our body's tissues, muscles, and nervous system has a vibration. Each samskara, be it from this lifetime or one from the past, is a stored charge, waiting to be released through our future karma.

Overlaying the Map of Consciousness with quantum physics, psychotherapy, and spirituality, we can hypothesize that shameful, guilty, and apathetic thoughts, memories, and trauma hold low vibrations. Thoughts of acceptance, reason, and love hold high vibrations.

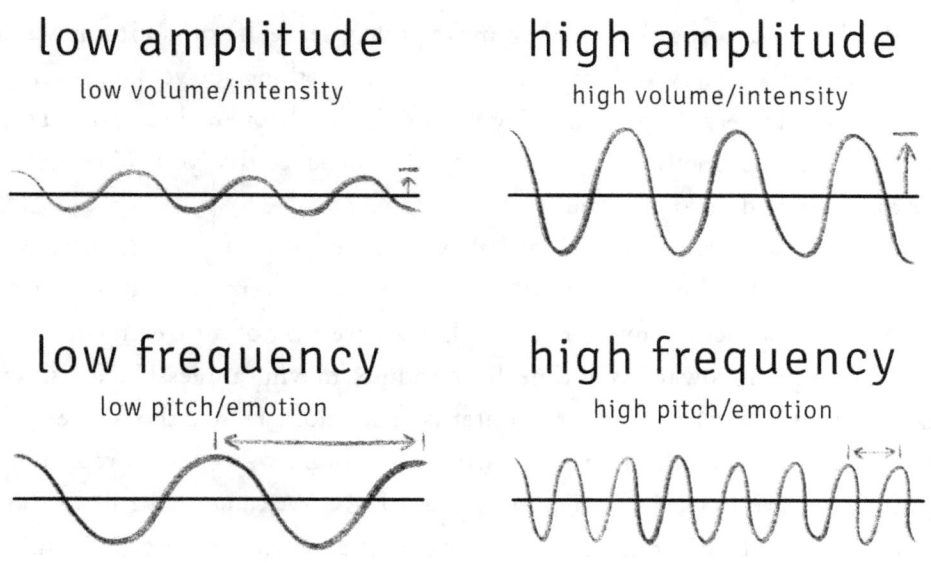

FIGURE 2. Amplitude and frequency of emotions

If we compare our emotions to a sound wave, we can expand this metaphor visually using the concepts of frequency and amplitude. The high-pitched sound of a violin would be like the high frequency of love. Conversely, the low-pitched sound of a tuba would be like the low vibration of shame. The stronger the emotion in our system, the higher the amplitude and the louder the volume—and the more intensely it disrupts our present-moment awareness.

As we will discuss further in chapter 17, "Activation," if our lives represent the average of our actions, then our consciousness is the average of all the vibrations stored in our body, mind, and spirit (BMS). I suspect that if science had instrumentation subtle enough to measure it, they could plot all the minute residue stored in our BMS on the Map of Consciousness. Unfortunately, this technology does not yet exist.

Healing Through Vibration

If we can appreciate that everything in our lived experience is just energy vibrating at different frequencies, and that the higher our average frequency, the better we feel, the natural next questions are "How can we feel better?" and "How do we heal?"

Self-love is one of the most overused tropes in the fields of therapy, healing, spirituality, and psychedelics. I frequently hear practitioners say, "Just love yourself," yet when I ask my clients, "Who taught you how to love yourself?" I am often met with a blank stare followed by the stark realization of "No one."

If this is you, don't be alarmed. You make perfect sense. If you don't know exactly what love feels like or how to love yourself, it's not something you've done wrong, and it isn't necessarily because of something traumatic that happened to you. Instead, it may be because of something that *didn't* happen to you, or that your biological caregivers didn't or couldn't do for you.

Emotional neglect is a pattern of behavior often seen when a caregiver consistently cannot meet a child's emotional needs. This can be very difficult to detect and treat because it's an act of omission rather than an overt act of mistreatment or abuse. Neglected children grow to become neglected adults, moving aimlessly, like fish swimming around without knowing what water is. They don't realize they've been living without the felt sense of love, because when their brain was open to receive it, the people who needed to teach them didn't have it to give. We can never truly love others any more than we love ourselves, we cannot give away what we don't have, and "hurt people hurt people," often unintentionally.

To overcome this deficit, we must take two distinct actions. First, we must find another human who knows what love is and is willing and capable of teaching us how to feel it within ourselves. That might look like a close friend, a teacher, or a helping professional. Second, we must soften and become vulnerable enough to receive the love being offered.

The saying "If you cannot be vulnerable, you cannot feel" refers to the idea that vulnerability is the basis of emotions and feelings. Most of the time, we cut off our vulnerability to protect ourselves when we're young. But when we avoid being vulnerable, we also prevent ourselves from experiencing a full range of emotions that includes love, joy, empathy, and belonging.

Consider all your emotions as chords played on a guitar. Love is one of those chords. If our parents attempted to teach us the sound of love with their guitar, which was out-of-tune, ours would also become out-of-tune. Most of us find out later in life that the definition of love we learned was more about action than vibration and resonance. Someone taught us how to strum the guitar, but most likely, we have been listening to a distorted love chord since birth.

If we abandon the trope that love is solely an emotion felt by poets, artists, and musicians, and respect that it's actually a vibration (500 on the MoC), we can then begin the gradual process of retuning our guitar to play a chord that's finally in tune. This goes for every one of our emotions, not just love.

In *A General Theory of Love*, author Thomas Lewis argues that our nervous systems are not self-contained and that our brains connect with the brains of people close to us from early childhood. This connection, called limbic resonance, creates a silent rhythm that can alter the structure of our brains, establish emotional patterns, and determine who we are.

Limbic resonance refers to how the emotional state of one person can be influenced or mirrored by the emotions of another. It explains how humans (and some other animals) can deeply connect emotionally with others. It plays a role in the nonverbal exchange of emotions, allowing people to feel empathy, form bonds, and attune to one another's emotional states.

For example, when you're with someone feeling joyful, your emotional state might uplift, reflecting that resonance. Conversely, when you're with someone who is anxious, you may also feel anxious. Lewis says, "The first part of emotional healing is being limbically known—having someone with a keen ear catch your melodic essence."

The discussion of limbic resonance frequently occurs in the context of close relationships, psychotherapy, and even spiritual or healing practices, since it underscores the significance of emotional connectivity for psychological and emotional well-being.

To visualize this vibrational concept, let's use the method of heart rate variability (HRV) to see how this manifests in our body. The HeartMath Institute provides us with some fascinating research:

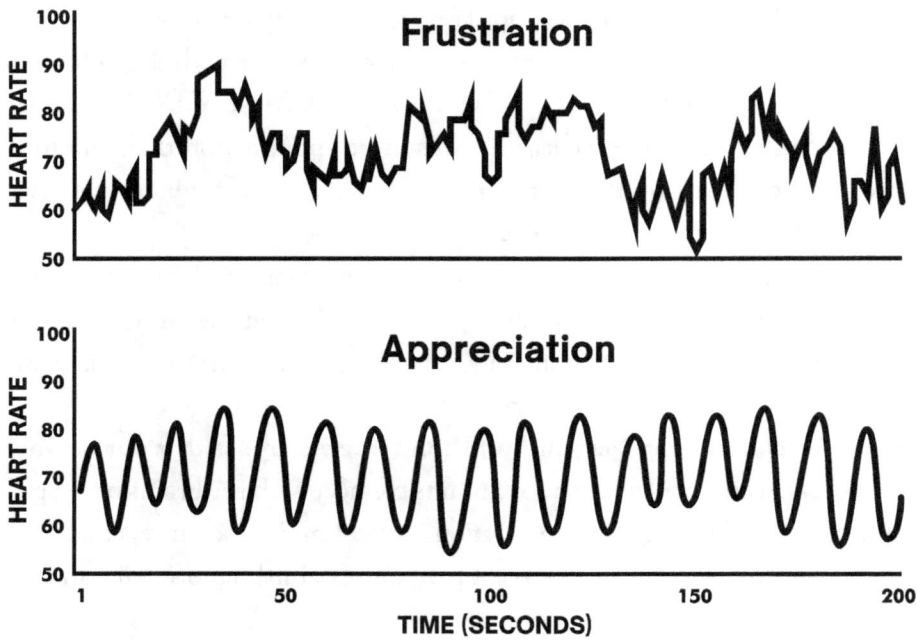

FIGURE 3. Frustration vs. appreciation in heart rate variability.

These graphs show examples of real-time heart rate variability patterns (heart rhythms) recorded from individuals experiencing different emotions. The incoherent heart rhythm pattern shown in the top graph, characterized by its irregular, jagged waveform, is typical of stress and negative emotions such as anger, frustration, and anxiety. The bottom graph shows an example of the coherent heart rhythm pattern typically observed when an individual is experiencing a sustained positive emotion, such as appreciation, compassion, or love. The coherent pattern is characterized by its regular, sine-wave-like waveform. It is interesting to note that the overall amount of heart rate variability is actually the same in the two recordings shown above; however, the patterns of the HRV waveforms are clearly different.[10]

The research continues to say, "… the magnetic field produced by the heart is more than one hundred times greater in strength than the field generated by the brain and can be detected up to three feet away from the body, in all directions, using SQUID-based magnetometers."[11] This adds credence that emotions are directly tied to our energetic field and that field can be felt and affect those around us.

Psychedelics as Cleansing Agents

We've come a long way, turning over nearly every piece of the healing puzzle. Now, we can flip over the last piece and learn how psychedelics complete this picture.

Consider this: When you take an ibuprofen, do you tell it where it needs to go to reduce inflammation? No. The stomach and intestines absorb the ibuprofen into the bloodstream, and it then circulates through the entire body. Since it is present throughout the bloodstream, it does not target a specific area but acts systemically. Wherever damaged tissues release inflammatory signals, the medicine eases pain and inflammation in those areas by inhibiting an enzyme that produces a chemical that causes inflammation.

If you sprain your ankle, that "traumatic residue" shows up as inflammation. Eventually, the body is smart enough to heal itself. Once the trigger of the inflammation is removed or healed, the lymphatic system carries the inflammation to the lymph nodes, where they process and remove it from the body.

At the risk of trying to oversimplify hundreds of years of psychotherapeutic theory, I propose that psychological trauma is not all that different from a sprained ankle, and that psychological "inflammation" is merely low-vibration energy stored in the BMS. Therapy and most spiritual philosophies, methods, and practices through the ages help us process and release these low-vibration patterns and integrate the Truth of our lived experiences. Each of these tools plays a similar role to the lymphatic system, cleaning out the traumatic residue of our BMS. The memory of a traumatic experience doesn't disappear from our consciousness any more than a deep scar disappears from our skin. But the energetic charge of that memory can shift from one of anger and shame to forgiveness and love. The memory stays but the "inflammation" is now gone.

What I have come to experience is that psychedelics vibrate at a rate lower than Brahman (∞) but higher than human enlightenment (1000). Using the MoC as our guide, we can see that psychedelics show us which parts of us are inflamed and vibrating at a low frequency, and help us release what is no longer in service to Brahman/Atman.

Psychedelics are frequently regarded as "nonspecific amplifiers," meaning they amplify whatever content is residing in our BMS. With this unique ability, they can shine a spotlight on whatever is hiding in our conscious or unconscious mind. I view them as a kind of powerful, energetic ibuprofen. They possess the unique ability to circulate through and scan our system; find low-vibration trauma, memories, and samskaras; and then transform, transmute, and liberate them from our bodies. With each release, our average vibration and level of consciousness increases. These substances have even been suggested to improve cancer treatment in a handful of cases.[12]

Step-by-step, we build greater strength in our BMS and raise our frequency. Because psychedelics operate solely on energy and vibrations, they have no interest in whether we call these things low-vibration patterns, thoughts, trauma, samskaras, imprints, illness, or disease. They don't care which lamp post we're standing under or how bright we think our individual light is. Words mean nothing to these substances, and are only necessary for humans, who need words to describe their experiences to others. Psychedelics heal outside of human understanding, and the only technology capable of measuring their effectiveness are the human bodies that experience their healing.

Psychedelics are not the only tools for energetic cleansing. Therapy also cleanses and releases energy. Deep forms of meditation, such as Vipassana, cleanse and release energy. Dancing, Reiki, acupuncture, and massage can release energy. A primary difference is that each of these activities originates from (or runs through) human consciousness and will therefore vibrate lower than their original source.

As a simple example, Reiki energy is said to come from the universal life force, known as *ki*. This energy may be as powerful as a psychedelic, but in most cases, it is channeled through a human being that has their own personality, process, residue, and trauma. This residue will attenuate the original frequency and amplitude as it moves through the practitioner's body, mind, and spirit. Conversely, the vibrational rate of a psychedelic substance is direct, so the speed and force with which it can clean our systems is higher.

To simplify, summarize, and illustrate this framework for healing, consider your BMS as a fish tank full of dirty water. The dirtier your water, the lower your vibration. Filter your water, and your vibration will rise.

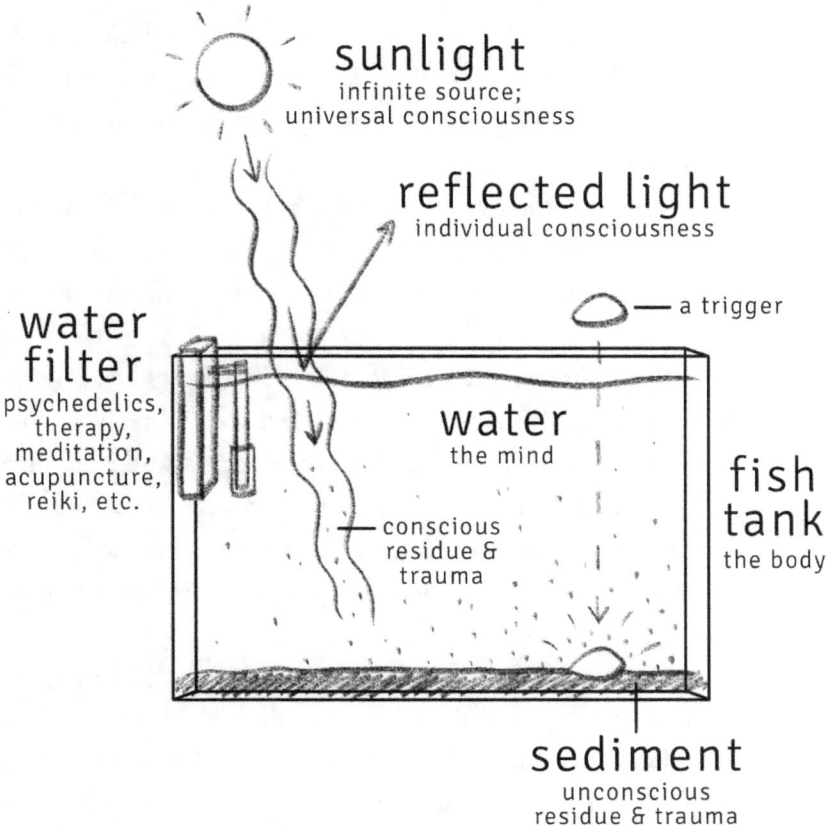

FIGURE 4. Your body-mind-spirit as a fishtank.

The illustration above encapsulates the entire process. Let me explain:

1. The fish tank represents our body. Over time, the sides of our tank attract dirt and algae, making it difficult to see in or out. Most people start their healing journey at the physical level because dirty glass is easier to see and clean. Metaphorically speaking, we can clean the sides of our tank with time, attention, and good old elbow grease.

2. The water within the tank represents our conscious and subconscious mind. Peering down from the top of the tank, we can easily see the depth of our conscious mind, which consists of the thoughts, feelings, and perceptions we are fully aware of. Below that, the murkier water represents our subconscious mind, which includes the mental artifacts that we can bring into consciousness with some effort. Our water always has some debris, but the messier our life, the dirtier our water.

3. The layer of sediment at the bottom of our tank represents our unconscious mind. Over time, debris from our conscious and subconscious mind sinks to the bottom and builds up an ever-thickening layer of mud. Unviewable in ordinary consciousness, the thicker our layer of sediment, the more uncomfortable our lives become.

4. The sun shining on the tank represents the Brahman, or Infinite Source. It vibrates at the frequency of infinity (∞) and sends an unlimited amount of high-vibration existence, consciousness, and bliss to illuminate our tank and water.

5. The reflection of the sun's rays represents our level of individual consciousness that can be measured with the MoC. A perfectly enlightened being would reflect a frequency of 1,000, but because our tank and water are dirty, what enters our system at a frequency of ∞ reflects at a far lower vibration. The dirtier our water, the lower the frequency of reflected individual consciousness. This level of individual consciousness is how we perceive ourselves and how the world perceives us.

6. The rock being dropped into our tank represents a situation or trigger in our lives. Depending on the size of the rock, once it hits the bottom, it might stir up a little (or a lot) of sediment, clouding our water and causing confusion and discomfort. If we ignore the sediment, it settles to the bottom again, eventually adding more debris and patiently waiting for us to start cleaning. If we address the sediment while it's floating in our conscious mind, we clean up our BMS a little more, minutely increasing our vibration and level of consciousness.

7. Psychedelics act as a powerful filter. When inserted into our fishtank, they clean the debris in our conscious and subconscious mind, and disrupt our unconscious mind, allowing built-up sediment to be dislodged and cleansed. It is a powerful process, and if our psychedelic dose is too high, the amount of disrupted sediment can cause such a disturbance that our lives may become unbearably cloudy and confusing for months—or even years. But with proper use, psychedelics can help clean our water and tank, increasing our frequency and our reflection of individual consciousness.

We are *sat-chit-ananda atma* (existence, consciousness, bliss), and over time, karma causes us to accumulate low-vibration residue from our current lifetime and our past lifetimes. Layer upon layer of residue builds up and negatively affects our body, mind, and spirit until that residue is cleaned and released. With each release, we remember the Truth: we are capable of infinite bliss. Until we make the conscious choice to clean our fishtank, we will continue to take actions that keep it dirty. Psychedelics have the remarkable power to help us turn that corner.

Now, before you decide to take a massive dose of psychedelics to filter all your debris, consider what it would be like for a kindergartner enroll in a college-level calculus class. Not yet knowing how to do simple addition and subtraction, calculus would be an impossible feat for a six-year-old. Depending on this youngster's emotional resilience and personality, this overwhelming experience might feel incredibly scary or wonderfully empowering. With the right mixture of consciousness and personality, the experience could make them feel superior to their kindergarten classmates. On the other hand, not possessing the requisite knowledge to understand the content and do the work, they could also find it a terrifying experiment, causing deep fear and shame.

This is what can happen when humans try to use psychedelics to move too quickly through higher planes of consciousness. Imagine meeting God (Brahman) with zero preparation. Suppose your system is vibrating at the level of shame (20), and you interact with an energy source vibrating at infinity. The delta, or difference, between your vibrations would be so profound it could be shocking—if not traumatizing—to your system. You wouldn't know what to do, how to feel, or even how to communicate on that level. Much like a kindergartener attempting calculus, you would not possess the consciousness required to understand and integrate the experience into your life. If you're the kindergartner who develops a superiority complex, you experience ego inflation. If you're the kindergartner who experiences fear and shame, you return to waking consciousness with an experience of ontological shock. Both are common risks of psychedelics that we will discuss further in chapter 7, "Risks."

When used with proper guidance, psychedelics act as a bridge to higher vibratory states. They cleanse our systems and teach us, step-by-step, how to experience these higher frequencies. They function as emissaries of Brahman, serving as finely tuned sensors for our body-mind-spirt system, scanning for low-vibration energy and helping us cleanse and release anything not aligned with *sat-chit-ananda atma*.

It may be helpful to think of each psychedelic substance (i.e., psilocybin, San Pedro, ayahuasca, and iboga) in the same way Hindus think of deities. Hinduism is often misunderstood as a polytheistic religion. In actuality, Hindus worship a single God (Brahman) that shows up in many aspects and with many names (Ganesha, Krishna, Shiva, etc.). I have found that psychedelics are very similar. While each of these substances may look and act differently, they all act as bridges to the same Infinite Source.

And if the thought of releasing old guilt or shame causes fear, don't worry. The vibration that entered your body (and caused your low vibration) does not need to be the energy that leaves it. I have found the fastest way to heal low-vibration emotions is with gratitude and forgiveness.

As our water becomes cleaner, our vibrations increase. As we vibrate at a higher frequency, our strength grows, and our lives become happier. The greater our happiness, the more we can enjoy our lives. This is the fundamental reason for using psychedelics for healing: to reorient our lives away from external pleasure seeking and toward a desire for freedom and true happiness. These medicines want you to be happy because that is your authentic nature.

An Enlightened Being Takes Psychedelics

Ram Dass, formerly known as Richard Alpert (of psychedelic lore and Harvard fame), was one of my earliest teachers on my spiritual path. Gv is actually short for Govind Dass, a name offered to me by Ram Dass in 2018 when I was studying with him in Hawaii. After being fired from his post at Harvard, Ram Dass became a well-known American spiritual teacher, guru of modern yoga, psychologist, and writer. One of his often-told stories is that of giving his enlightened guru, Neem Karoli Baba (also known as Maharaji), LSD in India.

During his first experience, Maharaji ingested roughly 900 micrograms of acid. Ram Dass watched him for an hour, but nothing happened. Nothing whatsoever. After returning to the US, Ram Dass began to doubt what had really happened. Had Maharaji palmed the pills? Maybe thrown them over his shoulder? Three years later, when he returned to India, Maharaji once again ingested LSD. This time the dose was 1200 micrograms (an amount eleven times greater than an average recreational dose). Once again, absolutely nothing happened.

Maharaji himself said, "These medicines were used in the Kullu Valley long ago. But yogis have lost that knowledge. They were used with fasting. Nobody knows now. To take them with no effect, your mind must be firmly fixed on God. Others would be afraid to take. Many saints would not take this."[13]

In his own retelling of the story, Ram Dass estimates that because Maharaji was already such an enlightened being and his consciousness was already vibrating at such a high frequency, the drugs were powerless to alter it. Since Maharaji's system was already free of all karmic debris, the psychedelics had nothing left to clean.

We rarely get to examine the intersection of such a high-vibration being with the high-vibrational power of psychedelics, but this story perfectly illustrates the theory being offered. If you're already enlightened, there is nowhere to go and no higher frequency to experience.

The Healing Paradox

A fundamental element of every mystic tradition is paradox. Healing with psychedelics is no different. We are simultaneously 100 percent human (with all our residue) and 100 percent Divine (perfect *sat-chit-ananda atma*). The process of healing is systematically cleansing and purifying our system. You don't need to acquire anything *new* to heal; you only need to release the low-vibration energy that is not your true nature. This idea is reinforced by verse 47 of the Tao Te Ching:

> *The student learns by daily increment.*
> *The Way is gained by daily loss,*
> *Loss upon loss until*
> *At last comes rest.*
> ###
> *By letting go, it all gets done;*
> *The world is won by those who let it go!*
> *But when you try and try,*
> *The world is then beyond the winning.*

After experiencing a decade of nervousness before every psychedelic journey, learning that psychedelics were only cleansing my system changed everything for me. It removed all my fears about doing deep work with these powerful medicines. I hope that it may also help ease some of your trepidation.

For years, I went into every psychedelic experience with some level of fear and anxiety, wondering what long-forgotten traumatic memory would be unearthed, requiring me to walk through the gates of hell to see it and purge it. Today, I know it's all just energy, and that these substances are healing. It is rarely the substances that should concern you—far more often the real concern comes from the humans who are serving them (a lot more on that in chapter 10, "Facilitation").

Anton Chekhov, a Russian-born playwright from the late nineteenth century, believed that when many remedies are proposed for a disease, it indicates that the disease cannot be cured. Modern allopathic medicine has repeatedly proven this accurate. Chronic autoimmune and inflammation-based illnesses have become pervasive in our culture, and no matter how many medications we try, the root cause remains unresolved—because these medications never remove the low-vibration energy causing the inflammation.

Humans have become drunk with the power of their intellect. Power and possessions have become the measure of a well-lived life, and colonialism and late-stage capitalism prioritize being smart and successful over being peaceful, joyous, and free. To heal, we must decouple net worth from self-worth. We need to remind ourselves to separate our packaging from our essence and clear away anything that isn't authentically us (*sat-chit-ananda atma*).

We've forgotten our true nature and how to find it, but psychedelics offer us something we cannot usually access in ordinary, waking consciousness. Healing in this way is like remembering. Psychedelics provide an expansive awareness for us to remember who we are at our core.

I propose that psychedelics operate at a level of consciousness far above the streetlamps of science, psychotherapy, and human spirituality. I believe that all these "lamps" are shining on something *partially* true, but that none address the fundamental how and why of psychedelic healing. Scientists might argue that psychedelics affect the brain, and that is the source of your healing. I theorize that what is happening in the brain is a downstream byproduct of the healing that comes before it. We don't need to know anything about the brain to heal with psychedelics. The billions of dollars spent to fund the ever-increasing body of research around psychedelics is merely mental masturbation supporting a medical and political structure that must crumble for true, large-scale healing to ever occur.

Today, science does not possess instrumentation that is sensitive enough to measure what is happening during psychedelic healing. The same was true before Rutherford discovered subatomic particles in 1911, or before Copernicus discovered the Earth revolved around the Sun. The only fundamental difference between science and spirituality is the subtlety and sophistication of our instrumentation.

For clarity and attribution, some elements of my theory are not new. Many of the broad concepts came from my teachers, directly from the medicine, or have already been published. My hope is to draw a theoretical through line between the known principles of three completely different disciplines to give psychedelics and spirituality, rather than science and psychotherapy, the long-deserved credit they are due.

Consider this: the most basic definition of spirituality is "self-knowledge." There doesn't need to be anything "woo-woo" about it. You don't need to believe in a giant marshmallow man in the sky or be fearful that if you don't behave, you'll end up spending eternity with Satan. Spirituality is only the process of self-remembering. When we direct our consciousness inwards, we remember who we are. The more we remember, the more we can experience the bliss that is our True nature.

Psychedelics have the unique ability to help us clean the dirty water of our consciousness. It's not a fast process. (If you're expecting it to be, you will be sorely disappointed.) Regardless of the path you choose to walk with psychedelics, remember this: You can take the psychedelics out of spirituality, but you can never take the spirituality out of psychedelics.

A Map to Guide Your Journey

"Shiva Feel" by DJ Drez & Jyothi Chalam

I f you are new to holistic healing and psychedelics, you should know you are intentionally leaving the mainstream and embarking on a new way to experience the world. The field of psychedelics is a complex and fascinating one. Humans have been exploring it for millennia, and it comes with its own unique language and terminology. These terms come from science, psychology, and spirituality—and often intertwine them. Depending on the person you're speaking with, they may use terminology from one, two, or all three disciplines. This complexity is part of what makes the psychedelic landscape so confusing, intriguing, and ultimately worth exploring.

This chapter aims to give you a lay of the land and provide you with a "normie-to-psychedelic" dictionary, offering just enough information to give you a head start on your new adventure.

Glossary of General Psychedelic Terms

When discussing psychedelics for healing, I have found it very helpful to shift away from a pejorative vocabulary (originating from the US war on drugs) to a healthier and more optimistic vernacular. You may be someone who's looking for healing but afraid of using "drugs." It may sound frivolous, but shifting your language around these terms makes a difference.

Activated — The period of time after ingesting a substance when the effects of the substance are felt in the body, mind, and spirit. This term intentionally shifts away from the phrase "getting high."

Aboveground — Legal use and institutionalized practices sanctioned by governments, medical institutions, and regulatory bodies.

Energy — The vital, unseen force or essence that permeates all of existence. Many consider it to be the fundamental substance, or flow, that connects all beings and elements in the universe, influencing physical, emotional, mental, and spiritual states. Other traditions might refer to this as *Qi, Prana, Ki,* or *Rauch.* It is worth noting that the term "energy" (along with all the practices surrounding the use and application of the word) is one of the most overused and abused concepts in spirituality today. Undoubtedly, there are many powerful energy practitioners whose access to this invisible source can be profoundly healing. There are also uncountable "TikTok shamans" and "Instagram charlatans" who want you to sign up for their twelve-week online energy healing course. When choosing an energy practitioner, a high degree of discernment (and maybe a dab of skepticism) is often required.

Entheogen — Another term for a psychedelic or hallucinogen, typically of plant or fungal origin. This term is frequently used in place of the word "psychedelic" and refers to substances that may be used in spiritual, religious, or shamanic rituals to induce altered states of consciousness, mystical experiences, or spiritual insights. The term comes from the Greek words *entheos*, meaning "full of god, inspired, possessed," and *genesthai*, meaning "to come into being." Some people prefer to use the term entheogen to signify using these substances in a more spiritual context, such as within an entheogenic church, ceremony, or ritual.

Experience — The subjective experience and inner exploration that a person undergoes while under the influence of a psychedelic substance. This term is an intentional shift away from the word "trip" and is used throughout this book. It is synonymous with "journey" or "ceremony."

Facilitator — A trained individual who guides and supports participants through their psychedelic experiences. This umbrella term is used throughout the book and can refer to guides, therapists, priests, ministers, ceremonial leaders, shamans, curanderos, or maestros. Because psychedelics cross the boundaries of science, psychotherapy, and spirituality, there is no single, accepted term to describe the role a facilitator will play in your experience or the qualifications they possess. If you are considering working with a practitioner who chooses to use one of these titles, I recommend asking them to describe why they have opted for their title of choice. The answer they give may offer insight into their philosophy and help you decide if they are someone you would like to work with.

Note: I intentionally excluded the role of "trip sitter" from this definition, as trip sitters do not typically possess formal training.

(Sacred) Medicine — The psychedelic substance you will ingest/receive within a ceremonial context. While many may consider this term to be synonymous with "entheogen" or "substance" (see below), pertaining specifically to a unique psychedelic molecular structure, I propose that Sacred Medicine is more than just the substance you are ingesting. This term represents the overlap between the substance and the facilitator. A facilitator with a deep connection to the substance they are serving may be able to manipulate or enhance the effects of the substance. In other words, receiving the exact same substance from two different facilitators can feel like two very different forms of Sacred Medicine.

Modern — The broad geographies, structures, ideas, and cultural belief systems surrounding today's psychedelic use. These are often aligned with the colonized, capitalistic, allopathic, and science-based systems that treat disease through diagnostic and drug-focused processes; as an opposing term to "traditional."

Note: I've come to realize that there is no easy way to name how, where, or why psychedelic substances are being used. Since psychedelics are used across the world and this book could be read anywhere, the term "the West" does not adequately represent geography and "Westernized" excludes populations that have also adopted modern ways of thinking and living. Terms like "the Global North" or "WEIRD" (Western, Educated, Industrialized, Rich, and Democratic) also come close, but both leave out parts of the "the East." Because I've written this book to be more practical than anthropologically exact, I've chosen to offer the short-hand term "modern" for better readability.

Psychedelic Church — A religious or spiritual organization that uses psychedelics as part of its rituals or spiritual practices. These churches view psychedelic substances, often referred to as "entheogens," as sacraments that facilitate spiritual awakening, healing, and connection to higher consciousness or the Divine. In the United States, two Native American Churches, the Santo Daime and the Centro Espírita Beneficente União do Vegetal (UDV), have fought and won cases at the United States Supreme Court granting them permission to legally serve a psychedelic substance as a part of their sincere religious beliefs. There are very few churches that have been granted legal authority to serve psychedelics, and most psychedelic churches operating in the United States today do so only from a stance of "legal defensibility."

Seeker — Someone who approaches the use of psychedelics intending to heal, explore more profound aspects of consciousness, gain spiritual insight, or achieve personal growth. This term is an intentional shift away from the term "drug user."

Serving (the medicine) — The actions of a facilitator who offers a psychedelic substance to seekers, usually in a healing or ceremonial setting. The phrase "serving the medicine" implies not just the physical act of giving someone a psychedelic substance, but also the more profound responsibility of ensuring safety and assisting the seeker through their experience in a meaningful—often sacred—way.

Sit (with the medicine) — The intentional experience of taking a psychedelic substance for healing. This is a conscious shift away from the phrases "getting high," "taking drugs," or "tripping."

(Holding) Space — A practice of being fully present and making space for someone else's experience without judgment, while allowing them to feel safe, seen, and heard. "Holding space" is a term used in many psychological and spiritual traditions. Your therapist, yoga teacher, meditation guide, or even a good friend or family member can hold space. We will discuss the qualifications of this skill in more detail in chapter 10, "Facilitation."

Substance — Any psychedelic compound you ingest for healing purposes. This term is an intentional shift away from the word "drug." This is a more generic and less spiritual term than "entheogen," "medicine," or "Sacred Medicine" that are used to describe psychedelics served in clinical, therapeutic, and spiritual settings.

(Infinite) Source — A spiritual concept of a higher power or Source of universal existence, consciousness, and bliss. This book takes a spiritual—but not religious—stance, and this term is an intentional shift away from the word "God" (and other common religious-specific names such as Brahman, Jesus, Krishna, Yahweh, or Allah). What you choose to call your Source is completely up to you. If "Infinite Source" causes you discomfort, please grab a pen, cross it out, and write in your preferred name.

Traditional — The geographies, structures, ideas, and cultural belief system surrounding historical psychedelic use. These traditions, often practiced by Indigenous communities and healers, have intentionally chosen not to modernize, and are based in centuries or millennia of experience; an opposing term to modern.

Underground — The informal, noninstitutionalized network of individuals and communities involved in the use, distribution, and facilitation of psychedelic substances, typically outside of mainstream medical, legal, or corporate frameworks. At the time of this writing (unless you are traveling out of the country or live in Oregon or Colorado, and until the government legalizes psychedelic substances), there is a better-than-average chance your psychedelic facilitator will be operating in the underground. While this may not be legal, it should be understood that many of the most experienced facilitators practice in this space.

(Doing the) Work — The conscious and intentional inner growth, healing, and self-transformation process. It often involves practices to cultivate awareness, align with one's higher Self, and address personal or emotional challenges.

Types of Psychedelic Substances

While the number of psychoactive compounds used for healing is vast, I have chosen to discuss eight specific substances in this book. Some are not technically considered a "psychedelic" (as we will further discuss in chapter 9, "Substances"), but still fall under the broad umbrella of psychedelic healing and represent the most frequently used substances in the industry today.

+ **Ketamine** — Originally synthesized in 1972, with more modern research continuing to discover ketamine's ability to treat depression and suicidal thoughts.
+ **MDMA** — Originally synthesized in 1912, the use of MDMA for therapeutic purposes began in the 1970s. It is now one of the leading and most successful substances used to treat post-traumatic stress disorder (PTSD).

- **Psilocybin Mushrooms** — Psilocybin mushrooms have been used for healing dating as far back as 6,000 to 9,000 years. Used across the globe, their popularity grew in the 1950s and 60s, and the psilocybin molecule was first synthesized in 1958. Today, this substance is used to treat a wide variety of conditions, including depression, anxiety, PTSD, substance use disorders, end-of-life distress, and more.

- **Lysergic Acid Diethylamide (LSD)** — Accidentally synthesized in 1938, LSD became one of the most widely studied psychedelics—until it began playing an overburdened role in the 1960s counterculture. Today, this substance is used to treat a wide variety of conditions including anxiety, end-of-life distress, depression, PTSD, substance use disorders, and more.

- **San Pedro and Peyote** — Used for spiritual and medicinal purposes by the Indigenous peoples of the Andes Mountains in South America and certain parts of North America, these cacti (and the psychoactive ingredient, mescaline, that they both contain) have been in use for 5,000 to 7,000 years. Deeply rooted in Indigenous traditions, these sacred medicines have been used for healing physical ailments, spiritual cleansing, existential healing, divination and visions, and connecting with the spiritual and natural worlds.

- **Ayahuasca** — Used for spiritual and medicinal purposes by Indigenous practitioners of many South American countries, ayahuasca use dates back 1,000 to 2,500 years—or possibly more. Deeply rooted in the Amazon basin, this traditional plant medicine most often comes from Peru, Brazil, Columbia, Ecuador, and Bolivia. It is used for healing physical and emotional ailments, spiritual cleansing and purification, divination, connecting with spirits or ancestors, and gaining insights and visions to solve problems.

- **5-MeO-DMT** — First synthesized in 1936, this substance was later discovered as a naturally occurring compound in plants (such as yopo snuff) and animals (such as the venom of the Bufo alvarius toad). Likely one of the most potent and fast-acting psychedelics, this substance is known for producing experiences of ego dissolution, unity consciousness, and transcendence. It is used to treat conditions such as depression, anxiety, PTSD, substance use disorders, and existential and spiritual crises.

- **Iboga/Ibogaine** — Native to Central Africa and one of the most powerful psychoactive plants on the planet, iboga is considered a "sacred teacher" by the Bwiti tradition of Gabon. Iboga has been used for at least 1,000 years, and its roots contain the powerful alkaloid ibogaine, first synthesized in 1901. It has since been deemed the "addiction interrupter" for its remarkable ability to break the cycle of addiction of opioids, alcohol, and other substances.

Each of these eight substances have a rich history, either scientifically or through Indigenous practices—many for thousands of years. The youngest of these substances, ketamine, still has over fifty years of modern use.

Trailheads for Psychedelic Use

In hiking, the trailhead is the place where the trail begins. In the world of psychedelics, most people find their way onto the landscape using one of these four "trailheads": recreational, clinical, therapeutic, or spiritual. Depending on the trailhead you choose, the substance you ingest, and the country, state, or city you ingest it in, the legality of many of these trailheads is highly variable. To view the current psychedelic laws by country, visit https://piq.lv/world-tracker. To view the current psychedelic laws by US state, visit https://piq.lv/state-tracker.

THE RECREATIONAL TRAILHEAD

Psychedelics for recreational use are nothing new and represent the broadest entry point for many people. While I hold no judgment for recreational use, this book does not cater to those entering through this trailhead. However, this book can prove beneficial if a recreational user decides to use psychedelics for healing, or if they "accidentally" have a healing or spiritual experience they cannot explain or integrate.

THE CLINICAL TRAILHEAD

The clinical trailhead is represented by researchers and scientists gathering data to study and understand how psychedelic substances work in a strictly physiological sense. If healing happens during this work, it is a fantastic byproduct. This entry point usually comes with an agnostic or atheistic approach, and attempts to avoid imposing a belief system of any kind onto study participants. Highly data driven, a clinical approach is often focused on the body and brain. It is designed for repeatable results, measurements, and protocols.

THE THERAPEUTIC TRAILHEAD

This trailhead frequently aligns with modern psychotherapeutic modalities, such as Internal Family Systems, as well as transpersonal, depth, and somatic psychotherapy, as supported by therapists and coaches interested in helping their clients heal with psychedelics.

THE SPIRITUAL TRAILHEAD

This trailhead is as vast, complicated, and often as misunderstood as spirituality itself. It is almost always accompanied by a belief system and supported by ritual or ceremony. In the Global North, entry onto this trailhead most likely involves an underground practitioner or psychedelic church. Working with psychedelics in non-Western countries usually includes a spiritual or ceremonial component.

Interestingly, no matter which trailhead you use to enter the landscape, your results are often the same. Psychedelics, unlike the humans that serve them or the different trailheads mentioned above, are agnostic in their ability to heal and offer mystical experiences. Pick the trailhead that most aligns with your level of consciousness, and the medicine will take care of the rest.

What I have found is that if you overlay these four trailheads onto a pyramid, the recreational trailhead represents the lowest level and has the greatest number of users. Moving up from there, the clinical trailhead attracts many users because of its legality, safety, and scientific backing. On the next level, the therapeutic trailhead is less accessible in our current legal landscape but is gaining in popularity. Most of the practitioners from this level have already been trained and licensed to deliver some form of psychotherapy, and are now parlaying that experience into healing with psychedelics. The spiritual trailhead represents the top of the pyramid. If you use psychedelics long enough, it's inevitable that you will have a spiritual or mystical experience. It is usually the facilitators with an understanding of spiritual concepts that are most effective in helping you understand and explain your psychedelic experience.

Each of these trailheads comes with its pluses and minuses. Many seekers, especially those without an existing spiritual belief system or any prior experience using substances, tend to want a clinical or therapeutic experience because it most closely aligns with their views of safety, therapy, and modern medicine. The challenge is that it is difficult to be admitted into a clinical study, and most licensed therapists who are practicing in a jurisdiction where psychedelics are illegal do not want to risk losing their license.

So, where does that leave an inexperienced beginner? Likely flying to a remote location or navigating the Wild West of the underground. This book dedicates much of its content to assisting seekers in safely and successfully traversing their healing journey within these domains. It might surprise you that many of the clinicians and therapists who are "certified" or "licensed" to conduct a clinical trial or serve you psychedelics in a therapeutic setting may have never ingested a psychedelic themselves, let alone guided hundreds, if not thousands, of seekers.

The underground comes with its own unique set of risks and benefits. The risks are that it may be illegal to ingest a psychedelic substance in your location, your facilitator may have no training in modern medicine or psychotherapy, and there is no governing body regulating psychedelic practitioners. The benefits are that your facilitator may have decades of experience working with these substances—without the cognitive limitations imposed by modern medicine or psychotherapy.

You must ask yourself, "How well has the system I've been working with served my healing?" If your answer is "Not very well," it might be time to consider a different system.

Styles of Psychedelic Use

Once you've selected a trailhead, you will often encounter a few different styles of how you can interact with psychedelics. Below is a summary of those styles.

CLINICAL STYLE

This style represents the epitome of a secular way of working with psychedelics. When working in a clinical setting, you must remember that you are a part of an experiment and that you will work with scientists or therapists in settings that may feel cold, impersonal, and like a doctor's office. The focus will be on measurable data, standards, practices, and protocols designed to remove as much variability from the experiment as possible. Clinical trials have a specific beginning and end. This may be fine for most participants, but others find that the rigorous methods of fairness limit their ability to receive the support they need after a challenging or dysregulating experience. Scientific trials are necessary to eventually merge psychedelics into modern medicine, but do not forget that this research may be driven more by data and funding than healing.

THERAPEUTIC STYLE

Also leaning more toward the secular, one of the most popular terms in today's landscape is "psychedelic-assisted psychotherapy" (also abbreviated as PAP). Interestingly, no one knows what this term actually means. PAP is generally thought of as a therapeutic approach combining the use of psychedelic substances with traditional talk therapy. Some describe PAP as the therapy sessions that happen before and after your psychedelic experience. Others include the experience within the definition. How that manifests depends on the therapist you're working with and the setting you're working in. The laws in Oregon, one of the few jurisdictions in the US where it is legal for a licensed therapist to work with psychedelics, explicitly say that psilocybin services will be "nondirective," meaning that facilitators will not direct or psychoanalyze you while you are in an altered state. Whether that approach is an accurate representation of PAP is up for debate.

SHAMANIC STYLE

A shamanic-style experience usually originates from a facilitator trained within a lineage or set of practices acquired from the Global South. Typically, this is represented by various rituals, ceremonies, prayers, and belief systems that center on the concepts of animism—a belief that all things possess a spirit. It is not uncommon for shamanic ceremonies to include the worship of higher beings, masters, and spirits which may include Mother Earth (Pachamama), mountains, rivers, or sacred animals such as the jaguar, puma, and condor.

RELIGIOUS STYLE

Some facilitators specialize in using psychedelics within a distinct religious context. It is possible to find facilitators who work specifically within a defined faith, such as Christianity or Judaism, to guide your preparation, experience, and integration. In this context, you will often encounter ritual, prayer, or devotional acts relating to a specific deity such as Jesus Christ, Yahweh, or Allah. This can take the form of a solo or group session and will often include some form of ceremony.

SPIRITUAL STYLE

The vast majority of underground facilitators fall into the spiritual style—and its precise definition is highly variable. Spiritual practitioners appear on a very broad spectrum. One side of that spectrum may represent practicing with ancient teachings from Buddhism, the Kabbalah, or Advaita Vedanta. The other side might present as "neo-spiritual" or "TikTok shamans." The spiritual use of psychedelics will most certainly lean toward the sacred and come with some ceremony and ritual, but will rarely be firmly enmeshed with a religious deity or belief system.

SINCERE STYLE

For some, taking a small amount of mushrooms and walking in nature can be a profoundly healing and beautiful experience. Sincere use has no defined setting, nor will it attach any specific structure or belief system. The sincere use of psychedelics may carry with it an intention of growth, but rarely focuses on healing deep wounds and trauma.

PSEUDOSPIRITUAL STYLE

Put a group of friends together, add some mushrooms, play a Joe Dispenza meditation followed by the healing vibes of Brian Eno or the Grateful Dead, and you have found yourself in the realm of pseudospirituality. If you created a Venn diagram of spiritual, sincere, and recreational, pseudospiritual would be the central overlap of all three. Psychedelic newcomers looking to do deep healing work should refrain from pseudospiritual experiences until they have a better understanding of how they react in an expanded state of consciousness. Using a powerful substance in a loosely held container (with an increased potential of boundary violations) can be a recipe for disaster.

Types of Psychedelic Facilitators

You will encounter many fellow travelers on your journey across the psychedelic landscape. No two facilitators are exactly alike, and each will have their own unique style of working with clients. Nevertheless, there are a few standard archetypes that show up more than others. I've listed the most common ones below.

GUIDES/COACHES/FACILITATORS

This is a vast category of individuals who use psychedelics in a professional capacity to help others heal. They aim to attend to their clients' physical safety and interpersonal needs. They are qualified to work with others through specialized training or apprenticeship. Working with psychedelics has become a part of their professional lives, and they are paid a fair wage for this labor.

SHAMANS/CURANDEROS/CEREMONIAL LEADERS

A shaman is loosely defined as someone believed to have access to, and influence over, the world of spirits. A curandero is a traditional folk healer who frequently incorporates the use of plants in their practice. This group usually works within an Indigenous framework that carries some implication of formal training, a lineage, and permission to do their work from a maestro—or the plant spirits themselves. Be aware that you could meet a few different kinds of self-described shamans on your path: Indigenous, modern practitioners, and plastic. The phrase "plastic shaman" describes individuals who present themselves as spiritual guides but lack genuine training, cultural legitimacy, or a deep understanding of the traditions and practices they claim to represent.

CLERGY

Psychedelic clergy are individuals who serve as spiritual leaders by integrating the use of botanical sacraments (e.g., mushrooms, ayahuasca, or San Pedro) into their spiritual or religious practices, under the umbrella of a psychedelic or entheogenic church.

MAESTROS

A maestro ("master" or "teacher" in Spanish) is a practitioner with a profound understanding of and deep connection to the spirit of the medicines they are serving. Maestros are master medicine carriers who communicate directly with the spirit of the plants and other energies. They facilitate healing on many levels of consciousness and on different planes of reality. Not unlike the guru of Eastern traditions, it might be said that while a guide or facilitator points to the way, a maestro *is* the way.

PSYCHONAUTS/ENTHUSIASTS

Using more colonial terminology, the three prior groups would be classified as "professionals" in their respective field. Conversely, psychonauts or psychedelic enthusiasts may be highly experienced, but would be closer to hobbyists than professionals. These psychedelic advocates often have a great deal of personal experience taking psychedelics and can offer tremendous practical information about their use, but they rarely have any training that makes them qualified to do deep work with others.

TRIP SITTERS

Trip sitters are those who offer support and supervision for someone experiencing a psychedelic journey. They primarily focus on ensuring the safety and well-being of the seeker. Trip sitters usually have some personal psychedelic experience and may have training in psychedelic support or first aid. They rarely have the level of training possessed by a facilitator.

NEOPHYTES

Neophytes emerge from a small number of psychedelic experiences, often with a single substance. These experiences may have been powerful in nature, causing them to experience a sense of singularity, a massive breakthrough in their thinking, or the release of past trauma. All of us start as neophytes in many areas of our lives, but just because we go to the gym a few times a week does not mean we are qualified to be personal trainers. Loosely hold the advice of a neophyte and show caution if invited to work with them in ceremony.

PROSELYTIZERS

A proselyte is a neophyte who tries to persuade others to accept a particular belief, idea, or way of life. This is very common in psychedelics. Those who have used psychedelics and experienced profound healing from a condition will often seek out others suffering from the same issues and try to persuade them that "this is the path to salvation." Should you come across a proselytizer, show appreciation for their experience and keep reading this book. If you have become one, please try to embody the idea that working with Sacred Medicine is based far more on attraction rather than promotion. It's okay to share your story, but there is no need to convince anyone to use psychedelics. When the student is ready, the teacher (and the medicine) will appear.

Private vs. Group Sessions

One final variable that you will undoubtedly need to solve for is whether you will work privately with a facilitator, find a group, or attempt to use psychedelics alone. A helpful suggestion is to think of psychedelic experiences like meditation. Meditation can be done solo or in a group, but it's always an "individual" experience. When you're sitting alone in meditation, it's usually quieter and easier to focus, because you are in full control of your environment. When you meditate in a group, participants do not touch or talk to each other, but all humans move, make noise, burp, and fart. A group environment (and all the people in it) is completely outside of your control, while a private experience can offer you more opportunity to dictate your surroundings and tailor your experience. There are challenges and benefits to each option, further explored below.

PRIVATE SESSIONS

Working one-on-one with a qualified facilitator can be one of the deepest and most profound experiences you will ever have. It can also offer one of the faster routes to healing with psychedelics because of its deeply personal and focused nature. When combined with proper preparation and integration, many people can experience profound and long-lasting transformation in a single session. Private work focuses completely on you, your process, and your content. Compared to group work, there is usually more time dedicated to preparation and integration, and everything from the experience to the music can be tailored to your unique needs.

The primary drawback to private work is cost—which can vary widely based on the experience of your facilitator, the amount of preparation and integration time, and the length of the experience. Using a typical mushroom experience as a template, the experience day could easily last five to seven hours. Once you add a few preparation and integration sessions, the total number of client-facing hours could be between fifteen and twenty. If you are working with an experienced facilitator, their billable rate may range from $100 to $200 per hour, similar to that of a therapist, and bringing you to a total cost of $1,500 to $4,000. This pricing can be inaccessible to many people, although many facilitators work on a sliding scale or offer scholarships to those in need.

GROUP SESSIONS

A group experience can come in many different forms. If you're doing work in the Global North, one common setting is a weekend retreat led by a facilitator and hosted by a local spiritual community. In these cases, the facilitator arrives, serves medicine for one or more nights, and then leaves to conduct ceremonies elsewhere. This is a common practice for Indigenous medicine carriers serving outside of their home country. The group experience typically costs anywhere from $250 to $1,500 (or more) per night, depending on the medicine, facilitator, and accommodations.

Entheogenic churches are another group option gaining popularity in the United States. In this scenario, local community members gather under the auspices of a religious entity to practice their beliefs. Psychedelic churches may have a membership agreement, a statement of beliefs, and a code of conduct to ensure the safety of themselves and their members. These group experiences also typically range from $50 to $300 or more per ceremony.

In clinical or therapeutic settings, providers may offer substances like mushrooms or ketamine in a group session, but—like meditation—the experience happens individually. In these cases, you may be in a room with a few other people but wearing eyeshades and headphones, allowing you to have a unique experience even while surrounded by others. Some ketamine clinics and legal psilocybin centers offer experiences like this, with prices ranging in the multiple thousands of dollars.

A final option for group work is traveling abroad to attend a retreat. Often hosted in the Netherlands, Jamaica, or South and Central America, retreats can be a life-changing way to have a legal psychedelic experience. If this is your chosen option, it is your responsibility to research the retreat center you will attend and clearly understand the container you will be working within. Depending on activities and accommodations, the cost of multiday retreats can range from $2,000 to $10,000.

Group work has the distinct advantage of reducing costs but also has a few built-in disadvantages. Because your experience will be in a room full of people you don't know, who are also doing deep work, it is easier to become distracted by others. If someone is having a powerful experience, it is not out of the ordinary to hear crying, laughing, screaming, or—especially with ayahuasca—vomiting. If you are a highly sensitive person or are already experiencing high levels of anxiety, this could make a group experience difficult.

Another downfall of many group experiences is the lack of individual preparation and integration time. In group ceremonies, the responsibility of prep and integration often falls on the participant. If you have a grueling experience that is challenging to integrate, you may have to find and pay for additional support from an integration specialist or therapist.

Before you decide to take part in a group setting, I recommend that you determine how much interaction you will have with other participants *during* your experience and take that into consideration. Unless you've been specifically told otherwise, participants typically do not interact with each other in any way during professionally facilitated group experiences. There is no talking, touching, or communicating of any kind between participants while the medicine is active. This is specifically implemented to ensure that each participant can have their own experience in a safe and supportive manner, without getting involved in the energetic or psychological processes of others.

WORKING SOLO

If you're reading this book, the chances are high that you are not a psychedelic expert. Without a strong skillset and expertise, I do not recommend working alone with anything other than a micro or very small dose. If you don't have familiarity with the work and the landscape of your mind, your session can pivot from pleasant to terrifying in a matter of seconds. Once you have gained more experience and have built safety into your process, doing a solo journey can be a wonderful way to heal. Until then, at a minimum, you should have a trip sitter available to help keep you safe.

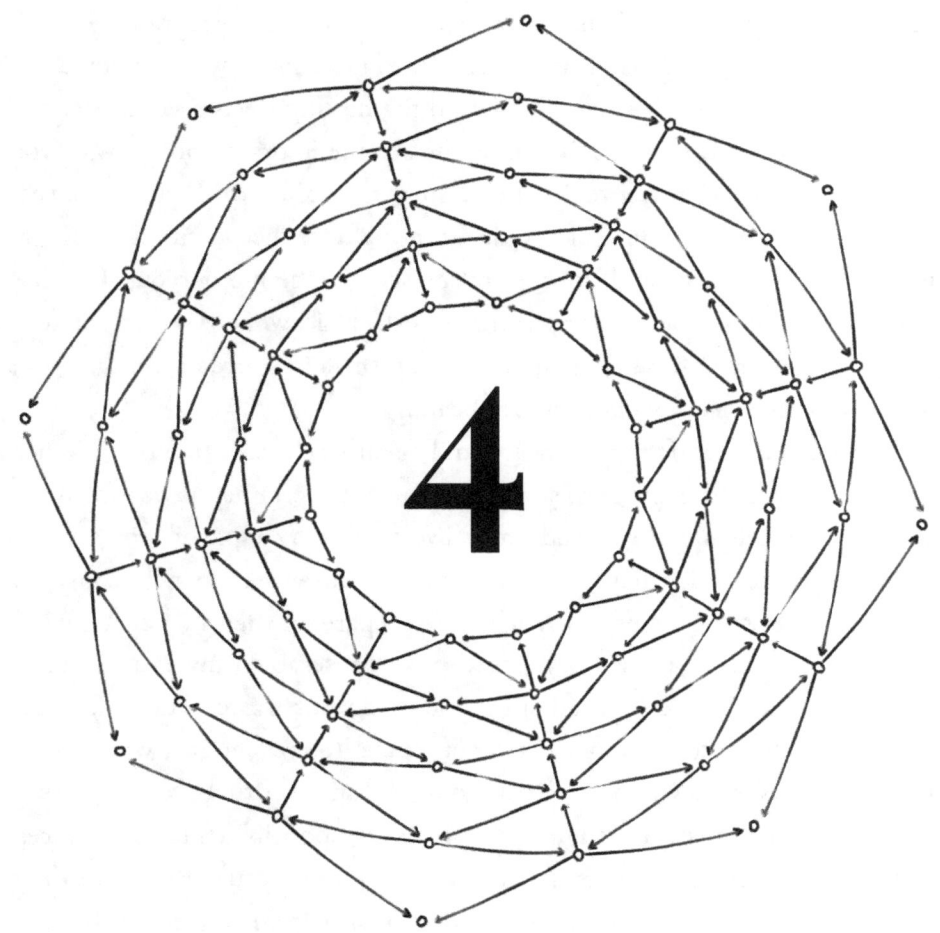

A New Psychedelic Framework for the Modern Era

"Sit Around the Fire" by Jon Hopkins, Ram Dass, East Forest

I n 2015, after eight years of therapy, yoga, and twelve-step programs, I felt I had
tried every healing modality I had access to. I knew how I was "supposed" to feel
after years of effort, but I still hadn't found the healing I was seeking—and didn't
know what to do next. Around this time, the shamanic practitioner I was working
with encouraged me to travel to Peru and sit with ayahuasca. With eight years of
alcohol recovery guiding much of my decision-making, the possibility of ingesting
a mind-altering substance and "losing my sobriety" made me nervous. So, like any
good former addict/people-pleasing control freak, I did what was familiar to me: I
combined my powers of obsession and perfectionism, and started my online research
adventure into the use of psychedelics for healing.

Nervous and excited for what lay ahead, I spent weeks scouring the internet and
reading trip reports, attempting to squeeze as much uncertainty as possible from my
upcoming trip to the jungle. A decade later, I've realized a couple of things: first, how
useless the trip reports of others are, and second, the absence of a single, consolidated,
and reliable source to help a psychedelic novice prepare for their first experience.

Spoiler alert: not a single story I read online resembled my experience in the
jungle—or any experience I've had since. Please do not waste your time gathering
information on the psychedelic experiences of others. Your experience will be different.

Each of us has our own physical, psychological, and spiritual process (in this lifetime and from past lives). So long as you proceed responsibly, these substances will
give you what you need, when you need it, and only when you're ready. Reading trip
reports automatically forces you into a state of comparison and creates both conscious
and unconscious expectations. I know from firsthand experience that setting expectations is the fastest path to resentment and disappointment.

The Need to Expand "Set and Setting"

Before my work as a psychedelic coach, I spent two decades working in corporate
America. Among the most beneficial skills I developed during that season of my life
were evaluating systems and developing repeatable processes for growth. "Systems
thinking" is a holistic approach to problem-solving that considers how different parts
of a system interact and influence each other within a whole.[14] What you will soon
realize is that the phrase "healing with psychedelics" covers a large, complex system,
and each of the variables is interdependent. Changing one input variable could create
the difference between heaven and hell, healing and harm.

Now, after a decade of working with psychedelics for healing and balancing
between the secular and the sacred, I'm using the same skills that benefited me in the

corporate world to aid to you on your healing journey—starting with the creation of the Psychedelic Safety Wheel (PSW).

Getting started with psychedelic healing can feel like hiking up a treacherous, windy mountain path in the middle of a dark and stormy night, while clouds cover the sky and the moon is invisible. Without a single star to guide your way, each step on the sliver-thin path feels uncertain and potentially life-threatening. All your feet can do is take one small step at a time, hoping they don't veer too far off in either direction. For many reading this book, this might be how you feel every day—struggling to constantly and precariously balance safety with forward progress.

Healing is deeply personal, often complex, and contains an infinite number of variables—some known, most unknown. This book offers a framework that honors this work's profoundly personal and complex nature. It is not prescriptive but still provides just enough scaffolding for each individual to heal safely and with long-lasting results. The PSW provides flexibility and freedom to choose the optimal path up your personal mountain.

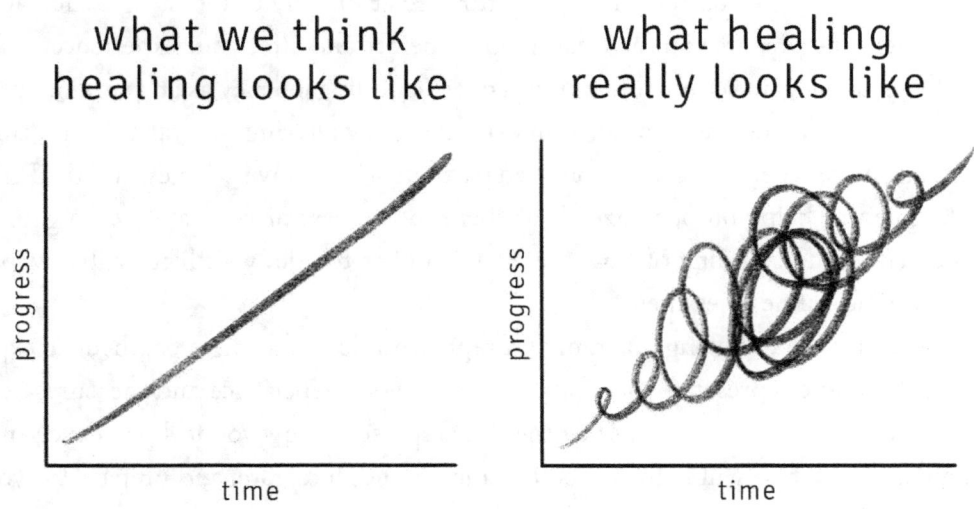

FIGURE 5. What healing really looks like.

We subconsciously tell ourselves that healing looks like the path on the left side of figure 5, but in reality, it looks much more like the line on the right. Martin Luther King Jr. once said, "The arc of the moral universe is long, but it bends toward justice." I believe the arc of our healing journey will always move up and forward, but when we're in crisis, we're unable to zoom out far enough to see the slope.

Let the PSW offer a bird's-eye view to help you safely and successfully prepare, experience, and integrate psychedelics into your path. Please hold the framework lightly and use it as a guide. At the same time, remember to cultivate a deeper sense of inner knowing and discernment. Learning to listen and trust your head, heart, and gut will eventually become far more helpful than anything you read in this book.

The Psychedelic Safety Wheel

The Psychedelic Safety Wheel was created to offer a modern-day framework that outlines the most critical elements of using psychedelics for safe and sustainable transformation. Unfortunately, there is no reliable GPS for navigating healing. Because everyone's lived experience is different, everyone's path to healing will also be different. The PSW is designed less as turn-by-turn directions and more as guard rails to keep you from veering over the edge. The framework allows you to approach each intersection with the right information and then choose the path that best supports your unique experience.

The PSW has twelve "spokes," or variables, to consider on your healing journey. Of the twelve spokes on the wheel, only three refer directly to ingesting a substance. The other nine prepare you for what happens before and after your experience.

I encourage you to think of your psychedelic healing journey as an experiment. In a perfect world, you could conduct an experiment by altering one variable at a time. But you and psychedelics are complicated partners with many variables, and the PSW is designed to help you optimize all of them to the best of your ability. To gain an immediate understanding of how the PSW applies to you, visit https://piq.lv/psw and take the online assessment.

Consider the following diagram as a representation of a single psychedelic experience. One line represents your formula before your experience and measures your perceived state of preparation. The other line represents how you feel postexperience. Comparing the two will help you better understand, integrate, and prepare for your next experience.

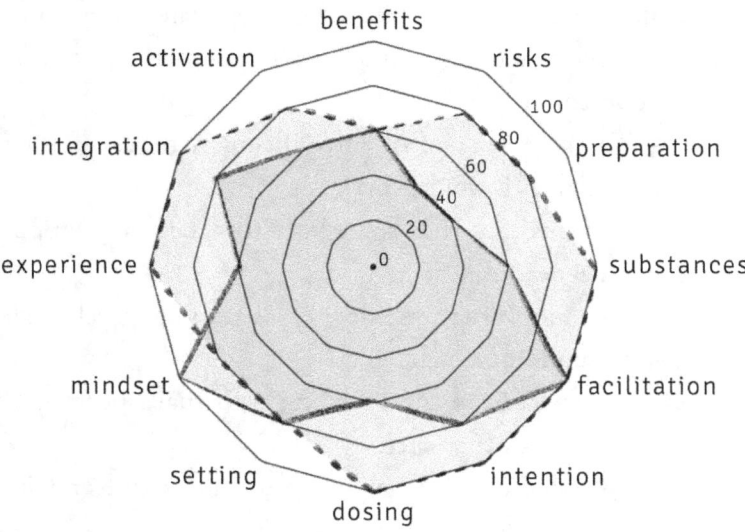

FIGURE 6. The Psychedelic Safety Wheel

The names of each of the twelve spokes are shown on the outside of the wheel. Your level of confidence with each spoke is measured on each axis. The lower your confidence, the closer to hub, with the lowest possible score being zero. The higher your confidence, the closer to the edge, with the highest possible being one hundred. The goal of the PSW is not to create a perfect circle around the outer edge—with so many variables out of our control, that would be impossible. But the more air in your tire, the smoother your ride will be. The PSW aims to help you see where you may be less confident in your preparation process, optimize each spoke to the best of your ability, and inflate each variable to maximize the surface area of your graph.

Here is an overview of the twelve spokes of the Psychedelic Safety Wheel, and what each one calls into focus:

1. **Benefits** — Common benefits of psychedelics and how to evaluate your personal goals against these known benefits.
2. **Risks** — Significant risk factors of psychedelics and how to evaluate your personal level of risk.
3. **Preparation** — Methods to prepare for your experience, and how to find the method most supportive of your process.
4. **Substance** — Common substances in current practice for psychedelic healing, and how to select a substance appropriate for your process and desired outcome.

5. **Facilitation** — The complex task of choosing a safe and qualified facilitator.

6. **Intention** — The benefits of setting an intention, and how to craft one appropriate for your experience.

7. **Dosage** — The complex and often confusing nature of dosing, one of the most critical variables in your experience.

8. **Setting** — The qualities that contribute to a safe and supportive setting, allowing your deepest transformation.

9. **Mindset** — The most crucial element of a successful psychedelic experience, ensuring your mindset is ready.

10. **Experience** — Physical, psychological, and spiritual aspects you will encounter on the day of your experience.

11. **Integration** — Methods for helping you understand and integrate your experience into your everyday life.

12. **Activation** — The role of conscious and intentional shifts in behavior, and how they create long-lasting, sustainable change.

Anyone beginning their research on psychedelics and healing will certainly come across the importance of "set and setting." If you keep searching, you'll discover dosage to be the third leg of this traditional psychedelic "stool." (It's not until after you start experimenting that you learn it would have been wise to include integration.) You may eventually be introduced to a reliable facilitator who already has a "substance of choice," eliminating your ability to choose the substance that may work best for your unique process. And sadly, if you're a novice, you may not know how to spot an unqualified facilitator until it's too late.

The problem with today's oversimplified view of psychedelic healing is that we're still using a 1960s aphorism and applying it to a completely new and unstructured model of usage. Set, setting, and dosage are simply not enough to accommodate the unpredictability of these substances when they're held in today's fragile, unstable, and underground container. In the best-case scenario, psychedelics can offer an excellent opportunity to explore your subconscious for greater self-awareness in a safe and enjoyable way. In the worst-case scenario, they can offer a horrific experience that triggers unpleasant emotions and memories, stress responses, depression, and even thoughts of self-harm.

Throughout the millennia of human history, psychedelics have healed and expanded consciousness, always within the context of tradition, wisdom, and community. Indigenous curanderos will rarely address integration directly because it is already central to the framework of their lives. These practitioners live each day based on the sacred teachings of their culture, community, traditions, and the medicine itself. In many modern cultures, those who are seeking healing with psychedelics are without that supportive social structure, sometimes going it alone and just hoping for the best. This subset of individuals needs a modern framework—one not solely based on scientific research, but still practical and accessible to an average person. We need guidance that doesn't require a PhD to understand, but still offers safe, responsible, grounded, and practical wisdom to a lay user. The PSW honors the entire life cycle of psychedelic healing and has been designed for those who do not live with direct access to community, tradition, and the Indigenous wisdom.

Donald Rumsfeld once said, "There are known knowns; there are things we know that we know. We also know there are known unknowns; that is to say, we know there are some things we do not know. But there are also unknown unknowns—the ones we don't know, we don't know." The PSW seeks to shift as many important "unknown unknowns" to "known unknowns," and eventually to "known knowns." The twelve chapters in part II of this book will help you do that by exploring each spoke of the wheel in greater detail.

If you are a psychedelic newcomer, I suggest reading through each of the chapters in the order in which they're presented. This will give you a wonderful step-by-step view of how psychedelics heal from start to finish. If you already have experience taking psychedelics recreationally and are now considering their use for healing purposes, consider skipping to the chapter on preparation. If you're coming to this book having had an unfulfilling, challenging, or even harmful experience, flip to the chapter you feel you need the most help with and start there.

One very important thing you must remember is that there is no one "right way" to psychedelic. If you meet someone on your healing journey who assures you that their way is the best way, demands you abide by their specific protocol, or guarantees you a particular outcome in a specified amount of time, I suggest you move on and continue your research. This is often an early warning sign of disappointment or potential harm. My definition of a "psychedelic expert" is someone who can accurately predict what will happen in your next journey. In my decade of experience, I've only met one true "expert." Beware of anyone who tries to convince you otherwise.

Bon voyage!

5

An Ideal (and Realistic) Healing Journey

"The Storm Approaches" by MARDELVA

In 1913, Eleanor H. Porter wrote a novel about a girl with an unwavering optimistic outlook. Her character, Pollyanna, has since become a byword for the cognitive bias of focusing on the positive aspects of experiences, situations, and information, often overlooking or downplaying the negative. Compared with the past half-century, the last few years of scientific research, mass and social media attention, and public discourse has forged a double-edged sword for the zeitgeist surrounding psychedelics. This shift has both dramatically improved and positively skewed the general public's opinion.

In many ways, this has been wonderful and is a change necessary to allow books like this one to be written, read, and openly received. But as in the yin-yang symbol of Chinese origin, darkness always rises up to meet the light. With all the positive attention on psychedelics, there has also arisen a belief that psychedelics are a magical cure and, once taken a single time, will heal all maladies. This "once and done" mindset has brought with it unreasonable expectations and ultimately caused harm. While the US Food and Drug Administration's (FDA) 2024 rejection of MDMA as a legal treatment for PTSD was some of the first widely publicized criticism of psychedelics since the 1900s, the majority of content the general public sees about psychedelics is positive. In fact, it is so positive that many newcomers think that if they take mushrooms or drink ayahuasca once, the problems they've suffered from for years will magically disappear. But not unlike learning to play the piano, you won't master a symphony after just one lesson at the keyboard.

Part II of this book will systematically demonstrate the complexity that popular media has all but scrubbed from the true process of healing. My hope is to remove any notion that psychedelics are magic pills. But before we dive into the deep end, I want to share with you a real-life healing journey that more accurately reflects reality. A journey that—in my opinion and that of the client—can still be considered miraculous, while filling in many of the details frequently left out of a thirty-second spot on the national news. I have been walking my own healing path for almost twenty years and working with psychedelics for a decade. Out of all the news segments, blog posts, or research papers you may have encountered before reading this book, I believe this single story most accurately reflects the amount of time, energy, effort, and trust required to safety and sustainably change your mind.

Scott's Story – In His Own Words

When I was fifty-six, I began experiencing what I now recognize as classic symptoms of depression. At first, things were mild enough that I didn't make the connection. I noticed I was experiencing less joy and laughter than before, but I didn't feel anything was seriously wrong. I figured I was just in a funk that would eventually pass.

Over the next year, however, my symptoms expanded and intensified dramatically. Eventually, I found it difficult to get out of bed in the morning, and it wasn't unusual for me to return to bed right after work. I felt an overwhelming sadness about almost everything, frequently breaking down in tears. I developed intense anxiety over things that had never stressed me out before.

Just thinking about what I needed to do in a day, even something as simple as a shower, would trigger waves of hopeless despair. I found myself asking, "What's the point?" Life felt meaningless. I'd often fall into negative thought spirals that could last for up to thirty minutes. When I finally managed to stand up and walk toward the bathroom, I would be engulfed by a sense of "NOPE!" and lie back down. I'd curl up into the fetal position, paralyzed and weeping, wondering, "What is wrong with me?"

The answer was that I had major depressive disorder (MDD). Given my family history—my great-grandmother, grandmother, and uncle had all experienced sudden, debilitating depression in their fifties—it wasn't entirely surprising. Both my grandmother and uncle underwent extensive treatment, including electroshock therapy, with varying degrees of success.

After seeing my doctor and receiving the diagnosis, I began treatment with antidepressants. Eventually, I found a combination of four medications that allowed me to function again. The feelings of hopelessness, despair, and anxiety were mainly eliminated. The minor side effects seemed like a fair exchange for getting my life back.

But even though I was functioning again, I wasn't truly living. The medications dulled everything. The joy and laughter were still gone, and my lifelong love of music, reading, theater, sports, and nature was reduced to a mild appreciation at best. Even worse, I found myself emotionally disconnecting from the people I loved, becoming distant and withdrawn. I felt like a functioning, soulless zombie.

Being a naturally analytical person, I dove into research on depression. That's when I learned about studies at Johns Hopkins on psilocybin for treatment-resistant depression. The results were promising enough for me to explore how I might access this treatment. I had tried mushrooms recreationally twice in my twenties, so I had some idea of what to expect.

Just as I was preparing to pursue treatment in Oregon, where psilocybin therapy was legal, I discovered a local underground resource. This facilitator administered mushrooms as a sacrament, with a spiritual aspect that included a ritual and the possibility of spiritual guidance during the journey. After speaking with them, I decided to move forward with a one-on-one session, which involved several hours of preparation, an eight-to-ten-hour ceremony using MDMA and psilocybin, and two follow-up integration consultations.

WHAT PSYCHEDELICS HAVE DONE FOR ME

Today, almost two years after that first session, I can confidently say I've never been mentally healthier. My life now feels deeper and richer than it did even before the onset of my depression—and my life back then was objectively great. I had a loving family, married the love of my life, had a wealth of friends, and enjoyed a fulfilling part-time job that gave me plenty of time to pursue the activities that brought me joy.

I still have all those things now, but with some significant enhancements. Before depression, my interactions with people were pleasant but cautious. I was fine discussing deeper topics once someone else made the first move, but I would always pull back when I sensed something vulnerable that could lead to discomfort. Now, I'm less afraid of things getting uncomfortable, and my interactions have become more vibrant and fulfilling. Instead of fizzling out, my connections with others now often burst into life, as if I can see the ember of potential turning into a full flame.

Beyond conversations, the world itself seems more decadent. I tear up with gratitude for the everyday wonders of life. I've remembered how to laugh at myself instead of dreading my own absurdities. I've also reconnected with simple, profound ideas I'd forgotten, like the concept that every moment holds infinite possibilities.

Perhaps the most surprising part of this journey has been the realization that I'm grateful for my depression. My symptoms aren't entirely gone, but I now feel equipped to manage (and sometimes even learn from) them. My journey is very human—I have good and not-so-good days—but it's now more conscious, tactile, and spiritual. If I were offered the chance to erase my depression but return to my previous, less engaged life, I would pass on that offer without hesitation.

WHAT HAPPENED DURING MY EXPERIENCE

One of the most impactful aspects of my psychedelic experience was the time my facilitator took to prepare me. I completed a "life inventory" exercise, which helped them get to know me and primed me—consciously and unconsciously—for the journey ahead.

This preparation phase also built my confidence that I was in safe hands. By the day of the session, I was a little nervous but mostly comfortable and ready to let go. A vital part of that confidence came from working with my facilitator to distill my intention for the journey down to a few words—something simple that I could hold onto while working with the medicine.

Another critical aspect of preparation was safely tapering off my antidepressants before the ceremony, since they can interfere with psilocybin. As the medication left my system, my symptoms returned in full force, a painful reminder of why I had been on them in the first place.

On the day of the session, my facilitator created a safe, intentional setting. Despite encountering some challenging moments, I never felt like I was in danger of losing control. They first gave me MDMA, and as we waited for it to take effect, we just "shot the breeze" and began listening to a playlist that had been curated for me based on the preparatory information I had given them. Gradually, the conversation shifted from light topics to more introspective ones. Under the influence of MDMA, I was able to face what I now recognize as a critical trigger for my depression. The medicine allowed me to get just enough distance from my emotions to start observing them. I noticed the specific physical sensations I was experiencing, the thoughts and feelings behind them, and the deeper underlying issues.

Later in the session, we added psilocybin. After I took the first dose, dissolved into a cup of herbal tea, we continued talking, exploring the specifics of my depression. When a wave of sadness hit, where did I feel it? Was it hot or cold? Did it have a color? My facilitator also helped me reconnect with my younger self—the exuberant, uninhibited ten-year-old inner child I had walled off after years of embarrassment and shame. The realization that I had hidden away this magical part of myself was profound.

When the booster dose of psilocybin kicked in, the experience shifted. I could no longer focus on conversation and instead went on a self-guided journey. I laid down, put on eyeshades, and let the medicine and my inner healer do their work.

What happened next was deeply personal, ineffable, and defies easy description, but it felt transformative.

By the end of the day, I had a clearer understanding of myself, and I haven't been in the fetal position since.

WHAT MY FUTURE LOOKS LIKE

Physiologically speaking, one of the most important things that happened is that the psilocybin created a meaningful amount of neuroplasticity. The realizations that arrived during my session seemed more amenable to becoming long-term thought patterns as I returned to them in our later integration sessions.

It is important to emphasize how crucial the follow-up sessions were in getting me from where I was to where I am today. The walls I had built around my more genuine self were created to last, and I don't believe it would have been possible to break them down without a lot of deliberate attention. They may never fall away entirely, but my ability to manage or ignore them has been strengthened.

That strengthening has taken the form of weekly coaching sessions. One advantage of working with the facilitator I chose is that they also offered this kind of coaching, allowing me to continue deepening my self-awareness and healing. Initially, I opted to take psilocybin every two to three months in a group setting led by my facilitator, which allowed me to go deeper into my process and build new thought patterns and habits that have strengthened my ability to live life to the fullest.

For almost a year now, I have not felt the need for additional macro doses of psilocybin. My ongoing mental health regimen consists only of continued weekly coaching and microdosing.

I don't intend to stay on this weekly schedule indefinitely, but I believe that I will always be healthier if I can return to coaching periodically. I also think that I have barely scratched the surface of what I can learn about myself from sacred interactions with psychedelic medicines, and when the time is right, I hope to continue those journeys.

In this moment, however, what really matters is that I have my life back—and that it is somehow richer and more meaningful than ever.

Dissecting Scott's Journey

Out of all the stories I've ever received about psychedelics, Scott's is one of my favorites, and that is why I've included it in this book. I appreciate his story because it touches on nearly every aspect of the framework you will be introduced to in the next section. It demonstrates what a safe, responsible, grounded, and practical approach to healing with psychedelics can look and feel like, and the benefits one can receive by being deliberate, slow, and consistent on their healing path.

The subtitle of this book explicitly states the goal of a "safe and sustainable transformation." It's easy to take psychedelics. It's frequently much harder to *heal* with psychedelics and cement positive changes into your life. Scott accomplished just that, and it didn't happen in a few hours. It happened gradually over months and years.

There are a few interesting aspects of his journey that I would like to call out. First, he did his homework. He developed a good understanding of both the benefits and the risks. Because he worked with a qualified facilitator he met through a trusted referral, he was also exposed to a deep and intentional preparation process, which included selecting substances and dosages that honored his current mental state and experience level with psychedelics. He and his facilitator crafted an intention and worked in a safe and supportive setting, which created a deep and meaningful experience.

After it was over, Scott began the phases of integration and activation, which spanned years. By consistently working with a coach, and adding additional group psychedelic work when needed, he continued healing and growing. Eventually, the positive changes in his life began to crystallize, almost permanently replacing the trauma and negative thought patterns from his past.

Another compelling aspect of Scott's narrative is that it never once veered into what is often called a "trip report," or a personal, highly detailed account of the moment-by-moment experience one has in their psychedelic journey. His psychedelic experiences are 100 percent his own and will be unlike yours in almost every way. Reading about someone else's visions—be they profoundly positive or horribly terrifying—will only set unnecessary expectations for you and slow down your healing process. Remember: comparison is the thief of joy.

Chapter six, verse twenty-four of the Bhagavad Gita, an ancient Hindu scripture offering guidance on various aspects of life, says, "Devotional service is successfully executed with enthusiasm, determination, and patience." The parable that goes along with this verse speaks of a tiny sparrow who conquers the ocean. In the story, a sparrow lays her eggs on the shore of the ocean, but one day, after a large rain, the ocean carries her eggs away as the tide recedes. The sparrow, struck with grief from losing her precious eggs, becomes very upset and asks the ocean to return them. The ocean laughs at her passionate appeal. With determination and utter defiance, the sparrow decides to dry up the ocean and begins spooning out the water, one beak full at a time. Everyone laughs at her for her impossible determination, but soon the news of her pluck reaches Garuḍa, the gigantic bird carrier of Lord Vishnu. Garuḍa becomes compassionate toward the blight of his small sister bird, and being very pleased by her determination, promises to help. Garuḍa asks the ocean to return her eggs, lest he take up the work of the sparrow himself. The ocean, frightened at the prospect, quickly returns the eggs to the little bird.

Whether you're using psychedelics or not, this parable accurately describes the journey we embark upon to heal. Love, determination, and patience are the qualities present within the little sparrow, and these qualities will also need to become a part of your ethos. Healing, regardless of where you're starting from and where you want to go, is never a fast process. We rarely understand the healing process while we're inside of it. But once we've emerged from the darkness, the brighter light of consciousness we gain throughout the process will shine a revealing beam on where we've been and help to further illuminate where we're going.

PART II

The Psychedelic Safety Wheel

"Footsteps in the Stars" by Deya Dova

Benefits

"Gran Maestra Curandera" (Live at Sugarshack) by Porangui

As we embark on this journey, let's begin with a broad and grounded approach to understanding the potential benefits of psychedelic healing through the modern medical lens of diagnosis.

In 2024, Allison Hoots, an attorney, advocate, and the president of the Sacred Plant Alliance, wrote a New York State Assembly bill to establish legal access to psilocybin.[15] Her bill includes a comprehensive list of conditions currently treatable with psilocybin. The list, which I've divided into two groups, comprises the following conditions:

Physical Conditions	Mental Conditions
• Amyotrophic lateral sclerosis • Arthritis • Bacterial infection or disease • Cataracts • Cancer • Chronic pain • Chronic fatigue • Cluster headaches • Degenerative disk or joint disease • Diabetes • Effects from stroke • Epilepsy • Episodic migraines • Fibromyalgia • Functional gastrointestinal disorders, including irritable bowel syndrome (IBS) and inflammatory bowel disease (IBD) • Glaucoma • Headache disorders • HIV/AIDS • Lyme disease • Motor neuron disease • Migraines • Multiple sclerosis • Muscular dystrophy • Neurodegenerative disease, including neuropathy • Parkinson's disease • Paresthesia • Premenstrual syndrome or premenstrual dysphoric disorder • Post-acute COVID-19 infection condition • Restless leg syndrome • Rheumatoid arthritis	• Adjustment disorder • Attention deficit/hyperactivity disorder • Autism • Alzheimer's • Anxiety • Anorexia nervosa • Behavioral/process addiction (gambling, pornography, shopping, etc.) • Body dysmorphia • Cancer-related distress • Depressive disorder • Eating disorder • Insomnia • Mood disorder • Obsessive-compulsive disorder • Panic disorder • Phantom limb pain • Prolonged grief disorder • Postpartum mental health disorder • Post-traumatic stress disorder (PTSD) or complex post-traumatic stress disorder • Psychogenic pain disorder • Sexual disorder • Sensory processing disorder • Sleep disorder • Substance use disorder, including the use of opiates, tobacco, and alcohol • Terminal illness or end-of-life distress

TABLE 3. Conditions treatable with psilocybin.

In a recent study, researchers from Emory University, the University of Wisconsin-Madison, and UC Berkeley determined that up to 62 percent of patients currently receiving treatment for depression in the United States—amounting to over five million individuals—could qualify for psilocybin therapy if approved.[16]

Beyond psilocybin, other psychedelics have shown promising clinical results. In their phase three clinical trial, MAPS (now Lykos) used a combination of MDMA and talk therapy as a treatment for post-traumatic stress disorder (PTSD). At the study's close eighteen weeks later, 67 percent of the participants in the MDMA group no longer met the diagnostic criteria for PTSD, compared with 32 percent of those in the placebo group.[17] (A cessation rate of 67 percent for PTSD is unheard of by any other treatment means available today!)

Sadly, it is normal for science and education to lag ten to fifteen years behind the anecdotal wisdom of the underground, and potentially thousands of years behind Indigenous healers. Yet it was underground efforts that sparked the launch of "Cluster Busters," the nickname of an online support group and message board, which eventually led to formalized research for effectively treating cluster headaches, a condition for which no other effective treatments have proven effective.[18]

But there's something even more fascinating about the above list of treatable conditions that may not be easily recognizable, much less understandable. As we will explore in the chapter on substances, there are five molecules most commonly used in psychedelic healing work. There are countless other substances and even more "designer drugs" being created every day, but researchers conduct the vast majority of studies using ketamine, MDMA, psilocybin, LSD, and 5-MeO-DMT (and two of those are not even considered psychedelics—more on that later).

The list of conditions that can be treated with psilocybin includes fifty-five items, roughly divided into psychological and physical diagnoses. Without a team of specialists, it is nearly impossible to determine how many pharmaceutical drugs modern medicine is using to treat all these conditions. However, only five different psychedelic molecules have been shown to improve, if not cure, all fifty-five conditions.

As of 2024, Statista shows 6,124 pharmaceutical companies worldwide with active research and development pipelines. In 2023 alone, the FDA approved fifty-five new drugs, and it's estimated that over 20,000 different prescription drug products are available in the US today.[19] A single substance, like psilocybin, being effective in treating so many varied issues is unheard of in modern allopathic medicine. How on earth can only five different psychedelic molecules heal or cure fifty-five different conditions?

If we regard psychedelics through only a scientific lens, we may never truly understand how they work. Modern science does not possess technology that can measure the subtlety of how these substances heal. As you will learn later in the book, trust plays a significant role in using these substances effectively. As Henry Ford said, "Whether you think you can, or you think you can't—you're right."

If you think psychedelics can, keep reading. If you think they can't, keep reading.

Major Benefits of Psychedelics

Researchers have concluded that psychedelics support the following primary categories of healing:

Mental Health

Psychedelics have been substantially proven to have positive effects on many mental health conditions, including PTSD, treatment-resistant depression, anxiety, OCD, and more.

Emotional Insight and Awareness

Psychedelics can create a sense of interconnectedness and self-reflection. These insights allow us to confront our feelings, better understand our mental and emotional states, and learn to be more loving and self-compassionate. These insights can uplift our mood and increase our sense of well-being.

Spiritual Insight

Psychedelics are known to provide mystical, existential, and spiritual experiences, which can be very beneficial for those of us struggling with an existential crisis or fear of death. These experiences can offer a sense of oneness and create a renewed sense of purpose, moving us closer to health and well-being.

Addiction

Iboga, a plant-based psychedelic often referred to as the "addiction interrupter," has proven to be one of the most effective solutions to our devastating opioid crisis. Psilocybin and ayahuasca have also shown great promise for treating alcohol and nicotine dependency. From a holistic point of view that considers the root cause of addiction to be trauma, almost all psychedelics (when offered safely, with proper preparation, intention, and integration) are beneficial.

Personal Growth

Exploring the hidden patterns of your unconscious mind can offer a profound opportunity for personal growth. Multiple studies from Imperial College of London,[20] Technische Universität Dresde,[21] and Leiden University[22] show positive outcomes for individuals struggling with self-acceptance, creativity, and empathy.

Anxiety, Phobias, and Negative Thought Patterns

Especially when combined with therapy and done within a safe and controlled environment, psychedelics have helped many people safely and healthily face their fears, leading to a reduction in phobias, anxieties, and negative thought loops.

Neuroplasticity and Cognitive Flexibility

Psychedelics have been proven to increase neuroplasticity (our ability to learn) and neurogenesis (the growth and development of nervous tissue in the brain). Combined with proper integration, this is the main reason people report lasting, positive changes in behavior, mood, and outlook after a psychedelic experience. Furthermore, psychedelics can increase cognitive flexibility, which allows users to break free from rumination and rigid mental models. A psychedelic experience can help people approach life's challenges with a fresh perspective by offering more creative thinking and problem-solving opportunities.

Enhanced Psychotherapy and Coaching

Psychedelic-assisted psychotherapy and coaching allows patients to deeply explore their psyche with the help of a trained facilitator or therapist. Combining traditional talk therapy with psychedelics can amplify benefits by helping clients process difficult emotions, memories, and traumas more safely and productively.

Lori's Story

For so long, I thought I knew the whole truth: I'm an alcoholic, and everything stemmed from there. But I think deep down, something else was stirring, and something didn't fit. None of the distractions I was using or solutions I was seeking were helping.

My struggles with alcohol started when I was young, and I got sober before I was of legal age to drink. My life has also been marked by struggles with an eating disorder as a teenager. I was always searching for some semblance of sanity. Twelve-step programs helped me to clean up my life and arrest some harmful behaviors. But after decades in recovery, I still felt crazy. Not always, but there was something underneath—deep down—that I couldn't touch or find, no matter how hard I searched. And I had searched a lot!

My life on paper and to the plain eye looked successful. I had a great career, a good marriage, and supportive family and friends. But I was also becoming depressed and anxious. How could I feel so crazy? What was wrong with me? That was my ever-present mantra. I noticed others living joyfully and accepting the difficulties and struggles of living a full life. But there was something missing for me, and I couldn't quite put my finger on it.

That's when I stumbled upon psychedelic therapies on social media, which piqued my interest. After researching and confiding in close friends, I decided, at age fifty-eight, to explore a new path. What I had been doing for decades was no longer working, and I was tired.

I was introduced to a coach who incorporated psychedelics into his practice and had been working with them for some time. I trusted him and honestly felt I had nothing to lose. I quickly overcame my hesitation and embraced the opportunity for change. After working with him for a short time outside the context of psychedelics, I was ready to take the plunge.

On March 8, 2024, I had my first experience with MDMA and psilocybin, a day I now celebrate as my personal "Independence Day." This experience set me free and provided a fresh perspective on life. I received insights that shifted my understanding, making me feel a bit more sane and somewhat liberated. It took several weeks to process and integrate this newfound knowledge. I engaged in forgiveness work for my family and myself, and I felt a sense of freedom I had never known before. I had a sense that I was okay, something I hadn't experienced in many, many years—if ever.

Several months after my first journey, I participated in multiple wachuma and ayahuasca ceremonies. These medicines had a profound impact on my IBS, which I had been grappling with for the past several years to no avail. My most severe symptoms were alleviated. The medicines also helped me release deep-seated anger and dark energy I had carried about men, while also introducing me to the Divine Feminine within myself—a side I had never truly experienced before.

Now, I no longer feel crazy or trapped. The benefits I've gained stem primarily from integration work. I continue to work with the same coach and have also started a microdosing practice. Intentionally microdosing with mushrooms has opened me up to a greater awareness of my unhealed wounds, as well as the parts of me that are beautiful and deserving of recognition. This subtle process has allowed me to access aspects of myself that remained buried beneath layers of trauma from an early age. I had never truly addressed that deep-rooted pain.

I don't look at working with these medicines as a source of fun or escapism; rather, when approached mindfully, doing so offers a safe and unique opportunity for introspection and deep healing. This work helps me confront the barriers that prevent me from embracing the beautiful spirit that is within us all. Of course, it's an ongoing process, not a "one-and-done" like I had thought it might be. But God willing, it is certainly one that I intend to continue as a way of life going forward.

Tailor-Made Healing

The process of healing begins when we really start to become aware of and honor our own true needs and desires. A simple yet profound teaching from the Quakers encourages us to listen to the "still, small voice within." No one knows your passion and purpose better than you do. Furthermore, no one must live with the consequences of your choices more than you. The first part of our life is spent conforming to the ways the world wants us to look and behave, but what you will soon discover is how important it is to be honest about which parts of your life "fit" and which do not. Consider how this parable might describe your life:

A dapper gentleman went to Zumbach the tailor to be fitted for a new suit. After Zumbach altered the suit, the man stood in front of the mirror to check the fit. Immediately, he noticed that the right arm of the jacket seemed rather short. Too much of his wrist was showing. He turned to Zumbach and said, "My sleeve is too short. Can you lengthen it, please?"

"The sleeve is not too short," replied the tailor. "Your arm is too long. Just pull your arm back a few inches and you'll see that the sleeve fits perfectly."

The man withdrew his arm a bit, and the sleeve fit perfectly. But this shift rumpled the upper portion of his jacket.

"Now the nape of the collar is several inches above my neck," he protested.

"There's nothing wrong with the collar," Zumbach insisted. "Your neck is too low. Lift the back of your neck and the jacket will fit perfectly."

The customer extended his neck a few inches, and sure enough, the collar rounded where it was supposed to. But now there was another problem: the bottom of the jacket crept up too high.

"Now my whole rear end is sticking out!" the man complained.

"No problem," Zumbach returned. "Just lift up your rear end so it fits under the jacket." Again, the customer complied, which left his body in a very contorted posture.

"But standing like this, the pants are too short," said the man.

Zumbach answered, "There is nothing wrong with the pants! If you'll just bend your knees a bit, you'll see the trousers fit just right."

The customer obeyed and, lo and behold, his new, gorgeous, and tailored suit fit like a glove.

Later that day, the sharp-dressed man was standing at the train station with his shoulders lopsided and his head straining forward, when another fellow stopped and said, "What a beautiful suit! I'll bet Zumbach the tailor made it for you."

"Why yes," the man said, "How did you know?"

"Because only a tailor as brilliant as Zumbach could tailor a suit for a body as crippled as yours."

The parable of Zumbach the tailor is timeless, and just as important today as when it was first told. Challenging childhoods, modern-day culture, a disconnection from nature, war and conflict, the climate crisis, and housing and food scarcity top the list of the ways life can bend and mold us into discomfort. But day after day, if we put on our crooked suit, we will eventually start to believe it's us, not the suit, that's crooked.

For many of us, when we tried to show our uniqueness as children, we were reprimanded and told to be "seen and not heard"— or even laughed at by our friends and family. I remind all my clients that none of us make it through puberty unscathed. If our "suit" didn't fit perfectly as a teenager, our classmates could be brutal. Instead of embracing our unique gifts, we were made fun of, and so we further contorted and hid our authenticity under the uncomfortable suit of adaptability.

These feelings of being "othered," shamed, and ostracized create powerful traumatic residue that doesn't leave our minds and bodies without effort. A popular statistic, often attributed to the National Science Foundation, is that humans have up to 60,000 thoughts per day, with 80 percent being negative and 95 percent being repetitive. While such estimates are challenging to empirically prove, with even one thought of fear, unworthiness, guilt, or shame played on repeat, minute after minute, day after day, and year after year, it's no wonder your body is so sore and contorted.

Most people I meet think the process of healing requires us to gain something new. In reality, we need absolutely nothing new to heal. Rather, we must learn to forget all that is not true. Healing is about letting go of all the untrue thoughts we had to believe to keep ourselves safe. Healing is remembering that all we need to do is stretch our arms, relax our shoulders, and stand up tall. The suit might not fit very well, and we may get a funny look or snicker here and there, but the freedom that comes with remembering your authenticity—of "re-turning" toward your authentic Self—is profoundly worth it.

Once your suit is off and your posture slowly readjusts, you'll eventually find just the right tailor to craft a beautiful new suit, one that perfectly fits your body and shows off your amazing and unique style. There are many ways to go through this unlearning process, but I can tell you from personal experience that psychedelics are one of the best and most powerful tailors I have ever met.

Psychedelics help us heal by allowing us to grow stronger, forgive, and release the memories and judgments that no longer serve us. The safe, intentional, and healing use of psychedelics may represent one of the most significant discoveries in medicine, with benefits as important and revolutionary as those of germ theory, organ transplants, and penicillin. What sets them apart from these human-made discoveries is that science may never fully understand psychedelics and their actions of operation.

Risks

"Coyote Dance" by Robbie Robertson, The Red Road Ensemble

I n October 2023, Joseph Emerson, a commercial aircraft pilot riding in the jump seat of Alaska Airlines Flight 2059 with two other working pilots, attempted to shut down the plane's engines midflight by activating the fire suppression system. Depressed and suffering from multiple nights of insomnia, Emerson told *The New York Times*, "I thought it would stop both engines, the plane would start to head toward a crash, and I would wake up."[23] Fortunately for Emerson and all those onboard, the flight crew was able to intervene, preventing a potential disaster. Upon landing, Emerson was arrested and faced eighty-three counts of attempted murder, as well as charges of reckless endangerment. His story prompted discussion about mental health support for pilots.

After an interview on ABC's *Good Morning America*, the pilot shared that he had taken magic mushrooms (combined with other substances) forty-eight hours before the flight and believed what he was experiencing was not reality. For most people, a typical psychedelic experience lasts a few hours. For Joseph, and some other individuals prone to psychotic disorders, these substances can have prolonged (and potentially catastrophic) effects. The *Diagnostic and Statistical Manual of Mental Disorders* (DSM) might classify this as depersonalization/derealization disorder (DPDR), which is one of the potential risks of using psychedelics.

Without a doubt, risks are involved in using psychedelics, but the likelihood of these risks is relatively low if they are used in a safe and controlled setting. DPDR is one of the very few severe risks associated with using psychedelics. Still, now that you've been made privy to perhaps the most extreme case of psychedelic risk the world has seen in the last century, let's step back and examine this topic from a more measured and practical perspective.

Psychedelics carry a relatively low risk when compared to many other substances you might already be using in your day-to-day life. For context, the data of a 2020 German study represented in figure 7, ranked the relative harm of thirty-three psychoactive drugs. LSD and mushrooms ranked in the midrange, just above nicotine but below cannabis. Crack, methamphetamine, heroin, alcohol, and cocaine topped the list as the most potentially harmful.[24]

If you consider and optimize the variables in the PSW, your likelihood of risk is considerably lower than many drugs regularly prescribed by doctors or used recreationally. This chapter is dedicated to reducing these risks. But remember, it is impossible to fully eliminate them.

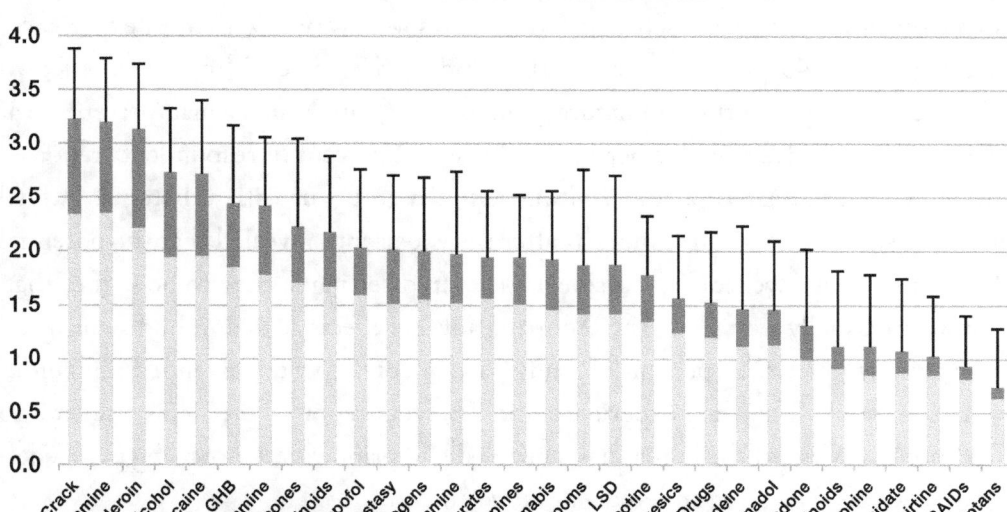

FIGURE 7. Relative harm by substance to users and others.

The Occurrence of "Bad Trips"

Two common questions from newcomers are "How risky is it for me to use psyche-delics?" and "What will happen if things go wrong?" Unfortunately, neither of these questions can be answered with 100 percent certainty. Many healthy individuals with no physical or psychological contraindications have tried psychedelics, and a small percentage (as we'll discuss below) experience a "bad trip" that can cause days, weeks, months, or even years of persisting symptoms.

Why does this happen, and what causes a "bad trip"? Sometimes, we have clues. The pilot mentioned above was mixing mushrooms with alcohol, was experiencing severe depressive symptoms and insomnia, and did no preparation or integration. No qualified facilitator interested in your safety would encourage this type of experience. Other cases have very little cause to support the adverse outcomes. Ultimately, it's tough to pin a "bad trip" on any one item, as the surrounding circumstances are usually more complicated.

A 2023 study by Johns Hopkins University surveyed 2,833 individuals taking psilocybin outside of a research setting.[25] The settings were varied, with most experiences occurring alone (43 percent), some with friends (25.7 percent), most in their own homes (69.7 percent), others in nature (15.8 percent), and even a small percentage at a concert or music festival (1.2 percent). Less than 2 percent of respondents reported working with a shaman or a guide, within a guided group, or with a therapist. A final follow-up survey two to three months after the experience revealed that the potential adverse effects of psychedelics outside a structured setting appear to be higher than what we are usually led to believe. Reporting adverse effects such as mood swings and depressive symptoms, 11 percent of study participants reported extended difficulties two to four weeks after their experience, and 7 percent reported problems after two to three months. Most of the individuals surveyed had prior experience using psychedelics, but even so, one in ten suffered a negative outcome.

In contrast, in other studies, where participants work in controlled environments and receive support before, during, and after their experience from trained facilitators, the likelihood of a negative experience is nearly nonexistent. A meta-analysis performed in 2024 evaluated 3,504 patients across 114 clinical psychedelic studies. The analysis discovered zero serious adverse events reported among patients with no preexisting neuropsychiatric disorders and approximately 4 percent of reported adverse events among those with a preexisting disorder.[26]

If you are a newcomer to psychedelics, the question I would pose to you is: are you willing to be one out of the ten people who experience long-term negative effects from taking psychedelics outside of a controlled environment? If your answer to that is no, my best suggestion would be to avoid working alone or in a pseudospiritual setting. Instead, work with a qualified facilitator in a controlled setting and with proper support. While many people can have a perfectly safe and gentle experience taking psychedelics alone or with friends, a one in ten chance of long-term postexperience difficulties is higher than most are comfortable with.

Unfortunately, people rarely discuss the risks of psychedelics—even in research papers and clinical trials. Most psychedelic zealots, influencers, and the media focus on highlighting the positive outcomes, while sweeping negativity under the rug. One of the stated reasons for the 2024 FDA denial of MDMA was that Lykos (previously known as MAPS Public Benefit Corporation) omitted adverse outcomes from their study data. Sadly, this might be a more common occurrence than we would like to admit.

The Challenging Psychedelic Experiences Project is a nonprofit founded in 2022 to learn more about post-psychedelic difficulties and what helps people cope with or recover from them.[27] Along with its slightly more brazen brother organization, Ecstatic Integration,[28] these projects specifically focus on exploring risks and exposing the seedy underbelly of psychedelics and spirituality. If you are interested in learning how to better spot psychedelic safety "red flags" or need a definitive reason to decide psychedelics are not right for you, I invite you to spend time exploring their resources. I believe accurate information on risks and negative effects is essential and critical to the long-term growth and health of the psychedelic industry.

Note: Organizations like The Challenging Psychedelic Experiences Project and Ecstatic Integration are operating as much-needed counterbalances to the positivity-focused psychedelic media. However, keep in mind that bearing the burden of this lopsided responsibility requires them to exert a heavier "negative thumb" in balancing the overadvertised benefits. Both these projects almost exclusively focus on gathering and exposing data from individuals who have already experienced discomfort or harm from their use of psychedelics. Therefore, the information presented is often biased toward the negative. The information offered is important, but I encourage you to make it just one of many sources for your research.

Psychedelic Contraindications

A contraindication is a reason someone should not receive a specific treatment because of a potential risk of harm, either physical or psychological. There are two types of contraindications:

+ **Relative contraindications** refer to treatments that have an increased risk of harm, but could still be considered if the benefits are deemed to outweigh the risks.
+ **Absolute contraindications** refer to treatments that should not be utilized because the risk of severe harm is too high.

In this instance, "harm" refers to both physical damage (such as stroke, heart attack, or even death) and psychological damage (including mental health issues like psychosis, emotional instability, or suicidal thoughts). Every substance, be it a psychedelic or a pharmaceutical drug prescribed by your doctor, comes with its own set of contraindications.

It would be impossible for this book to address every individual's unique needs, symptoms, and current physical and pharmacological situation, as well as how all of those factors intersect with each of the psychedelic substances available today. The following section offers a few broad contraindications and suggestions, but always work closely with your facilitator, therapist, prescribing physician, or a psychopharmacologist with specific expertise in psychedelics before proceeding with any psychedelic experience. Remember, you must be the responsible party in ensuring your own safety. Do not expect your facilitator to be an expert in your unique physical or mental health conditions.

PHYSICAL CONTRAINDICATIONS

Prescription Medications

The interaction of antidepressants and antipsychotics with some psychedelics can be incredibly dangerous. While new research has shown that mixing LSD or psilocybin with antidepressants may not be as big of a concern as we once thought it was, doing the same thing with ayahuasca or iboga could be life-threatening.

Cardiovascular Conditions

Psychedelics can increase heart rate and blood pressure. Combining psychedelics with conditions such as hypertension, heart disease, or a history of stroke or aneurysm could exacerbate or pose a life-threatening risk.

Neurological Disorders

Some psychedelics may lower the seizure threshold or even trigger seizures for individuals with epilepsy or prone to seizures. While some early research has shown psychedelics could improve conditions such as traumatic brain injury,[29] it is also possible they could exacerbate those symptoms.

Respiratory Conditions

Some psychedelics can cause bronchoconstriction and alter breathing patterns. These situations could present issues for those suffering from asthma or chronic obstructive pulmonary disease (COPD).

Pregnancy

Limited data exists, but people who are pregnant or breastfeeding should avoid using nonorganic substances and should show great caution if using classical psychedelics, especially in late-term pregnancy. It is unknown if psychedelics negatively affect the physiological or emotional health of the baby.

Active Addiction

Even though psychedelics have been successfully used to treat addiction, individuals in active, ongoing addiction should fully disclose and work closely with their care team to determine whether psychedelics are a safe treatment option. Many professionals frequently recommend that individuals remain sober for period of time before considering psychedelic use.

Blood Sugar Issues

Psychedelics may cause fluctuations in blood sugar levels, which could be problematic for diabetic users.

PSYCHOLOGICAL CONTRAINDICATIONS

Severe Mental and Emotional Instability

For those whose life already feels highly unstable, psychedelics may cause, rather than solve, problems. Many individuals who have powerful psychedelic experiences can become more destabilized before they get better. In lieu of a very stable and supportive care team that is able to provide daily life assistance, I recommend working to mentally and emotionally stabilize your life before starting your psychedelic work.

Primary Psychotic, Dissociative, and Affective Disorders

For those with a personal or family history of schizophrenia, schizoaffective disorder, bipolar 1, borderline personality disorder, or dissociative identity disorder, psychedelics can trigger psychosis or worsen symptoms.

Severe Anxiety, Panic, and Paranoia Disorders

Especially during challenging experiences or when using specific substances, psychedelics can initiate feelings of overwhelm and provoke or worsen symptoms of anxiety and paranoia.

History of Substance Abuse

Although the four classical psychedelics are not physically addictive (MDMA and ketamine are not considered classical psychedelics), a history of substance abuse could trigger a relapse or encourage misuse.

Suicidal Ideation, Severe Depression, and PTSD

Even though psychedelics have been proven to offer significant relief for suicidal ideation, severe depression, and PTSD, it should be known that symptoms may worsen before they improve. If you are already experiencing severe symptoms from these conditions, it is strongly advised that you only use psychedelics within a supportive and safe environment, and with a facilitator experienced in your conditions.

SPIRITUAL CONTRAINDICATIONS

Ungrounded Spiritual Identity or Framework

Similar to the psychological instability mentioned above, for individuals unstable or ungrounded in their spiritual practice, psychedelics should be used with caution. Powerful experiences may lead to confusion, disorientation, or disbelief about their spiritual identity. For those who hold atheistic beliefs (or other generalized lack of beliefs), having a powerful psychedelic experience could challenge or oppose the entire framework with which you have constructed your world, leading to ontological distress.

Traditional Morality and Ethics

Some spiritual traditions warn against, or expressly reject, the use of psychedelics or mind-altering substances. Existential confusion may arise when mixing traditions. Approach psychedelics slowly if your current tradition is highly rigid in its beliefs.

Risks of Psychedelic Use

If you possess any of the contraindications above, you may be more likely to experience one or more of the following risks.

PHYSICAL RISKS

Increased Heart Rate and Blood Pressure

Many psychedelics can increase heart rate and blood pressure, which can be dangerous for those with preexisting conditions or advanced age.

Overheating

Some psychedelics can dramatically increase body temperature to dangerous levels. Be cautious when using psychedelics in hot weather or with limited access to water and electrolytes.

Serotonin Syndrome

Many psychedelics affect serotonin levels in the brain. When combined with other substances that increase serotonin (e.g., antidepressants like SSRIs), it is possible to cause serotonin syndrome, a potentially life-threatening condition characterized by confusion, muscle rigidity, and seizures.

Death

While uncommon, the risk of death is possible with psychedelics. Mixing some psychedelic substances with pharmaceuticals or other dangerous substances could cause irreversible harm.

PSYCHOLOGICAL RISKS

Worsening of Negative Symptoms

A common phrase in psychotherapy and psychedelics is "things may get worse before they get better." It is essential to understand that you may see or experience challenging parts of your current (or past) life in a psychedelic experience, which could trigger an unraveling of past traumas that you will have to work through and integrate into your day-to-day human experience. Worsening psychological symptoms could involve increased or persistent anxiety and depression, impaired judgment or risky behavior, or feelings of being lost or emotionally overwhelmed by your life.

"Bad Trips"

"Bad trips" differ from what I would call "challenging journeys" when they trigger experiences that are so difficult and dysregulating, they register in the body as trauma or cause harm to our spirit. This will be discussed further in chapter 15, "Experience."

Depersonalization and Derealization

Depersonalization is the feeling of being outside yourself, or like you are observing your thoughts, feelings, or actions from a distance. Derealization is the feeling that you are disconnected from the world around you. You may feel like the world isn't real or like you're living in a dream and unable to wake up.

Hallucinogen Persisting Perception Disorder (HPPD)

While rare, HPPD involves long-term or recurrent perceptual changes in your day-to-day waking life. These could include visual distortions such as halos around objects, as well as trailing afterimages (where moving objects leave a lingering visual trace), flashbacks, or vivid reexperiencing of aspects of your journey.

Prolonged Psychosis

This side effect is very rare for most seekers, but it can be dangerous for those who have a personal or family history of psychiatric disorders like schizophrenia, schizoaffective disorder, or bipolar 1 disorder.

False Insights and Memories

Psychedelics can offer powerful insights and visions, but these substances often speak to us in metaphor and symbolism. Misinterpreting these insights without a grounded support team or guidance can create disruptive changes in your life.

Psychological Addiction

Classical psychedelics are not dependency-building substances, but it is possible to become addicted to the peak experiences they offer, especially as a means of escaping difficult elements of life and bypassing the healing work that needs to occur.

SPIRITUAL RISKS

Ego Inflation

Psychedelics may produce feelings of unity, oneness, or even God-like experiences. When these temporary states become transposed onto your everyday life, ego inflation may occur, and you may come to believe you are more spiritually advanced than you are.

"Spiritual Bypass"

When you use psychedelics to achieve a peak experience but do not do the corresponding work to integrate that experience or its teachings into your life, "spiritual bypass" occurs. This typically involves avoiding deep-rooted emotional issues or unresolved trauma, and prevents authentic spiritual development.

Ontological Distress or Shock

Going too far and too fast into a mystical or unexplainable experience may challenge your very understanding of reality and existence. This can occur when you encounter information, experiences, or events that contradict your deeply held beliefs about the nature of the world, yourself, or existence. It can lead to confusion, disorientation, or an existential crisis.

"Spiritual Overwhelm" or "Spiritual Emergency"

Psychedelics can cause profoundly mystical and spiritual experiences that may become overwhelming or difficult to integrate (More on this in chapter 15, "Experience"). Understanding the difference between spiritual emergence and a "spiritual emergency" is critical in this situation. Individuals experiencing the latter often feel lost, anxious, or unable to make sense of their lives.

Ruth's Story

Before my experience with 5-MeO-DMT, I read countless warnings about preparing properly that I ignored. I was desperate to find relief from anxiety and depression, and to save my domestic partnership. I wish I had known that the discomfort I hoped to escape would soon pale in comparison to the overwhelming anxiety, depression, and insomnia that consumed me and my partner after the experience.

Despite working with a psychedelic-informed psychiatrist to carefully wean off the psychiatric medications (SSRIs) I had been taking for twenty-five years, I barely felt the heroic doses (a very high, often overwhelming dose of a psychedelic, typically inducing profound ego dissolution and intense mystical experiences) of MDMA and psilocybin I took in my first intentional experience. After months of research, preparation, introspection, and conversations with my facilitator, I felt defeated. Broken. Inhuman. *Is there any hope for me?* I wondered.

I learned about another substance, 5-MeO-DMT, also known as bufo, from a friend who assured me it was a more potent medicine. She connected me with a facilitator who seemed confident, knowledgeable, and experienced, having served many others (including his own mother) and worked with the medicine frequently himself. He told me I would be the best judge of my dosage, encouraging me to continue until I could go no farther. If I felt unsure, that meant I needed more.

I should have listened to my instincts and my partner's concerns. The facilitator dominated our conversations, often veering into his own traumas and experiences. The setting for my journey was a futon mattress on a concrete floor in a loft where the facilitator was temporarily staying. Hopping out of the shower upon my arrival, he explained that he had been out dancing all night and was preparing to use some 5-MeO-DMT himself before I arrived. Despite the red flags, I was desperate.

We began with powerful breathing exercises, followed by drops of Sananga, a traditional psychoactive plant medicine, into my eyes, which made them burn intensely. Then he handed me the bufo vape pen, instructing me to inhale slowly, swallow, and hold. I was scared, and as I inhaled, I felt dizzy, jittery, and insecure—ultimately disconnected and unsafe. I took more hits, totaling upward of 150 mg (fifteen times the common dose) across eleven inhales over an hour. My discomfort grew. My body felt unbearably hot and tense. I vomited multiple times.

Are you breathing, Ruth? Are you still here? Breathe!! Don't forget to breathe— in and out... both in and out! I directed myself. The experience was agonizing, and something in me couldn't let go. My neck ached terribly, and no position felt comfortable. Finally, I called it off. He suggested a high dose of MDMA or LSD next time, followed by 5-MeO-DMT, stating I'd be more sensitive in the coming weeks. But he had no idea what was ahead—and neither did I.

For the next two days, I couldn't sleep a single minute. Even with nighttime stretching, meditation, and melatonin, I was restless. By the third day, I managed only brief, fragmented sleep. My primary doctor prescribed trazodone and melatonin, which worked initially, but then wore off. I alternated with Klonopin, which helped me sleep but left me groggy and disoriented.

My life spiraled. I became hypersensitive, constantly questioning my actions, my relationships, and my sanity. I was disconnected from my partner and overwhelmed with paranoia, anxiety, and unbearable neck pain that triggered migraines. Daily life became unmanageable. My sense of reality unraveled, leading to severe depression and suicidal ideation. For nearly a year, I felt trapped in a cycle of insomnia, pain, and mental anguish. Desperate for relief, I tried everything: reintroducing SSRIs and mood stabilizers, exercise, yoga, sound healing, breathwork, eye movement desensitization and reprocessing (EMDR) therapy, and various bodywork modalities. I even participated in traditional ceremonies and sought alternative therapies. Gradually, my mood and sleep began to stabilize, but my neck pain remains debilitating, and I am now consulting a neurologist for answers.

The lesson learned from my experience is clear: desperation can cloud judgment. Ignoring red flags nearly cost me everything. No one wants to talk about the potential downsides of psychedelic healing, but I assure you, understanding them is the most critical step you can take on your journey.

Trust Your Gut: Discernment over Desperation

The modern medical system is failing large portions of our population. Chronic conditions go unresolved, and millions of individuals are suffering, sometimes for years. Many reach for psychedelics like a life preserver thrown overboard in a raging storm. Many come to alternative healing from a place of sheer desperation, hoping that a single experience with iboga or ayahuasca will finally relieve their suffering or addiction.

Desperation is one of the most dangerous positions to operate from. It is all too easy to believe the charlatans, grifters, manipulators, "plastic shamans," and spiritual healers who guarantee that *their medicine* is the thing that will finally cure you. In reality, many of these people are not prioritizing their clients' health, and instead (consciously or not) seek only power, control, and money. If you are in a vulnerable population or have been suffering for years, working slowly and carefully to find a treatment path and facilitator that meets your needs is essential to your safety.

Discernment refers to the ability to understand and perceive things clearly and objectively. It is not a word often used in casual conversation. If you are new to psychedelics, it should quickly become a part of your vocabulary and daily practice. No one should focus more on your safety, health, and protection than you. If you abdicate this responsibility to an unfamiliar facilitator, you may end up experiencing more harm than healing.

The challenge with discernment in the early stages of your journey is that you may not possess the knowledge, wisdom, or nervous system attunement to make the right decisions. You simply won't have enough experience on your own to know when someone is lying or trying to manipulate you. As we will discuss in chapter 8, "Preparation," putting in place a knowledgeable and stable support team is critical to helping you make sound decisions.

If you and/or your support team all lack the requisite discernment, work only with trusted referrals or seek the advice of an independent and skilled third party. Don't travel to Central or South America to a random retreat center or meet someone at a psychedelic society meeting and have your first experience the weekend after.

When questions arise, make sure you ask your facilitator. If they are uninterested in addressing your questions, use that as information to make your next decision—which may be deciding to walk away. You are ultimately responsible for making an informed choice that best meets your needs. Even if you've already paid your deposit, if you feel unsafe walking into a ceremony, the physical and psychological costs of healing a new traumatic experience are so much higher than what you've already paid. Trust your gut and walk away!

Fast Changes vs. Slow Changes

The only thing humans hate more than change is uncertainty. But when we're suffering, all we want is change—and we want it now! We'll even put ourselves in abnormal amounts of uncertainty to feel relief. People often come to psychedelics because nothing else they've tried has worked, so they decide it's time to "pull out the big guns" and do something completely different.

Most facilitators do not address the difference between fast and slow change. To explore this concept, let's use dying as an example. We know we're all going to die. Most of us are pretty cool with that as we creep closer and closer to old age. With the "big change" spanning across the eighty or so years of a lifetime, our minds can get on board with this kind of slow change. However, if we receive a stage four cancer diagnosis and are told by a doctor that we have six months to live, our minds do not do so well with that kind of fast change. The result—death—is the same, but the speed at which the change occurs is very different.

Psychedelics are most definitely a way to initiate fast change in our consciousness. I often remind my clients that the vast majority of psychedelic experiences feel like drinking awareness from a firehose. Sometimes, learning how out of alignment you've been living your life in the span of a few hours can be very destabilizing. Other examples of massive shifts in awareness can come from remembering and reexperiencing parts of your past you've locked away for decades. This could look like early childhood abuse, prenatal trauma, or even committing heinous acts in a past lifetime.

As we'll explore in chapter 12, "Dosing," you have a lot of control over how hard and fast you travel on this journey. Some of the most challenging and dysregulating experiences I have witnessed—and helped reintegrate—have come from newcomers taking large doses of powerful medicines before they were ready. When it comes to dosing (and healing in general), consider using a phrase popularized by the Navy SEALs and co-opted by many in psychedelia as a rule of thumb: "Slow is smooth, and smooth is fast." The slower and more controlled you are as you approach this work, the less likely you will take on risks and expose yourself to harm.

"Trip Killers": What Happens if You Take Too Much?

An old psychedelic adage goes, "You can always take more, but you can never take less."

In both recreational and intentional work, it's not uncommon to hear someone to say, "I took the mushrooms and waited an hour, and didn't feel anything. Right after I took more, the first dose kicked in, and I quickly realized I had just taken too much." Delayed activation, a misinterpreted dosage, or the naturally unforeseeable nature of a psychedelic substance can create unpredictable experiences, sometimes with positive results and sometimes with negative ones.

Relatively recently, I was sitting in an Indigenous ayahuasca ceremony and had such an experience. During the first night of the ceremony, I had drunk two cups of ayahuasca and had a powerful, yet manageable, experience. On the second night, despite my familiarity with the strength of the medicine, I drank one cup and felt nothing. I drank a second cup and still felt nothing. Two hours later, a third cup kicked off an experience that forever changed my life—for the positive. You never really know what's going to happen on any given night with any given dosage.

I've learned to remove "hard" from my vocabulary, instead choosing to replace it with "powerful." For example, instead of saying, "It was a very hard night," I'll amend the phrase to "It was a very powerful night." This slight reframing of an experience comes with the understanding that the medicine knows exactly what I need, that I'm often just along for the ride, and that sometimes that ride can be intense. The night of my three cups of ayahuasca was filled with the most powerful experience of self-realization I've ever had in my ten years sitting with the medicine, and I wouldn't take it back for anything—regardless of how "powerful" it really was.

But what happens when you really have taken too much and want to get off the roller coaster? Researchers asked Reddit that very question. A 2024 study collating anecdotal evidence from thousands of anonymous Reddit posts found that benzodiazepines and antipsychotics were the most frequently used "trip killers" deployed in uncontrolled (recreational) settings, but the risks that these substances carry are rarely discussed.[30] These drugs have addictive properties, and using them to forcefully arrest a psychedelic experience before its emotional or psychosomatic closure can initiate long-term post-psychedelic difficulties. What clinicians today refer to as hallucinogen persisting perception disorder (HPPD) was more informally referred to in the 1960s and 1970s as "acid flashbacks." This is a phenomenon where a person experiences a spontaneous recurrence of the sensory or perceptual effects of a psychedelic long after the drug has worn off. Many have since speculated that these flashbacks were caused by psychedelic experiences that never reached a natural gestalt (a German word meaning "unified whole").

Unfortunately, law enforcement and medical personnel do not understand the downstream effects of this premature interruption and will frequently sedate unruly patients. They are often restrained or made to sit in silence in a padded room with bright, florescent lights—all horrible experiences when it comes to "set and setting."

There are much better and safer methods for assisting someone experiencing a "bad trip." Unfortunately, if you're the one having the experience, it's unlikely you will remember these helpful hints. If you've found yourself in a situation where you can safely offer support, consider a few of these tips before ingesting a trip killer.

Safety First

The first thing to do is ensure the individual is in a safe space, away from potential dangers like traffic, heights, weapons, or sharp objects. If possible, dim the lights, reduce the noise or change the music, and minimize any overwhelming stimuli.

Stay Calm

As we've already discussed in earlier chapters, we're all energy, and we're all vibrating at different levels. Consciously leveling your vibration by becoming a calm and grounding presence will go a long way toward reducing fear, anxiety, or panic in the journeyer.

Reassure Them

An individual having a challenging experience has temporarily lost touch with reality and is going through something you know nothing about. Rather than attempting to help them navigate their experience, simply reassure them with phrases like "You are safe," "You're not alone," "This is only temporary," and "I'm here for you."

Focus on Grounding

Helping someone ground back into their own body is one of the best ways to slow down a challenging experience. Gently encourage them to notice physical sensations rather than their visions or thoughts. Encouraging them to focus on and slow their breath, and to touch something physical (like the earth, a stone, or even a soft blanket or pillow), can be a very effective grounding technique.

Avoid Judgment

It can be easy to become engaged in the individual's story or even triggered by their words and actions. Try to validate their feelings without convincing them they're wrong for feeling a certain way. It's also critical to remember that while the person you're helping might be your best friend in a normal state of consciousness, they are not the same when they are in an altered state. What someone says or does in this state should never be taken personally.

Don't Overreact

Engaging law enforcement or emergency services is rarely required unless the individual is having a medical emergency or in danger of harming themself or others. Most law enforcement officers, and even many emergency medical service personnel, have not received training in working with individuals in expanded states of consciousness, and can unintentionally cause more physical or psychological harm than they solve. (If you are interested in engaging in this kind of training, please reach out to the Neuma Center for Psychedelic Safety & Response.) For most people, avoid arguing with the journeyer's perceptions or trying to rationalize their experience. What they are experiencing is "real" for them in that moment, and attempting to convince them otherwise will often only escalate the situation.

Seek Additional Support

At all times, your safety is just as important as the safety of the journeyer. Tagging in a trusted facilitator or mutual friend may be helpful (or necessary) if the experience lasts longer than you can handle. If the experience does not come to a natural conclusion, or if the person becomes a danger to themself or others, seek professional medical assistance.

Post-Trip Integration

While we will discuss this topic in more detail in chapter 16, it's important to give the individual space to reflect and process their experience once they are no longer activated. Encouraging them to journal, talk, or seek professional integration support are important ways to conclude the experience.

If you or someone you know has had a challenging experience and are seeking additional resources, please visit PsychedelicIQ.com.

Psychedelics and Pharmaceuticals

One of the most hotly debated topics in psychedelics is their use and interaction with pharmaceuticals. Many of those looking to psychedelics for healing may already be on one or more medications, including antidepressants, antipsychotics, and even benzo-diazepines. Depending on who you talk to, one "expert" may say you need to be off all prescriptions before you can engage in psychedelic use, and another may advise you to not go off your meds at all.

Interactions between pharmaceuticals and psychedelics are very complicated and often unpredictable. If you are on prescription medications that affect your heart, liver, nervous system, or brain chemistry, get more information from a qualified professional before proceeding. Psychedelic substances to be especially careful with are ayahuasca (due to the monoamine oxidase inhibitors [MAOIs] contained within its ingredients) and iboga/ibogaine (due to its cardiac risks, serotonin interactions, and liver metabolism).

If you are taking antidepressants, substances such as psilocybin or LSD may not cause severe harm but could potentially worsen your existing depression symptoms. In a 2024 study, researchers examined the effects of combining psilocybin with SSRI/SNRI antidepressant usage. They found that stopping antidepressants was linked to increased depression severity at the start of the trial.[31]

In my practice, I typically encounter two types of clients who take pharmaceutical medications. The first type is stable on their medications and does not necessarily want to be off of them. These people are not typically experiencing significant side effects, but they still want to address the underlying causes of their malaise. The second type of client is usually experiencing negative pharmaceutical side effects, wants to be off their medications, and is looking for an alternative treatment.

If you currently take medication that you no longer want to be on, it is critical to work with your support team to develop a slow and safe titration plan. If you want to consider taking psychedelics alongside your medications, I suggest working with a psychopharmacologist who also specializes in psychedelic interactions. These professionals can assist you in determining which of your prescriptions may interact with your substance of choice.

Remember, not all brains react the same way to all substances. I have worked with two individuals of roughly the same age and with very similar physical profiles, who were both taking the same antidepressant and dosage. Despite their similarities, they had completely opposing experiences with the same psychedelic substance.

For example, Seeker A can take three grams of mushrooms and have absolutely no experience. Seeker B can take the same amount of the same mushrooms and have a powerful experience. Science is unable to explain why this happens, and it's unlikely you will know if you're person A or B until you try. Sometimes, Seeker A can take more of the psychedelic substance and have a breakthrough experience. For mushrooms, if an average dose is three grams, someone on antidepressants may need to take seven to ten grams to achieve the experience they are looking for. On the other hand, I also have worked with an individual who took twenty grams of mushrooms and only experienced a light body buzz. Every body (and brain) is different!

Weighing the Risks and Rewards

If this chapter has caused you to feel some trepidation, that is an expected reaction. With today's constant barrage of positive media, it's uncommon to be exposed to the risks of using psychedelics. If this is your first real look at the potential dangers, this chapter may encourage you to slow down or pause your process. This is a good thing. My intention is, and will always be, to prioritize safety.

A 2023 study showed that 8.9 percent of study participants claimed they experienced functional impairment lasting longer than a day after using psychedelics.[32] Meanwhile, the National Institute of Mental Health (NIMH) reports that 23.1 percent of the US adult population has a mental health condition.[33] The sad reality of modern life is that you're twice as likely to experience a mental health issue just by living in the United States as you are to experience a negative effect from using psychedelics.

I tell all my clients that joy and vulnerability are two sides of the same coin. Most people who come to this work seek more joy in their lives. But newcomers often don't understand that to achieve a more profound sense of joy, they must first take a step toward vulnerability. Joy doesn't come without some pre-work. In his book *The Wisdom of Insecurity*, Alan Watts discusses an often-undesirable aspect of our healing journey, writing, "This is the human problem: there is a price to pay for every increase in consciousness. We cannot be sensitive to pleasure without being more sensitive to pain."[34]

While I do not believe healing always has to be hard and painful, there are usually segments of our healing journey that come with deep vulnerability and the risk of emotional harm. In these seasons, it's imperative to have a supportive family, community, or team to help you. Going it alone can be excruciating.

The risks of using psychedelics are pretty minimal compared to many other medically sanctioned treatments being offered today, but using psychedelics will never be risk free. Suppose you have none of the contraindications mentioned at the beginning of this chapter. In that case, the next most crucial element of your experience is finding a trusted facilitator to keep you safe. On the other hand, if you have one or more contraindications, it's best to slow down and evaluate the risks with your support team. Always be honest with your facilitator—weigh the risks and rewards together as a team. The goal is to make the best decision possible with everyone's eyes wide open.

In his song "Anthem," Leonard Cohen sings, "There is a crack in everything. That's how the light gets in."[35] There couldn't be a more appropriate way to think about a psychedelic experience. Psychedelics have the potential to shine a very bright light into our lives. But without a crack in our resistant exterior, it's tough for the light to get in. If you're still onboard, grab your hammer and chisel. It's time to create a few cracks and start letting some light in.

Preparation

"Seah Jahan" by Paul Horn

n episode six of the PsychedelicIQ podcast, Daniel Shankin, founder of TAMM Integration, says, "An ounce of preparation is worth a pound of integration." The responsibility to do this preparation is 100 percent yours, as the journeyer. Your preparation may be done with the help of a teacher, therapist, coach, or facilitator, but it is entirely up to you to do the work. And there is a very strong correlation between the amount of work you do ahead of time and the quality of the results you receive.

When you first begin your healing journey, you may find that things feel like they're getting worse before they get better. This is common. Letting go of the fears, resentments, deeply held beliefs, and stories we've been holding onto for years can shake us like an earthquake under our feet. With cracks forming all around (and within) us, it can feel like there's no safe and stable place to stand. If this is how you're feeling, I'll offer the comforting (yet paradoxically unsettling) words of Chögyam Trungpa: "The bad news is you're falling; the good news is there's no ground."

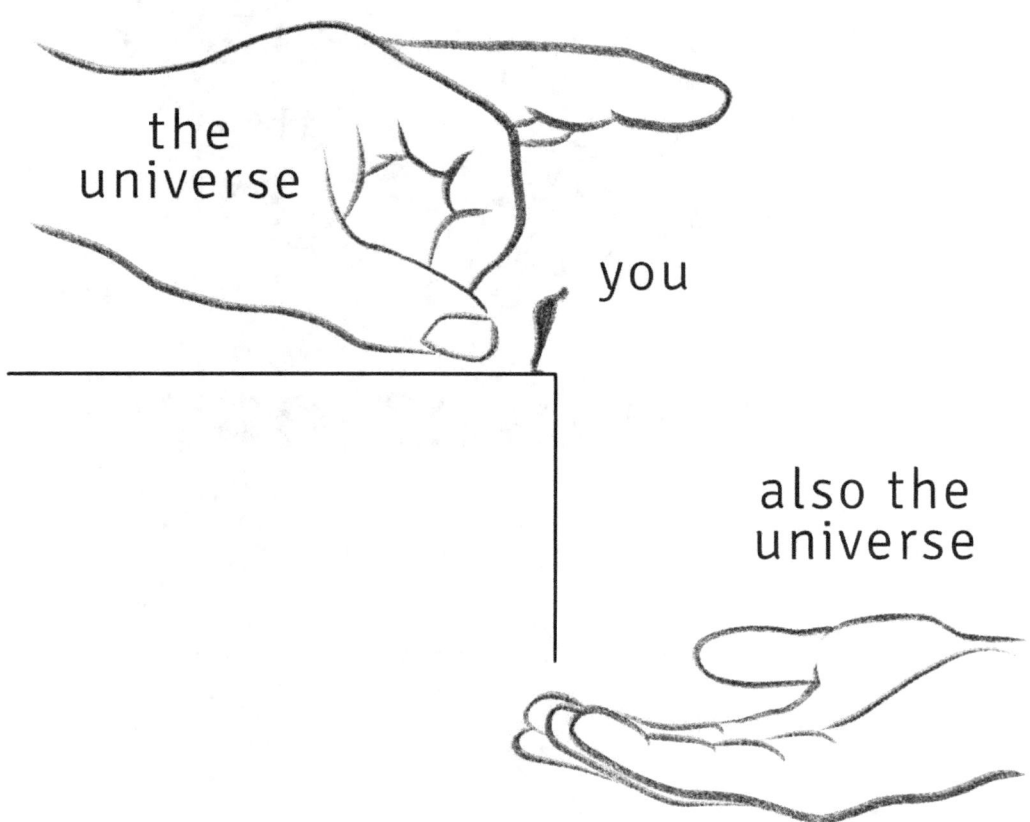

FIGURE 8. The bad news is you're falling. The good news is there's no ground.

This is exactly why preparation is so vital to the psychedelic process. Like almost every activity in life, it gets easier with practice. Psychedelics have a way of nudging us right to the edge of the cliff, then offering us an opportunity to take the next step and see and experience the unknown. Having some awareness of the terrain will make your experience much less nerve inducing.

Preparation is crucial in helping you change the way you think and address your core wounds to maximize your experience. Without a cursory understanding of ourselves, we embark on a trip without a roadmap. Without understanding where we are now or where we want to go, we're bound to get lost and waste a lot of time wandering in the dark. Preparation is where we start to examine what's really inside of us—our cravings, aversions, and all the thoughts that no longer serve us. We intentionally pull back the rug we've been sweeping dirt under for decades.

Does starting to learn the truth about who you really are make you a little nervous? Yes? Great! You're human. If you weren't nervous, I would be a little concerned. If you're still onboard, let's keep moving forward.

Focusing Your Preparation

Since using psychedelics for healing is a relatively new concept to most of the modern world, I find it helpful to explore the idea of preparation through two more ancient wisdom traditions: an Indigenous *dieta* (diet) and the three yogic *gunas* (fundamental qualities of nature).

For the first eight years of my ayahuasca practice, I was instructed to considerably limit my diet two weeks before ceremony. No alcohol, sugar, red meat, pork, or salt, and a focus on fresh fruits and vegetables. The maestro I study with today requires absolutely no dieta (outside of prescription medications) and tells his students that the medicine will teach us what and how to eat. My most recent experiences with this maestro have been the most life-changing of my entire psychedelic journey, leading me to believe that perhaps what you put in your mouth prior to ceremony may not be as important as I once believed. I've also learned that preparation is a highly individualized process, and one that should be approached together with your facilitator.

In more nontraditional settings, I have met practitioners who choose to use preparation and diet requirements more as rote protocols or hurdles to jump over, rather than tailored, helpful, and compassionate wisdom. Some practitioners may require you to only eat fruits and vegetables before a mushroom journey. Others will demand you abstain from caffeine and nicotine before you sit with the medicine. For my clients, diet *can* be a part of preparation, but it is not required. The harsh reality of this work is that some people have far more traumatic or challenging topics to address in their lives than cutting nicotine out of their system. My intention with those I work with is to have them come to ceremony in the most stable and safe state they can. If that includes red meat the night before or a cup of coffee before we start ceremony, so be it.

As you read on, please hold these two frameworks and the suggestions I offer very lightly. They are only to be used as guides, never requirements. The most important part of preparation is that *you* feel prepared and that you and your facilitator are in honest alignment with each other.

THE INDIGENOUS DIETA

When many modern minds think of a diet, we immediately focus on what we put in our mouths. In many traditional or Indigenous medicine traditions, a dieta goes beyond this, and is used to prepare the body, mind, and spirit to commune with a specific plant—or more specifically, the *spirit* of the plant. A traditional dieta is a contract between a practitioner and a particular plant spirit to deepen the relationship between themself and the spirit world. According to the Ayahuasca Foundation:

> One of the critical terms of the dieta agreement is the length of the dieta, meaning for how long the dieta will be kept. Sometimes, this is as short as eight days, although more common would be months and even years. The general agreement in a dieta is that the curandero or student will sacrifice the pleasures of physical stimulation by refraining from sex, alcohol, and sweet, spicy, salty, or rich foods. In return for this sacrifice, the plant spirits agree to teach, guide, protect, strengthen, or endow special abilities to the person doing the dieta. Usually, the dieta is done in near isolation to avoid temptations from interactions with people who are not doing or do not understand the dieta.[36]

This description reflects a deep and intentional relationship cultivated between a student and the plant spirit they seek as a teacher. This level of intentionality is not practiced casually. It is usually reserved for practitioners engaging in deep study with a specific plant, those preparing to serve under the instruction of a maestro, or those seeking deep healing or cleansing under the guidance of a curandero.

This level of preparation doesn't track well in many modern cultures due to the depth of commitment and time required. The intended physical, psychological, and spiritual sensitivity—and the relationship with the plant spirit in a true dieta—is impossible to achieve while watching Netflix, grabbing a coffee at Starbucks, and eating a standard American diet.

Even so, if you are considering using substance like ayahuasca, San Pedro, or iboga with the guidance of a teacher or healer, you can expect to be asked to engage in a dieta of some sort to prepare for your experience. For example, you may be instructed to refrain from certain behaviors for two or more weeks before a ceremony, and for one or more weeks following a ceremony.

The concept of a dieta can prepare you for any psychedelic experience, not just those with plant medicines like ayahuasca. Given that the dieta is about cleansing, it doesn't matter what substance you choose. Even if you opt for a different form of preparation, the intention should remain the same: filtering your proverbial fishtank to start with a cleaner body, mind, and spirit.

The cleaner your system is before entering an experience, the more productive that experience can be. When helping explorers prepare for an ayahuasca ceremony, I frequently offer, "The more cleansing you can do before the ceremony, the less cleansing the medicine has to do for you." Take it from me: it's easier to do this cleansing by choice than to have the medicine do it by force.

The Three Yogic Gunas

The other ancient wisdom that informs this preparation stage comes from yoga. This shifts us from a South American to an Eastern lens. The practice of yoga is incredibly complex, and it is a little unfair to extract one concept from thousands of years of philosophy. However, one idea further frames the purpose of the dieta and the preparation process in general: the gunas (pronounced "goo-nahs").

The Sanskrit word "gunas" translates to "qualities." There are three gunas: *rajas*, *tamas*, and *sattva*. These are the essential qualities that exist in the nature of all beings and all things. Each of the gunas is associated with a specific characteristic:

- **Rajas** — activity, passion, energy, and desire
- **Tamas** — impurity, lethargy, and darkness
- **Sattva** — consciousness, purity, knowledge, and harmony

While each guna is always present within us, it is believed that each of us are born with a unique balance of these qualities, influenced by our *prakriti* (innate nature or constitution). This balance can be shaped by factors such as genetics, environment, karma, and even our past lives. Ram Jain, a master yoga teacher and founder of

Arhanta Yoga explains, "The three gunas affect us deeply. They influence everything about us, from our thoughts and actions to the habits and activities that make us who we are. This means that whichever guna is more present within you will affect how you perceive the world."[37] In the context of psychedelics, the gunas are an invaluable lens through which we can examine ourselves and our lives. They create all that we are, all that we experience, all that we see, and all that remains to be seen.

For example, a person whose primary lived experience is driven by rajas is ambitious, restless, impulsive, competitive, and desires excitement. They likely lead a fast-paced, dynamic life characterized by energy and a constant pursuit of achievement. Rajas tends to be the primary experience of most developed nations and drives a continuous need for acquisition, growth, and achievement. Overlaying rajas onto the Map of Consciousness (see table 2, chapter 2, "How and Why Psychedelics Heal"), the overlap would include the emotions of desire (125), anger (150), pride (175), courage (200), and neutrality (250).

A person whose primary lived experience is driven by tamas will exhibit many of the opposite characteristics, including lethargy, procrastination, apathy, depression, dependency, addictive behaviors, and resistance to change. They will likely experience a sense of inertia and stagnation, characterized by a lack of energy, motivation, and engagement with the world around them. If depression represents a large part of your lived experience, tamas is your primary guna. Overlaying tamas onto the Map of Consciousness, the overlap would include shame (20), guilt (30), apathy (50), grief (75), and fear (100).

Finally, a person whose primary lived experience is driven by sattva will exhibit qualities such as clarity of mind, wisdom and insight, compassion and empathy, creativity and inspiration, self-discipline and moderation, gratitude and contentment, inner peace and serenity, service to others, and a connection to higher consciousness. They embody qualities of purity, understanding, and compassion, leading a life guided by higher principles and values. These individuals serve as a source of inspiration and upliftment for others, contributing to the greater good of humanity. A sattvic life embodies the phrase "strong back, soft front." Overlaying sattva onto the Map of Consciousness, the overlap would include willingness (310), acceptance (350), reason (400), love (500), joy (540), peace (600), and enlightenment (700–1000).

In addition to helping us develop a relationship with the plant's spirit, the gunas can indicate how to best prepare our body, mind, and spirit for a psychedelic experience, and also how we might react in the event of a challenging experience. Allow the gunas to move you toward the things and feelings you want. To rise from tamas, focus on activities that cultivate rajas. To transcend rajas, begin incorporating more sattvic practices into your life. Release any focus on pushing away from what you don't want.

For example, don't focus on the need to reduce a tamasic behavior—instead, focus on increasing feelings and behaviors higher up on the Map of Consciousness. We are already encouraged by marketing and media to pathologize and beat ourselves up over who we *don't* want to be. Don't make it even harder on yourself!

Considering the common stress response model of fight, flight, freeze, and appease/fawn, those with a stronger constitution of rajas may lean toward the fight response and may have trouble surrendering during a psychedelic experience (more on this in chapter 14, "Mindset"). Those with a heavier constitution of tamas may naturally respond with flight and have a desire to avoid or flee from difficult sensations or emotions. The more sattvic you can become, the more conscious and capable you are of trust and surrender, thereby creating a more gentle and productive experience.

In your preparation process, focus on behavior you *want* to cultivate in yourself. The practices I offer in the upcoming sections are designed to move you toward sattva while allowing rajas and tamas to fall away on their own. Act as if you're already sattvic, and with enough time and practice, you will find that this quality manifests from within with almost no effort at all.

When I assist my clients with preparation, I remind them, "There is no way to screw this up, and the less you can consciously *do* during your experience, the better." Hidden within this simple phrase is a deep acceptance of the transformative power of the medicine, a trust in a higher level of consciousness, and a movement away from action—each inherently sattvic qualities.

In the following sections, I will explore many different methods to prepare your system for a deep and productive psychedelic experience. Each of these methods share common goals:

1. Create a stable foundation by shifting out of rajas and tamas, and into sattva.
2. Develop trust and safety with yourself, your facilitator, and the medicine.
3. Create or further develop awareness of your involuntary reactions, as well as the art of responding, rather than reacting, to unexpected or challenging stimuli.

Preparation Methods

This section contains a complex and varied list of preparation methods. While it may feel overwhelming at first, remember that you shouldn't try to check off everything on this list all at once. Sustainable change happens slowly.

Think about your preparation phase like going to your favorite restaurant. You may want to try every item on the menu and feel tempted to overeat if your visits to the restaurant don't happen often. Luckily, you will have plenty of opportunities to explore *this* menu at a sustainable pace. If you're starving one day, you might order an appetizer, an entrée, and a dessert. On another day, when you're less hungry, you may only eat a salad. There's no urge to overindulge, because you can always come back and try something new tomorrow. This is the mindset with which you should approach your preparation.

Additionally, try not to make your preparation phase like a New Year's resolution, when you promise yourself that you'll go to the gym every day, stop eating sugar, and cut out caffeine all at once. A too-much, too-soon approach may leave you resenting your preparation, which will make it unsustainable. And despising your day-to-day life is the complete opposite of the reason you're doing this work. If you consider a gentle, middle-of-the-road approach to preparation instead of approaching it like training for a marathon, this stage of your journey will undoubtedly feel better, be easier, and become more sustainable over time.

In the spirit of sweet and easy, when choosing an item off this "menu," consider starting with dessert! Find something on the list that really want to try and know you will enjoy. What feels the most accessible right now? If you're feeling adventurous, pick one item from each category and see how it feels to practice those for a couple of weeks. If you want to go back for seconds, know that there is an all-you-can-eat buffet of opportunities to go deeper.

START WITH BREATHWORK

As we will further explore in the next chapter, I encourage every psychedelic new-comer to attempt breathwork as a first step in their psychedelic healing journey. An intense breathwork session has the greatest potential to offer an expanded state of con-sciousness and emulate a psychedelic experience—without ever ingesting a substance. Breathwork can also mimic the physiological changes of a psychedelic experience (like variations in blood pressure, temperature, and heart rate), along with the intense state of present-moment awareness. If you or your support team have any concerns about your physical ability to use psychedelics, breathwork is an effective way to measure your level of readiness and can be easily and legally practiced everywhere in the world. Specific methods of breathwork such as Holotropic, transformational, or rebirthing are incredibly powerful, and one of the best ways to prepare for your journey.

IMPROVE PHYSICAL HEALTH

Confucius said, "A healthy man wants a thousand things, a sick man only one." Regardless of age, your overall physical health should be one of your most important focuses in life. When any of my clients decide to "get healthy," it usually begins on this physical plane. The physical/material body is an accessible place for many to begin improvement, because we can more easily see and measure what is happening. Also, when our physical health is stronger, our mental, emotional, and spiritual preparations for psychedelics become more beneficial. These more subtle changes are easier to attain with a strong and healthy body. Below are some tips to improve your body's health:

Get Adequate Sleep

Without rest, all your body systems stop performing at optimal levels. You can no longer effectively metabolize your experiences and emotions. If you have been unable to get more than a few hours of sleep for multiple nights in a row, that is a suboptimal state to engage with psychedelics. Keep in mind that if you regularly take pharmaceuticals to sleep, they may be contraindicated and can severely blunt the effects of classic psychedelics.

Eat a Healthy Diet

In many cultures around the globe today, food is one of the most socially acceptable addictions. Addressing your unhealthy habits around food can be one of the most challenging (and life-changing) aspects of healing. In your preparation process, try to eat mostly nutritious, unprocessed foods, and do your best to reduce sugar, junk food, and caffeine. Some traditions, such as an ayahuasca dieta, will encourage you to cease eating most meats, spicy and fermented foods, and salt, while eating more fresh fruits, vegetables, nuts, and grains.

Explore Somatic Practices

When referencing psychedelic work, you may frequently encounter the word "somatic." Somatic simply means "relating to the body," and can refer to any method used to develop a deeper mind-body connection. This includes yoga *nidre*, guided body scans, breath awareness, shaking, and dance.

Combine Exercise, Breath, and Movement

One of my first teachers defined yoga as simply "breath and movement." With this definition, walking in the park, working out at the gym, taking a martial arts class, practicing tai chi or qigong, and doing poses on your mat can all be considered yoga, especially if done mindfully. Any practice that unites breath and movement is excellent for your psychedelic experience.

Incorporate Massage and Bodywork

These are excellent practices (and lovely treats) for before and after a psychedelic experience. Working with a trained massage therapist to help calm your mind and body is a fantastic tool for relaxing your nervous system and releasing tension and toxins stored in your body. If "deep tissue" is your standard order from the massage menu, try something gentler and see if you can embody a sense of rest and relaxation rather than hard work.

Refrain from Sex

Many Indigenous traditions and dietas recommend refraining from sex—with self or others—for some time before engaging with the medicine. Sexual energy is one of our body's most basic and potent energies (and a source of cravings). Metaphysically, your energy centers are very open at the moment of orgasm, and you can take on the energy of your partner. Many Eastern esoteric traditions believe that the release of semen can decrease our life force. Psychologically, refraining from sex, masturbation, and the use of pornography can help purify your mind and increase the sattvic qualities within your system.

Refrain from Drug Use

You should suspend use of alcohol, cannabis, and other recreational substances during your preparation time. If you're planning a healing experience with MDMA, you should refrain from taking "ecstasy" or "molly" in a recreational setting during this time. When used recreationally, these substances numb your life experience, hide what is true, and carry you away from your reactivity, essentially armoring the parts of you that most need healing. Additionally, the casual use of these substances may diminish or alter your psychedelic journey.

Evaluate Pharmaceuticals

The subject of how pharmaceuticals used to treat mental health diagnoses intersect with the use of psychedelics is complicated. Some facilitators will not work with individuals taking antidepressants, while others are not concerned. Current research and significant anecdotal evidence show that patients with no history of using antidepressant pharmaceuticals (e.g., Lexapro, Prozac, Zoloft, Celexa, etc.) showed measurable improvement after their psychedelic experience, compared to those who had suspended antidepressants during preparation. Yet, ceasing the use of antidepressants is also linked to increased depression severity before the medicine experience.[38] If your long-term desire is to stop using pharmaceuticals to manage your mental health, consider working with your prescribing physician to titrate safely off your meds. Or, if you would like to try using psychedelics while maintaining your medications, I recommend consulting with your facilitator and a psychopharmacologist who is well-versed in psychedelics. They can help you understand which medications may mute your experience and which ones may be contraindicated with your substance of choice.

Optimize Physical Environment

Readying your physical environment for your post-psychedelic return is an excellent way to prepare for your experience. Before you leave your house or apartment on the day of your journey, take some time to tidy. Do the dishes, make your bed, and have some comfort foods prepared for your return. Returning to a nurturing and cozy space will support your desire to keep your mind open and your nervous system relaxed for integration.

IMPROVE MENTAL HEALTH

Your mental body is comprised of your thoughts, and it is the first of the subtle levels to prepare. Everything you "know" in your conscious and subconscious mind resides in the mental body. Francis Bacon said, "Knowledge is power," but what I propose for psychedelic preparation is closer to "Knowledge is safety." For most people, the only thing more uncomfortable than change is uncertainty. And while every psychedelic experience comes with some uncertainty, removing as much of it as possible will increase your felt sense of safety—especially if you are a newcomer. Below are some tips to improve your mental health:

Increase Present-Moment Awareness

Unfortunately, many of us have little experience with the present moment because we spend most of our time ruminating on the past or planning for the future. Psychedelics act as a rocket ship to the present moment and are a potent tool for focusing our consciousness into the here and now. Preparing to have that experience is among the most important and valuable elements of preparation. Developing a meditation or contemplation practice, practicing pranayama (yogic breathing), or sitting quietly alone (without a book, journal, phone, or music) for twenty minutes each day to watch the grass grow and the birds chirp, are all beautiful ways to step into present-moment awareness.

Trauma-sensitive note: If your past includes abuse or neglect, spending time in the present moment may not sound pleasant, let alone enticing. The harrowing experiences you had in the past still live in your mind and body, and attempting to sit quietly in the now, without intrusion from those experiences, can be very difficult and potentially retraumatizing. Some people who have stored trauma even find the practices that cultivate present-moment awareness painful. If this is you, please do not increase your suffering. Find a trauma-informed or somatic-focused therapist, coach, or teacher with experience in mindfulness-based practices who can help you explore what works best for you. While sitting on a meditation cushion may feel excruciating, counting your steps while you mindfully walk through the park could feel like a calming balm for your nervous system. It is essential to find practices that work for you.

Spend Time Journaling

Second only to the practice of present-moment awareness, journaling is an excellent method for both mental preparation and for integrating your psychedelic experience. Consider buying a new journal dedicated to your experience (or to all of your psychedelic work), and spend time every day documenting your thoughts, feelings, dreams, and preparation steps. Writing is a powerful way to better understand what is happening in your mind while also releasing anxious or nervous thoughts and their energetic charge. For a deeper and more structured approach to journaling, consider reading Julia Cameron's *The Artist's Way: A Spiritual Path to Higher Creativity*.[39] Her twelve-week program guides readers through exercises and explorations designed to help amplify insight and creativity.

Increase Knowledge and Education

Congratulations! Reading this book is a form of mental preparation, so you're already on your way. Other educational books—along with blogs, podcasts, and videos—are also great assets when preparing for your psychedelic experience. Familiarizing yourself with some basic knowledge about altered states, psychedelic substances, and their subjective effects is excellent. On the other hand, refrain from content such as "trip reports" and sensationalized clickbait media that feeds unrealistic expectations for magical transformation—or fuels fears. As soon as you have enough information to make the decision to move forward with your experience, I advise putting away the educational materials and devoting your time to other preparation methods. Avoid filling your head with unnecessary information that will never increase the value of your experience.

Incorporate Daily Positive Practices

Returning to our earlier discussion, a dieta is not only about what you ingest through your mouth. Instead of using the common saying, "You are what you eat," try the substitute, "I am what I consume." What you consume with your eyes, ears, and other senses can profoundly affect your way of being. If you were performing a dieta in the jungle, spending too much time watching the news or doomscrolling social media would not be an option. Use your preparation time to take a vacation from all these tamasic habits. Instead, pick up a good fiction book with paper pages.

When it comes to your regular haunts, find positive venues that support your healing process. Instead of the pub, try a trip to the gym, a yoga class, or even a walk in the park. If a work-related event doesn't feel nourishing for your soul, tell your boss you're preparing for a "meditation retreat," and choose something more aligned with your preparation process.

The long-term benefits of stress management come from cultivating more intentional daily practices. An appropriate analogy compares a frog that immediately leaps back out when dropped into a pot of boiling water to a frog that simmers to death in water slowly heated from cool to boiling. The frog story illustrates how our lives get out of control. Slowly, over time, we say "yes" to things that don't feel good or are out of alignment with our deepest desires and authentic Self. These everyday misalignments pile up, and eventually, the stress of life becomes too much… we boil in our own decisions and resignation. Today, when I find myself in a position to either say "no" and feel better in the long run or say "yes" to make someone else feel more comfortable, I apply one of my favorite Brené Brown mantras: "I choose discomfort over resentment." Learning that "no" can be a complete sentence has changed my life.

Prioritize Time Management

If your calendar was a person, would it be tamasic, rajasic, or sattvic? Does your calendar accurately reflect your priorities? Constantly staying busy is a great way to avoid getting quiet and feeling your feelings. In most cultures, staying busy is equated with higher productivity and wealth generation, both highly praised activities. Before and after your psychedelic experience, try to slow down your life and clear your calendar. At a minimum, try to take a few days off before and after your experience. Slow down the month of your experience and leave the weeks before and after as empty as possible. Now, not everyone can take a vacation from their lives. Maintaining your commitments to your family and job is essential. But spending every night working late or going on a holiday with your neglectful parents the week before your experience is actually working against your goal.

Take Informative Assessments

Who doesn't like a good personality assessment now and then? You may have already learned your Myers-Briggs or Enneagram type. Still, when it comes to preparing for a psychedelic experience, there are other assessments that can help you determine how to approach your choice of substance and facilitator. Self-administered assessments like the Big Five Personality Test, the Adverse Childhood Experiences quiz, the Trauma Symptom Inventory, or the Life Events Checklist may light potential paths to explore during your work with psychedelics.

Set Intentions Instead of Goals

Expectations can be easily confused with hope and are a frequent source of discomfort. Expectations reflect attachment to a desired outcome. Hope shows up as a preference rather than a need. As we will cover in chapter 11, intention setting and expectation management are two high-impact elements of your journey. Shift your focus to intentions (while continuing to measure progress) rather than goals (which assume your healing can be checked off a list). This refocus enables living beyond a binary point of view—often called "black-and-white thinking"—revealing the many shades of gray in the process of healing. Exploring your conscious and subconscious expectations alone may prove challenging, so consider asking your therapist, coach, or facilitator for help.

IMPROVE EMOTIONAL HEALTH

Your emotional body, comprised of all your emotions, is the next subtle level of preparation. One challenge you may face is understanding and identifying certain emotions. Current research suggests we don't understand our feelings or what they actually feel like in our body. A *Time Magazine* interview with Brené Brown tells us, "In surveys taken by 7,000 people over five years, Brown and her team found that on average people can identify only three emotions as they are actually feeling them: happiness, sadness, and anger."[40] In her book *Atlas of the Heart*, Brown fills that all-too-common gap, as she illuminates eighty-seven common emotions in the human experience. Consider *Atlas of the Heart* an excellent choice to kick off your mental preparation, along with the tips listed below to improve your emotional health:

Adjust Your Attitude

Your belief in the transformative and healing power of these substances is critical to their effectiveness. Attitude is everything, and the placebo effect is incredibly powerful. If you are skeptical of the healing power of these substances, feel mistrustful of yourself or your facilitator, or generally have an attitude of negativity or resistance, there is a better-than-average chance that psychedelics will amplify those feelings, and your experience will not produce the results you are hoping for. Instead, adopt a positive attitude of trust, honesty, openness, and willingness.

Nurture Emotional Intelligence and Regulation

Most adults are disconnected from their emotions. Increasing your emotional intelligence helps you not only in your psychedelic experience but also in your daily life. One remarkable quality of psychedelics is they are some of the best "button pushers" I have ever worked with. They show us exactly where our reactivity is hiding, bring it to the surface, and ask us to deal with it… whether we like it or not.

One way to improve your level of emotional intelligence before going into your experience is by directly reflecting on your feelings. A beautiful way to start this practice is with The Feeling Wheel, created by Gloria Wilcox.[41]

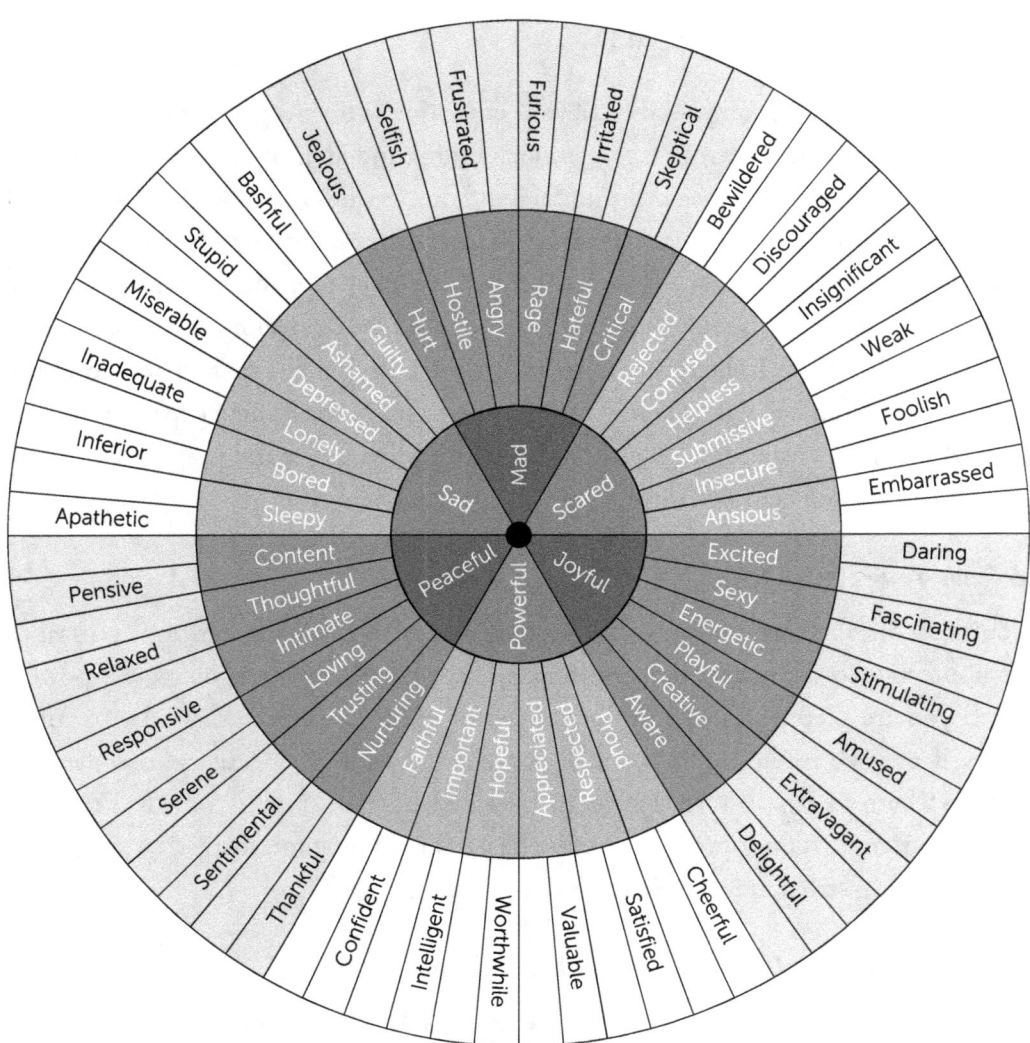

FIGURE 9. The Feeling Wheel by Gloria Wilcox

Wilcox identifies seventy-two feelings, organized into six primary categories. She offers the frame that "you cannot heal what you cannot feel" and suggests three opportunities to reflect on your emotions: directly (in the moment), daily, and long term.

Depending on your parents and the era in which you grew up, the space and permission to "feel your feelings" may not have been available to you throughout your life. Many adults I work with are severed from feelings of sadness and anger because those were considered unacceptable emotions in their childhood. This often happens when primary caregivers use the "I'll give you something to cry about" approach to parenting. If understanding your body's reactions to your feelings is not yet a tool in your toolbox, it will be helpful to work with a therapist or coach to help you reclaim this emotional bandwidth. Working with an experienced practitioner in somatic techniques who can help you connect to your emotions as you feel them in your body is a very effective way bridge your day-to-day consciousness and your psychedelic experience.

One reason people disconnect from their emotions is because they are afraid of what might happen if the connection is truly made. If you allow yourself to feel even a little bit of anger, will you turn into Yosemite Sam or the Tasmanian Devil? Most people have a few standard responses to stressful situations: fight, flight, freeze, or appease/fawn. Whichever is your default, psychedelics will open the doors to your unconscious mind and reveal what triggers that desire to fight back, run away, be invisible, or people-please.

When my clients report having strong reactions to the people in their life, I frequently remind them, "It's not their fault for pressing your buttons. It's your fault for having buttons to press." While blunt, it is true that you can only reclaim your place and power in the world when you accept complete responsibility for your emotions. No one else can feel your feelings for you. Owning your emotions is a potent approach to taking full responsibility for your life.

The work of emotional regulation falls on a continuum, and the work is never 100 percent complete. We all have many triggers, some close the surface and others lying dormant, waiting for just the right situation to appear. One easy way to use The Feeling Wheel to practice emotional regulation is by trying to embody the emotion directly opposite the negative one you're currently feeling. For example, if you're sad, practice joy. If you're mad, practice power. If you're scared, practice peace. Somatic experiencing, psychodrama, deep breathing exercises, and mindfulness meditation are also excellent ways to deepen your ability to emotionally self-regulate.

Learning how to appropriately respond to your triggers and their corresponding natural instincts will be very useful in your work with psychedelics—and this knowledge is also one of many benefits of psychedelic healing. As we'll discuss in future chapters, where you land on the emotional regulation continuum should play a part in your choice of substance and dosage.

Seek Coaching and/or Therapy

Working with a qualified coach or therapist is a great way to develop greater intelligence about your emotional body. Your chosen path will depend on your current state of being and what you want to accomplish. Therapy is fantastic for developing greater awareness of your emotional body's real-time responses, building a strong sense of safety in your system, and exploring and integrating childhood wounds. A few therapeutic modalities that align well with psychedelic work include somatic therapy, Internal Family Systems, transpersonal, dialectical behavior therapy, and psychodrama. If you've already spent years in therapy with little progress to show for it, it may be time to consider a skilled and qualified coach. Coaching is often more future-focused and concentrates less on resolving trauma, creating safety, or dealing with crises. Coaches tend to be more direct and push their clients harder and faster than their therapeutic brethren.

Find People, Community, and Support

Indigenous shamans have little to offer in the way of formalized preparation and integration planning, since so much of this work happens naturally in their daily lives. Spending time with and learning from the elders of a tribe (and Mother Earth herself) is built into the fabric of their community and culture. Unfortunately, this community-focused way of living has largely disappeared in many modern societies.

While social media may have been designed to keep us connected, it has done the opposite. Not only has it destroyed the bonds of authentic community, but it has also divided us more than ever before. The modern-day absence of community bonds is one reason why gathering together and developing a healthy support system is so important for deep work with psychedelics. The powerful feelings and transformation that arise in your psychedelic experiences can be challenging to process without proper support. Having an open and compassionate friend to talk to about your experience can be a wonderful resource in life, even in addition to a trusted therapist.

Motivational speaker Jim Rohn famously said, "You are the average of the five people you spend the most time with." While I think our lives are a bit more complex than this, the intention of Rohn's perspective is quite meaningful when preparing for a psychedelic experience. Spending time with nervous or anxious people who are always on the go, constantly striving for more productivity, money, and control, ignites the rajasic qualities within your own system. Likewise, spending time with people who are severely depressed, negative, unhealthy, or generally apathetic about life will encourage you to slip into the lethargy of tamas.

During the days and weeks leading up to your experience, do your best to spend time with the most healing and grounded people (and community) you can find. Temporarily—or perhaps permanently—clearing your life of toxic or overly dramatic people is a great way to prepare for both your experience and your integration. Filling your days with loving and supportive relationships that expand your positive energy is a fantastic way to take care of yourself.

Try to develop these healthy relationships before your psychedelic experience. Social community can be a soft net to fall into after your journey. And if a healthy community is something you're looking for but don't know where to start, try joining the free online community at PsychedelicIQ. With live trainings, integration calls, and Q&A sessions, this virtual community may be a perfect place to start while you discover or develop your own local community.

Incorporate Your Integration Plan

Including your integration plan in your preparation process means one less thing to worry about after your experience and sets the groundwork for long-term, sustainable transformation. Much of your preparation work is about replacing uncertainty with stability. An integration plan explores what life could look like after your experience and is another way to allow your nervous system to relax. Beyond the support of your facilitator, your research, and your social community, consider finding an integration circle (in person or online) where you can continue processing your experience. Sharing your experiences with others doing similar work and hearing their experiences can be profoundly nurturing. Community and integration circles can help soften feelings of loneliness and confusion that you may encounter after coming down from a powerful experience.

Relax with Sound and Music

One fun and relaxing way to work with your emotions is through sound. A Brighton and Sussex Medical School study found that "playing 'natural sounds' affected the bodily systems that control the flight-or-fright and rest-digest autonomic nervous systems, with associated effects in the resting activity of the brain."[42] With this in mind, consider spending regular time in music meditation. Find a comfortable seat or reclined position, play some of your favorite relaxing music, and let your mind wander. If anything interesting arises, take a moment to write it down in your journal. If you want to step outside the box of spa music or nature sounds, consider trying some binaural beats,[43] Solfeggio frequencies,[44] or a guided yoga nidra (yogic sleep) meditation.[45]

IMPROVE SPIRITUAL HEALTH

While psychedelics can heal our body, mind, and emotions, they can also operate on our spirit in ways that may never fully make sense to the human mind. And while many people have never believed that a power greater than themselves exists, psychedelics can quickly change and shift this perception.

A survey conducted by Johns Hopkins researchers gathered data from thousands of individuals who reported that they'd experienced personal encounters with God—with or without psychedelics. Over two-thirds of these participants, who had all previously identified as atheists, no longer embraced that label following their experience. Moreover, a majority of respondents attributed lasting positive changes in their psychological health—e.g., life satisfaction, purpose, and meaning—even decades after their initial experience.[46]

Approaching this topic from the opposite direction, in a paper written by The Challenging Psychedelic Experiences Project, 50 percent of their participants stated their post-psychedelic discomfort resulted in "ontological difficulties"—referring to the way one understands reality and existence.

Essentially, these two measurements say that many people who didn't believe in God before their experience suddenly started believing in God—and that if you have no way to explain deeper planes of reality or the mystical nature of the psychedelic experience, integrating your experience grows substantially more difficult. We'll dive further into this topic in chapter 14, "Mindset."

Whether you have a mystical experience depends on an uncountable number of factors, but it is often highly correlated with dosage. Still, there is never a guarantee. I encourage you to release expectations and embrace the journey no matter how it unfolds. The minute we want something to happen, it becomes harder to get. Ram Dass said it best: "The most exquisite paradox… as soon as you give it all up, you can have it all. As long as you want power, you can't have it. The minute you don't want power, you'll have more than you ever dreamed possible."

While mystical experiences tend to be positive, they can also be distressing, especially when dosages are increased. Having already done some preparation to improve your spiritual health can make the experience more meaningful, less scary, and easier to metabolize. To put it bluntly, we're not always ready to meet God. The energy differential between you and the Divine can be so great that even witnessing such powerful energy can feel very uncomfortable. Below are some tips to improve your overall spiritual health:

Consider a Spiritual Philosophy or Framework

Having a spiritual philosophy or framework can help build a foundation, prepare, and even relax your mind toward the ineffable experiences you may have during your journey. It is by no means a requirement.

Many atheists I have worked with over the years have become agnostics, if not full believers, as a part of their psychedelic practice. For "recovering Christians" or those who have suffered abuses at the hands of a church, spirituality and religion may be very closely intertwined, and might even cause their system to recoil at the thought of reengaging in an esoteric practice. If this is you, consider orienting toward a spiritual philosophy instead of traditional religion. Mystic philosophies exist at the roots of most religions. By removing the present-day dogma and doctrine, you can explore the basic, universal theme of enlightenment. Furthermore, you can study many of these philosophies from their original texts and scriptures, without the need for an intermediary like a pastor or rabbi.

Once you've found a path that feels good for your psyche, I recommend working with a skilled teacher in your tradition of choice. It is nearly impossible to deepen into any tradition without a navigator who knows the way and can act as a clean mirror for you to see yourself. For a teaching to be truly effective, it must be delivered in context to the student receiving it.

If you pursue a long-term practice with psychedelics, you will almost certainly find yourself wading into the waters of shamanism. Shamanism (a spiritual practice centered on connecting with spirit realms, typically through rituals, altered states, and healing work) has deep roots in South American Indigenous healing and psychedelic traditions, but different varieties have been found all over the globe and can be traced back thousands of years. Shamanism, in its highest integrity, is a beautiful practice. Please engage a high degree of discernment when deciding who you want to learn shamanism from, and choose teachers who have received training, apprenticeship, and permission from their Indigenous teachers.

Contemplate Reciprocity

Within South American shamanic traditions, ayni (pronounced "eye-knee") is a word that means "sacred reciprocity" and, more specifically, "today for you, tomorrow for me." From an energetic perspective, ayni is the balance and equilibrium among all life—including people, nature, animals, and the cosmos. Sacred reciprocity is frequently offered in rituals such as *despacho* ceremonies or gratitude practices. It helps ensure that those assisting you on your spiritual journey are fairly and equitably treated and compensated.

Communicate Through Prayer and Contemplation

The most concise way to address these ephemeral topics is to say that prayer is talking to the Divine, meditation is listening, and contemplation is having direct awareness. Offering your prayers to the spirit of the medicine and cultivating the quiet spaces necessary to receive insight directly from the spirit of the plants are good ways to begin shaping your experience before ingesting any substance. The basis for almost every good friendship is intention and time. In this spirit, one beautiful way I have encouraged clients to build this relationship is to write a letter to the spirit of the plant. Express your deepest desires and thank the spirit for its incredible wisdom and healing power.

Spend Time in Nature

In a 2019 study, researchers found that "forest bathing" (a therapeutic practice originating in Japan that involves spending intentional, mindful time in nature to enhance mental, physical, and spiritual well-being) has positive physiological benefits, including a reduction blood pressure and the improvement of autonomic and immune functions. It also improves psychological symptoms of depression and boosts overall mental health.[47] While you may not be near a forest, spending time in any nature setting can go a long way toward calming an otherwise frazzled nervous system. Bringing reverence for Mother Earth into your psychedelic experience, allowing yourself to let go of doubts, and opening your heart can all contribute to your physical, mental, and spiritual preparation. Take time to offer gratitude to nature, the potent force responsible for giving you everything you have in your life.

Build Your Support Team

If you are doing deep work of any kind, whether it be with psychedelics, therapy, coaching, or even meditation work, having a loving support system makes a tremendous difference in creating and sustaining positive transformation.

With psychedelics, you will be venturing into parts of your physical, psychological, and spiritual well-being that you may not have ever known existed. That alone can be a destabilizing experience. This is why building a team that will help support you before and after your experience is so important. For starters, this could mean reaching out to supportive friends and family members to share about your current well-being, why you've decided to do this kind of work, and what your intention is going into your experience.

If you are already working with other helping professionals, it is best to involve them as much as possible. This could be your current therapist or coach, your general practitioner, your psychiatrist, or even your recovery sponsor, pastor, priest, or spiritual director. If you have a complicated pharmaceutical regimen and need additional support to explore potential drug interactions, I advise you schedule a consultation with a psychopharmacologist who specializes in psychedelics.

How to Talk to Your Family and Friends About Psychedelics

Ideally, the people on your team are already psychedelic friendly and supportive of your healing process, but that may not always be possible. You may have to become your own advocate and psychedelic educator when talking to others about your journey. Here are a few helpful tips for discussing psychedelics with your friends, family, and support team:

Do Your Research

Being prepared to answer the first round of questions is important—and your responsibility. Having your facts straight and knowing the basic information about what you're getting yourself into will go a long way toward calming their nerves. You do not need to know everything, nor do you need to act like you know everything. "I don't know, but I will find out," is a perfectly acceptable response and will demonstrate humility and a willingness to keep learning.

Put Yourself in Their Shoes

If you have been studying the possibility of using psychedelics for some time and have already made the decision, remember that your support team may need time to catch up. Remember who you're talking to and ask yourself a few questions: Are they already supportive of therapy and healing in general? Have they had their own experience with substances in their past? Were those experiences positive or negative? Were or are they active supporters of the "war on drugs?" Are they generally open to new ideas? The answers to these questions can help you build a reasonable path and timeline for your upcoming conversations.

"Set and Setting" Matter for the Conversation

Just like set and setting are important for your psychedelic experience, the mindset of your care team and the setting for your discussion is also important. Block off a dedicated time on everyone's calendar and find a quiet and comfortable place to talk. Rushing your conversation or having it a public place where other people could over-hear is not the best way to gain the support of naysayers.

Don't Rush the Process

This goes both for your own process and for the process of gaining the support of your care team. It would be a big red flag if you made a decision to use ayahuasca on Friday and booked a plane ticket leaving for Peru on Monday. Demonstrate how responsible you are by mapping out your preparation and integration plans, and showing your care team the confidence scores from the Psychedelic Safety Wheel Assessment.

Watch Your Language

If you've spent research time on Reddit, there's a good chance you've come across some psychonauts discussing ego death, aliens, or the "DMT elves." As we discussed in part I, the language surrounding psychedelic use is incredibly important. Speaking a new, shared language of psychedelic healing rather than the language of recreational drug use will offer everyone a better way to communicate before and after the experience.

Start with Facts

A less emotionally intense way of approaching your support team is to lead with data—maybe even offer them a copy of this book. There are countless studies avail-able today demonstrating the efficacy of psychedelics for treating all kinds of condi-tions. Showing them data alongside your own individual risk profile is a great way to decrease negative emotions.

Help Bridge the Gap in Understanding

There is a better-than-average chance that some of your support team will think you're "using drugs," may become addicted, or believe that you are putting yourself in a highly risky situation. It's partially your responsibility to educate them on what they do not know in the most empathetic way you can. This book can be a great start, but there are also many other books, podcasts, and documentaries that may help them feel more comfortable with understanding your process. One helpful hint to remember: it can be easier to learn from a stranger than to be taught by someone you love.

Be Honest About the Risks

As we've discussed, there are risks and elements of this process that no one can measure or predict. Attempting to hide or ignore this will be a red flag for your support team (and maybe for you). Share the Psychedelic Safety Wheel with them and show them your confidence scores for the risk variable. Do your best to ensure you're doing your homework and removing as many unknowns as possible from your process.

Honor Their Process

Everyone has their own process for dealing with challenging new situations. It is important to honor each person's process and give them the time they need to take in the information, do their own research, and come to their own conclusions. It is possible you may never get exactly the level or type of support you're looking for, but it is still important to at least give everyone a reasonable amount of time to adjust.

Finding the Right Support

There is a chance that the preferred members of your care team will not support your decision. Unless they are legally responsible for you, this may mean you have to seek support elsewhere. This could involve getting a second opinion from a new doctor or psychiatrist, or finding a more supportive friend group and community. As you begin to heal, letting go of people who are not growing with you will become a recurring part of your journey.

Building your support team is incredibly important. If those on your team have witnessed your suffering for years or decades, they may be more supportive than you think. I have worked with many therapists and psychiatrists who are deep believers in the power of psychedelics. After trying everything else to help their clients, many will even proactively refer people to this work. The best advice I can offer is to be open, honest, and willing to hear everyone's opinions. Once you've done that, you may have to make the difficult choice of honoring your own healing above the feelings of others.

For additional resources to build your psychedelic support team, please visit PsychedelicIQ.com.

Meet Yourself Where You're At

Remember: the above methods and practices should be considered a "menu" rather than a checklist. It's crucial to meet ourselves where we're at with all of our preparation work. Demanding too much of ourselves before our journey may increase, rather than decrease, our suffering. If your facilitator demands that you perform a specific preparation method that does not feel good, please have a conversation with them. This could be a fantastic opportunity to deepen the trust in your relationship and learn more about each other in the process.

Each of the options in this chapter is simply a recommendation. None of them—except for the consideration of specific health issues and pharmaceutical contraindications—are required for a successful psychedelic experience. Preparation (like going to the gym or self-care in general) is additive by nature. It is something to build upon and continually strive to improve.

EMBRACE DISCOMFORT

For nearly a decade, I have organized group experiences for ayahuasca, San Pedro, and mushrooms. Anywhere from five to thirty people typically attend these group ceremonies; some have waited years to become ready and spent months preparing. One consistent feature of each ceremony is that the closer participants get to the experience, the more intense their life becomes.

Within Indigenous traditions, there is a belief that once you decide to sit with a medicine, the medicine begins working. In his book *The Alchemist*, Paulo Coelho states that "When you want something, all the universe conspires in helping you to achieve it."[48] Coelho doesn't mention that when the universe steps in to help, you may get more of what you *need* than what you *want*. Your world is designed to be a curriculum for your soul. It has been perfectly crafted to burn out your reactivity to the things separating you from peace, joy, and freedom.

Some ancient parts of your psyche were created to protect you from these external stimuli, and the closer you get to touching, healing, or liberating them, the fiercer and more active they become. As you move toward the light, your ego will become more savage. These old protector parts of your mind don't want to go away, and they will do everything they can to convince you not to have your experience. This may come in the form of chaotic life circumstances, relationship struggles, or even physical illness. While it is critical to always listen to your intuition, I also caution against abandoning your efforts at the last minute—unless you feel your safety is in jeopardy or the experience no longer feels in alignment with your highest good. Those unhealed parts of yourself are rooting for you to give up. Surround yourself with as much support as possible and lean into the discomfort.

Leira's Story

When I told my sister I use psychedelics for healing, she made intense side-eye contact, raised an eyebrow, and asked, "Aren't you afraid of having a bad trip?"

The metaphor that came to mind, and that I replied with, was, "It's like going to a party. Some people open the door expecting a party. One day, though, their psyche, or the spirits, decides it's time for an intervention instead. They are not prepared. When I open that door, I am not expecting a party—I'm prepared to participate in that intervention. I have cleared my schedule. I go in expecting what others call a 'bad trip.'"

So, what happens during this "intervention?" Many say psychedelics are non-specific amplifiers. This has been my experience. They magnify and illuminate issues, making some seem easy to address. Some are still hard to face. There is a good reason we hide or block out painful memories, knowingly or unknowingly. Preparation makes it possible to do the work. Without it, the experience can feel shocking, overwhelming, even horrifying—what most would call a "bad trip."

For me, preparation is about shifting my mindset. Instead of shying away from painful thoughts, I face them. I listen to my small, inner voice that says, "I hurt," rather than drowning it out. I prepare myself to sit with discomfort, fear, and pain. I prepare myself to be willing to change by releasing what is familiar and moving toward the unknown. I create spaciousness in my mind and my life. Practical preparations—like clearing my schedule—help me feel safe enough to confront these challenges. It can still be excruciating, but unearthing that pain is the first step toward healing.

For most of my life, there was a constant screaming in my brain. Only recently has it started to quiet. During one of my first ceremonies, the nonspecific amplification turned this internal chaos into a time-dilated, synesthetic experience. My intention was to surrender to the medicine spirit and heal, but all I felt was agony. At the time, I didn't understand its meaning. Had I not been prepared for the possibility of a painful experience and had the right support around me, I don't know what I would have done. Yet even that difficult journey wasn't a "bad trip." It was part of my healing path.

That painful journey eventually led me to discover something I had hidden deeply. Over eight months of intensive work, which included additional work with psychedelics, I uncovered deeply buried memories of being repeatedly abused as a child. I had no idea that was what I was looking for, but once it came to the surface, I began a full year of intense healing work. Confronting that trauma and the patterns I built around it has brought me a sense of relief and stability. My life has changed completely—my career path, my relationships, and my understanding of my purpose have transformed.

Taking psychedelics and hoping they'll miraculously fix everything is a huge gamble. Intentional preparation is what makes healing with psychedelics work. For me, this preparation has become part of my life.

I create spaciousness by reducing external input and quieting internal chatter. This quiet was difficult at first; I had relied on these distractions to avoid my own thoughts and feelings. Now, I'm learning new patterns and a new framework for my life. I practice silence, meditation, and walking in the park without music. I've stopped watching the news and cut back on media consumption. I read articles and books, and listen to podcasts on healing. I've taken classes on shamanism, energy medicine, and Buddhist philosophy. I study the Bhagavad Gita weekly—it's so invaluable that I joke with my study group, "If I'm not here, call the police, because I'm probably dead." My relationships have shifted, too. I've created healthy boundaries. I seek out supportive communities. I show up. I also have a great therapist.

I focus on understanding and integrating what comes up during my journeys. Part of preparing for the next ceremony is integrating the last one. I intentionally sit with discomfort, turning toward it during meditation or contemplation. With each feeling or memory or pattern I examine and process, I create more spaciousness and calm in my life. This allows even deeper, more subtle issues to be revealed. It's hard work, but it's necessary. The true healing happens outside of the psychedelic journey—in the preparation before and the integration after.

"Slow Is Smooth, and Smooth Is Fast"

Consider this: if we accept the premise that all humans are strands of energy, tightly bound together to appear solid, and that those strands are all vibrating at different frequencies, it also stands to reason that everything we take into our bodies is also vibrating at a certain frequency. Sugar vibrates at a lower frequency than a vegetable. A nature documentary vibrates at a higher frequency than a horror movie. Preparing for a psychedelic experience is a way to slowly, gently, and intentionally increase our vibration by ingesting as many high-vibration things as we can in the days and weeks preceding our experience.

As a newcomer to the practice of psychedelics, it might feel pretty scary to venture into the unknown. It can be unnerving to let go of control and explore the parts of your mind you've kept locked away for years or decades. But here's the rub: as the self-awareness teacher Leland Val Van De Wall puts it, "The degree to which a person can grow is directly proportional to the amount of truth he can accept about himself without running away." Learning the truth about ourselves can frequently be difficult and uncomfortable. Trauma is real, comes in many forms and severities, and can often act as a blinder to the truth—much like the dirty fishtank we discussed in chapter 2.

"Big T" trauma is frequently categorized as significant life events like car accidents, assaults, or disasters causing major distress, each of which introduces a large amount of residue into our fishtank in a short amount of time. Big T trauma is frequently the cause of post-traumatic stress disorder (PTSD). "Little T" trauma might include stressors like neglect, criticism, or bullying. These smaller—but still uncomfortable—life circumstances add dirt to our water more slowly, but eventually, this residue builds up to degrade our physical and mental health. Years or decades of Little T trauma can be the source of complex PTSD, especially when the trauma is chronic, cumulative, and occurs in relationship context (e.g., childhood, partnerships, workplaces). Sometimes, no matter how badly we want to see through the absurdity of our predicament, our trauma prevents us from seeing anything clearly. And if we can't see it or feel it, we can't heal it.

Remember, slow and steady wins the race. I can't tell you the number of dysregulated clients I've worked with who wrongly prioritized speed over safety. As evidenced by the many preparation methods mentioned in this book, you can do a great deal of work ahead of time to make your experience safer and more successful. But if you rush into the process out of desperation, the benefits of all your preparation work disappear.

There is no way you can ever be fully prepared for a psychedelic experience. No matter the preparation, what we receive in our experience is not up to us. In all honesty, this is probably the reason you're turning to psychedelics to begin with. The knowledge and experiences that got you to this point in your life will not get you to where you want to go. It's high time to try something new—pun intended.

9

Substances

"Humankind" by Dhafer Youssef

Most newcomers who stumble their way onto this adventurous path have very little practical knowledge or experience with psychedelic substances. When starting your journey, you should carefully consider different substances before you choose a facilitator, not the other way around.

In this chapter, I discuss eight of the most common substances currently being used for healing. As you explore less-traveled paths, you may encounter other substances, as well as people who swear by their healing powers. While I don't intend to discount any of the substances outside this list, I have chosen to focus on these eight for several reasons:

- They each have decades, if not millennia, of practical experience behind them to guide their use.
- They each come with a pedigree of practitioners operating above and below ground.
- They each have history of being used in clinical research settings, making their path to healing slightly more straightforward, accessible, and predictable.

When it comes to psychedelic substances, there are a couple of broad categories that are frequently considered: classical vs. nonclassical and organic vs. synthetic.

Classical vs. Nonclassical

The four psychedelics that fall into the classical category are psilocybin, LSD, DMT, and mescaline. These substances primarily act on the 5-HT2A serotonin receptors of the brain and are considered non-habit-forming. Contrary to what we have been led to believe by the war on drugs, none of the four classical psychedelics are addictive in a physiological sense, but as we'll discuss later, frequent use can become psychologically addictive and a form of escapism. On the other hand, nonclassical psychedelics could include dissociatives (which induce a detachment from reality, one's body, or the surrounding environment) such as ketamine and entactogens/empathogens (which promote feelings of emotional connectedness, empathy, and introspection) such as MDMA. Many nonclassical psychedelics can be physiologically habit-forming.

Organic vs. Synthetic

The second broad classification describes the origin of the substance. While the term "plant medicine" is frequently used to describe all forms of organic substances, mushrooms are not technically plants, but rather fungi. Therefore, the term "organic" tends to be more accurate than "plant medicine," and refers to substances such as psilocybin (from mushrooms), mescaline (from peyote or San Pedro cacti), 5-MeO-DMT (from the Bufo alvarius toad), ayahuasca, and iboga. The synthetic category refers to substances created in a laboratory, including ketamine, LSD, MDMA, and the synthesized versions of psilocybin, mescaline, and 5-MeO-DMT.

María Sabina, the renowned Mazatec curandera from Oaxaca, Mexico, often regarded as the "grandmother of modern psychedelics," was instrumental in introducing the Western world to the sacred use of psilocybin mushrooms. In 1962, Sabina and her daughter ingested roughly thirty milligrams of synthetic psilocybin (just over the standard twenty-five milligram dose used in most clinical trials) provided to her by Albert Hofmann, a renowned chemist who created LSD and synthetic psilocybin. After a full night of ceremony, Sabina claimed there was very little difference between the synthetic pills and the natural mushrooms. Organic versus synthetic is likely a debate that will never end, but a 2024 study comparing synthetic psilocybin, whole mushrooms, and mycological extract expressed a consensus that all three forms were helpful and similar, though the overall quality of experience of synthetic psilocybin was inferior to the organic forms.[49]

Comparing Different Substances

One very intentional choice I've made in this chapter is the order in which I present the substances: on a relative scale of increasing power. To revisit the analogy of filtering water in a fishtank from part I, think of power as indicative of the speed at which each filter is capable of cleaning the water. A good rule of thumb is the lower the power, the more tolerable a substance may be for beginners.

It is also worthwhile to address the concept of durability. In a medical context, durability refers to the long-term effectiveness or persistence of a treatment, intervention, or medical device. It is a measure of how well a treatment maintains its intended effects over time. In psychedelics, durability refers to the persistence or longevity of the positive effects and transformations resulting from a psychedelic experience. While never guaranteed, there is a strong correlation between power and durability. The lower the power, the shorter the durability of the experience—and the greater the likelihood that negative symptoms will return.

For comparison's sake, think of each of the following substances as a different model of hammer, starting with a rubber mallet (relative power = 1) and going up to a wrecking ball (relative power = 5). There is no need to use a wrecking ball to drive in a tenpenny nail to hang a picture, yet many seekers are keen to do this. Many modern ways of thinking have trained us to optimize and supersize, rather than carefully select the right tool for the job. The problem with this approach is that when we use a wrecking ball to hang a picture, we will likely cause more damage than benefit. Please trust me when I tell you that it is much easier to repair a hole in the wall than it is to repair the damage from a harmful psychedelic experience.

The power of each substance is also important when choosing a facilitator. When considering the potential harm a substance can cause, you want to work with someone with the requisite experience and training. The more powerful a substance (and the greater the speed with which it might heal), the more potential damage it can cause. An unqualified crane operator swinging a wrecking ball in the wrong direction can cause an enormous amount of long-term damage in a very short period of time.

One very important variable that is intentionally omitted from this chapter is substance-specific dosing. Dosing most often—though not always—correlates to intensity and power. The more you take, the more intense your experience could be. The challenge lies in offering dosing recommendations without intimate knowledge of your constitution and the exact substance you're ingesting—substance potency is extremely variable. In today's marketplaces, one dried gram of mushroom strain A could contain ten milligrams of psilocybin, while mushroom strain B could contain double that amount. Ingesting two grams of strain A might represent a very manageable experience for a first-time journeyer. But the same weight of strain B could turn into a very long, uncomfortable, or even frightening journey. This variability holds true for all of the organic substances mentioned in the following pages. Dosing is highly variable, dependent on many factors, and should always be determined with the help and collaboration of a knowledgeable facilitator.

This chapter is not intended to teach you everything you need to know about these substances, but rather to give you just enough information to begin your own research and search for a facilitator who can safety and responsibly create an experience for you.

Should a Substance "Kill Your Ego?"

Short answer: No!

A few common terms heard in many psychedelic conversations are "ego death," "ego dissolution," and "killing the ego." Rather than these, I prefer to use the term "ego rest" because your ego always comes back—sometimes for the worse, as we'll discuss in chapter 15, "Experience."

The "ego" in each of these terms refers less to one's personality and more to our innate sense of Self. Approaching the concept from a scientific perspective, ego is closely tied to the default mode network (DMN), interconnected brain regions responsible for self-referential thinking, introspection, and maintaining a cohesive sense of self. Psychedelics disrupt and reduce activity in the DMN, leading to a loosening of the ego's grip and allowing for experiences of interconnectedness and unity. "Dropping the default mode network" is another common term that describes a profound psychological experience, in which an individual temporarily loses their sense of personal identity.

Common characteristics of this state include:

- **Loss of Self-Identity** — The absence of feeling like a distinct individual with a personal history, preferences, and boundaries.
- **Perception of Oneness** — A heightened sense of interconnectedness with everything around you, where the boundaries between "Self" and "other" no longer exist.
- **Time Distortion** — A diminished sense of time or the experience of timelessness.
- **Absence of Egoic Control** — Your internal dialogue or "personal narrator" becomes quiet or ceases altogether.
- **Spiritual or Mystical Insights** — Often described as a spiritual awakening or a direct experience of the Divine, fostering deep insights about existence, love, and interconnectedness.

If you've been scanning research papers (or Reddit), you may have already set your sights on killing your ego because you've heard it's the fastest and most powerful way to heal. Well, before you set that as your intention, let me offer a few "yellow flags" to encourage you to slow your roll.

Ego dissolution is no joke. The primary role of your ego is to keep you alive, so if it feels threatened (as we'll discuss further in chapter 12, "Dosing"), it will undoubtedly fight back. While ego dissolution can be a profoundly positive experience, it can also be overwhelming, or even distressing. Common experiences that come with ego dissolution are anxiety and fear, difficulty understanding and integrating your experience, and the potential triggering of severe mental health issues.

St. John of the Cross, a sixteenth-century Spanish mystic, wrote a poem called "La Noche Oscura del Alma" (translated to "The Dark Night of the Soul"). Some people who go through a profoundly mystical experience like ego dissolution may enter a period of profound spiritual or existential crisis—a dark night of the soul. Some of the characteristics often attributed to this intense season of transformation include spiritual despair, loss of meaning, and emotional pain. If you are a newcomer to psychedelics with an intention to kill your ego, I must warn you to be careful what you ask for!

To help reframe this conversation, let me remind you that your ego is an essential part of your daily life. Without it, you would die. Your ego is what wakes you up every morning, keeps you safe from harm, and holds your sense of self together so you can operate effectively in the world. Regardless of the number of times you've heard it repeated online, killing your ego is *not* the goal of using psychedelic substances. Instead, set an intention to make friends with your ego—become a teammate rather than opponent.

Unfortunately, there are occasions when an individual can have a powerful ego-dissolving journey, and their ego returns even stronger than it was before the experience (more on this in chapter 15, "Experience"). Trust me when I tell you that this is not the outcome you're hoping for.

Ease into a Substance with Breathwork First

If you are a newcomer to psychedelics or expanded states of consciousness, I strongly encourage you to consider the practice of intense breathwork as a way to prepare for the use of a substance. In 2023, I had the pleasure of attending the Psychedelic Science Conference in Denver, Colorado. As one of the preconference activities, I participated in a Grof® Breathwork workshop for two and a half days. The power of this work left me completely amazed. During these sessions, I witnessed emotional releases far beyond what I have seen using incredibly powerful psychedelic substances.

Intense breathwork practices can mimic many aspects of a psychedelic experience. In fact, breathwork is a common tool used to train psychedelic researchers operating in clinical settings. Because you're not ingesting a substance, you maintain a great deal of agency throughout the experience. The ancient "protector" parts of your mind are far more comfortable with your breath than they are with a foreign substance. Breathwork is gentle enough not to cause damage, but safe and strong enough to expose and sand off some of the rougher edges of your psyche.

Breathwork is a part of many ancient cultures and mystical traditions. *Pranayama*, which has its roots in India and has been practiced for thousands of years, is one of the eight limbs of Ashtanga yoga, and is defined as "learning to control one's breath." The word *prana* is often simplified to mean "breath of life."

Today, breathwork is a trendy term frequently used in the health and wellness industry to represent many different breathing techniques. Some of these could be as simple as breathing deeply into your abdomen. Others add counting to your breath (like 4-7-8 breathing), designed to elongate your exhale and activate your parasympathetic nervous system. You may also find some yogic methods being offered, such as alternate nostril breathing (*nadi shodhana*) or "breath of fire" (*kapalabhati*).

While these breathing techniques can have tremendous benefits for calming the nervous system and providing focus to an overactive mind, none are specifically used to induce an expanded state of consciousness. To do that, we must shift our focus to a subset of breathing techniques first conceived in the 1970s and stemming from Holotropic breathwork.

"Holotropic," means "moving toward wholeness." It comes from the Greek words "*holos*," meaning whole, and "*trepan*," meaning moving in the direction of something. Holotropic breathwork was created by Stanislav and Christina Grof in 1974 at the Esalen Institute. It is a potent form of breathwork conducted over multiple hours and is usually done with a one-to-one ratio of breathers to sitters.

Breathwork has many advantages. The health risks are incredibly low, the accessibility is high, and it does not require you to stop using any of your current medications. It is also an excellent way to dip your toe in the water of expanded states without ever needing to ingest a substance. When looking for opportunities in your area, you can search for specific terms such as "Holotropic," "Rebirthing," "clarity," "transformational," or "Vivation" breathwork. These are all subtypes or "brands" of breathwork known to induce an altered state of consciousness.

As we begin exploring the ingestible substances, I would like to remind you that most of these substances are considered illegal in most US jurisdictions. To view the current psychedelic laws by country, visit https://piq.lv/world-tracker. To view the current psychedelic laws by US state, visit https://piq.lv/state-tracker.

Ketamine

Power: 1/5
Type: Nonclassical
Source: Synthetic
Street Names: K, special K

OVERVIEW

Ketamine is not actually a psychedelic, but rather a "dissociative anesthetic." This means that it can make you feel detached from your body and environment. It can also alleviate pain. Out of all the substances discussed in this chapter, ketamine is the only fully legal substance (when prescribed or administered by a physician). It is often the gentlest and most easily tolerated of all the psychedelic substances.

ACCESSIBILITY

Since the 1960s, people have been legally using ketamine aboveground as an anesthetic. In the last decade, it has emerged as an off-label treatment for depression. Although people frequently use it as a recreational substance, it is also commonly used underground for healing purposes.

RECOMMENDED SETTING

Providers typically offer ketamine as an individual experience, though it can also be provided in groups while still allowing each individual to have their unique experience. Low doses can be given for in-home or in-therapy use. Because ketamine is a nonorganic substance, it is less connected to any spiritual tradition.

COMMON ROUTES OF ADMINISTRATION

Ketamine can be administered in many forms, including lozenges, rapid dissolving oral tablets, or as an IV or intramuscular (IM) injection administered in a clinical setting. The pharmaceutical drug eskatamine (sold under the brand name Spravato), a more refined version of ketamine, was approved by the FDA as a treatment for depression in 2019 and is available as a nasal spray.

DURABILITY

A ketamine experience typically lasts for one hour or less. Because it is frequently offered in a clinical setting and rarely combined with any therapeutic process, ketamine's durability can be as low as two to four weeks, though it sometimes lasts up to ninety days.

BENEFITS

Ketamine does not interact with most antidepressants or antipsychotics, and is well suited to treat major depressive disorder (MDD), treatment-resistant depression (TRD), bipolar disorder, suicidal ideation, PTSD, anxiety disorders, and more.

RISKS

As a synthetic, ketamine carries with it a risk of both physical and psychological addiction. It also carries an increased risk of harm when combined with other substances, such as alcohol, and large amounts can be toxic or fatal. When the source is unknown, ketamine also runs a higher risk of being adulterated with other substances.

MDMA

Power: 1.5/5
Type: Nonclassical
Source: Synthetic
Street Names: Ecstasy, molly

OVERVIEW

MDMA (short for 3,4-methylenedioxymethamphetamine) is a laboratory-made compound. First manufactured in the early 1900s to help control bleeding, it became more widely by psychiatrists used in the 1970s and early 1980s to assist with the treatment of PTSD and in couples counseling. Around this time, people also started using MDMA as a recreational drug in the party/rave scene. In 1985, authorities classified it as a Schedule I illegal substance. MDMA is particularly known for its ability to facilitate deep feelings of connection, empathy, and love, and it is frequently referred to as a "heart-opening" medicine uniquely qualified to heal trauma. It also tends to be one of the gentler and more manageable psychedelic substances, especially for newcomers.

ACCESSIBILITY

MDMA is largely illegal around the world. Since 1986, the US-based nonprofit Multidisciplinary Association for Psychedelic Studies (MAPS, now Lykos) has been valiantly trying to reverse this decision. Despite a very successful phase three clinical trial, the FDA rejected approval of MDMA in August 2024 for legal use. There is currently no legal channel for use in the United States outside of a clinical study.

RECOMMENDED SETTING

When intentionally used for healing, people usually experience MDMA individually, as it often involves verbally processing information, emotions, and trauma to make sense of them. Because MDMA is a nonorganic substance, it is less connected to any spiritual tradition.

COMMON ROUTES OF ADMINISTRATION

MDMA usually comes as a pill or a powder, and is most often consumed orally.

DURABILITY

A typical experience lasts around five hours and (when combined with proper preparation, therapy, and integration) is incredibly effective when treating conditions such as PTSD, as evidenced by the MAPS phase three clinical trial. The trial reported that 67 percent of participants no longer met the diagnostic criteria for PTSD two months after treatment.[50]

BENEFITS

Because of its empathogenic and mood-enhancing effects, MDMA allows you to open up emotionally and process difficult memories. It is most effective when used in a controlled set and setting. MDMA is well suited to treat trauma, PTSD, treatment-resistant depression, and anxiety, and is frequently useful in couples therapy and all forms of relationship challenges.

RISKS

As a synthetic, MDMA poses a risk of both physical and psychological addiction. A large amount can be toxic or fatal. When coming from underground sources, it also runs the risk of being adulterated with other substances.

Psilocybin (Mushrooms)

Power: 2.5/5
Type: Classical
Source: Typically organic, synthetic for most clinical work
Street Names: Magic mushrooms, shrooms, boomers

OVERVIEW

Psilocybin is a naturally occurring compound found in over 200 species of fungi. Made famous in the West around 1955, the compound was first synthesized in 1963. Psilocybin is one of the most common forms of psychedelic compounds used today. Its power and shorter duration makes it a popular choice for many researchers and facilitators.

ACCESSIBILITY

Psilocybin is largely illegal around the world, but access is widening in some US states and municipalities. Many people use psilocybin as a recreational substance, but it is also frequently used underground for healing purposes.

RECOMMENDED SETTING

It is common for psilocybin to be offered in both individual and group experiences. Depending on your facilitator, the use of mushrooms could be clinical, spiritual, or anywhere in between.

COMMON ROUTES OF ADMINISTRATION

People typically dehydrate the mushrooms and eat them whole or mix them with other foods. Seekers can also grind or chop mushrooms, and brew them in tea. The mushrooms are sometimes soaked in lemon or lime juice (known as "lemon tekking") to enable faster activation.

DURABILITY

A typical experience lasts four to six hours and has been shown to create long-lasting and positive changes in one's physical, psychological, and spiritual health.

BENEFITS

The list of benefits of psilocybin is long and continues to grow. Mushrooms are best known for the treatment of PTSD, end-of-life anxiety, treatment-resistant depression, anxiety and distress, addiction, OCD, cluster headaches, and more. Physically, psilocybin treats chronic pain and inflammatory conditions. Spiritually, psilocybin assists with existential or spiritual crises, as well as death and grief processes.

RISKS

When used in a controlled setting, psilocybin carries relatively low risks. Individuals may or may not experience "blunting effects" (when the psychedelic experience or its impact is reduced, dampened, or becomes less intense) when combined with antidepressants or antipsychotics. As psilocybin is one of the four classical psychedelics, there is no possibility of overdose and no risk of physical addiction.

LSD

Power: 3/5
Type: Classical
Source: Synthetic
Street Names: Acid, lucy, blotter, tabs

OVERVIEW

LSD (lysergic acid diethylamide) is a laboratory-made compound originating from a substance found in ergot, a fungus that infects rye grain. First synthesized in 1938 by Swiss chemist Albert Hofmann, LSD rose to fame as a hallmark of the 1960s counterculture. Undoubtedly one of the most powerful compounds by mass, even incredibly small doses can cause very powerful effects.

ACCESSIBILITY

While LSD is largely illegal around the world, some US jurisdictions have chosen to decriminalize it. Many people use LSD as a recreational substance, but it is also frequently used in the underground for healing purposes.

RECOMMENDED SETTING

Because of its long-lasting effects, LSD is most commonly offered in individual experiences. While many people do use LSD as a means of conscious exploration and healing, as a relatively young and synthetic substance, LSD is not used in Indigenous ceremonies and is not often connected to any major organized spiritual traditions.

COMMON ROUTES OF ADMINISTRATION

Individuals typically take LSD orally, either in liquid form or by placing the liquid on a small piece of blotter paper or something like a sugar cube.

DURABILITY

A typical experience lasts around twelve hours and has been shown to create long-lasting and positive changes in one's physical, psychological, and spiritual health.

BENEFITS

The list of benefits of LSD is long and continues to grow. LSD is best known to treat anxiety and distress, PTSD, treatment-resistant depression, OCD, and more. Physically, LSD treats addiction and substance use disorders, chronic pain, and cluster headaches. Spiritually, LSD assists with existential or spiritual crises, as well as death and grief processes.

RISKS

When used in a controlled setting, LSD carries relatively low risks. Individuals may or may not experience "blunting effects" when combined with antidepressants or antipsychotics. As LSD is one of the four classical psychedelics, there is no possibility of overdose and no risk of physical addiction.

Mescaline (San Pedro and Peyote Cactus)

Power: 3.5/5
Type: Classical
Source: Typically organic, synthetic for most clinical work
Street Names: Wachuma, buttons, mescalito, big chief

OVERVIEW

The psychoactive ingredient in peyote and San Pedro (also known as *wachuma* or *huachuma* in the native Quechua language) is mescaline. Native traditions in both South and North America have used these cacti ceremonially for centuries, making mescaline likely the oldest known psychedelic substance, dating back over 11,000 years. It was first synthesized in 1919. Ceremonially, the experience of using these cacti can be gentle and heart opening, or incredibly powerful and mystical—you'll never know which kind of journey you'll get until you're already in it.

ACCESSIBILITY

Mescaline is largely illegal around the world. In the US, special exemptions were made in 1993 via the Religious Freedom and Restoration Act, allowing certain Native American groups—specifically the Native American Church (NAC)—to legally use peyote in their religious ceremonies. San Pedro and peyote are not popular recreational substances, but are frequently used for healing in the underground.

RECOMMENDED SETTING

San Pedro and peyote are almost always offered in traditional ceremonial group settings. These ceremonies often last anywhere from six to twelve hours. In many South American traditions, San Pedro is served in the morning, followed by an all-day hike. Peyote is often served in all-night ceremonies. Traditional songs and music frequently accompany both.

COMMON ROUTES OF ADMINISTRATION

Oftentimes, people cook and distill San Pedro into a cough-syrup-like consistency before drinking it. People frequently consume peyote by eating the fresh or dried cactus "buttons." Both cacti, when dried, can be ground into a powder and mixed with another liquid for drinking.

DURABILITY

A typical experience lasts around twelve hours and has been shown to create long-lasting and positive changes in one's physical, psychological, and spiritual health.

BENEFITS

Indigenous healers have used these cacti for centuries to treat and heal many conditions, including emotional trauma, PTSD, depression, anxiety, and more. Physically, mescaline treats addiction and substance use disorders, chronic pain, cluster headaches, and psychosomatic conditions. Spiritually, mescaline assists with existential or spiritual crises, death and grief processes, and healing intergenerational trauma.

RISKS

When used in a controlled setting, mescaline carries relatively low risks. When combined with antidepressants or antipsychotics, individuals may or may not experience "blunting effects." Mescaline should never be combined with MAOIs. As mescaline is one of the four classical psychedelics, there is no possibility of overdose and no risk of physical addiction.

A SPECIAL NOTE REGARDING PEYOTE

In the wild, a peyote cactus can take thirty years to grow to the size of a golf ball. Cultivated cacti can take up to ten years to mature from a seed. Environmental disruption and overuse have ravaged the peyote supply, and the non-Native use of these plants has become a very complicated topic. When activist groups proposed the decriminalization of peyote, the Indigenous Peyote Conservative Initiative (IPCI) and the National Council of Native American Churches issued a statement citing "… broken treaties in [the] land, the preciousness of native traditions, ecological threats to the medicine itself, and the importance of spiritual respect in its use" as reasons to exclude peyote from decriminalization efforts. If you are presented with an opportunity to sit with this sacred plant, I encourage you to respectfully work in alignment with the Indigenous elders who have shepherded and kept its use sacred for millennia.

Ayahuasca

Power: 4/5
Type: Classical
Source: Organic
Street Names: Aya, hoasca, yagé, the vine, la purga

OVERVIEW

The ayahuasca vine and a chacruna shrub are combined and cooked for many hours to create a brown tea. Ayahuasca is famous for its purgative qualities, which often induce vomiting or diarrhea. Much less traumatic than it sounds, this purging has a cleansing effect that frequently makes participants feel better rather than worse. Due to its strength, you must observe great care with your physical, psychological, and spiritual health before sitting with this medicine, especially if you consume it in a foreign country. Ayahuasca (and its active ingredient, DMT, often called the "God/spirit molecule") has deep traditions in the Amazon jungle. Indigenous healers have used it for centuries, and it has drawn a new wave of psychotourism to Central and South America.

ACCESSIBILITY

Ayahuasca (and its active ingredient, N,N-Dimethyltryptamine, or DMT) is largely illegal around the world. In the US, authorities have granted special exemptions for a few entheogenic churches to use it in their religious ceremonies. Ayahuasca does not have a popular reputation as a recreational substance, but it finds frequent use in the underground for healing purposes.

RECOMMENDED SETTING

Practitioners almost always offer ayahuasca in a traditional group setting, and they often encourage participants to sit with the medicine for multiple nights. Sometimes, participants in a retreat setting can experience three to seven ceremonies in close proximity. The ceremonies typically happen at night and are accompanied by traditional songs (called *icaros*) and/or music.

COMMON ROUTES OF ADMINISTRATION

Participants frequently drink the tea in multiple cups, or servings, throughout a single ceremony.

DURABILITY

Ayahuasca often provides a highly visionary experience that lasts five to seven hours. People have experienced long-lasting and positive changes in their physical, psychological, and spiritual health because of this powerful medicine.

BENEFITS

Indigenous healers have used ayahuasca for centuries to treat and heal many conditions, including depression, anxiety, trauma, PTSD, and OCD. Physically, ayahuasca treats chronic pain, addiction and substance use disorders, autoimmune and chronic inflammatory conditions, and psychosomatic conditions, as well as improving gut health. Spiritually, ayahuasca assists with existential or spiritual crises, death and grief processes, and healing intergenerational trauma.

RISKS

Ayahuasca carries more risks and contraindications than many of the prior substances in this chapter. Mixing ayahuasca with antidepressants (particularly SSRIs, SNRIs, MAOIs, or other serotonergic drugs), stimulants, antipsychotics, blood pressure medications, and opioids can lead to serious and potentially life-threatening conditions. Additionally, ayahuasca may further destabilize individuals with severe mental health conditions and is a frequent source of ontological difficulties. As the active ingredient in ayahuasca is DMT, which is one of the four classical psychedelics, there is no possibility of overdose and no risk of physical addiction.

5-MeO-DMT

Power: 4.5/5
Type: Classical
Source: Organic and synthetic
Street Names: Five, toad, the God molecule, bufo

OVERVIEW

If you compare the long-lasting effects of an ayahuasca journey to a NASCAR race, 5-MeO-DMT would be more like a drag race. Its potency is four to six times greater than that of its closely related cousins DMT and Bufotenin (5-HO-DMT or "the Toad"). Five produces a fast-acting and powerful experience that often results in a full and nearly instantaneous—though temporary—ego dissolution. Its most potent effects last around ten to fifteen minutes. Because of its strength, you must observe great care with your physical, psychological, and spiritual health before sitting with this medicine, especially if you consume it in a foreign country.

ACCESSIBILITY

Five is largely illegal around the world. It is not commonly used as a recreational substance but is frequently utilized underground for healing purposes.

RECOMMENDED SETTING

Five is typically offered as an individual experience, but it can also be provided in groups, with each individual having their own unique experience. Having only come into popularity in the 1980s, Five is the proverbial "baby" of modern-day psychedelics and is not often connected to a spiritual tradition. This is unfortunate, because this substance has the highest potential to instantaneously connect seekers to unitive/God consciousness. This can, however, result in ontological difficulties or shock.

COMMON ROUTES OF ADMINISTRATION

Smoking Five can result in effects that last only ten to fifteen minutes. When insufflated (snorted up the nose), its effects can last up to two hours.

DURABILITY

Its most potent effects last around ten to fifteen minutes. However, Five's ability to merge seekers into higher planes of consciousness can permanently change the user— for better or worse. This powerful medicine can create long-lasting changes in one's physical, psychological, and spiritual health.

BENEFITS

Five is best known to treat depression, anxiety, trauma, PTSD, and OCD. Physically, Five treats chronic pain, addiction and substance use disorders, and psychosomatic conditions. Spiritually, Five is best known for its ego-dissolving properties and ability to induce a profound sense of oneness with the universe. It also assists with healing intergenerational trauma and addressing existential or spiritual crises, as well as death, rebirth, and grief processes.

RISKS

Five has a relatively low risk profile for physical health, but it should not be combined with antidepressants (especially MAOIs) without first consulting with a qualified psychopharmacologist and your facilitator. High doses of Five can lead to ontological shock and worsening of physical and mental health issues.

A SPECIAL NOTE REGARDING FIVE

Five carries some unique psychological risks that other psychedelics on this list do not. Because of its short experience length, lack of lineage/spiritual underpinnings, and its unique ability to almost instantaneously transport users into Ultimate Reality (an experience often caused by ego dissolution), this substance can be dangerous. The potential of ontological shock is much higher with Five than with almost any other substance.

Five's relative immaturity as a substance used for healing has left it without generally accepted professional standards or "best practices." This unique set of circumstances has attracted many untrained "healing enthusiasts" who wish to share its speed and power with as many people as they can. I suggest that newcomers considering Five for healing work only do so with qualified professionals. Many of these professionals are beginning to use a "step-up" method that allows seekers to start "low and slow," and work their way up to more intense and full experiences.

Iboga and Ibogaine

Power: 5/5
Type: Classical
Source: Organic, synthetic for most clinical work
Street Names: Root bark, sacred wood, tree of knowledge

OVERVIEW

Iboga has been traditionally used for centuries by African cultures such as the Bwiti. More recently, scientists have synthesized a clinical version of one of its alkaloids, called ibogaine. Of all the substances in this book, iboga and its synthesized brother, ibogaine, offer the most potential gains but also come with the highest risks. Iboga gives seekers a panoramic view of their lives and an extended opportunity for deep reflection.

ACCESSIBILITY

Iboga is largely illegal around the world and in the US. Often referred to as the "addiction interrupter," ibogaine has been considered by multiple US states for use in special access programs to combat the growing addiction crisis. Ibogaine is not widely used as a recreational substance, and its complex contraindications and long journey length make it uncommon in the underground. Most individuals seeking iboga or ibogaine will need to travel to another country and work with a specialized clinic or facilitator to receive treatment.

RECOMMENDED SETTING

Iboga can be offered in group or individual experiences, and is usually served within an African shamanic ceremony—primarily originating from the Bwiti tribe of Central African origin. As such, using iboga comes with a deep lineage and spiritual tradition.

COMMON ROUTES OF ADMINISTRATION

The highest concentration of iboga is found in the root bark of the iboga plant. This bark is usually ground and eaten.

DURABILITY

An iboga experience is one of the most powerful and long-lasting journeys of any available psychedelic substance. The most powerful phase can last over twelve hours, with an additional twenty-four to forty-eight hours dedicated to grounding and returning to ordinary consciousness. This powerful medicine has been shown to create long-lasting and positive changes in one's physical, psychological, and spiritual health.

BENEFITS

Ibogaine is best known to treat severe addiction and withdrawal from substances such as heroin, morphine, and other opioids. It can also be used to treat chronic pain. Psychologically, it treats depression, PTSD, anxiety, mood and neurological disorders, and more. Spiritually, iboga can be used for spiritual awakening and insight, healing ancestral trauma, and ego dissolution and transformation, as well as rites of passage.

RISKS

Iboga/ibogaine is the most dangerous substance in this book due to its sheer power and complicated list of interactions. It is strongly recommended that individuals seeking treatment of iboga or ibogaine work with a well-qualified practitioner or specialized treatment facility.

What About Cannabis?

Many US states and local jurisdictions have legalized or decriminalized medical and recreational cannabis. Its use has become ubiquitous, and for many, more frequently used than alcohol. Though cannabis is not typically classified as a psychedelic substance, high doses can lead to psychedelic-like experiences, and many users tout its healing and spiritual benefits. Without question, individuals can effectively use cannabis medicinally and ceremonially. We know it is being used to significant positive effect in treating many health conditions like chronic pain, inflammation, seizure disorders, nausea, multiple sclerosis, glaucoma, cancer symptoms, and more.

However, there has arisen a great deal of societal and energetic confusion regarding this substance, and it is often being chronically used to self-medicate and avoid healing our maladaptation to life. For those who have no experience with mind-altering substances, cannabis might be an excellent (and more likely legal) substance to begin your intentional work with Sacred Medicine. Taking a low-dose cannabis gummy and quietly sitting in meditation could be a fantastic way to experience an altered state of consciousness. But when cannabis use occurs every day, multiple times per day, or throughout the day, it no longer qualifies as ceremony and has shifted to habitual use, no different than a common cigarette. Much like cold medicine, cannabis use in this fashion isn't healing you. It is only masking your symptoms.

Psychologically, cannabis is frequently used to numb discomfort and dull the pain of daily life. Rather than feeling and addressing this dis-ease head-on, you avoid confronting your feelings. The Center for Disease Control (CDC) reports that approximately three in ten people who use cannabis have cannabis use disorder. It is estimated that people who use cannabis have about a 10 percent likelihood of becoming addicted.[51] Society has been told cannabis is not addictive, but that simply is not true. Any mind-altering substance can encourage addictive behaviors and dependence.

My teachers have often said cannabis is a very "loud" plant that can quickly "dirty the waters" of our mind and body. Its communication goes to great lengths to interrupt our daily lives, and the energetic residue it leaves behind can take years to thoroughly cleanse from our system.

Molecule vs. Medicine

A few months ago, I was speaking with the maestro with whom I study in Peru. He asked me if ayahuasca was legal in the United States. When I said no, he genuinely could not understand why. After I explained to him that DMT was a controlled substance, he looked at me, somewhat puzzled. It was in this moment that I realized he had no intellectual knowledge of the chemical compound of DMT (the psychoactive ingredient in ayahuasca) that he has been serving for decades.

As the most profoundly connected and enlightened human I've ever met, he has no need for knowledge about a scientific molecule. Instead, he possesses a deep, personal relationship with the substance and speaks directly to the spirit of the medicine—in this case, Doctor Ayahuasca. This is a fundamental difference that exists between more traditional and modern perspectives on psychedelic use.

Modern science has taken an extractive approach to psychedelics, reducing their power to a series of molecules and brain functions. Animism, on the other hand, is a metaphysical belief that all things have a spiritual essence, including animals, plants, rocks, rivers, and weather systems. The Global North does not operate from a place of animism and often relies on the belief that if something cannot be measured, it does not exist.

I came to my work with psychedelics through a more modern and psychological lens—an adjunct to the psychotherapy I was already doing. This path offered a safer, more accessible model for my mind to comprehend. But through the years, my acceptance of scientific materialism has begun to fade. As my practice with Indigenous traditions expands and my relationship with the spirit of plants and fungi continues to deepen, I understand how much my modern mind struggles to see—in large part because of our lack of belief.

If you are a newcomer to this path, you get to choose which path you want to take with psychedelics: recreational, clinical, therapeutic, or spiritual. Each path comes with its own set of rules and customs. The therapeutic model is well adapted to modern expectations. When you ask your facilitator for a softer approach, a slower pace, or very specific boundaries, these requests are usually accommodated. But when you choose to enter the spiritual level, especially in a foreign country or Indigenous tradition, you are giving up some of those options. If you make the choice to work within an Indigenous lineage, you must also accept the responsibility of honoring that lineage's agreements and traditions. Not doing so demonstrates a lack of respect for the medicine and for those who have been serving it for decades.

If you have opted to sit with a curandero in an Indigenous ceremony, you are consciously stepping into a belief system of which you may have little to no understanding. The curandero may ask you to "say a prayer to Mother Earth" or request that you "ask for help from the spirit of the medicine." Just remember, if you are coming to these healers for *their* medicine, it's probably because *your* medicine hasn't worked. As I have often heard in the rooms of twelve-step programs, "If you continue to do what you've always done, you'll continue to get what you've always got."

So rather than getting upset that you're being asked to do, say, or believe in something you're uncomfortable with or don't understand, pause and consider why you showed up in the first place. When you work with psychedelics, the medicine comes in different forms—many of which you may not currently possess the consciousness to understand. That's why you're coming to psychedelics to begin with.

As a closing reminder: be open-minded with your experience, but never agree to anything that risks your personal safety, no matter what situation you are in.

Start Lower Than You Think

Many people come to this work desiring to break off the biggest chunks of trauma they can. This is frequently why many people skip the first few substances on this list and go straight to more potent substances, like ayahuasca. If you're not ready or properly prepared for using a high-power substance, your risks for harm will increase. Taking on too much, too soon can even cause you to experience worsening symptoms of depression and anxiety—or even ontological shock or HPPD.

When Carl Jung said, "Beware of unearned wisdom," he was specifically referring to altered states of consciousness with psychedelics. He believed that profound spiritual or psychological insights gained without the necessary groundwork could be overwhelming, misinterpreted, or even harmful. Bypassing the natural development process of personal growth can be hazardous to your health.

If your self-assessed level of dysregulation (be that anxiety, depression, PTSD, etc.) is a seven out of ten or higher, I recommend starting with a substance that ranks lower than three on the relative power scale. This might look like low-dose, psychedelic-assisted therapy with ketamine or sitting intentionally with MDMA. One way to evaluate your current level of dysregulation is by using the "Window of Tolerance Self-Assessment" from KOI Education, which can be downloaded at https://piq.lv/wot.

Use Caution When Combining Substances

Indigenous medicine carriers have been mixing substances for many years. Whether combining multiple medicines in their ayahuasca brew or incorporating tobacco into their ceremonies, these master practitioners use the power of Mother Nature to their clients' benefit.

In the modern world, you may encounter many practitioners combining (also referred to as "stacking") substances for a more significant effect. Many times, combining substances can prove incredibly effective (such as combining MDMA with psilocybin or LSD). Certain combinations allow seekers to receive the benefits of both substances and often create a more pleasant or tolerable overall experience.

Conversely, combining substances to achieve more speed and power can also be disastrous. I have helped clients integrate traumatic experiences, many stemming from unsuccessful attempts to combine multiple substances that led to catastrophic psychological outcomes.

Anytime you combine substances, the risk profile of your entire experience increases. Your facilitator must have extensive experience or training in understanding how these substances interact with each other and how each individual substance may be contraindicated within your unique system. Remember, there's already twelve variables on the Psychedelic Safety Wheel. Introducing a new substance into an experience doubles the number of variables and exponentially increases the number of potential outcomes.

For more information on how substances may interact with each other, visit the resource section on PsychedelicIQ.com.

Test Your Substances

If you decide to work in the underground, it is crucial to understand what substances you will use and where they come from. If you choose a botanical substance, there is a smaller chance it has been adulterated with other harmful substances. On the other hand, substances such as ketamine or MDMA can frequently be adulterated with drugs such as fentanyl, a highly addictive chemical that, even in small quantities, can result in overdose or death.

It is also not an uncommon practice in today's psychedelic landscape for a facilitator to ask you to acquire your own substances. This shifts the legal burden of acquiring and possessing a controlled substance to you rather than them. If you find yourself in this situation, I highly recommend that you test your substances before using them. Home tests are available that measure the quality and potency of many substances.

To find one of those tests, visit the resources section on PsychedelicIQ.com.

Escapism vs. Confrontation

I place most psychotropic substances into two broad categories: escapist and confrontational. Substances like alcohol, cocaine, methamphetamine, and opioids are escapist. They distract us from our life and true nature by numbing our experiences. Psychedelics, when used intentionally, are confrontational. As nonspecific amplifiers, they can direct our attention to the present moment, show us what lies within, and reveal what is True. They open the aperture of our consciousness and ask (if not demand) that we examine the truth of our reality.

One of my favorite quotes from researcher Andrew Huberman is "Addiction is a progressive narrowing of the things that bring you pleasure. Happiness is a progressive expansion of the things that bring you pleasure. The former emerges passively. The latter takes work." It is crucial to appreciate that psychedelics can be used in a confrontational way to increase pleasure or in an escapist way that will progressively narrow what brings you pleasure. A hammer can build a wall just as quickly as it can tear one down. The one swinging the hammer plays an oversized role in the outcome. If you consider these substances as tools, it is the intention of the user that largely determines whether they will heal or harm.

Practically speaking, individuals who take 1.5 grams of mushrooms while drinking alcohol and partying at a music festival are pointing themselves toward escapism. But those same mushrooms, when used with a facilitator in a safe and private setting, could be healing.

These substances are largely agnostic. They do not inherently come with a belief system. What you choose to do with them is entirely up to you.

10

Facilitation

"Aum (the Primal Shabda)" by Russill Paul

I consider most deep psychedelic experiences similar to surgery. Sometimes you're doing surgery on the body, sometimes the mind, and sometimes the spirit. And just like in an operating room, highly trained surgeons carefully prepare their patient and their surroundings. To ensure as little potential for infection as possible, the surgeon takes great care in sterilizing the environment. The surgeon makes an incision, carries out their work skillfully, and sutures the wound to prevent scarring, and then the medical team transfers the patient to the recovery area.

While using psychedelics may depend a little less on the surgeon and a little more on the substance, this analogy still holds true. In fact, during my third night of sitting with ayahuasca in the Amazon jungle, I can specifically remember the curandero performing an "energetic surgery" on me to remove heavy energy from my chest. The healer had me open my shirt and he then spread *Agua de Florida* (a mixture of grain alcohol and various botanical scents often used to clear energy) all over my chest. He began singing an *icaro* over top of me. I felt like my chest was being literally opened for surgery. It was not painful, but my insides felt completely exposed to the elements. While nothing was changing in my physical body, my energetic body was being opened in a way I had never experienced nor could understand.

After putting Agua de Florida in his mouth, the healer sucked this dark energy from my chest and spat it out. Throughout three or four of these extractions, this heavy energy was purged from my system. He then applied more Agua de Florida to my chest and sang another song to "close" my body. I felt like I had experienced soul surgery, something not available using modern medicine. This kind of "surgery" has happened many more times with my current maestro, who uses tobacco as a protective barrier rather than Agua de Florida.

Here is a question to consider: "Would you be willing to have surgery performed on you by an unqualified facilitator?"

As a newcomer, one of the most essential variables to optimize in your early psychedelic experiences is finding the right facilitator *for you*. The right facilitator for one person may not be suitable for another. And it's also possible that a facilitator may not be right for you *right now*.

Your needs will change throughout your healing journey, and what you need today may not be what you need a year from now. Your chosen facilitator should align with your current body, mind, and spiritual needs. If you're unable to articulate those needs, then it's even more important to slow down and get the help you need to figure it out.

There are many people wandering around the psychedelic landscape today. Most facilitators find a system, a substance, and a protocol that works for them, then create or adopt a belief system to support their choices. This is not inherently wrong; it's simply looking at the landscape through a telephoto lens. Think of it this way: when you are looking to buy a car, it's important for you to know all your options and make the best choice for your needs. If you're driving every day in the city, you wouldn't want to drive a gas-guzzling pickup truck. If you had to choose a pickup truck because that's all the dealership had, you'd be doing yourself a disservice. You need the right tool from the right person. Alignment is essential when choosing a facilitator.

Earlier in the book, we reviewed the various kinds of guides and facilitators you might meet on your healing journey. And just like someone traveling the Oregon Trail, your chances of making it west dramatically increase if you have the right guide.

Why Do I Need a Facilitator?

Not a week goes by that I don't see a social media post encouraging seekers to abandon their desire for a facilitator in favor of a supportive friend or doing a journey alone. Many of these comments come from longtime psychonauts who may have used substances for years but have little to no experience with healing, much less holding or mending complex trauma. Unless you're frequently working with newcomers, it's easy to forget how scary it can be to explore the depths of your consciousness without a map.

The following image helps illustrate the benefits of working with a facilitator. If you're new to psychedelics, you will have absolutely no idea how to navigate the maze of psychedelic healing. This is precisely the reason you should work with someone qualified to help you through this process, especially if you know your work includes trauma.

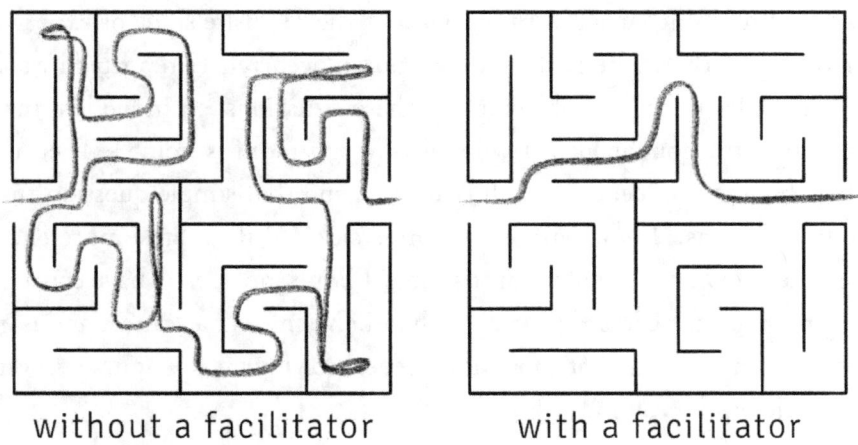

FIGURE 10. Working without vs. with a facilitator

Once it's all said and done, it might appear that your facilitator did very little work *during* your experience. Your initial reaction might be, "Well, what did I pay them all that money for?" What can be difficult to understand is all the work they did *before* your experience that allowed you to have a successful journey.

After a quarter century working in corporate America, one valuable lesson I learned was the importance of the "Six Ps"—an abbreviation for the phrase "Prior Planning Prevents Piss Poor Performance." This rather blunt mantra has proven very worthwhile both in my own medicine work and in working with my clients. Try to appreciate that there is a lot more happening before and during your experience than may be visible to your naked eye. Do not discount your facilitator's ability to help you feel safe and seen, and to create and maintain the energetic container that allows your system to intuitively heal itself.

But let's be honest: countless humans have used psychedelics through the ages. Many, if not most, have not worked with a trained facilitator. If you're a physically and psychologically healthy individual, taking psychedelics in a responsible setting and using a reasonable dose, the likelihood of harm is pretty low, right?

A lot depends on your end goals. Data suggests recreational psilocybin use has a significantly lower rate of harm than alcohol. It's true that many people regularly consume psychedelics recreationally at festivals and friendly gatherings across the globe, and most of trips turn out just fine. However, seeking recreation and self-exploration is very different from working through deep-seated trauma or attempting to alleviate symptoms of PTSD, substance addiction, or treatment-resistant depression. Taking a tab of LSD at a music festival differs greatly from opening up a Pandora's box of adverse childhood experiences. If healing is what you aim for, working with someone prepared to help you safely hold and explore this delicate content is paramount to having a positive experience.

Venturing into uncharted territory without the requisite skills or experience can be a harrowing journey. One of the most common occurrences reported by solo journeyers is an undesirable "thought loop." In these situations, an individual may think a perfectly benign thought like, "I wonder how my mom is doing?" Then they will remember she was not feeling so well last week, and that simple question turns into a subtle fear, such as, "I wonder if my mom is sick?" With a little more energy and attention, the thought suddenly morphs into, "I hope she doesn't have cancer," which then can grow into the catastrophizing realm of, "My mom has cancer and is going to die." Now imagine playing that thought on repeat for four to six hours without being able to turn down the volume.

Another rather dark and unfortunate experience reported to me by an integration client involved a thought loop that spiraled into paranoia. This individual had taken LSD alone in the safe confines of their apartment. The thought loop that crept into their mind became conspiratorial, and the individual thought they were being watched. For hours, their mind and nervous system felt like they were under the threat of surveillance, and the discomfort caused by this repetitive thought loop lasted far longer than they expected. It took months of therapy to fully flush it from their system. If they had worked with proper support, a facilitator could have quickly intervened and helped avoid this harmful thought loop.

If you are having a challenging solo psychedelic experience and need support, there are resources available. The Fireside Project, founded in 2021 by Joshua White, is the world's first psychedelic peer support line. Open every day from 11 a.m. to 11 p.m. US Pacific time, trained operators offer free, confidential, and nondirective support to anyone experiencing a difficult psychedelic experience.[52]

In 2023, psychologist Dr. Mollie M. Pleet conducted a study on the Fireside Project. The study reported the outcomes through an anonymous survey sent to callers twenty-four hours after their contact. Out of the 4,047 calls received between April 2021 and September 2022, 848 callers completed the study. In terms of results, 29.3 percent of individuals stated their phone call helped them avoid being physically or emotionally harmed, 12.5 percent said it helped them avoid calling 911, and 10.8 percent said it helped them avoid an emergency room visit.[53]

To connect with the Fireside Project, download their app or visit firesideproject.org.

How to Choose the Right Facilitator

On your psychedelic journey, you'll encounter many people claiming to be healers or guides. Early on, you may lack the discernment to differentiate between those who are genuinely qualified and those who simply talk a good game. It's essential to acknowledge this lack of knowing as simply a part of your learning process and to approach these relationships with curiosity and caution.

Much of the pain we seek to resolve with psychedelic healing stems from relational trauma—emotional, psychological, or physical harm we experienced within close, trusted relationships, often in our formative years. The good news is that while relationships may have been a source of deep wounding, they also hold the potential for profound healing.

When we are harmed in relationship, we must heal in relationship, but a relationship with those who've harmed us is *never* required. Instead, healing can involve building safe and supportive relationships with practitioners who have traveled the path you wish to take. These relationships can create the trust and safety necessary for deep emotional repair, helping you return to wholeness. Do not discount the possibility that the relationship you have with your facilitator can represent an amazing opportunity to repattern old traumatic relationships.

Another common mistake among newcomers is forming judgments about a prospective facilitator's capabilities based on their outward appearance. Remember that how someone looks and dresses has no bearing on the medicine they serve. The price of the chalice that they use to hand you your mushrooms makes absolutely no difference in the healing power of those mushrooms. After almost two decades of working within the spiritual, yoga, and psychedelic communities, one thing I've learned is that the more elaborate the costume, the more time I will need to spend with someone before deciding to work with them. No amount of special clothes, Indigenous headwear, necklaces, mala beads, or crystals can make up for a lack of intentionality and integrity with which they serve medicine. Just because someone is wearing white clothes on the outside does not mean that they're full of light on the inside. And to make the process even more complicated, the right facilitator for you *initially* may not be the one you need in a year or two. The following guidance will help you get started finding a reliable and trustworthy facilitator.

Seek Trusted Referrals

Work with someone referred to you by a trusted friend, community member, or helping professional. Ideally, the individual doing the referral will have already worked with the facilitator and be willing to offer a personal account of their experience and outcome. If they're willing, take the person giving you the referral out for coffee and spend quality time talking to them about their experience.

Hidden within this referral system is the esoteric dictum of "attraction rather than promotion." While it's true that a commercial venture such as a retreat center will likely advertise its services, many of the best facilitators I have worked with do no advertising at all. They focus on building an impeccable reputation by caring for their clients and producing positive outcomes. When this happens consistently over many years, advertising is no longer required.

Talk to Multiple Facilitators

If possible, interview multiple facilitators and choose the one that best suits your needs and personality. If you are new to this work and only interview one facilitator, that's the only context you'll have for how the process could unfold. There could still be other ways that better suit your needs and are worth exploring. Until you've talked to two or more people, you will have little context for what you like or don't like. This may require you to go outside of your local geography. While this may not feel ideal, if you are able to travel, keep an open mind and consider all your options.

Try to spend time with each facilitator you are considering. Most facilitators doing one-on-one work will offer a free introductory call for you to get to know each other. If you feel more time is needed before making your decision, or if you have additional questions you'd like to ask, see if they offer an hourly session rate that might allow you to continue working together before you make your final decision.

Research Your Options

It is a good idea to conduct some online research about your facilitator before meeting them for the first time. See if they publish content online. Check their social media accounts. Have they participated in any podcast interviews? Do they write articles on their blog, Medium, or Substack? These are all ways to better understand your facilitator before your introductory call. If their content raises questions, the call is your opportunity to seek clarification. Pay attention to how they respond to questions or criticism. A defensive posture is something to pay attention to and may represent a "red flag" or misalignment. An openness to explaining or clarifying their position is a much better sign.

The advice I've received from my Peruvian teachers is: "Never sit with someone with a lower vibration than you." Recalling the Map of Consciousness from chapter 2, if your primary lived experience hovers around fear (100), avoid a facilitator whose lived experience is lower than yours. How do you figure this out? Ask questions and spend time with your facilitator. Much of this is a gut feeling. If you sense your facilitator feels or embodies a quality that you want in your life, that is a good sign.

Another way to use the Map of Consciousness in this process is to know what level of work you're trying to reach and choose a facilitator who's already working from that level. For instance, if you're trying to do work focused on self-love (500), but your facilitator's primary level of consciousness is reason (400), they will not be able to correctly retune your chord of love. This is not a criticism or an implication that the facilitator is unqualified. It's simply an observation that they may not yet possess the level of consciousness you seek. This is also not to suggest it's impossible to explore self-love during your experience. It is, however, unlikely that this facilitator will be the one getting you there. (In some cases, the medicine will offer this experience with no human intervention.)

Trust Your Gut

Finally, always trust your gut. Ask yourself if you would want to work with or spend time with this facilitator if psychedelics were not involved. So many people over the years have said, "I knew something didn't feel right, but I didn't trust my instincts." I can't stress strongly enough that your body will help you decide, but only if you listen to it. At any point during your preparation process, pay attention if a part of you feels unsafe or unseen. Bring these feelings to your facilitator and take notice of how they respond. A good facilitator will take ownership of their words and actions by making a helpful correction.

Facilitator "Green Flags"

Volumes could be written on the qualifications and characteristics to look for in a psychedelic facilitator, and there would still always be some disagreement. The fact that there is no one "right way" to psychedelic complicates things. The training and qualifications required to work in a clinical context are completely different than those required in a spiritual or Indigenous context.

Psychedelics are like a scalpel. They can be used as a tool to heal or to harm. They primarily work on the mind, which is exponentially more complex than the body, and science cannot predict or map thoughts. Two bodies of similar demographics will work relatively the same way, while two minds—not so much.

Keeping this in mind, here are a few of the most important characteristics and "green flags" I've experienced while working with psychedelic facilitators. I have done my best to order this list by criticality. For instance, if your facilitator is dishonest, everything that comes after that is moot. This list is not exhaustive, but it will get you started in the right direction.

Honesty

If your facilitator has a tenuous relationship with honesty, then nothing else matters. Pay attention to details from the first time you speak or meet with your facilitator. Write down important points of your conversation. These might be qualifications, pricing, protocol, dosing, etc. If you sense inconsistency, bring it up with your facilitator. Their response to being confronted with potential discrepancies may give you all the information you need to proceed or walk away.

Humility

Practitioners should remain humble, keep an open mind, stay curious, and realize they don't have all the answers. Humility allows a facilitator to put you and the medicine in the driver's seat rather than prioritizing their skills, knowledge, experience, or desired outcome. It's a quality that honors your inner healer and allows for a genuine exchange of ideas, perspectives, and insights. It creates a space for your process to unfold exactly how it needs to, rather than being directed along a path predetermined by the facilitator.

Empathy

Considered by many (myself included) to be one of the essential qualities of any healing professional, empathy refers to the ability of a practitioner to understand and share the feelings and experiences of their client without experiencing those feelings themself. Having a deep sense of empathy will allow your facilitator to perceive your emotions, perspectives, and struggles without judgment or personal bias. This quality is crucial in creating a safe container for work that allows you the freedom to feel all your feelings. Rather than needing to "fix" or solve your problems, an empathetic facilitator will make you to feel heard, understood, and accepted as you navigate your journey of self-discovery.

Ethics

Ethics are among the most important and frequently overlooked issues within the psychedelic landscape. Unsatisfactory ethics are more often seen in the underground but can also occur in aboveground work. Because of these substances' boundary-dissolving nature and the ensuing hyper-suggestibility, your facilitator must have a solid ethical foundation. And just because someone is ethical in their personal life doesn't mean they have a firm grasp on the ethics of working with clients. Each style of psychedelics (i.e., clinical, therapeutic, spiritual, Indigenous) has its own set of standards when it comes to ethics and responsibility. One of the most common causes of harm I see in psychedelia today is when a seeker's definition of ethics differs from the facilitator's (more on this in chapter 15, "Experience"). When evaluating your facilitator, consider their clear understanding of and ability to communicate agreements, boundaries, confidentiality, touch, and scope of practice.

Safety

If your facilitator honors the first four qualities listed, safety should already be a part of their process. That said, once you connect with a potential facilitator, you should start to feel safe from your first phone call, and safety should be a through line to the end of your process. From the start, safety should present itself during preparation, integration, and exploring contraindications and risks. It should extend to confidentiality, set, setting, and dosage, and ensure you are physically, psychologically, and spiritually safe throughout your work. If there is ever a point in your process where you feel unsafe, address it openly with your facilitator. Their response should create more safety in your system. If it doesn't, this may be a sign that they are not your ideal facilitator.

Experience

Would you want someone who has no experience with the inner workings of the brain to perform your brain surgery? Definitely not! The same should be true with psychedelic healing. Your psychedelic facilitator should have extensive experience with both taking and serving the substance they are offering. No two psychedelic experiences are ever the same, but your facilitator should have an expert-level understanding of the terrain they're asking you to explore. Your facilitator should have something you want and have gone "where you want to go." One quick and easy way to discern how much experience your facilitator has is to pay attention to how rigid they are in their thinking. The last decade of my work has taught me that the more I know, the more I realize I don't know. Absolute surety in the ways of the cosmos or the Divine may be cause for concern.

Doing Their Own Work

To relieve suffering in others, we must first remove it from our own system. It's not enough to only serve medicine to others. Facilitators must have done—and continue to do—their own work, both in and out of the medicine. This usually involves deep and ongoing work with a therapist, coach, mentor, or teacher. If your facilitator tells you they don't have any work to do or that they've already finished their work, that may be a good reason to walk in the other direction. You should also be wary of a modern facilitator who tells you they do *all* their work *in* the medicine. This line of thinking may indicate psychedelic bypass and represent an avoidance of the actual work we must all do in our human experience.

Accountability

Hand in hand with doing their own work, a facilitator should have some form of accountability built into their practice. This may involve ongoing work with a teacher, supervisor, or peer group. Client work with psychedelics is complicated, powerful, and often messy. If a facilitator has been working long enough, mistakes will eventually happen, and complex situations will arise. They must have a plan to support and address these mistakes, so they do not continue to happen. Accountability, along with honesty, is an essential quality when working with psychedelics.

Qualifications

I've listed qualifications lower on this list than you might expect, because this quality doesn't always make sense for those who have been educated in a Westernized school system or capitalistic society. Qualifications in this work can be acquired in unconventional ways that may not seem valid when looking through a more modern educational lens. Many new facilitators pay thousands of dollars and spent hundreds of hours learning about psychedelic facilitation in an online course. (This in no way makes someone qualified to serve medicine.) A facilitator may have spent years apprenticing within a South American lineage but never cracked open a book. (This individual is probably more qualified than the former to serve psychedelics.)

I recommend working with a facilitator that has experience in one or more modalities or cosmologies that address root causes in the body, mind, and spirit. Some of these approaches could be considered traditional, some not. Some may be Indigenous or spiritual, others secular. They may originate from Western, Southern, or Eastern philosophies. Regardless of the approach, facilitators should know and operate within their scope of practice, which refers to the protocols, conditions, and substances an individual is qualified to address in their work. Those operating outside their scope of practice have a greater chance of harming their clients.

Groundedness

Being "grounded" refers to a state of being where an individual is mentally and emotionally present, centered, and connected to their surroundings, body, and reality. Not only should your facilitator be a grounded person, but their work should also demonstrate a sense of groundedness. Their practice should be stable and, within reason, mistakes and surprises should not be commonplace. Possessing a grounded quality allows a facilitator to sit and engage with a comprehensive presentation of emotions or trauma without becoming disturbed or unseated from their own emotional center.

Attunement

Attunement refers to a facilitator's ability to understand and resonate with their clients' emotions, experiences, and needs. Doing this requires a deep level of empathy, sensitivity, and responsiveness to both the client's inner and outer worlds. A facilitator well attuned to your needs will sense subtle cues from your body language, tone of voice, facial expressions, or even shifts in your emotions and energy bodies. These will assist them in guiding you through your experience.

Vulnerability

Healthy vulnerability is a potent attribute for any healing professional. Not only does modeling healthy vulnerability help create and deepen an authentic relationship between the facilitator and the seeker, but it also serves as a bedrock for the safe space a client needs to explore their innermost feelings and experiences without fear of judgment. Vulnerability is mandatory for anyone "doing their own work." Without vulnerability, facilitators cannot receive feedback, improve their practice, or develop a greater sense of self-awareness.

Facilitator "Red Flags"

While you can certainly inverse the previous list of "green flags," to automatically create a list of "red flags," there are a few other examples of inappropriate behavior I want to specifically call out. Though not an exhaustive list, staying away from the following traits could save you significant pain and suffering.

Ego Inflation

While psychedelics can "kill" or temporarily "dissolve" one's ego, they can also inflate it. This often equates to facilitators taking too much ownership of your healing process. If your facilitator has deeply attached themself to the need to heal you, watch out. Anyone too strongly attached to "being the healer" desperately requires someone to heal. This kind of ego inflation can appear as an unwillingness to receive feedback and a lack of humility, accountability, vulnerability, and empathy. Unhealthy facilitators may also position themselves as having a great deal of power or claim to have a "special" technique or substance that can heal you. Be cautious of anyone who focuses more on themself, *their* process, and *their* medicine than you. Comparing this to a flesh wound, a facilitator should only act as the stitches that will assist your body, mind, and spirit to heal in exactly the way it knows how to do.

Lack of Screening, Preparation, or Integration

Anyone leaving these steps out of their protocol may be more of an enthusiast than a professional. The screening and preparation processes should include a discussion of potential risks as they relate to your medical history and psychedelics. You may encounter Indigenous practitioners practicing in Western locales, often with substances such as ayahuasca, San Pedro, or peyote, who do not include these steps in their process (more on this in chapter 16, "Integration"). If you choose to sit with an Indigenous practitioner, be prepared to accept a greater degree of responsibility for these aspects of your experience.

Overpromising

Contrary to what the media would like you to believe, psychedelics are not "magic pills" or "silver bullets." If your facilitator is overpromising results or claiming that a single, high-priced journey is all you need to heal, take that as a warning and walk the other way. Consider regarding this work as an ongoing practice rather than an event.

Claiming "Enlightenment"

Facilitators claiming high levels of consciousness such as enlightenment, satori, nirvana, or even being "done" with their own work should be regarded with caution. To this day, I've never met a human walking this earth who has completely healed themselves and attained enlightenment. Approaching this from an Eastern perspective, anyone who outwardly claims enlightenment is most assuredly not enlightened.

Lack of Professionalism

If you are paying someone good money to assist in your healing journey, there should be a reciprocal level of professionalism in their process and way of being. Reliable and clear communication, healthy boundaries, well-developed informed consent practices, and a deep understanding of their medicine, protocol, and belief system are the bare minimum requirements for psychedelic professionals.

Radical Cosmology

An individual's cosmology refers to their meta-understanding or belief system regarding the origin, nature, and structure of all things. Your cosmology is substantially influenced by the location or environment in which you were raised or live. Psychedelics (and many other esoteric or spiritual traditions) can carry with them a disconnected, radical, or "out there" view of the way things work. Once again, an individual's cosmology doesn't make them bad, but you must ask yourself if you want your facilitator to encourage (or even demand) that you believe in their cosmology. It is often said that amateurs (or, in this case, "enthusiasts") think in absolutes, while experts think in probabilities.

Overuse or Co-Use of the Substance

It is normal for Indigenous facilitators to ingest medicine with their clients. I've never met an Indigenous curandero who did not ingest some amount of their own medicine while guiding clients through an experience. Unfortunately, unqualified psychedelic enthusiasts will frequently ingest more than a small amount of a substance and journey *alongside* their clients. This, along with chronic or recreational substance overuse, suggests addiction, a use disorder, or dependency, and should be approached with great caution. It is a sign of poor ethics if your facilitator is "doing their work" at the same time you're paying them to do yours.

Instability

Instability is the inverse of groundedness. Self-help author Bob Proctor offers an excellent frame with which to consider this: "Your outside world is a reflection of your inside world. What happens on the inside, shows on the outside."

If your facilitator has no permanent place to live, this might be an outward sign of their inner instability. If the setting for your experience seems unsafe or unclean, these can also be outward signs of inner instability. Be extra cautious of a facilitator who is emotionally unstable or constantly surrounded by drama within their community or social group. While just one of the examples listed above may not be enough for concern, multiple outward signs of potential instability should cause you to slow down and reevaluate your situation.

Question Avoidance

If you ask your facilitator a simple question about the substance they're using or the protocol they're working with, and they don't know the answer, this may be a cause for concern. Another way this kind of avoidance can present itself is with a lack of transparency or deflection. If you ask a question and your facilitator responds with "You don't need to worry about that" or "That's not important," this is also cause for concern. If you ask a second time and they get defensive, consider this is a "double red flag." Alternatively, if you ask your facilitator a question and they honestly respond with, "I don't know. Let me get back to you," and then they do—this shows integrity rather than avoidance.

Constant Relocation and Lack of References

A common outcome of a facilitator acting inappropriately within their community is that they become shunned and are forced to find a new pool of unsuspecting clients in a new location. If your facilitator is "new in town," slow down your process and do more research. Not unlike job-hopping, frequent relocations can be a red flag. If this is the case for your facilitator, make sure you ask for references. A professional in good standing should have no issue offering multiple references from former clients.

Friction

This seems relatively simple, but if you experience "friction" with your facilitator during your preparation process, this is a good sign they may not be the right facilitator for you at this stage of your journey. This doesn't mean they're a lousy facilitator, but it may indicate that they're not the best fit for your personality. Not every facilitator is safe for every client. Sources of friction could be a lack of attunement, limited experience with your specific condition or symptoms, or even a fundamental difference in a belief system or cosmology. If this arises in your process, bring it up to your facilitator and see if they are open to discussing it further. It could be a simple misunderstanding that can be quickly resolved. If not, a professional and ethical facilitator will understand your process and may even help you find a better fit if they know one is available.

JJ's Story

How do I safely enter the world of psychedelics? Should I even try? These questions haunted me as I contemplated my first psychedelic journey. On paper, I had an incredible life—a strong marriage, three amazing kids, a fulfilling career, and a circle of friends in a thriving community. I wasn't trying to escape trauma or struggling with addiction. By all measures, I was happy. There was no crisis, but there was a void: spirituality. As an avid reader of personal development books, I encountered the idea that spirituality is vital to a meaningful life. I didn't follow a religion, so spirituality felt elusive—something I couldn't even define.

I saw psychedelics as a gamble, one that could ruin my greatest asset: my mind. My wife supported me, but I saw the fear in her eyes. What if this breaks me? What if it breaks us? Still, I had a deep respect for "the medicine." I wouldn't move forward unless I could be reasonably sure I'd come out the other side okay—or better than when I entered. I was being so cautious, it took 4,362 days after deciding to do it for me to finally participate in a ceremony.

So, what took so long?

Years earlier, I heard about DMT. A college friend mentioned his upcoming film, *DMT: The Spirit Molecule*. He explained that DMT is a hallucinogenic substance that some believe simulates death or a near-death experience. It's non-habit-forming and already exists in our bodies, secreted when we dream. A DMT trip lasts fifteen to thirty minutes and, like a dream, can be hard to remember. Or I could drink ayahuasca, a tea brewed in the jungles of Peru, and have a longer experience, likely involving vomiting.

DMT seemed appealing, and the idea of experiencing death without dying intrigued me. I thought it might ease my fear of death or even give me some insight into what happens afterward. Though technically illegal, I decided that night that I would take DMT if the opportunity arose. That was June 5, 2009.

I became obsessed. For years, I absorbed everything I could find on DMT. Yet, I never took the plunge. Then, in August 2019, I met with a potential business client, a trusted referral. After discussing his project, he casually mentioned organizing a local ayahuasca ceremony. I was floored—here I was, sitting with a local expert on plant medicine. This was my moment. We talked for another half-hour, and he invited me to connect about a future ceremony.

Then COVID hit, and everything changed. During the pandemic, I wrestled with life's biggest questions: Where did we come from? What is our purpose? Spirituality felt within reach, yet I couldn't quite grasp it. After a year of contemplation, I reached out again. He was open to having me join a future ceremony but advised against starting with ayahuasca—it could be too intense for a beginner. Having never experimented with psychedelics before, he recommended a one-on-one mushroom journey first, with the possibility of sitting with ayahuasca six months later.

At his suggestion, I read *How to Change Your Mind* by Michael Pollan. By the time I finished, I was certain mushrooms would not only be safe, but transformative. I was ready. In preparation, I also completed an extensive packet of paperwork outlining my life and intentions. The facilitator also had me bring photos and props related to those intentions, ensuring the environment felt safe and personal. Despite my nerves and lingering paranoia, I trusted him.

The journey exceeded my wildest expectations. His facilitation was perfect, and he has constantly supported me during my integration. He helped me process my experiences and incorporate them into my life. It wasn't just about the trip, but the work that followed.

Since that first journey, I've had many more, each healing and profound. With this new confidence, I've also sat with other facilitators. I'm deeply grateful to that first facilitator for showing me this path with such safety, care, and professionalism. Because of these journeys, my universe has expanded, and my life has become more prosperous. It all started with trusting the right guide.

Drawing *Your* Line Between Safety and Growth

Each style of psychedelics (i.e., clinical, therapeutic, spiritual, Indigenous) has its own set of expectations when it comes to safety, ethics, and responsibility. One of the most common causes of harm I see in psychedelia today is when a seeker's definition of these words differs from their facilitator's.

How each of us define these terms relies a great deal on where and how we were raised or taught. If you grew up in the United States and are expecting a level of care similar to psychotherapy, but your facilitator grew up in South America and was trained in the jungle, there is a high likelihood that your definitions of these terms will be different. This doesn't mean either of you are inherently right or wrong, but a lack of clarity could end up being the source of severe discomfort, if not the felt experience of harm.

We've already discussed that feeling safe and being seen are two of the most important prerequisites for healing. To this end, modern society has been built (and maybe overcorrected) to keep us cozy—safe from discomfort and risk. But what I've found in both my coaching and psychedelic practices is that real healing starts where your comfort zone ends. Avoiding discomfort may be holding you back from growth. When holding on to your trauma becomes a higher priority than healing, there is no room for growth to occur. This pattern might be referred to as "learned helplessness."

If you choose to step out of the modern psychotherapeutic style of healing, or if you are considering heading south to sit with Sacred Medicine, consider how you have been cared for up to this point and how you expect to be taken care of during your experience. Without an understanding of these expectations, a serious clash of beliefs and values may cause a lot of discomfort. It is very easy to misinterpret harm when someone doesn't meet your personal demands and expectations. Yet one does not necessarily equal the other.

To offer informed consent, you must first completely understand what you are consenting to, including the action, treatment, and participation required. Part of this responsibility lies on the facilitator, and the other part on you. It is important that you ask questions that help you both determine your needs, boundaries, and expectations. Your facilitator may have been working for decades serving group ceremonies to thousands of people all over the world. If this is the case, they may not take the time to personally explain every detail of how and why they do what they do.

If you are used to a more psychotherapeutic style of healing, you may be familiar with the concept of trauma-informed care (TIC). This framework considers an individual's past experiences of trauma and violence, responding in a way that promotes safety, empowerment, and healing. The approach is rooted in empathy and aims to actively avoid retraumatizing by supporting recovery and resilience.

To put it rather bluntly: Indigenous medicine carriers and the ceremonies they offer are not trauma informed. In these ceremonies, trust is shifted to the Divine intelligence of the medicine. If you have a hard process or a grueling journey, that's simply the experience you were supposed to have. There is no judgment, only love and trust that the medicine is working in exactly the way it needs to support you in your healing journey.

There are many kinds of psychedelic experiences, and many different expectations unique to each seeker. There is a fine line between safety and growth that you must take the responsibility to draw yourself. It is essential for your safety that, before you begin your psychedelic experience, you have established clear boundaries between yourself, your facilitator(s), and any other co-journeyers. You must have an understanding of what (if any) physical touch may or may not be used during your experience, and what type or level of communication (or lack thereof) will be allowed. Asking questions about what will and won't happen during your journey is crucial to keeping everyone safe and comfortable.

Due to the tremendous power of and suggestibility brought on by these substances, it is considered unethical to redefine boundaries once you have taken a substance. Since the "activated you" is in an altered state, it can no longer offer informed consent for the "sober you" that will return to normal consciousness in a few hours. A desire to shift boundaries mid-journey could feel good in the moment, but may cause a great deal of shame, guilt, rupture, and necessary repair work after the experience. It shouldn't have to be said, but unless you have explicitly decided that physical intimacy or sex will be a part of your experience, this should never occur in a professional psychedelic setting.

Stuck in a state of desperation, many seekers may spend more time researching an upcoming appliance purchase than they will their psychedelic facilitator, retreat center, or experience. It's important to recognize there is no lemon law or return policy for your psychedelic journey. If you don't know if your values align with your facilitator and aren't sure how to make that determination, slow down or pause your process long enough to figure it out. Ask for help from someone who has experience, or better yet, only work with referrals from people you trust. It is your responsibility to become an informed consumer.

Without question, some behavior will always be unethical and irresponsible. In no way am I condoning that behavior. But before you decide to go deeply into this work, it is incredibly important for you to have an understanding of where you draw the line between safety and discomfort. If you are unsure, please start your psychedelic journey at the level where you're currently working (clinical, therapeutic, or spiritual), consider first gaining some experience with breathwork, and start with substances lower on the relative power scale.

Nondirective vs. Directive Approaches

Imagine you've just ingested some magic mushrooms at a music festival. While you only took a medium dose, you're having a much more powerful experience than expected. You head to the back of the festival grounds and lie on your blanket. Your body starts trembling, you close your eyes, and you go deeper and deeper into your experience. The tremble turns into a noticeable shake, and you begin audibly moaning loud enough to draw the attention of those around you. A nearby festivalgoer notices what's happening and comes to your aid. Depending on their background and experience level, a few things could happen next:

1. They could call the medical team, who might arrive and use a high-powered pharmaceutical to sedate you.
2. They could call law enforcement, who might arrive and arrest you.
3. They could be a trained therapist and inform you that your body is simply releasing old childhood abuse.
4. Or they could calmly sit next to you, prevent you from harming yourself or others, and allow your process to unfold in whatever way it would like.

The first two options would not be ideal. At first, the third option seems reasonable, but what if you never experienced childhood abuse? Because of the hyper-suggestibility induced by psychedelics, after the experience, you might fixate on this possibility and start questioning your memory. You might wonder if you've actually repressed memories and if maybe someone did abuse you as a child. With this uncertainty, you might begin a new quest to uncover these lost memories, never fully knowing if they were true or simply implanted by a well-meaning bystander. We then come to the fourth option, the only truly nondirective solution. Here, the kind stranger holds space for you, allowing your inner healing intelligence to arise naturally. Volunteers use this nondirective approach at the Fireside Project and the Zendo Project (harm reduction initiatives that frequently provide on-site support for festivals, concerts, and other events where psychedelics are commonly used) as a very effective harm reduction method.

One oversimplified way to think of an experience is to ask yourself, "Who will be in the driver's seat of my experience?" If your facilitator is in the driver's seat, they are choosing the destination and deciding how you'll get there. Conversely, a completely nondirective approach will put your facilitator in the back seat. They will make sure you don't fall asleep and crash the car, but they'll be very "hands-off" throughout your experience. This shifts all the responsibility to you, your inner healer, and the medicine to figure out where to go and how to get there.

I like to think of this as a spectrum. Directive and nondirective are at either end, but there's a "Goldilocks path" that feels just right and sits somewhere in the middle. This middle path allows you to remain in the driver's seat with your facilitator sitting next to you—sometimes helping you drive, sometimes letting you do all the work yourself. You still get to choose the path and the speed of your journey, but they'll use their years of experience as a teacher to help you make more progress and learn a bit more quickly and easily.

A NONDIRECTIVE APPROACH

Some facilitators rely almost entirely on the medicine to heal. While they will keep you safe and hold a grounded seat during the experience, should difficult things arise during your process, they will often let you handle the situation on your own. This is a nondirective approach, and it is frequently seen among Indigenous practitioners and those who have studied with an Indigenous teacher.

While assisting during a group ayahuasca ceremony many years ago, I encountered an individual who began having a very frightening experience. Approaching the boundaries of ego dissolution, blackness began to converge from both sides of their consciousness, and they felt their boundaries of Self disappearing. They called out for help, prompting myself and the *ayahuscaro* to approach. Again, they said, "Help! I cannot do this," to which the facilitator calmly and compassionately replied, "Yes, you can. Just breathe and pray." The participant, while having had a challenging experience, was perfectly fine after that.

It's possible to perceive this approach as cold and detached, but there was also deep healing, safety, and wisdom behind it. With complete trust, a facilitator allows the medicine and the participant to work together to achieve exactly what is necessary to heal. Even though the seeker may not have felt that way in the moment, at no time was their safety compromised. On the contrary, the firm physical, psychological, and energetic boundary held between facilitator and participant is a very clean and safe way to hold space, allowing each individual and their inner healer to do the heavy lifting.

A DIRECTIVE APPROACH

Now let's look at an example of a directive approach. Imagine you have chosen to work with a trained facilitator in a private session. You and your facilitator have worked together for some time, the facilitator has deep knowledge of your psychological process, and a great deal of trust has been developed within your relationship. As a part of your preparation work, it becomes very evident to you both that perfectionism and codependence are frequent causes of discomfort in your life. You've both agreed this is something you'd like to address in your work together.

Midway through your experience, a conversation arises that begins to expose your anger, resentment, and unhappiness with your parents. You begin talking about how emotionally unavailable they were during your childhood and how hard you had to work to receive their praise and affection. Dots begin to connect, and you start to realize that the behaviors you learned in childhood are the same unconscious thoughts that drive your perfectionism and codependence today.

At this point, your facilitator invites you to stand up and asks you to slip a large canvas ruck sack onto your back. What starts out as empty and light quickly changes when your facilitator begins filling up your backpack with rocks… heavy rocks. You quickly begin to feel the weight of this experience on your shoulders. In an instant, you realize how frequently your neck and shoulders hurt. Somatically, you begin to understand how much unnecessary weight you carry by holding on to responsibility that is not actually yours. The pack gets heavier and heavier, and your facilitator invites you to walk around the room and feel what it's like to walk through your life with all this unnecessary weight. The invitation is made to take it off whenever you're ready—but only when you've decided to let go of all the ruminations, perfectionisms, and codependence, and not a second before. The choice is all yours, and you are 100 percent responsible and in control of the experience.

Finally, after the discomfort of holding onto all these old beliefs gets too intense and you realize in your body, mind, and soul just how heavy and hard it is to walk around with all that weight, you slip the backpack off your shoulders and immediately feel a sense of freedom. In an instant, the need to manage other people's feelings is gone. You clearly feel the contrast between your old life and a new life, and you realize just how heavy those old thoughts truly were. In this moment, your facilitator asks if you're willing to commit to not picking the backpack up again. You pause and genuinely ask yourself if this is an agreement you're willing to make. You experience a full-body "yes." In that moment, you release your codependence for good.

This story is a real-life example of a directive approach. At some points, the facilitator was sitting in the driver's seat of your experience. A behavior that has plagued your life for decades was directly targeted and addressed because of the skilled approach of your facilitator and the trust and understanding developed during your preparation sessions. What may have taken years to unravel in therapy was somatically and energetically discharged in a mere moment.

A more directive approach can have advantages and disadvantages. The most significant advantage is that it can bring focus and speed to your process. Yes, it is possible that you and the medicine could have handled the issue on your own, but it's impossible to predict when that might have happened. It could have been addressed in that experience, or you may have had to wait years for an opportunity to arise. On the other hand, situations can quickly go awry if a facilitator makes broad assumptions or introduces new and unfamiliar content that had not been previously discussed within a session. Introducing irrelevant or unexpected content is a frequent cause of harm and confusion, and is often a sign of a poorly trained or unqualified facilitator.

A qualified facilitator who is knowledgeable of your background and unique process can bring awareness to parts of you that you are unaware of. A skilled facilitator can help you see your "shadow" (the unconscious parts of yourself that you reject, suppress, or are unaware of), then skillfully employ various healing and therapeutic techniques, offering more directive methods to explore and release those old patterns and beliefs. It is important to note that the disclosure, discussion, and mutual agreement of these patterns during your preparation sessions are a critical element when working in a directive manner.

A "GOLDILOCKS" APPROACH

So, how can you combine the best elements of a nondirective and directive approach? What might that scenario look like?

Imagine you have done multiple preparation sessions with an experienced and well-qualified facilitator. You know you have childhood trauma; you have shared this with your facilitator, and you've set an intention to begin safely addressing it. You and your facilitator have selected a private and safe setting. Emotionally evocative music is playing, and you start to feel a tremble in your body. Your facilitator, noticing your subtle movements, gently asks you questions that help you more deeply explore these sensations.

You hear a prompt like "Tell me what's happening." You bring some awareness to the trembling and share your response. Your facilitator encourages you to continue noticing the trembling, allowing it to simply be there, or maybe even grow in size and strength. The trembling then moves into an almost uncontrollable shaking. Tears well up in your eyes. Your facilitator asks, "If those tears had words, what would they say?" This question transports you back forty years, to when you first began experiencing the neglect and abuse you suffered as a child.

Wave after wave of violent shaking and sobbing arise from your body. Your facilitator is calmly sitting next to you, holding your hand, and encouraging you to stay with your experience and let go of anything that no longer serves you. In this moment, the mental image of your abuser comes into focus, and fear races through your body. Your facilitator asks if the adult version of you could go back in time and support the six-year-old "you" who is afraid and vulnerable. This feels possible, and you retreat into your most painful inner experience.

With the soft, slow, and gentle guidance of your facilitator, the adult you returns to the six-year-old you, you grasp the hand of your inner child, and you take this younger part of yourself to a safe place, far away from your abuser. Finally, out of harm's way, your facilitator asks the six-year-old version of you if they would like to say anything to your abuser. You can stand up for yourself for the first time in your life. You finally have the strength and willpower to be angry and say "STOP!" You shout and scream and say, "Leave me alone!"

Having regained some of the power that was viciously ripped away from you as a child, your facilitator asks how it might feel to try and send forgiveness to your abuser. At first, you're repulsed by the idea. There is still more anger and hurt inside. More space and time are given to allow these emotions to fully express themselves. After finally releasing all these emotions, there is nothing left to do but forgive.

With a kind heart and the tenderness of a loving mother, the words "I forgive you" come up as a whisper, and for the first time in your life, you experience a deep sense of peace. Your longtime tormentor can no longer hurt you. Your work with them is done, and they are left in the past. Your nervous system is no longer on high alert, and it feels like your anxiety has finally been turned down to a comfortable level.

If this story feels authentic, it's because it is. It could be told by countless souls who have healed using the power of psychedelics, combined with elements of somatic therapy, parts/inner child work, soul retrieval, and the incredible power of forgiveness. In many ways, it's Joseph Campbell's "hero's journey" (which we'll discuss further in chapter 15, "Experience"), encapsulated into mere minutes.

In this scenario, the sole reliance on your inner healer does carry some benefit. Allowing your process to unfold at its own rate offers a great deal of safety for your system. The content arises in the speed and order it desires, and the facilitator is there to hold space and offer compassion, empathy, and support only as needed. A nondirective style is more "hands-off" and may take on a clinical feel, though it benefits from not introducing any outside belief system into your process. This "middle-of-the-road" approach that combines elements of nondirective and directive styles is a very safe and practical approach to modern psychedelic-assisted psychotherapy, provided the facilitators can still show empathy and emotional support when needed.

WHICH APPROACH IS RIGHT FOR YOU?

Bruce Lee used the phrase "It is like the finger pointing to the moon…" in his movie *Enter the Dragon*. This phrase originates from an ancient Buddhist text called the *Shurangama Sutra*. In this text, the Buddha tells his students to imagine someone trying to show them the moon by pointing at it. It is the pointing finger that allows you to see the moon. But it is not the pointing finger that matters.

Think of your true Self as the moon; the finger represents the guidance and teachings of your facilitator. A skilled facilitator knows that the true goal of their work is for you to see your own moon, not to focus on their finger. They act as a bridge, rather than a gatekeeper, for you to experience your true Self.

When choosing an approach, you should carefully evaluate your options and communicate your desires to your facilitator. If you're considering a more directive approach, a great deal of trust in your facilitator and their medicine (in substance, training, and philosophy) is important. If the facilitator is more invested in you seeing their finger than the moon, then maybe that's not the facilitator for you.

If your facilitator ascribes to a different belief system than you, it's worth exploring this in more depth. I have found that almost every mystical tradition carries many similar beliefs, but they may use different words to describe those beliefs. When you peek underneath the covers of all the major religions, you will see many of the same teachings. The people delivering these teachings and the terminology may differ, but love, forgiveness, compassion, and acceptance are common characteristics of almost every healing tradition.

The best way to decide the right approach is to spend time with your facilitator. This could start with a free introduction call and continue throughout your preparation sessions. (If your facilitator does not do preparation, that could be all the information you need to decide not to do directive work with them.) When choosing a facilitator to do individual work—especially one with a more directive approach—you should avoid desperation at all costs. Once again, discernment is critical. Listen to your heart and trust your gut instincts.

Facilitator Training vs. Experience

When medical doctors progress through their training, they spend years studying in a classroom before they work directly with patients. Even after meeting their psychometric qualifications, more experienced doctors closely monitor and supervise all their patient interactions. The same goes for psychotherapists. After many years of study, therapists must complete thousands of supervised hours before becoming fully licensed. Conversely, most Indigenous psychedelic practitioners will have read no books on psychedelic facilitation, nor will they have taken an exam or become licensed by any certifying body you would know. Their expertise is all based on practical experience. Those working within an Indigenous lineage probably spent thousands of hours studying with their teachers, and many of their teachings will have come directly from the medicine they're serving rather than a book.

Facilitating psychedelics will continue to evolve as more legalization occurs throughout the world, but at the present moment, there are no universal standards, curricula, or educational prerequisites in place for becoming a psychedelic facilitator. Today's training in the psychedelic landscape is like the Wild West.

A "certification" from a training program may not be worth the paper it's printed on, because no agreed-upon standards exist for any of these programs. As a seeker, simply hearing "I am a certified guide" should mean nothing to you. One facilitator's certification could be three years of study and include substantial practical use. Another certification could be a three-month, self-guided, online course without a practicum of any kind. Both courses come with "certifications," but neither holds any weight beyond that of what the certificate holder feels it should hold. To make things even more complicated, some of the most experienced underground facilitators have no formal training, though they have been successfully helping clients heal for decades.

Many psychotherapists are interested in the healing potential of psychedelics, but do not want to risk their therapy license by serving psychedelics outside of the legal system. Many of these therapists may have received classroom education on the use of psychedelics but have little to no practical experience in expanded states of consciousness.

This begs the question: would you rather work with a facilitator with lots of book knowledge and no practical experience, or lots of practical experience and no book knowledge? Most seekers would say, "I want both." Unfortunately, because of the relative newness of psychedelics in Western culture and the fact that using psychedelics is still illegal in most jurisdictions, the possibility of finding practitioners with thousands of classroom hours *and* thousands of hours spent with the medicine will be difficult.

If your path feels unclear, my best suggestion is to work with a facilitator that:

1. Has been referred to you by a trusted source
2. Is qualified and able to serve a substance that's a three or lower on the relative power scale (discussed in chapter 12, "Dosing")
3. Makes you feel safe and seen
4. Doesn't have any of the "red flags" previously mentioned in this chapter

In the beginning, you simply don't know what you don't know, and all the quantitative analysis in the world cannot prepare you for the experience you're about to have. In this case, the best thing you can do is optimize for safety.

The Importance of Good Facilitation

If you are genuinely interested in doing deep healing work with psychedelics, the facilitator you choose to work with may be the single most crucial variable in your experience. This individual (or multiple individuals) will be responsible for nearly every aspect of your experience. They will play a large part in selecting and serving the medicine, preparing the setting, helping prepare your mindset, and assisting with integration.

A good facilitator can help you integrate a challenging experience into a profoundly positive outcome. A bad facilitator can wreak havoc on what could have been a positive experience. In all my years doing this work, I have found that healing can happen in a harmful journey just as readily as harm can happen in a healing journey. I can also assure you that healing is much sweeter and easier to integrate when we don't have to simultaneously untangle the complexities and confusion of harm.

When searching for a facilitator, try to let go of reductionist thinking. A reductionist analyzes and attempts to describe a complex phenomenon in terms of its simple or fundamental parts. If this is the strategy you employ when selecting your facilitator, you are doing yourself a disservice. Instead, slow down and zoom out. Ask yourself if you trust this person and if you would want to spend time working with them if psychedelics weren't involved. Do not choose to work with someone solely because they have access to the substance you would like to sit with. This is not a good enough reason to put your mental health in jeopardy.

Most importantly, learn to recognize who and what makes you feel safe. If shame, guilt, and self-judgment are common aspects of your everyday experience, do not sit with someone who intensifies these feelings. Bedside manner is critical in psychedelic work. With psychedelics, you are not only conscious but hyper-suggestible, lacking many of the boundary-creating faculties your psyche has developed to keep you safe. Your facilitator should make you feel safe, comfortable, and seen—and maybe even encourage you to be more vulnerable than you have ever been in your life.

There are good and bad facilitators, just like there are good and bad doctors, attorneys, and therapists. Finding opportunities is not complicated, as long as you're looking in a relatively populated area. Today, the main challenge is not with the supply of facilitators, but rather with their safety and ethics. After reading this chapter, you now have the information needed to seek and choose wisely.

Intention

Adagio for Strings op. 11 by Samuel Barber

Psychedelic use is a journey, but if you don't know the destination of that journey, how will you know when you've arrived?

It's important to create an intention for your experience before you begin. Think of an intention less as a "destination" and more as a "direction." If your intention is to "heal acute trauma," you may eventually arrive at your destination. There is no guarantee it will happen in one, five, or ten journeys, but releasing all the heavy residue and charge from a traumatic experience is absolutely possible with psychedelics. In other cases, with intentions such as "fostering more self-love or compassion toward others," there is literally no end to the size your heart can swell, and the work may be forever ongoing. A well-structured intention can act as a beacon of hope, guiding you in the direction of unlimited positive healing and growth.

At a practical level, an intention should be a few words (or a short phrase) to set the course for your experience. Some intentions are more straightforward than others. With acute trauma, your intention will probably relate to a specific incident, but it can also be much broader. Perhaps you want to focus on a pattern of underlying thoughts or behaviors. You might be struggling with a core emotional theme, such as fear, abandonment, guilt, or anger. People often orient their intentions toward releasing something they no longer need, cultivating a quality they desire, achieving the clarity to move forward, removing a negative behavior, or transforming, transmuting, or liberating stored energy in the body-mind-spirit.

Intentions represent our first and most powerful method of communicating our desires with the medicine and with Infinite Source. They frequently act as a rubric for integration, help us explore the meaning of the content we receive, and act as an anchor to ground us when the waters of our journey get rough. Intentions should be the opposite of goals. You can check a goal off your list when it's complete, but it is impossible to ever fully achieve an intention. However, you *can* consistently and consciously keep moving in its direction.

Crafting a Well-Formed Intention

Depending on the type of work you're doing, you can have intentions that are very targeted or very broad. "Help me release the fear and trauma from my assault" is a very targeted intention. A more generalized intention might be "Please show me what I need to see."

If you are a newcomer, I recommend starting with a more specific and practical intention. This approach can motivate you, bring focus to your work, and make you feel empowered and ready to begin your journey. Over time, should you choose to use psychedelics as an ongoing practice rather than a discrete experience, your intentions can raise in elevation and address broader themes. We'll explore this further in the following sections.

One way to evaluate a well-formed intention is to consider what your life would look like, or how it would feel or improve, if you made certain progress. If you cannot connect your intention to your day-to-day life and how you'd like it to change alongside the progress, then you may need further guidance.

Below are a few helpful guidelines for creating a well-formed intention.

Keep It Short

Your intention should be short and powerful. If you can't memorize it and say it in a single breath, it's too long. When you need it most, you should be able to recall your intention immediately.

Address the Root Cause

I like to think of intentions as trees. The further away you are from the roots, the less different the tree will be when you remove or heal one of its parts. You may require multiple journeys, integration work, or sessions with your coach or therapist before you are ready to address your core/root wounds. (You, your facilitator, and trusted care team members can help you determine the level at which to begin your work.) To the best of your ability, set your intention to go as deep as you feel comfortable. Remember that going too deep, too quickly could result in postexperience difficulties and even retraumatization.

Have a Positive Focus

One of my first spiritual teachers used to remind me that the Universe only responds to and with "yes." If you constantly say, "I am sick and tired of the life I'm living," then the Universe will affirmatively respond with, "Yes, you are sick and tired." When wording your intention, focus on what you're moving toward, rather than what you're moving away from. Instead of saying, "I want to let go of self-hatred," which has a negative focus, try incorporating a more positive approach by saying, "I want to embrace my ability to love myself."

Incorporate Virtues

Many ancient spiritual traditions, philosophies, and virtues can help us align our intention to what we need most. Scott Jeffrey, a transformational coach and author, explains that a "virtue" is an ideal quality or attribute considered beneficial for every individual in society.[54] After consolidating several sources, from various religions to positive psychology, he compiled the below list of primary virtues:

- Benevolence / Compassion / Kindness / Charity / Liberality / Love / Magnanimity
- Temperance / Moderation / Patience / Frugality
- Truthfulness / Honesty / Integrity / Sincerity
- Prudence / Wisdom / Knowledge / Intelligence
- Courage / Fortitude
- Justice / Righteousness / Honor
- Friendliness / Politeness / Courtesy
- Modesty / Humility
- Equanimity / Tranquility / Contentment

You may also want to consider incorporating the universal healing qualities of forgiveness, peace, harmony, humility, and gratitude.

For your intention, choose a virtue that is the opposite of the root cause of your suffering. For example, if addiction is the root cause you are addressing, incorporate the virtue of temperance. During your psychedelic experience, ask for guidance from the medicine or Infinite Source to teach you how to cultivate this positive virtue within yourself. And remember, you have to believe it to see it.

Let Go of Your Task List

Many newcomers arrive at their first experience with a notebook full of goals they'd like to achieve, tasks they'd like to complete, or problems they'd like to solve. This tracks well to the modern mindset and its desire for productivity, optimization, and achievement. Unfortunately, optimization and healing rarely pair well together.

If we follow the word "priority" back to its Latin root *prior*, the word was originally singular in nature and meant the "first and most important thing." Today, modern society complicates our lives, and many of us struggle with "prioritizing all our priorities." Overlying this scattered mindset onto your psychedelic experience can frequently cause more confusion than resolution.

Psychedelics do offer a higher-octane fuel for rapid transformation, but treating your journey like a race to be won will only serve to disappoint—and may even cause harm. On the path of healing, it is far better to walk than to run. Running dramatically increases your risk of falling and hurting yourself.

Intention comes after facilitation because your facilitator can be of great help in setting the heading on your compass. If you're starting with what feels like a long list of healing "tasks" or are engulfed in the fog of depression and malaise, work with your facilitator (or another helping professional) to examine the commonalities between the items on your task list. With enough curiosity and exploration, you should begin to find a common thread tying many of them together. Select the thread that is most important or reachable, and remember: the closer to the trunk or roots you can work, the more leaves will fall away all on their own.

How to Use Your Intention

Once you've documented your intention, it's important to consider how you'll use it—not just during your experience, but throughout your entire healing journey.

BEFORE THE PSYCHEDELIC EXPERIENCE

One of the most common methods of journey preparation is to meditate on your intention. If your intention is short enough, try using it as a mantra in your daily meditation practice. If your intention is longer, try sitting quietly and gently thinking about it, allowing your mind to wander and seeing what thoughts or feelings it brings up. This is the act of contemplation. Allow your unconscious mind an opportunity to play its part and show you what you need to see.

You can also ask yourself how you would feel if you made progress on your intention or imagine what your life would be if your intention had already come true. If your intention triggers positive sensations, soak in them and recognize what "feeling good" really feels like.

DURING THE PSYCHEDELIC EXPERIENCE

If you're doing a private journey, you can write your intention down on a large whiteboard and make it visible throughout your entire experience. Even in journeys where eyeshades are being used, there are many moments where you can reflect on your intention and see how it relates to the present moment.

If you're working in a group ceremony, you can write your intention down on a notecard and keep it near your mat or under your pillow. You can think about your intention from a shamanic or energetic perspective by selecting a small crystal, rock, or talisman, and blowing the energy of your intention into the object. When you hold this object throughout your experience, it will act as a powerful reminder of your desire and will help you remain centered and focused.

Another helpful method I use myself and with my clients is silently repeating my intention as I wait for the medicine to activate in my system. This anchors the intention in my psyche, helps me focus on why I'm doing the work, and is a wonderful tool to remember my intention when I really need it. Once you feel the medicine working, try not to hold on too tightly to your intention and allow the content of your experience to take the place of your recitation. When your journey starts to take you to a new place, try not to resist, trust the process, and learn from the sentience of the medicine. There is an old saying that goes, "If you want to make God laugh, just make a plan." Allow yourself to follow the medicine and resist the urge to direct and change the experience to meet your exact needs.

Note: there are a few exceptions to this rule of nonresistance. One is if things feel like they're going really great, and the other is if things feel like they are going very badly. During very positive moments of our journey, it's easy to get lost in feelings of bliss. Remember to consciously connect these positive feelings back toward your intention, which can be a powerful way to shift your negative beliefs around a challenging topic. Conversely, if the waves of your experience get super rough and the content becomes challenging, you can get lost in negativity. One of my best suggestions to keep yourself grounded during these difficult moments is to ask yourself, "How does this experience or content relate to my intention?" By asking yourself this question, you can easily transform a terrifying experience into valuable content that can give you deep insight into your unconscious mind, both in the moment and later during integration. Remember, as a nonspecific amplifier, the medicine is only showing you what lies within. These experiences are a powerful and visceral opportunity for you to see and experience your outer world represented by your inner experience.

AFTER THE PSYCHEDELIC EXPERIENCE

Your intention should act as the through line connecting each phase of your experience. Continue revisiting your intention as often as you need. We will discuss specific ways to use your intention after an experience in chapter 16, "Integration." Keep in mind that your intention should be your "true north" until you have successfully integrated your experience to the best of your ability—keep moving toward it.

SAMPLE INTENTIONS

In the early stages of your journey, crafting an intention can be hard. Having worked with thousands of journeyers over the past decade, I've documented many intentions that have proven very effective. If one of these can be a helpful starting point, by all means, incorporate it into your work. Remember, a very unique soul doing their very unique work created each of these for their very unique experience. Please work with your care team to craft an intention that moves *your* soul.

- Learn to relax
- Experience (self-)love, rest, and inner peace
- Turn down the volume
- Let go and be more present
- Remember who you are
- To reveal and heal the parts of me that are depressed, lazy, and undisciplined
- Feel safe with my thoughts and feelings
- Find my voice, stop blaming, and let go of being a victim
- Love and express my emotional, sexual, and loving self
- Receive clarity and perspective on my priorities
- Experience more peace and worthiness from within
- Allow myself to feel worthy
- Stop fighting and believe in myself
- Let go of fear and criticism; experience safety
- F*ck It! And have FUN!
- Rediscover a life of play
- Open, observe, discern, reconcile
- Surrender and connect to the universe
- Release obsession; find rest and confidence
- Authentically show up in my life
- Accept my true nature
- Experience joy and love myself
- Release judgment to accept help and belonging
- Connect and make friends with my survival brain
- Trust, surrender, and be me
- Make friends with my inner critic
- Safely release the past
- Receive help letting go of skepticism
- Learn to love when I feel out of control
- To be seen and believe in myself
- Love, accept, and "be" authentic
- Trust and release

I asked some psychonaut friends for a few of their favorite intentions. Considering they have more experience in their practice, these intentions place more trust in medicine and their own inner healing intelligence:

+ "Show me whatever I need to work through for the highest good of the collective."
+ "Show me what I need to know, see, hear, or feel in this moment."
+ "Help me connect more deeply and freely."
+ "Connect me with everything I am—show me truth, love, and clarity."
+ "Help me come home into myself and let go of what does not align with who I am."

Notice that none of these intentions have anything to do with surface-level symptoms or changes. All of them show trust in the medicine's power to give them exactly what they *need*, assigning little value to what they *want*.

A Journey into the Unknown

As a newcomer, a strong intention may be one of the most helpful elements of your early psychedelic experiences. As you journey into parts unknown, a compass is your most valuable tool. Your intention serves as your compass, reminding you of your true north.

While we may try our best to maintain our compass heading, it's also important not to force it. In many of life's journeys, the unexpected will happen. Stormy weather may take you off course, and you may find it challenging to reorient toward your heading. That's okay. Remember, one of the primary benefits of psychedelics is that they show us what we cannot see in normal waking consciousness. Focusing too heavily on your intention can cause you to miss some beautiful and vital teachings on your new and unexpected path. As we'll discuss in chapter 14, "Mindset," surrender is one thing even more important than intention.

Regardless of your intention or how much progress you make toward it, keep in mind that a single psychedelic experience rarely offers full resolution. The goal of each experience is to receive greater awareness and insight into the next step of your healing journey. Without an intention, you don't know where you're going, and if you don't know that, there's a good chance you'll never get there.

Dosing

"Third Cup" by Larimar Sound Alchemy

Archimedes said, "Give me a place to stand, and I shall move the earth." In physics parlance, he taught us how to use minimal effort to achieve maximum impact. It was Archimedes who explored using a fulcrum and lever (of just the right size) to mechanically move objects. If we think of the heavy residue stored in our body as objects to be moved, the length of our lever can equate to dosage.

After set and setting, the three-legged "psychedelic stool" regards dosage as the third-most critical variable. And while dosage is such an essential factor in the success and productivity of one's psychedelic experience, it is also one of the most inconsistent and confusing to understand.

With most modern pharmaceutical prescriptions, a doctor prescribes a specific medication and dosage, proven with high accuracy to address an acute condition and achieve a desired outcome. One place in modern medicine where the formula is rarely this straightforward is the prescription of pharmaceuticals for mental illness (see the appendix for further exploration on this topic). The brain and the mind are variables that make dosing pharmaceuticals—and psychedelics—very complicated and require additional patience, expertise, and nuance.

Many people on antidepressants, antipsychotics, or other similar medications spend months—if not years—continually tailoring and tweaking their cocktail dosage to reach some measure of stability, all the while trying to reduce as many adverse side effects as possible. Selecting the appropriate substance and dose in psychedelics, especially for first timers, is a lot like prescribing SSRIs. There's no perfect formula or guaranteed effect.

Let's think about the substance and dosage of psychedelics in terms of air travel. The dosage is the amount of fuel you need to get to your desired destination. The lower relative power of MDMA might be akin to jet fuel, while ayahuasca might be more like rocket fuel. The MDMA passenger jet leaves the ground at a gentler and slower angle of ascent than the ayahuasca blast of a launching rocket. The higher the dosage, the more extreme the forces leaving the ground, all compounded by the relative power of your substance of choice.

There's a reason astronauts have a great deal more training than airline passengers. As I often say, "Mushrooms for the masses, ayahuasca for the brave." Keep this in mind as the variables of dose and substance intersect.

Dosing Sizes

Every substance discussed in this book has unique dosing guidelines. On top of that, the number of variables that affect how a substance will interact with your system during any given journey is truly unmeasurable. Taking three grams of mushroom one night may cause little to no effect; taking the same dose for a subsequent experience may be a roller coaster ride you never expected. Furthermore, the more experience you gain and the cleaner your system becomes, the less medicine you will need to ingest to achieve a powerful experience.

Broadly speaking, there are four categories of dosing will be helpful to understand in your psychedelic work:

MICRODOSE

Microdosing is probably the fastest-growing practice among new psychedelic users today and refers to taking a tiny amount of a psychedelic substance (frequently psilocybin or LSD) to improve neuroplasticity and overall mood, and even reduce symptoms related to depression. Microdoses are intended to be *subhallucinogenic* compared to the larger doses noted below. This means that if you feel a change in physical sensation or visual perception, you've taken more than a microdose.

Microdosing is typically performed using some specific cadence or protocol. Some people take their microdose for one day, then take two days off. Others may dose for four days and then take three days off. Unlike going to your doctor and receiving a daily prescription, microdosing requires patience and self-awareness to determine the substance, dosing, and frequency best suited for your body-mind-spirit.

There is debate about the long-term benefits and risks of microdosing. Many people report positive effects while taking the substance but find that their symptoms return upon cessation. This begs the question of whether microdosing is truly creating long-term change, or if it's simply another "medication" for reducing symptoms. (Even if it is the latter, the organic nature of these substances may be better for your body than the ones coming from your pharmacy, and they usually come with far fewer side effects.)

Microdosing is often reported to widen our window of tolerance and make us more conscious of our thoughts and actions. This could be of considerable benefit when working with a coach or therapist. The greater cognitive flexibility that microdosing offers may allow you to go deeper and work faster with your care team. For many, microdosing acts as a gateway into more profound journeys.

Note: One of the more common requests I hear is a desire to use microdosing to be more "creative and productive" at work. If this is your intention, I invite you to reflect on the energetic signature of *what* you are creating. If you can confidently say that your work is either a) furthering your true purpose in life, or b) is in service to love, acceptance, unity, peace, harmony, and a holistic reduction in suffering, then by all means, use microdosing to further your pursuits. On the other hand, if your intention to be more productive is in service to power, control, and money, then there is a better-than-average chance the microdosing may help you achieve that at the cost of prolonging your suffering. What you're actually doing is cultivating a short-term reward that feels good in the moment, rather than cultivating a deeper sense of peace, joy, and freedom from within. When you think about why you want to microdose at work, ask yourself where the energy of that thought would intersect with the Map of Consciousness. Is that the energy you are seeking to cultivate in your life?

MINI DOSE

Most people classify a "mini dose," or a "museum dose," as having both physical and mental effects while still being manageable in most settings. A mini dose is the area above a microdose, where one feels the physical and psychological effects of the substance, but below a dose capable of pushing you into new and unfamiliar psychospiritual realms or barriers.

Ram Dass described a mini dose as allowing the user to operate on the astral plane without the danger of losing one's sense of conscious awareness. When considering using psychedelics with a sincere intention, a mini dose is a safe place to start for a hike or a walk in the park.

MACRO DOSE

Users engaging with a "macro dose" are most often moving into the realm of clinical, therapeutic, or spiritual use. For those who have no psychedelic experience, it is not recommended to use a macro dose alone. Individuals in this category should work with a facilitator (or, at a minimum, an experienced trip sitter), as the potential for new and challenging thoughts and experiences grows exponentially as a dose increases.

Those with more psychedelic experience will often use a macro dose to expand conscious awareness. Macro doses of any of the classical psychedelics carry with them the potential of "ego death," where an individual can lose consciousness, awareness, and connection with subjective reality. In this temporary dissolving of the ego, an individual may—metaphorically or spiritually—experience their own "death." It is recommended to have support during and after an experience like this, as it can be extremely disorienting for newcomers and experienced users alike.

MEGA DOSE

Because the four classical psychedelics cannot cause death from overdose, some dedicated explorers choose to take extremely high doses. The late Kilindi Iyi, head instructor and technical adviser of the Tamerrian Martial Art Institute, frequently discussed mega dose journeys of mushrooms—sometimes upward of thirty to forty grams, or ten times a normal dose.

In a paper published in the *Journal of Alcohol and Drugs*, entitled "LSD Overdoses: Three Case Reports," authors Haden and Woods discuss the eventual outcomes of three separate cases where individuals accidentally consumed massive doses of LSD (in one case, 550 times the regular recreational dose). None of these instances ended in fatality or long-term negative outcomes. In fact, one of the participants experienced a complete discontinuation of her bipolar symptoms.[55]

By mentioning it here, I am not encouraging the use of mega doses, only offering information for anyone interested in attempting more profound work above the macro dose range. Mega doses are rarely enjoyable and should never be attempted without adequate support before, during, and after the experience.

Two helpful words to consider when discussing dosage ranges are *power* and *force*. Think of power as a natural and organic ability to influence outcomes without overexertion or manipulation. Force, on the other hand, involves exerting pressure or coercion to achieve a result. Revisiting the filter analogy from part I, power is the natural speed at which a filter is capable of cleaning the fishtank without unnecessarily taxing the motor. Force could be applied by plugging the motor into a 220-volt outlet, hoping to achieve higher-than-normal outcomes. While this strategy may work, you also run the risk of burning out the motor.

Each of the substances discussed in chapter 9 was given a relative power that aligns to the Macro Dose category above. With all the classic psychedelics, pushing beyond generally accepted dosing sizes will undoubtedly cause an increase in force. Quadrupling an average dose of mushrooms could result in an ayahuasca-like experience, but using force to achieve this outcome could be challenging for your body, mind, and spirit to metabolize. Please keep power and force in mind when evaluating the intersection of substance and dosage.

Methods for Determining Dosage

There are many methods available to determine dosage, and they each have pros and cons. Until you have experience with a substance, you will have little understanding of how your body will react. Each organic strain, recipe, and brew will have different concentrations of the psychedelic you are ingesting. A typical Golden Teacher mushroom may have less than half the amount of psilocybin as an Albino Penis Envy mushroom of the same weight. If you don't know the strain you're taking, you could have some very intense experiences that you may not be prepared for.

Ideally, you will do enough preparation work with your facilitator that both of you can confidently select an appropriate dose for your experience. If you have no context for the substance you'll be ingesting, it's best to rely on the dosing direction of a qualified facilitator. As you gain more experience and develop a personal relationship with the medicine, you can play a more active role in the dosing conversation.

A great way to begin the process of determining the right dose for you is by asking yourself one simple question: During your experience, do you want to feel underwhelmed, overwhelmed, or "just right"? Understanding your intention and communicating that to your facilitator ahead of time can go a long way toward creating the experience you're looking for.

Additionally, many online sources provide generally accepted dosing guidelines for almost every substance imaginable. For example, a quick look on the Erowid website for LSD dosing shows a threshold/micro dose to be 10–20 μg, a strong/macro dose to be 150–400 μg, and a heavy/mega dose to be 400+ μg.[56] Having some awareness of these standard metrics may help you and your facilitator decide on a dose that is appropriate for you and your intention. Even so, some body-mind-spirts are more sensitive than others and require less medicine. Others are much more resistant and require higher doses. Factors like metabolism, neurosis, and personality also play an important role in dosing. As a general rule, go "low and slow." And remember: you can always take more, but you can never take less.

Remember, it is crucial to consider all factors when determining the appropriate psychedelic dosage, such as your overall physical and mental health, trauma history, medical history, previous experience with psychedelics, and the specific goals of the treatment. Working with a qualified facilitator is very helpful in ensuring a safe and tailored approach to dosing.

Below, you'll find two additional methods that may be helpful in determining the right dose for you.

For links to other dosing-related websites or to acquire an at-home kit to test the potency of your substances, visit the resources section of PsychedelicIQ.com.

SPIRITUAL/INTUITIVE METHOD

Depending on the type of facilitator you're working with, dosing could feel less scientific and more intuitive. Facilitators who've worked with their substances for some time usually have a good idea of the potency needed to get you where you want to go. Ask your facilitator how they determine dosage and see how their explanation feels in your system. It's all just information; you should be able to offer feedback and ask as many questions as you need to feel comfortable.

I think it's important to note that for substances that have a potential for overdose, it's absolutely critical to pay attention to the generally accepted guidelines. For classical psychedelics, higher doses may be incredibly difficult but are not life-threatening. For substances like ketamine and MDMA, high doses could cause a medical emergency or death.

BODY WEIGHT METHOD

In most clinical studies, dosing is determined by body weight. The typical psilocybin dosage in these studies varies but usually falls within twenty to thirty milligrams (mg) of psilocybin per seventy kilograms (kg), or 154 pounds, of body weight. This dosage is usually high enough to maximize the chances of a mystical experience while minimizing the potential for adverse reactions.

Because of the scientific nature of these experiments and the synthetic nature of the psilocybin, researchers can measure the exact amount being served to their patients. Unless you're participating in a clinical study, it's doubtful you will have access to synthetic psilocybin or measurements of this accuracy. As noted above, psilocybin content can change dramatically between strains and even individual batches, so testing any new substance or batch is always a best practice.

Keep in mind that body weight is not the only factor considered when determining the appropriate dosage. In clinical research settings, weight-adjusted dosing is often used to account for potential differences in drug effects among individuals of different body weights. This approach aims to provide a more standardized and personalized dosing regimen. However, it is essential to note that the relationship between body weight and psychedelic effects is complex and not fully understood. Other studies have suggested that body weight may not significantly impact the subjective effects of psilocybin within a specific dosage range. For example, one recent study found that the intensity of psychedelic experiences after taking a twenty-five-milligram dose of psilocybin was unaffected by differences in body mass index (BMI).

When Dosing Triggers Your Natural Defenses

When working with psychedelics, bigger doesn't necessarily mean better. Consider this: the higher the dose, the more your mind and body will experience stress. The greater the stress, the more strongly your instinctual, mental defense mechanisms will activate. The more strongly your defense mechanisms activate, the harder they fight against the psychedelic. This is your ego attempting to ensure your safety.

Unfortunately, it's impossible to know what size of dose will activate these defenses. One person may not even feel three grams of mushrooms, but another could have an incredibly powerful experience. This makes dosing, especially for beginners, challenging. All that said, doses that trigger our natural defense mechanisms often result in one of four types of experiences: a nonexperience, a painful experience, a delayed experience, or a second-chance experience. More on each of these below.

NONEXPERIENCES

When some people ingest a moderate to high dose of a psychedelic, their natural defenses can activate so strongly that they negate the effects of the medicine alto-gether. For example, I have often served two individuals (similar in age, size, and physical health) the exact same dose of mushrooms. One of these individuals can feel absolutely nothing, while the other has a profound experience. There is no definitive, rational, or measurable explanation for these nonexperiences, though I suspect they are highly correlated with hypervigilance, a strong desire for control, and an unconscious inability to surrender.

PAINFUL EXPERIENCES

This type of experience is one I would never wish on anyone. As dosages increase, it's possible that your ego can become savage. This is not the type of psychedelic misery you've read about, where you're slaying demons in the pit of hell. In this type of experience, there is little to no psychedelic experience at all. Instead, you simply feel the misery in your mind and body, and you can't wait for it to end. Body aches and pains, severe fatigue, and mental confusion are common symptoms of a painful experience. Depending on the dose and the substance, this miserable experience could last anywhere from four to twelve hours.

DELAYED EXPERIENCES

Delayed experiences can be a surprising type of psychedelic experience. In rare cases, individuals may take a macro dose of a psychedelic and feel nothing for hours. Then, upon shifting their focus to another activity or lying down to rest, they begin having the journey they intended to have hours before.

It is important for individuals to handle nonexperiences with patience and be extra cautious, just in case a nonexperience becomes a delayed experience. Ideally, seekers should not drive or put themselves in unsafe or out-of-control settings after a nonexperience until they're sure the lingering effects of the substance have passed. Getting behind the wheel of a car or being in a public setting when your journey starts to happen can be frightening and dangerous.

SECOND-CHANCE EXPERIENCES

These experiences start out as nonexperiences or painful experiences but could transform and become incredibly profound, emotional, or mystical beyond your wildest imagination. If you find yourself in the middle of a painful experience, ask for help, do your best to relax, focus on your breath, and practice being in the present moment. With enough surrender, relief could be a breath away. There is a Taoist principle I find helpful in these moments that says, "You are the maker of music stands, who makes no music stands, yet music stands are made," which paradoxically exemplified the ancient Chinese principle called *wu wei*, which translates to mean "effortless action."

Seeking the Minimum Effective Dose (MED)

One of the best proactive measures for dealing with difficult experiences is to rely on the pharmacology principle of minimum effective dose (MED). Coined by Dr. Theodore Woodward, MED emphasizes the importance of using the smallest amount of a drug or treatment that produces the desired therapeutic effect.

MED is meant to minimize the risk of side effects and complications associated with higher doses of medications or treatments while still achieving the intended outcome. Thought leader Tim Ferris popularized the concept more recently, and people have since applied it broadly in various fields (including fitness, productivity, and personal development) as a principle for optimizing results with minimal effort and resources.

When we look at the four types of challenging journeys above, all of them represent complications associated with higher dosages. Many modern mindsets are attuned to optimization and intent on squeezing every drop of productivity out of a single experience. This is the same mindset that encourages seekers to bring task lists into their experience, hoping to leave their journey full of dopamine—less from the medicine and more from a boost in productivity.

Unfortunately, I've had to assist countless seekers in untangling their "heroic dose" journeys. In reality, heroic doses don't make heroes. These journeys frequently cause us to feel worse than we did before the experience. Taking too high of a dose might make us feel less like a hero and more like a lightweight boxer who spent four hours in the ring with Mike Tyson.

We have a window of tolerance toward situations that stimulate us. When situations or individuals trigger us in our everyday lives, we set healthy boundaries to limit our exposure to those situations and keep us within our safe and comfortable window of tolerance. In psychedelics, if you choose a dose that is too far outside your window of tolerance, you may end up with more than your system can handle. (This is where f*cking around a little too much may help you find out more than you bargained for.)

Something not discussed nearly enough is the idea that higher dosages are not required to do deep work. This is yet another belief encouraged by the idea that "more is better." I have worked with countless clients who have had incredibly powerful experiences on 1.5 grams of mushrooms, a single dose of MDMA, or 100 µg of LSD. But with more experience and further healing, and as our vibrations rise, two things happen: we discover we *can* do higher doses, and we discover that they are unnecessary to our healing journey.

If you have been suffering for years or decades, desperation may be calling you to the path of psychedelics. This desperation often leads you to the dosing mistake of "too much, too fast," which frequently causes more harm than good.

If you've already had a difficult or challenging experience and would like more information on how to work through it, please refer to the section titled Bad Trip vs. Challenging Journey in chapter 15, "Experience."

Tips for a Smooth Journey

For many years, I thought my healing had to be "strong and hard." This mindset caused a lot of undue harm and countless delays in feeling more happiness and freedom in my life. Today, I do not believe that this work has to be so hard. While many facilitators work from set standards and practices they were taught, I believe getting the most out of any experience in the sweetest and easiest way possible is the optimal path to healing. With this in mind, I'd like to offer a few helpful suggestions I've learned in my own work and in working with many of my clients.

KNOW YOUR DOSAGE

Knowing your dose can inherently cause bias. I once worked with a client who adamantly stated they could never take more than 1.5 grams of mushrooms because their last experience was so horrible. In fact, this same client went on to have a beautiful and healing experience taking three grams. It would have undoubtedly activated their defenses if they had known they were taking three grams before the experience, and it could have turned a healing journey into a challenging experience. Their anxiety, need for control, and preconceived beliefs about dosing were getting in the way of their healing far more than the actual dose.

Customizing dosing to each individual is critical, especially in the early stages of your medicine work. When working with a trusted facilitator, they should offer you a dose within your tolerance and agreed-upon range. In my practice, I frequently tell clients, "A medium dose is around three grams of mushrooms. Most clients fall within the range of two to four grams." If clients are okay operating with that level of certainty, I will intuitively select a dose that I sense will work well for them.

Conversely, things can quickly go awry when individuals sit in a more dogmatic group or tradition, where dosing is strict and preset. For instance, some *ayahuascaros*, lineages, and traditions require participants to drink a specific number of "cups" during a ceremony. For a newcomer, this removes all power of choice and could be very challenging, if not harmful. If you are going to be sitting in a group ceremony, it is wise to ask more about this before you decide to participate. Unfortunately, the increased suggestibility, dissolved boundaries, peer pressure, and power dynamics in the moment may encourage you to do something you wish you hadn't.

If you sit in a session without knowing your dosage, please remember to inquire after the fact. Knowing this and comparing it to the depth of your experience can help you better plan for future experiences.

DIVIDE YOUR DOSE

A common practice for many facilitators is to take a first dose, then wait sixty to ninety minutes before taking one or more booster doses. The first, small dose allows the energy to build in the body at a gentler slope (think about the trajectory of an airplane taking off). Then, once you've been lifted off the ground, the booster dose more rapidly propels you deeper into the experience, creating a hockey-stick-like effect.

If you have previously struggled with higher doses, work with your facilitator to space out doses in a way that gives you the effects of a higher dose but does not overly tax your body and nervous system or push too hard against your natural defenses.

WAIT LONGER THAN YOU THINK

It happens all too often. You take a dose of a substance, wait, and when nothing happens, you take a second dose—only to have the first dose kick in late and catapult you further than you intended to go. Lo the intelligence and sneaky unpredictability of the medicine!

Sometimes, factors like metabolism or the amount of food in your stomach can slow down the onset of a psychedelic, but more often, it can be traced back to our natural defense systems. Putting it another way: a watched pot never boils.

If you get stuck asking yourself, "Is it happening yet? Is it happening yet?" you are likely to slow down the onset. This is a common thought rumination pattern for newcomers that can frequently be driven (consciously or unconsciously) by uncertainty and fear. If you're in the appropriate setting, consider doing a little yoga, dancing, or just chatting to take your mind off "watching the pot." If you're sitting in a group setting where these things are not possible, try meditating and focusing on the breath coming in and out of your nose. The goal is to distract and shift the focus of your "protector parts" just long enough for the psychedelic to sneak in through the back gate. You can always take more but never less, so wait a little longer than you think before doubling your dose.

WATCH OUT FOR THAT SECOND EXPERIENCE—IT'S A DOOZY

Another thing I frequently see is individuals that have a profound and life-changing experience on their first journey and then crash into hurricane-sized waves during their second experience. I attribute a lot of this to expectations. You're just along for the ride on your first journey, and you and your nervous system don't know what to expect. But once you've had that mind-blowing, mystical first experience, a part of you—conscious or not—wants to go back to that place. The part of your mind trying to achieve the same experience is the same part preventing you from actually having it.

Much like a meditation practice, the minute you want something to happen, it won't. You'll get there only when you let go of your desire to be somewhere. My suggestion for second-time seekers is to cut your dose by one-third (or even one-half) and flatten your ascent by dividing the dose into multiple servings. Let the medicine come on slowly, allow your body to get used to the sensations, and then use your booster to go deeper.

Sometimes, Dosage Doesn't Matter

About two weeks before writing this section, I was in a ceremony with my teachers, sitting with one night of ayahuasca and two nights of wachuma. Because I was traveling the next day, I opted only to take a small amount of wachuma, roughly one-third of my usual dose.

This specific substance continues to be one of the most challenging medicines for me to understand and explain. During a regular ceremony, it's not uncommon for me to ingest three cups of wachuma and have an incredibly gentle experience. I might even put some of these ceremonies in the nonexperience category.

But on this particular night—after ingesting only one cup of the same medicine as the previous night, with the same preparation, location, facilitators, food in my stomach, and pretty much all the other variables being equal—I had one of the most powerful experiences of my life.

Why this happens is more of a question for philosophers than scientists. Richard Tarnas, an author, cultural historian, and former instructor at the California Institute for Integral Studies, believed that archetypal astrology (a branch of astrology that emphasizes the patterns and archetypes that appear in human experience and their correlations with planetary alignments) could affect our psychedelic journeys. In his book *Cosmos and Psyche: Intimations of a New World View*, Tarnas explores the connections between planetary cycles and historical events, proposing that cosmic alignments relate to major shifts in history and culture. Applying these theories to individual consciousness, the possibility exists that the alignment of the planets at the time of a journey could affect the outcome.

While Tarnas's theory could be true, my teachers would chalk it up to the spirit of the medicine. These spirits are in charge, and regardless of our plans, the way they decide to work within our physiology is far more up to them than it is to us. To be clear, wachuma is not the only medicine that can cause this reaction. I have had many experiences with both mushrooms and ayahuasca where the exact dosing of the same medicine on two consecutive nights offered a radically different experience. The moral of the story is to expect the unexpected and plan for safety.

Always Plan for Safety

There are so many factors that affect one's ability to work with psychedelics. Trauma, control, neurosis, and rumination play major roles in the dosing equation. All of these should be considered and will shift from experience to experience.

It usually requires a few journeys to begin developing a relationship with the medicine. Once this relationship begins to form, you will have a better understanding of how the medicine works in your system. Safety—internally and externally—is something you should always prioritize. If you plan for safety, you can rest assured that while you may not get what you want, you will get what you need—no matter the dosage.

Setting

"Heart Song (Heart Chakra)" by Jonathan Goldman,
Sarah Benson, Andi Goldman

I n a fascinating and almost unbelievable story first reported in 2022 by *Outside Magazine*, Jim Harris, a mountaineering instructor turned adventure photographer, was involved in a snow kiting accident that left him paralyzed from the chest down. [57] He needed to use a wheelchair, and doctors told him he would never walk again. Jim's life had changed forever.

Later, when a friend invited him to a jam band concert at a local music festival, he opted to go and enjoy himself to the best of his ability. Jim could no longer consume alcohol because of his fragile nervous system, so while the String Cheese Incident played onstage, Jim opted to try some magic mushrooms.

Enjoying the music and setting sun, Jim noticed something strange: some activity had returned to his hamstring muscle, which had been completely inactive since his accident. With wonder and some degree of hesitation, he showed his friend who was a physical therapist. They marveled together at what had been impossible for Harris earlier that day. He felt excited, but also confused. He'd been looking for a recreational experience, a way to feel normal and connect with other people. Instead, the trip was therapeutic: his mind and body communicated in a way that they hadn't since his accident.

Today, almost a decade after his original accident, Jim successfully walks with a cane and can even ski and ride a mountain bike.

I've included this story for three purposes. First, besides healing the mind and the spirit, we are discovering more and more about the profound healing potential psychedelics can have on the physical body. Second, what started with an entirely recreational intention miraculously morphed into a healing one. And finally, and most appropriately for this chapter, this shows that individuals can heal anywhere, without the need for a clinical setting or the jungles of South America. The substances themselves are rather indiscriminate with setting. The counterpoint is that we—and more specifically our minds—are not.

In Jim's case, the setting didn't seem to cause significant negative issues with his experience. Because so many variables can affect the overall journey, it's impossible to fully understand how a recreational intention combined with a recreational setting initiated such profound healing. We also don't know exactly what kind of dosage was being used, or exactly what strain of mushrooms. The tricky part of working with psychedelics is that it's just as likely that one of these variables could turn a healing experience into a harrowing one.

What Is Setting?

Setting refers to "the physical, social, and cultural environment in which the experience takes place."[58] Physically speaking, this could include the room you're in, the art on the walls, or the comfy blanket you're holding. Socially, it includes the people you're with. And culturally, it includes the influences, norms, and laws of wherever you're journeying.

Setting is one of the most critical variables to optimize for your psychedelic experience. More than sixty years after its importance was first declared by Timothy Leary, most psychonauts still agree that "set and setting" are the most highly appreciated elements of any psychedelic preparation.

Though he coined the phrase, Leary was not the first to cultivate these concepts. Indigenous *ayahuascaros* have been using specially crafted structures, drumming, singing, and tobacco for thousands of years to create and cultivate an ideal setting for their work. If we zoom out farther than psychedelics, setting has been important since humans first began performing rituals. Almost every spiritual and religious tradition or rite of passage honors the concepts of set and setting when performing important rituals and ceremonies.

In his review, "The Evolved Psychology of Psychedelic Set and Setting: Inferences Regarding the Roles of Shamanism and Entheogenic Ecopsychology," Michael James Winkleman writes:

> *There are features of optimal psychedelic ritual, set and setting derived from of our evolved psychology. For example, most prefer psychedelic sessions at night and would feel it strange to start a ceremony at midday. Singing, drumming and dancing are frequent aspects of psychedelic rituals, but not wrestling, swimming or mountain climbing. Feeling compelled to sing a song or heal is normal in psychedelic sessions but explaining a mathematical solution or football strategy is not.*[59]

In most Indigenous traditions, people serve psychedelics once the sun goes down because they believe that nighttime is when the vibration of the outside world settles, the veil becomes thinner, and it becomes easier to work with energy. Yet, in most scientific and therapeutic experiences, people typically serve psychedelics during the day.

Like all the variables offered thus far within the Psychedelic Safety Wheel (benefits, risks, preparation, substance, facilitation, intention, and dosage), setting should also be evaluated on a spectrum. On one end of the spectrum, setting can be relatively simple, like where you decide to ingest a substance. On the other end of the spectrum, setting can be very complex, including all things around you—seen and unseen. It can also mean the cultural norms, laws, beliefs and thought forms held by the facilitator and the other people you're journeying with.

Setting can include everything around us, what scientists call the "unified field." The term was first coined by Albert Einstein, and now modern-day scientists studying quantum mechanics and string theory are attempting to prove that everything we experience in our world is created from a single source, an idea referred to as the "theory of everything."

If we examine setting through a spiritual lens, this unified field implies that all existence is interconnected and originates from a single, underlying reality or energy source. Agnostically, this concept is referred to as Infinite Source. In the Hindu tradition, it is called the Brahman. In Taoism, the Tao represents this fundamental nature of the universe. And in almost all methods of arriving at an expanded state of consciousness—be it through prayer, meditation, breath, or the use of psychedelics—it is this shared vibration and energy that can cause participants to experience a deep sense of interconnectedness or "oneness" with everything. This is a widespread experience reported by many who have used psychedelics for experimentation, recreation, or healing, and it can occur just as easily in a scientific setting as it does in a spiritual one.

Regardless of your perspective, whether sacred or secular, both anecdotal and quantitative evidence demonstrates that setting is critical to a positive psychedelic experience.

The Importance of Setting

Both modern and Indigenous practitioners know that setting is critical when using psychedelics. Clinical research provides further insight into this. A 2023 study published in the *Journal of Affective Disorders* notes that a "disagreeable social and physical environment" represented the cause of a reported negative experience (15 percent and 14.5 percent, respectively).[60]

Another study by The Challenging Psychedelic Experiences Project shows the following adverse experiences and their correlation to setting:[61]

Social Setting	Type	Frequency	Percentage
With a friend, partner, or group of friends	Unguided	213	35.0
On my own	Unguided	115	18.9
In a group ceremony	Guided	73	12.0
At a rave, nightclub, or festival	Unguided	57	9.4
Other	Unguided	42	6.9
On a psychedelic retreat	Guided	39	6.4
At a psychedelic therapy session	Guided	32	5.3
At a party	Unguided	18	3.0
At a clinical or medical trial	Guided	17	2.8
Information not provided	N.A.	2	0.3

TABLE 4. Adverse experiences by setting

A high correlation between negative experience and sitting "on my own" tracks well with anecdotal evidence of challenging experiences. There is also dissonance in the data when comparing "in a group ceremony" and "at a psychedelic retreat." Those two settings are fundamentally the same, so presumably, other factors contributed to the negative experiences. Furthermore, "at a rave, nightclub, or festival" ranked high, while "at a party" ranks near the bottom. So, what gives?

If that data doesn't clearly explain why the physical setting is so important, then there must be other reasons. The next section offers a few potential factors that intersect with setting and that you should consider when planning your experience.

Factors to Consider When Evaluating a Setting

Not unlike the menu of options offered in chapter 8, "Preparation," creating a safe and comfortable setting offers a bevy of levels to push and pull. Depending on the type and location of your experience, you may not be able to control many of these variables, but when you have the choice, optimizing as many as possible will only make your experience feel safer and more comfortable.

Experience of the Seeker

When you combine a psychedelic newcomer with an unfamiliar setting, the possibility of something going sideways increases. Experienced psychonauts have a much better understanding of what they're getting into. This allows them to look over the edge of a negative experience, take a moment to recenter themselves, and retreat to safer ground. Inexperienced seekers do not have this awareness and can quickly get overwhelmed by a negative thought or uncomfortable engagement with another human.

Intention Alignment

Your setting should align with your intention. If you want to have a fun and recreational experience with psychedelics, then by all means, enjoy yourself at a party, rave, or music festival. If you hope to do deep psychological or spiritual work, choosing a quiet place for a private session or sitting in a ceremonial setting would be a better choice. Undoubtedly, it is possible to have a healing experience at Burning Man, but having a meltdown on the playa while you process your childhood trauma is ill-advised.

Depth of Work

In my practice, I frequently encounter clients who know they have deep and traumatic work to do, but rarely want to do that level of work in a group setting. When you combine this depth of work with an inexperienced seeker, the fear and hesitation of having a powerful experience in a room full of strangers can cause anxiety—to the point where a seeker may not even feel the effects of the psychedelics. For psychedelic newcomers, finding a one-on-one or small group opportunity may be best.

Substance

Like intentions, your substance should also align with your setting. People frequently use MDMA at raves and music festivals because the same feeling of open heartedness is effective for both connecting with fellow partygoers and healing PTSD. Ayahuasca is not a suitable substance for this kind of setting, or even one of a pseudospiritual nature. As substances increase in power, you should pay greater care to the setting.

Dosage

The intersection of dosage and setting is essential. Taking a high dose of a psychedelic in a public setting could prove to be the makings of a "bad trip." With so many variables out of our control, it's all too easy for an unexpected person, place, thing, or situation to create a disturbance that spirals into an emergency. If you don't have enough experience to make these determinations, seek the advice of an experienced friend, facilitator, or coach.

Personalities

Notice in the table above that the most likely setting for a challenging experience is "with a friend, partner, or group of friends." You might say to yourself, "But I love my friends! It sounds like so much fun to have this experience with them." What is easily overlooked is that these substances can surface new and unconscious material or behaviors. The friend you know and love may also have their own trauma that surprisingly manifests as sadness, guilt, shame, or even rage. If this content unexpectedly bubbled to the surface of their experience, it could splatter onto you and quickly turn your good trip into a challenging journey.

Mixing of Substances

It's not uncommon, especially in recreational settings, for substances to be mixed. Cannabis and alcohol are the two most socially acceptable substances available, but when you combine either of these with psychedelics, the possibility of unexpected results grows. I have heard several horror stories that started with, "The psychedelics weren't kicking in, so I took a puff of weed, and then things got really out of control." Any substance that can almost instantaneously alter your consciousness (cannabis and alcohol being prime examples) can turn a gentle journey into an out-of-control roller coaster ride.

Risk of Boundary Violations

Taking all the above variables into account, many of the worst harms perpetrated in the psychedelic space are due to physical, psychological, and spiritual boundary violations. Physically speaking, having someone place their arm around your shoulder or give you an unwelcome hug might feel like a boundary violation when you're in a highly vulnerable state. Worse yet, unwanted and inappropriate intimate or sexual touch is sadly an all-too-common report in the world of psychedelics. Additionally, a friend taking advantage of your permeable state to tell you all the things they disapprove of in your life, or attempting to convince you of a God you don't believe in, may later feel like a severe violation of your psychological or spiritual boundaries. Addressing appropriate boundaries with your facilitator (and fellow journeyers) is essential to a safe and productive experience.

Critical Elements of Setting

When we look at creating a healthy and supportive setting, there are several elements we can easily control to help optimize our experience. While some of these variables can apply to ceremonial settings, this list most closely aligns with a one-on-one thera-peutic style. This style, more than any other, allows for highly tailored adjustments to each client's unique and individual needs.

Safety as Priority

First and foremost, your setting should be safe and allow you to feel at ease with yourself and those around you. Ensure that the space is physically secure and free from potential hazards. Remove any sharp objects or obstacles that could cause harm. If you use substances that may alter your perception or coordination, take extra pre-cautions to prevent accidents or injuries. This safe space could be your home, a trusted friend's place, or a natural outdoor setting you are familiar with. Being in a familiar environment can also help reduce anxiety and promote relaxation.

Access to Privacy

Privacy is critically important for those new to doing deep personal work and trauma work. No one wants to have their dirty laundry aired to the world, so working in a space free of unwelcome passersby is paramount to putting your nervous system at ease. Create a space that minimizes distractions. If working in a natural setting, choose a private area where encountering a stranger will not occur. Having a stranger interrupt a deeply emotional process could cause fear, panic, or even retraumatization.

Trustworthy People

"Familiar and trusted" is the best scenario, but that may not be possible when working in a group. Consider this a good rule of thumb: the less you know your fellow travelers, the less interaction you should have with them during your experience, and the more clear physical and social boundaries should exist between everyone. Putting together a group of people who are unfamiliar with each other and encouraging them to interact during an experience can often produce less-than-positive results. If you choose to have others present during your journey, make sure they are trusted individuals who understand and respect the importance of set and setting. They should be supportive, nonjudgmental, and knowledgeable about psychedelics. Their presence can provide reassurance and guidance if needed.

Ideal Soundscape

Music and song are very important aspects of any experience and can significantly influence the mood and atmosphere of the journey. Within Indigenous traditions, most curanderos will whistle or sing songs (known as *icaros* in the ayahuasca tradition) to work with the energy and call in various spirits and energies.

In most modern traditions, recorded or live music is a common and highly effective tool to support you through your experience. Every facilitator will have their own style and approach. Some opt for music that feels relaxing, pleasant, or reflective, similar to what you might hear while getting a massage at a spa. This style provides background support to the seeker and allows them to control their experience more. Another style uses music to guide the seeker to explore different feelings and aspects of their inner experience and content. This music is typically more powerful, moving, and inspiring. It supports the seeker and helps them dynamically move through the various stages of their journey.

Some facilitators will encourage participants to wear headphones during their experience. This may be ideal if you're doing individual work while in a group setting, since it allows you to have your own auditory experience without engaging in the process of other journeyers. Keep in mind, though, that wearing a pair of headphones for four to six hours can also feel cumbersome and uncomfortable.

Finally, it's also essential to have access to silence during your experience. Having silent periods during your journey where your mind can wander can unlock enlightening (or sometimes unsettling) elements from your unconscious mind.

Limited Distractions

For anyone who has ever "drunk-dialed" their friends, know that inclination doesn't disappear with psychedelics. It might be even more intense. At a moment's notice, you might have an urge to call your partner and tell them how much you love them, or on the flip side, tell them how horrible they are and that you want a divorce. Neither is acceptable while under the influence of a psychedelic or immediately following your experience. When you consume a psychedelic substance, it heightens all your senses, so it's best to eliminate any potential distractions from your environment. Turn off your electronic devices and tell others you will be unavailable during your journey. Minimizing external distractions will help you stay focused and fully present in the experience.

In my work with clients, I've also discovered the importance of limiting a client's ability to move around from room to room or shift from indoors to outdoors.

Experiencing your journey in your own home might sound like a great idea until you're an hour in and realize you forgot to load the dishwasher. Then, while you're in the kitchen, you decide you'd also like to make a cup of tea for yourself and your facilitator. These movements and distractions often demonstrate that a part of you is avoiding the call to go within. Taking a quick break to play with your pets or check the mail are also ways we use our setting to distract us from the inner work we're being called to do.

One often heralded aspect of taking psychedelics outdoors is the ability to connect with nature. Frequently, seekers will experience a deep connection with the plants or animals around them, feeling a sense of "oneness" with everything. This can be a highly positive element of doing work outside, but if you become too focused on external factors, your ability to go within will be lessened.

If your intention is to go deeply into your mind and address the memories that are negatively affecting your life, I suggest finding an indoor setting that is not your own home. It's all too easy to be swayed and influenced by your surroundings. Aligning your setting with your intention is essential.

Optimized Energy

The energy of a place can readily affect your experience. The yogic gunas (see chapter 8, "Preparation") of rajas, tamas, and sattva apply as easily to settings as to our internal systems. A festival venue is somewhere we would consider very rajasic. Someone's dirty basement would be tamasic. A clean yoga studio or temple would be sattvic. When doing your deepest work, your nervous system should feel relaxed and comfortable. If stepping into a certain room or space makes you nervous before you take the substance, there is a good chance you will be exponentially more uncomfortable once you're activated.

Maximized Comfort

Journeyers are often sitting up for the first part of their journey, but most will inevitably want to lie down at some point. Access to reclining chairs, a bed, or even a mattress are all great ways to ensure you will be comfortable and safe. Many psychedelic substances can also cause significant fluctuations in body temperature. It is ideal to have a way to adjust the temperature or ensure you have access to blankets or layers. Don't be afraid to bring your own blanket or pillow—you want to do your best to create a space that feels more like home than a hospital room. Comfortable clothing that stretches and breathes is one of the best recommendations I can offer for your experience. Psychedelics can quickly and unexplainably cause you to sweat one moment and feel freezing the next. Having the ability to add or remove comfortable layers is highly recommended.

Awareness of Sensitivity to Smells

Depending on the facilitator and the setting, you may encounter a variety of smells during your journey. A therapeutic style may include a scented candle or essential oils. A more spiritual practitioner may burn things like sage or palo santo. (Palo santo means "holy wood" in Spanish and is a type of fragrant wood native to South America). The smoking of tobacco is a common element of Indigenous traditions and is used to cleanse, heal, and protect the space from outside energy. If you are very sensitive to smells, bring this up to your facilitator before the experience. As the journeyer, you should wear nothing with a powerful scent on the day of your experience. Under the influence of the medicine, you or your fellow seekers may become extremely sensitive to smells, and even a tiny application of essential oil to your wrist could be overpowering.

Ambient Decor and Lighting

Once in a highly suggestible state, artwork on the walls, symbols in a space, or even statues on an altar could affect your experience. Many Indigenous and spiritual practitioners will bring a belief system into their space and ceremony using visual elements. As a seeker, you should feel comfortable asking your facilitator to explain anything you see that you don't understand. If something in the space makes you feel uncomfortable, express this to your facilitator. Depending on their practice and belief system, they may have no issue removing it. If something in their space makes you deeply uncomfortable, trust your gut. This may not be the right facilitator or setting for you.

Having access to darkness during your experience is recommended. It's valuable to be able to remove light from the room or use eye shades, as periods of darkness during your journey can frequently lead to more powerful visions and a deeper experience.

Helpful Accessories

Bringing something from your personal practice or environment into the space can be comforting. From an emotional perspective, the act of bringing a personal item into the space with you and then taking it home after the experience can act as an ever-present reminder of the deep work you did. This item can be a token, trinket, crystal, religious symbol, or good luck charm—anything that makes you feel safe and supported. Some more practical personal items you can bring include your eye shades, pillow, blanket, journal, and water bottle. When working in group settings, try to avoid bringing anything too large, anything that makes a lot of noise, or anything that may break if it is kicked or knocked over.

Cultural Considerations

It is undeniable that elements of our culture make up a significant aspect of our setting. These elements may be buried deep within our subconscious or unconscious mind. The reality is that drug laws have harmed many populations. In his article, "Race as a Component of Set and Setting: How Experiences of Race Can Influence Psychedelic Experiences," Logan Neitzke-Spruill offers:

> *Differences in motivation for psychedelic use between African American and White psychedelic users may be one area where differential interpretations of psychedelic experiences occur. Regarding setting, the history of race relations in the United States and stigma toward minority drug users may contribute to broader concerns about drug use among African Americans. Furthermore, lack of representation in psychedelic using subcultures may limit the extent to which African American users share in harm-reducing sanctions and rituals, as described by Zinberg (1984).*[62]

For most of the world, the use of psychedelics is still illegal. And for many living in this modern world, the penalties of illicit drug use have been incredibly harsh, unfair, and devastating to their lives or the lives of their families and friends.

This reality can undoubtedly make one feel unsafe in what may normally be perceived as a "safe setting." Zooming out even further, imagine if an African American journeyer, during their experience, saw someone in their family lineage being tortured by a white male enslaver. If the facilitator for this experience was also a white male, the potential projection of fear or rage could be alarming and severe. This is an overly simplified example of the incredibly complex dynamics that may need deeper exploration between you and your facilitator.

Even though these cultural elements are baked into the setting, they may also occupy conscious (or unconscious) space within a journeyer's mindset, which we will discuss further in the next chapter. These subtle energetic "signatures" can create fear and paranoia that can seep into the setting. Once those energetic signatures manifest, they may not be easily assuaged and could necessitate additional post-journey support and integration.

Flexibility

Do your best to build some flexibility into your setting, within reason and where appropriate. You may decide that you want different music or that you'd like to add or subtract light during your experience. The ability to quickly and easily change your setting can be a tremendous benefit during one-on-one work.

Test Run Your Setting Before Your Experience

One final way to increase the feeling of safety is by doing your preparation work in the same location that you will have your experience. If you are working with a private facilitator, this could mean having your preparation sessions in the same location as the journey. If you're working in a group, knowing where the session will be held or even spending some time meditating in the space before your experience can be a fantastic preparation technique.

Being able to spend time in your setting before your experience will go a long way toward creating safety within your system. Feeling into the energy of a space, knowing where you will be sitting/lying, and your position in relationship to your facilitator will help answer many unconscious questions your nervous system is seeking answers to that you don't currently possess the awareness to ask.

Trust Your Intuition

Many variables contribute to the creation of a truly safe and supportive setting. One of the biggest advantages of working with a skilled facilitator is their assistance in optimizing your environment. Many times, your facilitator will take care of the setting for you so that you can simply walk in, slip your shoes off at the door, and have one of the most powerful experiences of your life.

As one final and repetitive reminder: it is essential to trust your intuition. If you enter a setting that does not feel safe, it may not be the right time and place for you to ingest a powerful, mind-altering substance. Regrettably, many individuals who have been harmed during an experience admit, "I sensed something was wrong, but I didn't trust my intuition." This can apply to a setting just as easily as it can to a facilitator. Please remember to prioritize discernment over desperation.

14

Mindset

"Paris, Texas" by Ry Cooder

O ut of all the variables in our framework, mindset is anecdotally (and scientif-ically) the most crucial to optimize before entering a psychedelic experience. While you may find it odd that it comes ninth in our framework, there's an excellent reason for this. Mindset represents the culmination of all the preparation you've done up to this point. Suppose you took all your work with the prior variables (benefits, risks, preparation, substance, facilitation, intention, dosage, and setting) and combined it together. The sum would equal your mindset.

Timothy Leary and Ralph Metzner state in a 1967 article that "set is understood as anything related to the internal state of a person, including personality, preparation for the experience, intention, as well as 'mood, expectations, fears, wishes.'"[63] Prepar-ing your mind is essential in this work, as it indicates the most significant difference between a positive and a negative experience. Shamanic practitioners, researchers, and philosophers have known this for centuries. It is now your responsibility to build it into your process.

In his 1902 work, *The Varieties of Religious Experience: A Study in Human Nature*, Williams James describes two qualities that most frequently occasion a natural mysti-cal experience: facing a "strong turning point or existential crisis," and "fully [commit-ting] to an unknown future."[64] He characterizes this second quality as "passivity, not activity; relaxation, not intentness," moving toward one's ability to "give up the feeling of responsibility, let go your hold, resign the care of your destiny to higher powers, be genuinely indifferent as to what becomes of it all." Doesn't this bear a striking resem-blance to the sattva guna?

The challenge with James's proposal is that the concept is almost entirely foreign to most modern ways of thinking. Unlike many Indigenous, traditional, or animistic cultures and traditions across the globe, the majority of modern culture isn't well-trained to connect with and put faith in a higher power. Without that trust, giving up the feeling of responsibility or resigning ourselves to destiny feels nearly impossible. At best, if you believe in an Infinite Source, the desire to surrender may live within you. But actively turning your will over to the care of that power is often far more complex, comes with a lot of hesitation, and requires practice. At worst, if you have a strong leaning toward atheism or a belief that we have 100 percent free will, holding a posture of faith in a higher power may feel entirely out of reach.

No matter what you believe, when the pain of life begins to exceed the pleasure, you may find yourself in just enough of an existential crisis (James's first quality) that the only choice left is to let go of everything you thought you knew and try a new way to live. This has been the experience of many clients I have worked with over the past decade.

Qualities of a Well-Prepared Mind

Knowing that mindset is essential to the positive outcome of our psychedelic experience, it's essential that we explore what a well-prepared mind might feel like. In a 2019 paper, authors Russ, Carhart-Harris, Maruyama, and Elliott found that:

> *Despite including set and setting factors in our model, both [mystical experiences (ME)] and dread in this study related most strongly to mental state at the time of ingestion. Specifically, a state of surrender at the time of ingestion substantially and significantly explained ME, and a state of preoccupation with time and one's daily tasks or concerns in conjunction with low surrender explained dread. It thus appears that an ability to set aside one's preoccupying interests and goals, place oneself in a fully receptive state, and commit or surrender to the psychedelic session fully and completely increases the extent to which MEs can be experienced, and decreases the likelihood of dread.[65]*

Here, the authors offer further proof that Williams James's 1902 research highly correlates to the practice of psychedelics. Using their terminology, "surrender" is the single most significant predictor of a mystical experience, and a lack thereof serves as a high predictor of dread.

Sorry to be the bearer of bad news, but the opposite of surrender is control, one of the most well-developed traits of the modern mind. You cannot force yourself to surrender any more than you can force yourself to fall asleep. Though, just like good sleep habits, surrender can become a learned skill.

So, how do we actually surrender? That could be the most complicated question posed in this entire book. An excellent quote that aptly describes my own experience with surrender is from David Foster Wallace, who says, "Everything I've ever let go of has claw marks on it."

Humans most commonly think of surrender as loss, and if we tug long and hard enough on the thread of loss, we almost always end up in a situation where our lives are in danger. Here's a simplified example of a thought process in great need of surrender:

If I don't make the big sale, then I won't be a top-tier salesperson in my company. If I'm not a top-tier salesperson in my company, I might lose my job. If I lose my job, then I can't pay the bills. If I can't pay the bills, then my spouse will divorce me. If my spouse divorces me, then they'll take the kids away. If I lose my kids, then I no longer have a reason to live, so my only option will be to take my own life.

This may sound reductionistic, but it's a real-life example. At its core, our ego's purpose is to keep us alive. So, if we want to explore surrendering and unclenching our death grip on life, we will need to closely examine our relationship to control, loss, and even death.

Usually, when something unexpected happens in our life, especially something that doesn't feel good, our systems clench (remember our "ancient protective parts" from chapter 8, "Preparation"). We might notice it in our physical body as muscle tension, an increased heart rate, sweating, or the feeling of a pit in our stomach. We can also recognize this in the psychological body by observing our emotions. Anger, shame, guilt, and fear are common signs. Our default trauma responses of fight, flight, freeze, or appease/fawn become activated. These somatic and psychological symptoms are indicators that we are no longer resting in a posture of surrender.

7 Steps to Surrender

When I was growing up and playing competitive sports, we were always taught that the best place to improve our skills was in practice, not in competition. The stakes are higher when it's game time; people are watching, and someone's usually keeping score. Practice, on the other hand, is safer. It's a place designed to allow us to fail repeatedly without negative consequences. With no one keeping score, we could focus on improving our skills and performance without fear of failure or retribution.

Suppose we holistically extrapolate this concept and use our lives to begin practicing surrender. This means that improving our surrender skills needs to become a daily practice, not just something we expect to be good at when the stakes are high.

Below is the simple, step-by-step process I use to teach and facilitate surrender for my clients—and for myself. When you practice these steps enough times in your daily life (before you ingest a substance), the chances you will be able to more easily surrender during your experience are much higher.

1. **Notice Your Resistance**
    The first step requires noticing that you're not in a state of surrender. With a sense of curiosity, start exploring what you're resisting, see what happens in your mind or body when this resistance is present, and take a moment to acknowledge that you're in resistance. If you instinctively react (rather than respond) to a situation, your "fuse" isn't quite long enough to perform this investigation. If that's the case, refer back to the practices mentioned in the chapter on preparation and consider starting a meditation practice. Meditation

is the single best method I have found for lengthening my own fuse. It can also be helpful to work with a coach or therapist to better understand the cause of the reaction and learn ways to work with that intense energy before it over-powers you.

2. **Accept the Present Moment**

There is a beautiful passage in *Alcoholics Anonymous: The Big Book* that states, "Acceptance is the answer to all of my problems today. When I am disturbed, it is because I find some person, place, thing, or situation—some fact of my life—unacceptable to me. I can find no serenity until I accept that person, place, thing, or situation as being exactly the way it is supposed to be at this moment."[66] Once you recognize you are in resistance, any suffering that you experience is caused by either your judgment that the situation is not as it should be or your desire for that situation to be different. The suffering will dissipate, if not completely disappear, once you learn to accept life on life's terms. Period, end of story.

3. **Trust the Process**

Trust is the second most important quality of a well-prepared psychedelic mind. Trust is essential in allowing a situation to unfold precisely how it's meant to, regardless of your plans and desires. The only thing humans hate more than change is uncertainty, but if you can develop a deep sense of trust that you are safe and things will eventually work out, surrender becomes a much easier proposition for your mind and your nervous system.

4. **Investigate Your Lack of Control**

Once you realize, either on your own or with the help of a friend, loved one, or helping professional, that your desire to control the uncontrollable is the root of your suffering, it's time to work with that control. If your belief system includes something like Infinite Source, try asking for help from this power. One of my favorite mantras for moments when I find myself grasping for control is "I bless you and I release you." Another beautiful practice is to recite the Serenity Prayer: "Grant me the serenity to accept the things I cannot change, courage to change the things I can, and the wisdom to know the difference." (If you do not believe in any such power, refer to the section titled "A Unique Challenge for Atheists" later on in this chapter.)

5. **Control What You Can**

If you've made it this far, you're doing great. There's good news, and there's bad news from here. The bad news is you've realized how little you're actually in control of. The good news is what you are in control of is all yours to manage.

To start, take a deep breath. In his podcast with Tim Ferris, Dr. Andrew Huberman shows a highly effective technique to quickly reduce stress and anxiety called the "Physiological Sigh," a breathing pattern consisting of a deep breath in through the nose, followed by another quick breath in through the nose, then a slow exhale through the mouth, which helps regulate the nervous system by reducing stress and promoting relaxation.[67] In his words, "use the body to control the mind." Next up, decide what thoughts you want to believe instead of the thoughts you're believing right now. This can be challenging, but having a regular "thought practice" and learning to consciously choose new, healthier ways of thinking has truly changed my life.

6. **Let It Be**

Contrary to many spiritual teachers and TikTok shamans, I despise the phrase "let it go." I've learned over time that instead of trying to let something go, it's a lot easier to let something be. In step 2, you brought awareness to the present moment and—likely begrudgingly—realized that you could not change it. With your mind and nervous system in check, it's time to consciously drop into the uncomfortable feeling. Without trying to change anything or push it away, allow the discomfort to fill you up. Welcome whatever needs to be seen and experienced. The magic of this practice is that once you're ready to let the feelings be exactly the way they are, they will subside or disappear on their own. No "letting go" required.

7. **Cultivate Self-Compassion**

The last step in this process is to offer yourself compassion and grace. All those judgments, reactions, beliefs, and feelings were given to you—whether by society or the people around you in this lifetime, unconsciously through epigenetics, or even from a past lifetime through reincarnation. The reality is you don't get to choose your triggers, and we're all doing the best we can with what we've got. A very helpful practice is to stop judging who you *were* with the consciousness of who you *are* today. When you notice yourself judging something or someone, try shifting that judgment to appreciation. As in, "Thank you for showing me what I still need to heal within myself." Slow down, take a deep breath, pause, and send some love, compassion, and forgiveness to yourself and others. You may not immediately feel it, but your inner child will appreciate it.

Finally, I'd like to highlight a few subtle but essential qualities hidden within these steps. Incorporating these qualities into your daily practice and preparation plan will do wonders and help you shift your perspective from "strong and hard" to "sweet and easy":

- Surrender
- Curiosity
- Trust
- Acceptance
- Openness
- Self-compassion
- Nonjudgement
- Mindfulness

Mindset Evaluation Exercise

Yogananda, one of the great Indian Yogic saints, was fond of saying, "Our mind is like a restless, drunken monkey who has been stung by a scorpion." Other people, life circumstances, and psychedelics can provoke a well-prepared, calm, and centered mind into this drunken monkey at the drop of a banana. Having already examined the more subtle qualities of a well-prepared mindset, it's time to get down to the nuts and bolts of your experience. There are several ways that you can evaluate your mindset before going into every psychedelic experience.

This evaluation exercise offers important insights to help you understand how your mind works and whether you need to slow down or pause your process. Grab your journal and a pen, find some quiet time, and write down your answers to the following questions to check in with yourself and evaluate how you're feeling. (Note: If something on the day of your experience feels strongly out of alignment, please discuss it with your facilitator. Remember: discernment over desperation.) It's a great idea to revisit this exercise at the following intervals: a week before your experience, a few days before your experience, the day of your experience, and after your experience.

Directions: For each evaluation below, rank your answers to the questions on a scale of 1 to 5, 1 being the most negative and 5 being the most positive. Average your score for each inventory. As you move closer to your experience, pay special attention to any sharp decreases in your score. A reduction of 50 percent or more on the day of your experience is a good reason to hit the brakes.

TRUST LEVEL EVALUATION

As we've discussed, trust is a critical ingredient in the recipe of surrender, and it can also act as a valuable indicator in your preparation process. Ask yourself:

Do I trust my Self?

Do I trust my facilitator?

Do I trust the substance?

If the answer to any of these is "no," you should discuss this with your facilitator and determine if there are conscious or unconscious fears that can be addressed. If your facilitator is uninterested or incapable of helping you address these fear or concerns, this is a red flag you should not ignore. If your facilitator gives you an ultimatum in the direction of "You have to sit or else...," run in the other direction. This is not someone who holds your best interests in mind.

Without a certain level of trust, it will be impossible for your mind and body to relax into the experience. Without relaxation and trust, many odd and unexpected things can occur. Sometimes, you may not feel the medicine. Other times, your anxiety and fear may increase to uncomfortable levels, leading to a painful experience, a trip to the hospital, or even a psychotic break.

If you are showing up for a group ceremony and meeting your facilitator for the first time, I encourage you to make space for "game-day decisions." If your intuition does not trust the facilitator or the container, you should pause or step away altogether. The cost and mental anguish experienced by seekers who failed to trust their gut can be far greater than the money they paid to sit in the ceremony.

EMOTIONAL STATE EVALUATION

Considering that a positive emotional state will contribute to a more positive experience, and vice versa, ask yourself:

What Is My Cognitive State?

Take inventory of your overall thoughts, beliefs, and mental clarity. A racing and cluttered mind oriented toward pessimism can lead to a more challenging experience.

What Is My Physical State?

Take inventory of your overall physical body and health. Are you well-rested, hydrated, and nourished? Have you followed the agreed-upon plans for medications and supplements? Two frequent causes of challenging experiences are dehydration and not getting enough sleep.

What Is My Current Life Situation?

Take inventory of what's happening in your life right now. If you were feeling well-prepared, but then a close member of your family is in an accident the day before your journey, it may not be the right time to go into an intensely altered state of mind. If there are challenging stressors in your life or if you have experienced recent negative events, consider pausing your process until things restabilize.

What Is My History with Psychedelics?

Take inventory of any emotional baggage you're carrying from past psychedelic experiences. It's not uncommon for individuals seeking healing to have already had recreational or pseudospiritual experiences in the past. If your past experiences were challenging or harmful, checking in with yourself about any emotional baggage you're still carrying is a good practice. Sharing these experiences with your facilitator and discussing how your coming experience could be similar or different is also a great way to assuage these fears and leave the baggage at home.

What Are My Expectations?

Take inventory of your conscious expectations about your experience and ask your facilitator, coach, or therapist to help you uncover any hidden, unconscious expectations you may have. Your expectations may not directly affect the experience, but they can cause negative feelings afterward if those expectations go unmet. Get expectations out in the open beforehand to avoid placing unnecessary blame on yourself, your facilitator, the group, or the medicine.

Nervous vs. Anxious: What Mindsets Are Cause for Concern?

I have been working with psychedelics for over a decade, and there hasn't been a journey where I don't experience some amount of nervousness. And it's reasonable to be a little nervous before your experience—you're stepping into the unknown. For most people, the nerves fade quickly once the substance begins working and they're no longer worrying *about* the experience—they're *in* the experience.

But there are some distinct differences between being "nervous" and being "anxious." An underlying sense of anxiousness may be precisely the reason you want to work with psychedelics. But if you're explicitly experiencing anxiousness *about your experience*, you may need to investigate.

Nervousness is typically an acute, short-lived sensation that goes away after a stressful event. It's often directly tied to a trigger (in this case, taking a dose of psychedelics, especially if it's for the first time). It may be uncomfortable, but it should be manageable and dissipate once the triggering event has passed. Nervousness can coincide with a sense of fear.

Anxiety is a persistent and chronic condition. There is often no identifiable trigger, and it can cause you to feel out of control. It can even manifest as physical symptoms like increased blood pressure, body aches, and sweating. Anxiousness disrupts your daily life.

A restless night of sleep caused by nerves before a journey is nothing to be concerned about. Losing sleep for days or weeks because of overwhelming anxiousness is a cause for concern. If you are anxious and have feelings of panic, dread, or paranoia directly related to your psychedelic experience, this is a powerful sign you are not in a conducive mindset. A lack of safety, whether perceived or actual, shows that you have not yet generated enough trust in your system to do the work.

Encountering Religion and Spirituality

If you've chosen to engage with psychedelics within a clinical or therapeutic framework, the more physical aspects of the experience have likely been scrubbed of religion and spirituality. Even so, countless studies performed in these settings show that participants ingesting macro doses of classical psychedelics—regardless of their prior spiritual or religious beliefs—can have "God experience encounters" or "entity encounters." **You can try to take psychedelics out of spirituality, but you can never take spirituality out of psychedelics.**

I have worked with many people who have strong negative feelings toward both religion and spirituality—some for good reason. According to a 2023 study published in the *Socio-Historical Examination of Religion and Ministry Journal*, one in three adults in the United States have experienced religious trauma (RT) at some point in their lives.[68] This type of trauma refers to the physical, emotional, and psychological harm caused by involvement in or exposure to harmful religious beliefs, practices, or environments. It frequently stems from experiences within authoritarian religious systems, punitive or fear-based doctrines, spiritual abuse, or rigid social structures that suppress individuality. Religious trauma can manifest in a wide array of symptoms, including intrusive thoughts, perfectionism, identity crisis, guilt and shame, fear and anxiety, or grief and loneliness. With numbers like these, it's no wonder that many people have abandoned or actively distance themselves from anything that looks or feels like an organized religion.

Intersecting these deeply held beliefs with psychedelic work frequently presents obstacles. Many Indigenous traditions are built on rituals or prayers that, at least through a modern lens, can resemble religion to an outsider. Adding to that confusion, psychedelic churches are springing up within the modern landscape to provide a legally justifiable mechanism for psychedelic use. The mere mention of the word "church" or ritualistic practices can understandably trigger someone to run in the other direction.

The resulting dichotomy has caused significant popularity in the "spiritual but not religious" (SBNR) movement. With origins dating back to Williams James, the SBNR moniker has seen a resurgence in the last twenty years. In 2017, a Pew Research Center study found that 27 percent of US adults identified as "spiritual but not religious."[69] That number only continued to rise, with a Gallup poll in 2023 showing an increase to 33 percent.[70]

If you are considering using psychedelics within an Indigenous tradition or with an underground facilitator, the chances are high that you will encounter spiritual (if not religious) beliefs or traditions you may not understand or believe in. Applied appropriately, these belief systems may become helpful. Having had many unexplainable or ineffable psychedelic experiences myself, the spiritual traditions practiced for millennia have helped me understand and integrate these mystical experiences into my daily life. If possible, try to keep an open mind.

Unfortunately, like almost every spiritual path throughout the centuries, psychedelics are not immune to those cultivating cult-like behavior and power trips.

So, what's the difference between religion and spirituality? They can look very similar on the surface, but there are some important differences that can go a long way in ensuring your safety and maintaining your cognitive freedom.

Key Differences Between Religion and Spirituality

Religion	Spirituality
Religion offers teachings based on faith and believes that if you act in a prescribed way *today*, you will receive your reward *later* (e.g., you'll go to heaven once you're dead).	Spirituality offers teachings and practices that help you achieve peace, joy, and freedom *today*. If you're being told to do things that don't make you feel better in this lifetime, consider stopping.
Religion demands you *believe* in a set of authoritative teachings, whether they can be proven or not.	Spirituality encourages you to *learn* via direct experience. Spirituality asks that you trust the teaching until you've tested it for yourself. If the teaching doesn't work, you need not believe it. Approach these teachings in the spirit of "trust prior to verification."
Religion focuses on being the vehicle that brings individuals closer to the Divine through a prescribed set of rituals and moral codes.	Spirituality removes the middleman and encourages individuals to have a *direct connection* with their own version of the sacred.
Religion eliminates individuality and actively promotes a single path to achieve a prescribed goal.	Spirituality takes an "all roads lead to Rome" perspective, allowing each seeker the freedom to choose their own path toward self-realization.
Religion has a name for their deity (or deities) and asks that you believe in it with them.	Spirituality offers seekers the ability to select a name that resonates with their path. Some people prefer a defined term for God. Spirituality makes space for the Infinite Source, Universe, Consciousness, the Divine, Mother Nature, or even the Force. You choose!

Religion	Spirituality
Religion occurs in a specific place (e.g., a church).	Spirituality can happen anywhere. Four walls and an altar not required.
Religion requires group participation and focuses on organizational and communal dimensions.	Spirituality is an individual activity focused on the well-being of the Self, including one's body, mind, and spirit. While spirituality can involve group participation (e.g., joining in meditation or psychedelic ceremonies), each individual has their own personal experience.
Religion has one leader who directs followers in the proper methods of practice.	Within spirituality, *you* are your own supreme leader. You may have teachers or guides along the way, but they only lead you down the path of direct experience.

TABLE 5. Religion vs. spirituality

In an idyllic world, religion would be a springboard into spirituality. Almost all of the world's religions teach and promote positive virtues such as peace, joy, love, and community. The challenges arise when the human ego distorts those teachings to gain power and control. Spirituality can undoubtedly exist within religion, but it is not guaranteed.

My go-to definition of spirituality is, quite simply, "self-knowledge." We hypothesize in chapter 3, "How and Why Psychedelics Heal," that we are all made of the same energy, and the deepest part of us hold the same characteristics as this Infinite Source. Spirituality, the act of self-knowledge or self-realization, is actually an act of knowing that Source. *You* are that which you seek.

Any teacher or teaching that helps you develop a more definitive sense of Self is a part of spirituality. It doesn't have to be any more complicated or mystical than that.

A Unique Challenge for Atheists

Some of the most challenging healing journeys I've witnessed were those of self-identifying atheists. Each of these individuals possessed a deeply held perception that made them believe they had more control over the outcome of their lives than they actually did.

By denying the existence of a "giant marshmallow man in the sky," they possessed total control and ultimate responsibility for their destiny. When things didn't go as they wanted or planned, there was no one to blame but themself. This, dear reader, is an uncomfortable place to stand when something horrible and unexplainable happens in your life.

In no way do I want this to be a critique of atheism. I staunchly believe that every individual should have the cognitive liberty to choose their beliefs, or lack thereof, about God and spirituality. I share this not from a place of judgment, but as an invitation. Developing a mental model or thought process around the concept of surrender before you find yourself forcibly shoved into this state of mind is an excellent idea to explore before your first macro dose.

In 2019, a team at Johns Hopkins University interviewed over 4,000 psychedelic users about their "single most memorable God encounter experience." Quite remarkably, two-thirds of those who identified as atheists before the experience no longer identified as atheists afterward.[71] The study states, "Most participants reported vivid memories of the encounter experience, which frequently involved communication with something having the attributes of being conscious, benevolent, intelligent, sacred, eternal, and all-knowing."

I mention this research only to add further support for investigating a spiritual philosophy or framework before you begin macro dose work with psychedelics. Considering one of the most common post-psychedelic challenges is ontological difficulties, a rigid-thinking atheist will likely struggle to understand and integrate the experience of being literally introduced to God in the span of a few minutes. They would have to either challenge their lived experience or abandon a deeply held belief system that makes up the entire foundation of their life. A double bind of that magnitude is not a desirable position to find yourself in.

As Rachael Peterson wrote in an article titled "Taking Mushrooms for Depression Cured Me of My Atheism," "When, during a follow-up session in the clinical trial, a researcher asked if I still identified as an atheist, the question didn't surprise me as much as my inability to answer. Suddenly, the label felt like a shirt that had shrunk in the dryer: something that served me for a time, but no longer fit."[72]

Here is a gentle suggestion for any atheists considering macro dose work with classical psychedelics: before you work with higher doses, please consider your willingness to change your mind. If you have firmly shut and bolted the door to spirituality, I suggest starting with breathwork, using low doses, or maybe avoiding psychedelics altogether. If you're not careful, you may get more than you bargained for.

Surrendering Means Winning

As children, most of us received the recognition, support, and emotional validation we deeply craved by getting good grades or winning a big sports match. Not achieving those things sometimes forced us into a state of shame, guilt, fear, or neglect. As adults, it's no wonder we burn ourselves out trying to "keep up with the Joneses." The American Dream and our pursuit of happiness is based on power, achievement, and acquisition. Over the past hundred years, our world has only reinforced these notions with each election cycle, tech billionaire, and social media influencer.

If you genuinely have a desire to heal, you will quickly understand that working with psychedelics is an entirely different game. All the "rules" you've learned up to this point in your life won't serve you while sitting alone on your mat, processing years of memories or trauma in a matter of minutes. The intentional use of psychedelics teaches us to release rather than acquire. It teaches us that we need nothing new to end our suffering, and that letting go is actually the fastest path to happiness.

All the protection mechanisms your mind created through the years to keep you safe are precisely the things that you will have to give up, as they will only get in the way of your healing. A healthy psychedelic practice represents one of the few opportunities in life where surrendering actually means winning.

Our mindset is a fundamental part of our daily activities. "Powerfully" educated minds are advertised as accomplishing amazing feats in most modern societies. Many incredibly successful people train their minds for optimization, control, and the acquisition of resources, and they're often handsomely rewarded (materially, at least) for their talents. This strategy works well for a while, but it will never provide a lasting sense of fulfillment. Everything gained eventually disappears. Everything we can see, touch, taste, smell, hear, or think is impermanent. *Everything*!

Those who wish to find happiness from within can nurture a very different mindset. Minds like this are often more relaxed, curious, and authentic. So, I ask you, dear reader, are you willing to believe, have faith, and trust that these substances will teach you and take care of you in ways you've never thought possible? If you're willing to agree that what got you *here* will not get you *there*, then you might just be ready. If you're ready to jump headfirst into a pool of uncertainty that could introduce you to unlimited creativity, bliss, fear, intelligence, sorrow, or possibility, then by all means, please proceed.

But if all of this scares the shit out of you, please do not pass Go, do not collect 200 dollars, and return to the chapter on preparation. If your mindset doesn't feel right, there's a better-than-average chance your journey won't feel right.

In our past, we have almost always chosen a familiar hell over an unfamiliar heaven. This chapter represents the demarcation line between those two ideas, so before you decide how to proceed, pay attention to what's happening in your heart, be honest with yourself, and choose your next move wisely.

15

Experience

"The Eye" by Brandi Carlile

The big day has arrived. If you've diligently followed the steps in the book, you've completed your assignments and made significant preparations. Believe it or not, after all the hard work you've done to get to this point, my best suggestion for your journey day (and the journey itself) is to do as little as possible.

The most common question I get asked from psychedelic newcomers is "What will happen during my experience?" There is no way to answer that question. As the saying goes, the more you f*ck around, the more you're going to find out. The more you explore and experiment, the more you will discover about yourself, your relationship to the world around you, and potentially collective consciousness, other planes of reality, good and evil spirits, and even the Divine.

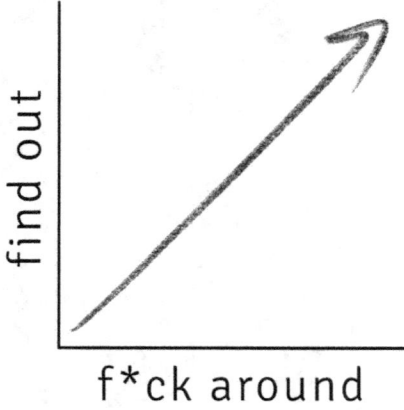

FIGURE 11. F*ck around and find out

When we measure the surface area of f*ck around and find out, a few variables can significantly affect how much you're going to find out. You can move farther along the x-axis by modifying three primary variables: increasing your frequency of use, using more powerful substances, and increasing your dosage. The harder and faster you push these variables, the more you will "find out." And what many newcomers and experienced psychonauts have discovered is that sometimes we don't always like what we find out.

As Erika Perez from Psychedelic Passage states, "We will never be able to predict the trajectory of our psychedelic trip accurately. We should see that as a benefit because if we could, we'd likely steer the experience using the same counterproductive mental narratives and behavioral patterns that led us here in the first place."[73]

Parallels can be drawn between a psychedelic experience and what author and mythologist Joseph Campbell called "the hero's journey." Campbell explained the common story of a hero goes who on a quest, faces challenges, and returns transformed. He outlined the steps of the hero's journey as follows:

1. **Ordinary World** — The hero begins in their everyday life. (Your ordinary waking consciousness.)
2. **Call to Adventure** — The hero is presented with a challenge or quest. (Your call to healing.)
3. **Refusal of the Call** — The hero hesitates to accept the challenge. (Your reluctance and fears.)
4. **Meeting the Mentor** — The hero meets a guide (the medicine) who helps them prepare for and take the journey.
5. **Cross the Threshold** — The hero leaves their familiar world and enters the unknown.
6. **Tests, Allies, and Enemies** — The hero faces challenges, makes allies, and confronts enemies. (Your beliefs and emotions, or even entities and spirits you may meet from other planes of reality.)
7. **Approach to the Inmost Cave** — The hero approaches a critical challenge or confrontation. (Encountering your core trauma, your unconscious mind, your shadow, or even Infinite Source.)
8. **Ordeal** — The hero faces a significant crisis or challenge, often risking death or failure. (Feelings of surrender and ego dissolution, or letting go of the armor that's protected you for so many years.)
9. **Reward** — The hero gains a reward or insight after overcoming the ordeal.
10. **The Road Home** — The hero begins the journey home, often facing more challenges. (Your return to waking consciousness and first steps toward integration.)
11. **Resurrection** — The hero faces a final test, emerging transformed. (The last components of integration and, more importantly, all the activation work required to change your life.)
12. **Return with the Elixir** — The hero returns to the ordinary world with newfound wisdom or a boon to benefit others. (When you heal yourself, the ripples from your work spread to your friends, family, loved ones, and community.)

If we take these twelve steps of the hero's journey and add them to the twelve spokes on the Psychedelic Safety Wheel, we end up twenty-four distinct variables. If we oversimplified these variables to "yes or no" options, that represents a potential

16,777,216 possible outcomes. But as you've recognized by now, every one of these variables is unlimited in their scope. So, when someone asks me, "What should I expect when I take psychedelics?" my best answer is, "It could be heaven, it could be hell, and it will most likely be somewhere in between."

Your Final Pre-Journey Checklist

Before my clients ingest the medicine, I advise them to write down three things:

- **"Note to Self"** — One or two affirming sentences you can refer to if the waters get rough. If confusion or fear sets in, the experience becomes more intense than expected, or a desire for the experience to end becomes overwhelming, revisiting a few words of encouragement you wrote to yourself can often bring you back into enough safety to get through the next wave.
- **Grounding Contact** — Your grounding contact represents your "phone a friend" option. This could be someone from your support team that you love and trust, and who is directly supporting you through your process. If the need arises, they have agreed to be available if you choose to contact them during your experience.
- **Emergency Contact** — This could be the same person as your grounding contact, but I've often found that not to be the case with my clients. Should a true medical emergency arise, if 911 is called, or if you require immediate professional medical attention, your emergency contact would be contacted immediately.

What to Do Right Before Your Experience

The days, weeks, and hours leading up to your experience can profoundly affect its outcome. You may have spent weeks or even months preparing for your experience; it's now time to reap the benefits of all that hard work. In chapter 8, "Preparation," we discussed creating a safe environment for our body, mind, and spirit. As you arise on the day of your experience, keep that goal in mind. Do everything you can to embody the qualities of sattva: peace, harmony, positivity, goodness, truth, balance, and serenity.

Enjoy Some Quiet Time

Meditate, journal, walk in nature, and focus on the task at hand. It is typically recommended to cease eating three or four hours before your experience. This ensures there is no excess food in your stomach to impede the speed or effects of the medicine. Remember to discuss day-of preparations with your facilitator, which should include diet.

Avoid Caffeine

Many facilitators encourage seekers not to drink caffeine on the day of their experience. If that is possible for you, great. If your morning routine includes a cup of coffee to get you started and settle your nerves, rest assured that this will not pose any significant issue for your experience. What is most important is that you stay in alignment with the agreements you've made with yourself, your facilitator, and the medicine.

Dress Comfortably

When dressing for your experience, remember to wear layered, breathable clothing. Psychedelics can quickly change your body temperature, so it's helpful to easily add or remove layers to maintain comfort. Pack your favorite blanket, pillow, or pair of fuzzy socks, so you'll be as comfy as possible in the expertly crafted setting your facilitator has created for your experience.

Set Expectations and Review Boundaries and Agreements

Before starting, you and your facilitator should revisit any expectations, boundaries, and agreements governing your experience. Remember that you cannot offer informed consent once you've taken the substance. Unless absolutely necessary, additional consent should not be asked of you by your facilitator during the experience.

Reviewing your informed consent could involve things like how and where you can be physically touched, how much medicine you will take and the approximate time intervals at which it will be offered, what you should do or say if you need help, how much interaction you will have with the facilitator or other participants, if talking is allowed or expected, and if you will be confined to a specific space or allowed to move freely about your chosen setting. Discussing these boundaries with your facilitator before you start your experience is an absolute necessity. Not doing so is a "red flag."

Reflect on Your Intention

Before entering any experience, take ample time to reflect on your intention. This may involve writing your intention down and tucking it under your pillow, meditating on your intention, or even treating it like a mantra and reciting it 108 times with the beads on a *mala*. Infinite Source and the medicine "hears" your intention and will offer you what you need to move toward it.

What to Do During Your Psychedelic Experience

"Inner healing intelligence," a term first coined by authors Stanislav and Christina Grof, is fundamental to many Indigenous and modern psychedelic-assisted therapy teachings. The MAPS manual for MDMA-assisted psychotherapy states: "It is essential to encourage the participant to trust their inner healing intelligence, a person's innate capacity to heal the wounds of trauma. It is important to highlight that the participant is the source of their own healing."

If you have been struggling with your health for years, it may seem almost impossible to believe that you are the one who holds the secret solution to your healing. I can assure you from my prior experience (of both ingesting and supporting others) that this is almost always the case. As we've previously discussed, so much of this work comes down to is trust. Can you trust yourself and the medicine to give you precisely what you need?

Understand How Psychedelics Cleanse Us

As we discussed in chapter 2, psychedelics are very powerful cleansing agents. They scan our system and seek out low-vibration energy that needs to be shifted or released. How those shifts and releases happen is incredibly varied. In the middle of your experience, it is not uncommon to feel any or all of the below symptoms. Unless these symptoms reach an abnormally high severity or they don't stop in a reasonable amount of time, they are all very normal signs of your body's many methods to cleanse itself.

- Heavy breathing
- Rapid temperature changes
- Sweating or shivering
- Tears (with or without emotion)
- Increased mucus production

- Passing gas
- Vomiting
- Diarrhea
- Tremors, shaking, or trembling
- Muscle spasms

Seek Support from Your Facilitator

You may ask yourself, "If I've got all I need within me, and I'm the one doing all the healing, why do I need a facilitator?" This is a fantastic question, and knowing the answer could save you from a great deal of harm. Think of yourself as a roped climber, clinging to the rock face of a mountain. Your facilitator is acting as a spotter and will skillfully handle the rope on the ground so you stay safe. If you get stuck, they will offer help. And most importantly, should you slip and fall, they will catch you. They're there to offer assistance when needed, and ultimately, to keep you safe.

During a one-on-one psychedelic experience, having done proper preparation and understanding your unique history, a skilled facilitator may invite or remind you to explore certain thoughts or examine relationships that you've already expressed cause you difficulty. Your facilitator does not come into the experience with a set agenda and acts more as a follower than a leader. When you're wandering around in a dark room, your facilitator will only switch on the light for you to see more clearly what's already inside.

Let Go of Inner Resistance

In the immortal words of Carl Jung, "What you resist will persist." When the going gets rough, pay attention to your breath. Sit up straight, focus your concentration, and remind yourself, "I am safe. I trust myself, the medicine, and my facilitator." Sometimes, taking a few deep breaths while repeating this mantra (out loud or in your head) is enough to get you through even the steepest inclines.

Remember that you are strong, that avoiding the experience will only prolong your suffering, and that whatever challenging or uncomfortable experience you are having will end in a few hours. I always recommend newcomers have a facilitator so that if the climb gets too hard, the facilitator can help you breathe and navigate your difficult experience. They're your life preserver and act as stable ground when you're unable. They can help remind you that the only way out is through.

Simply Be Present

Once your journey starts, try and resist the temptation to "do" anything. For many of my clients, a psychedelic experience might represent one of the first times in their adult life that they transform from a human "doing" to a human "being."

One of my favorite reminders to tell clients before their experience is, "You cannot f*ck this up." Once you've taken the medicine, there is no need to do anything but be present with yourself. The medicine will take you exactly where you need to go.

What to Do After Your Experience

Some people complete their experience feeling lighter and filled with energy. Others, who may have had a deeper or more emotional process, may feel emotionally and physically exhausted. Some degree of physical discomfort is not uncommon after a psychedelic experience. This could feel like muscle tension or soreness, nausea, brain fog, headaches, and often feeling much more tender and sensitive to your emotions. I often remind my clients that after a powerful experience they will "feel" better—they may feel pain better, anger better, sadness better, and even happiness better. Give yourself grace postexperience. Clear your calendar for the next day, so you have plenty of time to feel and be however you need. If you are in severe discomfort, you should immediately consult your facilitator or trained medical personnel.

Plan for Recovery Time

It is best to think of your experience as a two-day event; one day is for medicine, the next day is for fully landing. Directly after your experience, you will probably feel a little "wobbly," altered, unstable, and ungrounded. Plan ample time after any experience before needing to drive, cook, or interact with others not in your support team or close peer group. You will also remain very sensitive to the energy of others. Going straight from a psychedelic experience to a party, pub, or competitive sporting event is not recommended.

Eat Simple, Light Foods

Once you return home, you may or may not be hungry. It's best to have simple, healthy food and snacks available. Try a light meal first to see how food sits in your stomach. Then, if you feel hungry and your stomach feels settled, it is reasonable to have a full meal. If you've had a powerful emotional experience, temporary nausea is not an uncommon side effect and should disappear after sleep.

Have a Support Person

From an emotional support perspective, having a trusted friend or loved one keep you company can also be very helpful and comforting. You may or may not feel like chatting, but having the loving presence of someone with you can be a very calming experience.

Anticipate Possible Sleep Disruptions

You may feel very depleted and have the desire to go to bed early, or you may find it difficult to fall asleep. It is common for the first sleep cycle after your experience to be disrupted. Sometimes, your dreams may become a rich source of new unconscious content. Try to take advantage of the liminal state between waking and dreaming consciousness and use it to begin your integration process.

Avoid using any sleep aids and allow your process to unfold on its own. If absolutely necessary, you can usually take a natural sleep aid (such as herbal tea or melatonin) without any risk of harm, though it is best to check with your facilitator before ingesting any new supplements and pills after your experience.

Steven's Story

Sometimes, the phrase "nothing happened" can feel more disheartening than a painful or exhausting psychedelic experience. It stirs up mixed emotions: anger, confusion, disappointment, and a sense of being let down. We hear so much about the transformative power of psychedelics and the profound experiences others have had, and it's natural to hope for the same. I certainly did.

Before my first journey, I immersed myself in books like Dr. Fadiman's *The Psychedelic Explorer's Guide* and Michael Pollan's *How to Change Your Mind*. They filled me with hope for change, especially after battling hopelessness and despair for years. Having been diagnosed with PTSD, anxiety, and depression, I had already tried pharmaceuticals, professional therapy, self-help books, and even faith in a higher power. None of it seemed to be enough. When I learned about the therapeutic potential of magic mushrooms and LSD, I felt like I had nothing to lose.

And then, during that first carefully prepared sit, what happened? Nothing.

At least, that's what I thought. But is it ever true that *nothing* happens? Reflecting on it now, I realize that what I initially judged as "nothing" was simply my expectations going unmet. I began to question if I was different from those having mystical encounters with God, aliens, or spiritual teachers. But recently, a profound experience helped me reframe this idea of "nothing."

After three years of working with psychedelics, I'm finally starting to understand. It's taken that long because my mind, like many others, is a master of control. Even though I had been told—and even advised others—to "let go of expectations," I was still unconsciously carrying some. That's the tricky thing about our minds; even when we craft a simple intention and surrender to the outcome, our hidden expectations often linger.

I want to pause here and acknowledge that some experiences of "nothing" are due to physiological factors, like medications (such as SSRIs) interfering with the effects of psychedelics. But outside of that, even when we sign up for a cosmic journey and end up staring at the floor for six hours in sober disbelief, *something* is always happening. Life, after all, is always happening.

In hindsight, the experience I once labeled as "nothing" was a profound lesson in observation. What I did at that moment was react. I felt uncomfortable and resisted the sensations that were coming on more forcefully and later than I'd anticipated. My aversion to the experience became so intense that I began to panic—sweating and feeling regret for taking "too much." Within minutes, the sensations faded, and I spent the next eight hours in a sober, yet foggy, state of discomfort.

Not exactly "nothing" when I describe it that way, right?

Through ongoing practice and integration, I've realized how deeply ingrained my expectations were. In a world where we're constantly bombarded by others' declarations of how things should be, I'm slowly learning to let psychedelics do their work on their own terms. My role is to "let go," "surrender," "receive," and "be" with nonjudgmental curiosity. Whether it's rage, body spasms, bliss, distant thoughts, or even a growl—it's all part of the experience. It only becomes "good," "bad," or "neutral" when I decide it is.

There's always something happening. That's the lesson. Maybe it's different for you. But I encourage you to explore the possibility.

What If You Don't Get What You Wanted?

Often, when we examine our journey and reflect on our intention, we feel like we didn't get what we came for. Sometimes, this can feel like we've failed. The integration process can help us realize that we had conscious and unconscious expectations coming into the experience that affected our journey.

I have also found that individuals often document one intention for their journey but have a completely different intention in their mind. Or the intention they wrote has an energetic signature that feels more like a goal. For instance, I recently worked with a client who intended to "let go of guilt, say yes to enjoyment and clarity." As discussed in chapter 11, "Intention," intentions are directions we can move toward, not goals that we can ever fully accomplish. Here, the client felt disappointed at the end of their experience because they never experienced a "total" sense of enjoyment and clarity. What they came to understand was that their intention had turned into a goal. Deep down, they were seeking an experience of bliss and ultimate clarity to resolve the challenges they had in their life. Rather than the experience itself, their expectations were the source of their resentment.

They received tremendous clarity on why they had trouble feeling enjoyment. When we consider these substances to be sentient and to have an intelligence significantly greater than ours, we can trust that we're getting exactly what we *need* rather than what we *want*. In this specific instance, the client realized there were questions they hadn't even asked. They thought happiness was going to be the natural next step on their journey, then realized that healing some untreated childhood neglect was going to be required before that could happen.

It's important to remember that the only goal of an experience should be to move us one step further on our healing path. If we get lucky, we may take more than one step— but expecting that to happen will only set us up for disappointment.

Was It a "Bad Trip" or a Challenging Journey?

Psychedelic experiences vary widely. Every trip, every time, is a brand-new experience. There are two kinds of negative experiences—"bad trips" and challenging journeys— and there are key differences between the two.

A "bad trip" usually stems from a sense of being completely overwhelmed or lost, resulting in the body-mind-spirit metabolizing the experience as trauma. Feelings of paranoia, self-doubt, or downright terror can occur. The vast majority of "bad trips" I encounter usually start with poor preparation, an unsafe setting, a dosage that was too high, or a lack of proper support. What might start as a fun experience at a music festival can spin into a horrifying experience where your entire conception of reality is shifting under the watchful eyes of hundreds of onlookers.

A challenging journey is often intense and can bring up difficult emotions, memories, or fears. While this "retracing" of the painful past can feel like reexperiencing sensations or symptoms that were felt during an original injury or trauma, it's part of the mind-body-spirit's effort to release and resolve what was previously unmetabolized. This can lead to significant personal growth and healing. Many who work with psychedelics therapeutically describe these challenging moments as opportunities to confront and heal deeply held traumas or limiting beliefs. Knowing how to handle this difficult process in the moment can be very helpful.

For many years, I believed there were no "bad trips" and that all those journeys were just challenging. That is, until I started hearing from journeyers who actually had their systems traumatized and exhibited PTSD-like symptoms after their experience. Some of these people experienced depersonalization or HPPD, began having chronic thoughts of self-harm, couldn't sleep anymore (even on high doses of antipsychotics or benzodiazepines), and watched their lives fall apart. Most of these individuals were not harmed by their facilitators, did not take a mega dose, managed their set and setting correctly, were not on any contraindicated medications, and did not engage in any inherently "wrong" actions during the journey. So, what triggered a "bad trip" for them? In episode two of the PsychedelicIQ podcast, doctor and facilitator Erica Zelfand offers the phrase "too much, too hard, and too fast." Most "bad trips" happen when a journeyer's mind and nervous system is unable to handle the physical, psychological, or energetic load these substances can bring.

After ten years of working with various substances, dosages, experiences, and clients, one thing I have learned is that with the proper work and support, almost every "bad trip" can eventually turn into a challenging journey. The time that takes and your unique path to get there will be different from anyone else's.

A "bad trip" can make you feel incredibly isolated and misunderstood. If this is you, and you are continuing to struggle, please visit the resources section on PsychedelicIQ.com for additional support. You are not alone.

Techniques for Navigating Challenging Journeys

Keep these helpful practices in your back pocket in case you find yourself experiencing a challenging journey. If trauma is the low-frequency residue of challenging life experiences, then finding and releasing that residue is essential to your healing process. Better out than in!

Ask for Help

Provided you are working with a skilled facilitator, they should have experience assisting clients with difficult experiences. Communicating what is happening and asking for help is the first-best option to navigate your challenging experience.

Surrender

As we discussed in the previous chapter, "surrender" is the ideal method to manage a difficult experience. In his poem "A Servant to Servants," Robert Frost offers, "… the best way out is always through." Try to relax and allow whatever needs to happen to happen.

Breathe

One of the reasons meditation is such a powerful preparation method for psychedelics is that it is perfectly designed to bring us into the present moment. Physically speaking, taking long, slow breaths can help to calm your thoughts and regulate your heart rate and nervous system. During a challenging journey, focus on your feelings and physical experience using strong, powerful breaths. Your intention should be to release this energy with every exhale.

Adjust Your Posture

Changing your physical posture is a very simple and effective way to manage your experience. If laying on your back causes intense sensations, rolling onto your side, shifting into child's pose, or even sitting up in a cross-legged meditation posture can offer an increased level of awareness that enables you to address your difficult experience.

Open Your Eyes

Contrary to popular belief, most of the visionary components of a psychedelic experience happen with your eyes closed. While some psychedelics and higher dosages can cause open-eye hallucinations, this is far less common than folklore might suggest. Sometimes turning a challenging experience into a tolerable one is as simple as opening your eyes.

Seek Help from the Medicine

From a more esoteric perspective, try asking the spirit of the medicine for assistance. Asking for a gentler experience or requesting guidance for dealing with a powerful entity are both common shamanic practices. I've often received a break in the middle of an ayahuasca journey simply by asking for it.

Move Toward the Discomfort

While somewhat counterintuitive, moving toward—rather than away from—the discomfort is one of the fastest ways to make it disappear. If you're being confronted with a terrifying entity or a real-life person who has harmed you in the past, confronting this energy with curiosity, love, compassion, and forgiveness can be incredibly powerful and healing medicine. A Buddhist practice known as Chöd (pronounced "chö"), which means "cutting through," is colloquially referred to as "feeding the demon." The term "demon" in this practice symbolizes internal obstacles, such as fear, attachment, or anger. Rather than avoiding or fighting these obstacles, the practice involves embracing and transforming them through a five-step method of compassionate engagement. For more information on this powerful practice, consider reading *Feeding Your Demons* by Tsultrim Allion and remember that attempting to avoid pain will only create more.

Shift the Vibration

The same frequency that caused the trauma does not need to be the frequency that heals it. If a person or experience in your life injected a tremendous amount of fear within you, it is not necessary to reexperience all that fear to heal or release the trauma. If fear is the first sensation you notice in your psychedelic experience, try using higher frequency emotions like love, forgiveness, peace, or harmony as an antidote to the heavier energy. Remember, the medicine you've ingested is already vibrating higher than the low-vibration frequencies that originally caused the harm and trauma, so asking your substance for help in transmuting these low frequencies to higher frequencies can offer near-instantaneous resolution.

Sometimes, healing is hard. There's just no way around it. Until we can learn more gentle ways of processing our traumatic residue, there will be challenging aspects to our psychedelic experiences.

If you can reassure yourself that what you're feeling is temporary, and that if you do this work now it will be over in a few minutes (or at worst, a few hours), that can help lessen the distress. I also find it helpful to remember that once I've done a specific piece of work, I'll never have to do it again. Once that energy has been released from your body, you will never have to face, process, and release it in the same way ever again. That is not to say there's not a deeper or more subtle process underneath, but rest assured, once it's gone, it's gone (unless your future actions replicate it, which we will discuss further in the chapters on integration and activation).

Spiritual Emergence or "Spiritual Emergency"?

Spiritual emergence is a positive and manageable experience for most—a gradual, natural process of personal and spiritual growth. It may include feelings of unity, increased sensitivity, intuitive abilities, joy, and a sense of purpose. However, sometimes a psychedelic experience can be so powerful or profound that it triggers a personal awakening at a level beyond your normal comprehension. Often referred to as a "spiritual emergency," this occurs when the process of spiritual emergence becomes overwhelming, disorienting, or distressing. It feels much more like a crisis, and the spiritual experiences are too intense or happen too quickly to be easily integrated.

Stanislav and Christina Grof, authors of *Spiritual Emergency*, offer ten distinct types of manifestation for a spiritual emergency:[74]

1. **The shamanic crisis** is a transformative journey of disintegration and rebirth, mirroring the ancient path of the shaman.
2. **The awakening of Kundalini energy** can lead to profound spiritual transformation but may bring disorienting physical and emotional symptoms.
3. **Episodes of unitive consciousness ("peak experiences")** bring fleeting glimpses of oneness and higher consciousness that can be both inspiring and destabilizing.
4. **Psychological renewal through return to the center** is a symbolic death of the old Self that paves the way for a new sense of identity and purpose.
5. **The crisis of psychic opening** is the opening of psychic abilities, which can feel disorienting without a framework for understanding them.
6. **Past-life experiences** can reveal unresolved traumas or spiritual lessons.
7. **Communications with spirit guides and "channeling"** can offer wisdom but also provoke doubt or fear of losing touch with reality.
8. **Near-death experiences** may bring a deepened sense of purpose and connection to the spiritual dimensions of life, but may also be experienced as life-threatening.
9. **Experiences of close encounters with UFOs and beings** may challenge perceptions of reality and can provoke a spiritual crisis.
10. **Possession states** can signal a profound inner conflict or spiritual awakening masked in symbolic form.

The Grofs further state:

One of the most critical implications… is the realization that many of the conditions, which are currently diagnosed as psychotic and indiscriminately treated by suppressive medication, are actually difficult stages of a radical personality transformation and of spiritual opening. If they are correctly understood and supported, these psychospiritual crises can result in emotional and psychosomatic healing, remarkable psychological transformation, and consciousness evolution.

It is helpful to consider spiritual emergence and spiritual emergency on a continuum. When you successfully integrate new, powerful states of energy and consciousness, and function well in daily life, the scale tips toward *emergence*. When life becomes disrupted or unmanageable, it tips toward *emergency*. If you feel like you are somewhere on this continuum, first flip to chapter 16, "Integration" and review the section entitled "When Your Experience Won't End."

If you're still unsure what to do next, visit the PsychedelicIQ.com resources section for support. There are organizations and practitioners who deal specifically with this type of post-psychedelic difficulty.

What to Do If You've Been Harmed

Unfortunately, harm can and does occur within the fields of psychedelics and spirituality. Sometimes bad actors intentionally prey on vulnerable victims, but much more often, harm is unintentional. However, no matter the intention, harm can be very confusing to experience.

Instances of harm are incredibly complicated, made more complex under the influence of a powerful, mind-altering substance. There are so many subtle variables in each experience—a simple gesture, word, or even shift in the energetic field—that could drudge up an old memory or trigger a past trauma that becomes a surprise to both you and your facilitator.

Below is a scale created in 2018 from a meta-analysis of collected harms in the medical profession:[75]

LEVELS OF HARM SEVERITY

Severity	Definition
1. No harm	Any incident that ran to completion, but no harm occurred to the patient.
2. No harm outcome due to mitigating action	Any incident that had the potential to cause harm to a patient but resulted in no harm.

Severity	Definition
3. Mild harm	Incident in which: (i) patient was harmed, with mild and short-term impact, on physical, mental or social functioning, that was expected to resolve in a few hours; (ii) patient was harmed but required no or minimal intervention/treatment, e.g.… patient or their loved ones experienced transient emotional distress but no long-term consequences and incident report contains words, e.g., angry, anxious, confused, distressed, frightened, frustrated, humiliated, or upset, that might describe a feeling that occurs at the time of the incident but soon passes.
4. Moderate harm	Incident in which: (i) patient was harmed, causing a medium-term impact on physical, mental, or social functioning that was expected to resolve in days; (ii) patient required medical intervention in the form of treatment… and/or patient or their loved ones experienced psychological difficulty of a more long-standing nature but not requiring formal treatment, e.g., as indicated by evidence in the report of more long-standing anxiety, insomnia, or low mood.
5. Severe harm	Incident in which: (i) patient was harmed, causing a major long-term or permanent impact on physical, mental, or social function or shortening of life-expectancy;… (ii) patient was harmed and required prolonged hospitalization or admission to critical care unit, high-dependency unit, or intensive care unit; and/or… (iv) patient or their loved ones experienced enduring psychological difficulty that required specialist treatment, e.g., as indicated in the report by evidence of chronic anxiety or depression or psychosis.
6. Death	Incident in which, on the balance of probabilities, death of the patient was caused or brought forward in the short term by the incident.

TABLE 6. Levels of harm severity

Harm should always be perceived from the vantage point of the one who feels harmed, rather than the one accused of causing harm. What feels harmful to one person may not feel harmful to another. But that does not mean that it wasn't harmful or traumatic.

So how should you deal with harm if it happens to you? The answer depends on the severity and your comfortability with your facilitator. Based on the scale above, the next section lists a few potential considerations for repair.

SUGGESTED RESPONSES TO HARM BASED ON SEVERITY

1. **No Harm**

    If there was a moment during your experience that bordered on harmful and made you feel unsafe, consider discussing this with your facilitator. If you feel comfortable discussing it during or right after your experience, this is best, as it will leave no lingering questions or energy for either party. This could be an amazing learning opportunity for you and your facilitator to deepen your therapeutic relationship and trust.

2. **No Harm Outcome Due to Mitigating Action**

    Same suggested action as for No Harm: discuss with your facilitator.

3. **Mild Harm**

    In the event of mild harm, you may need time and support to process your experience entirely. If you feel comfortable bringing it up to your facilitator during or directly after your experience, please do so. If you need more time to process your feelings, possibly with the help of your care team, take the time necessary and schedule a follow-up session with your facilitator. If you feel that having someone support you in that conversation would be beneficial, let your facilitator know ahead of time who will be joining you to offer that support. Mild harm is often caused by misunderstandings, confusion, or being pushed outside of your window of tolerance by your facilitator or the medicine. In some cases, you may find that with enough time and awareness, what you initially perceived as harm might actually be projection and transference (redirecting your feelings, desires, or expectations onto your facilitator), and with the right support, could be an opportunity for growth. Mild harm is rarely intentional and not likely illegal or unethical.

4. **Moderate Harm**

    In the event of moderate harm, you will probably need time and support to process your experience. This type of harm could look like an improper touch or a violation of your personal, emotional, or spiritual boundaries. With moderate harm, having the help of a third party to help you process and better understand what occurred is wise. Document harm that occurred at this level, as memory can quickly shift the further away you get from your experience. Consider written/electronic communications with your facilitator until you feel stable and comfortable enough to meet in person. Having the support of a trusted friend, family member, or therapist may also be helpful. Boundary violations, which could be intentional or unintentional, can often cause moderate harm. While these violations may not be illegal, they are almost certainly unethical.

5. **Severe Harm**

In the event of severe harm, immediately distance yourself from your facilitator and seek medical, psychological, or legal help as necessary to begin the process of healing and resolution. This type of harm may involve intentional improper touch or gross negligence. If you experience severe harm, it is important to document as much detail as possible from your experience and keep electronic records of all communication with your facilitator. If you are communicating directly with your facilitator, consider copying someone from your care team on the communication for additional support. In cases of unintentional severe harm, you may or may not want to work with your care team to repair the relationship. If what occurred was not illegal or happened in another country, it may be difficult to prosecute the offender formally. In these situations, it may be wise to abandon the relationship and work toward your own healing. When the harmful actions are illegal, you and your support team should work directly with law enforcement to report your experience and file charges as you feel appropriate.

6. **Death**

I pray that this never happens, but the sad truth is that there have been documented instances where a fatality occurred—and it will likely happen again. The location where the fatality occurs and the facilitator/church/retreat center/etc. will have a lot to do with the process and resources made available for closure. If the fatality occurred in the Global North, your first call should be to an attorney, the proper authorities, or both. On the other hand, challenges may arise if the incident occurs in Central or South America. The legal system of many of these countries is far laxer than what we're used to in the North, and sadly, what happens in the jungle, often stays in the jungle.

One of the best ways to prevent harm is to prepare for it. Before your experience, take time to ask your facilitator how they would like to handle situations that feel harmful. A qualified facilitator should welcome this type of conversation. If your facilitator shies away or seeks to avoid the topic of harm altogether, this is a "red flag" and an opportunity for you to practice greater discernment.

As I mentioned before, harm is often neither conscious nor intentional. Truly good people with pure intentions do their best to help others. Sometimes humans make mistakes, things go wrong, or facilitators operate outside their scope of practice. It's possible that the harm experienced may be no one's "fault," but that doesn't make it disappear. In these cases, it can be very beneficial to understand the process of rupture and repair, and have a way to work through this with your facilitator. The repair process can often be incredibly healing for all parties involved.

If you have been harmed and need support, please visit the resources section on PsychedelicIQ.com.

Preparing for the Integration Process

The things that can occur during a psychedelic experience are truly uncountable and unquantifiable. These experiences often carry with them profound experiences of uncertainty. The best antidote I have found for uncertainty is curiosity. Curiosity turns uncertainty into opportunity—and that's the whole reason you're doing this work to begin with.

Now that your experience is complete, it's time for your actual work to begin. The vast majority of the healing that occurs with psychedelics comes after the experience. This is what's known as the integration process, where genuine and sustainable transformation begins.

Integration

"Simply The Best (Acoustic)" by Ben Haynes

Many astronauts who have had the privilege of looking at Earth from space have experienced what is called the "overview effect." Researchers have explained this phenomenon as "A state of awe with self-transcendent qualities... The most prominent common aspects of personally experiencing the Earth from space are appreciation and perception of beauty, unexpected and even overwhelming emotion, and an increased sense of connection to other people and the Earth as a whole. The effect can cause changes in the observer's self-concept and value system, and can be transformative."[76]

This definition could just as easily describe a psychedelic experience. Like an astronaut returning to Earth after a powerful experience, you may never feel the same again. If your experience was solo and you do not have a support team or an understanding community to return to, this can be a challenging time for newly minted psychonauts. Most (if not all) of the people around you will not understand what you've experienced. It becomes even more challenging if you have difficulty putting your journey into words. Some have referred to this sensation as the "post-ecstatic blues."

This feeling can represent a crossroads in your healing journey. During this period, you are offered an opportunity to redefine who you are as a sovereign being and, more importantly, who you want to become. You have an opportunity to begin the practice of self-governing your thoughts, words, and actions. It's an opportunity to stop comparing yourself to those who do not understand or support you, and start living your life for yourself. For many, a single psychedelic experience is a "re-turning" toward the true, authentic Self.

Here's the good news: if you spent quality time preparing for your experience, you've already got a great start on integration. Almost every practice covered in the earlier chapter on preparation will also support your integration process. If you've already developed positive new habits during preparation, do not stop them just because your experience has ended. Integration is the time to crystallize those good habits into your psyche (more on that in "Critical Periods" as follows).

What Is Integration and Why Is It Essential?

Integration is a valuable opportunity to gain clarity, perspective, and wisdom from your experience. If you think about your psychedelic journey like baking a cake, integration helps you thoroughly mix all the ingredients of your experience together, so the final, fully baked product tastes the way you want it to.

Interestingly, if you asked different professionals to define integration, you'd get different answers. There is no single "best" approach to integrating your experience.

If you choose to work with a coach or therapist, their methods will be more closely aligned with their training, personal style, and preference than any quantitative data and outcome. Yet we know one thing for sure: integration dramatically increases the durability of your psychedelic experiences and is one of the best indicators for long-lasting and sustainable transformation.

It can also be helpful to think of integration on a spectrum: one end is more fluid and natural, the other more directive and intentional. Walking in the park the day after your journey is the former. Individual sessions with an integration coach are the latter. Your process should naturally unfold through your own unique needs.

It may feel overwhelming to incorporate everything from your experience into your daily life. This is perfectly normal. Profound realizations could take months, or even years, to implement and integrate fully. Sadly, I've met countless seekers who return to the same medicine, repeatedly abdicating all their personal responsibility for change to the substance they've ingested. Most of the time, these seekers have never taken the time and effort to complete the integration phase of their prior experiences. The harsh truth is that if you're not integrating your experience, you're really just getting high.

One of the earliest known mentions of "psychedelic integration" is from Stanislav Grof in his 1980 book, *LSD Psychotherapy*. He states, "The general suggestion for the day is to rest, relax, and stay in a meditated state of mind," and suggests that if your experience remains unintegrated, you miss the opportunity to absorb the wisdom and meaning your unconscious mind offers.[77]

If your first journey resulted in a profound mystical experience or shift in consciousness, you may have been introduced to an entirely different worldview. The phrase "we're all one," which once sounded like nonsense, may now have profound significance to you. Atheists have been known to become believers in a few hours. You might metabolize decades of memories and trauma, and now feel like you're living in a different body. Or even trickier, you may know that something's different, but be unsure of exactly what that is.

Each of these experiences is surprisingly common but can feel challenging without support. This is the true purpose of integration.

Neuroplasticity and Neurogenesis

Psychedelics can do wonders to show us our path forward. Unfortunately, old habits and beliefs can quickly snap back into place unless we're willing to do the work to prevent that from happening. Fortunately, psychedelics have a unique ability to increase neuroplasticity and neurogenesis in the brain, allowing us the opportunity to get the most out of our experience.

Neuroplasticity refers to the brain's ability to reorganize itself by forming new neural connections. This allows the brain to adapt to new experiences, learn new information, and recover from injuries. Neuroplasticity is essential for cognitive development, memory formation, skill acquisition, and recovery from neurological conditions. It refers to the brain's remarkable flexibility and ability to change, even in adulthood.

Neurogenesis is the process by which the brain generates new neurons (nerve cells). Neurogenesis occurs throughout a person's life, although it is most active during prenatal development, when the brain first forms its initial structures.

The duration of psychedelic effects on brain function can vary depending on the substance and individual. Multiple studies suggest that the effects of psychedelics on neuroplasticity can last from several days to several weeks—or even longer. The real-world, practical implications of this are that you have an increased opportunity to grow and learn new things for a limited amount of time after your psychedelic experience.

Lead researcher Joshua Siegel and his team at Washington University performed a breathtaking visual study of the brain's response to psychedelic use. The researchers measured participants' brains roughly eighteen times using functional magnetic resonance imaging (fMRI) before, during, and three weeks after they ingested a high dose of psilocybin. The first study of its kind, researchers were able to specifically correlate activity in participants' brains to corresponding measurements of the Mystical Experience Questionnaire (MEQ30). Interestingly, they found that a disruption in the functional connectivity of the brain most strongly correlated with a feeling of transcendence (for example, "loss of your usual sense of time or space"). More importantly, their imaging showed that brain activity remained altered for weeks after the experience, stating:

> *Psilocybin massively disrupted functional connectivity (FC) in cortex and subcortex, acutely causing more than threefold greater change than methylphenidate.... Psilocybin caused persistent decrease in FC between the anterior hippocampus and default mode network, lasting for weeks. Persistent reduction of hippocampal-default mode network connectivity may represent a neuroanatomical and mechanistic correlate of the proplasticity and therapeutic effects of psychedelics.*[78]

This study, though slightly more technical than your typical light reading, demonstrates just how vital the days and weeks after your experience are. Never in your adult life is your brain been more flexible to change and learning than after a psychedelic experience.

Ask yourself, "What is my true goal in working with psychedelics, and how do I want my brain to change when I'm done?" If you are clear on the answer to these two questions (and hopefully you are, especially if you have completed the intention and preparation steps), you should be able to create an integration plan specifically designed to accomplish these goals.

If the old adage "You are the average of the five people you spend the most time with" is true, what kind of people would you like to surround yourself with after your experience? Ideally people you love, admire, and who challenge you to be a better person, rather than people who do not respect you and the changes you're trying to make in your life. Since your brain is temporarily and profoundly primed to learn new things, carefully consider how to best use that time. Would you rather watch reruns of *The Walking Dead*, or would you prefer to try journaling or reading *Autobiography of a Yogi*?

Take a moment to return to your intention and make choices that best align with it.

Critical Brain Development Periods

Critical brain development periods are developmental windows during childhood when your brain is especially open to learning and improving specific skills like language, vision, and social behaviors. During these periods, the brain's neural circuits are highly adaptable or "plastic," allowing for increased learning and development. Once a critical period ends, the brain's plasticity decreases, making it harder to learn new skills or behaviors later in life. These periods are crucial for normal development, and disruptions can impact cognitive, emotional, and social growth.

The early years of a child's life, usually between birth and age five, represent the most crucial period of critical brain development. A rich educational environment surrounding a child during this time presents terrific opportunities for learning and growth. Yet, as offered in an article from Verywell Mind, "Events such as abuse, neglect, trauma, or extreme stress—collectively known as adverse childhood experiences (ACEs)—can be detrimental to brain development. These adverse events can impede the formation of neural connections and lead to behavioral, emotional, and cognitive difficulties later in life. Once a critical period has been closed, it is very difficult to be reopened."[79]

With the help of a 2023 study from Johns Hopkins University, we are beginning to understand that psychedelics have the remarkable ability to reopen these periods.[80] Researchers showed that a single dose of psychedelics reopened critical brain development periods in mice, lasting anywhere from two days to four weeks. By reopening these developmental periods, psychedelics could help adults improve social skills, which may have applications in treating conditions like social anxiety, PTSD, and autism. This flexibility to changes in the brain's cortical circuitry could enhance social reward learning, a process closely linked to forming social connections. The research further revealed that different psychedelics have varying effects on its duration. MDMA was reported to have the longest-lasting effect.

After a psychedelic experience, it is impossible to ever truly know how long our brains will remain in a higher state of plasticity or how long our critical periods will stay open. The most opportune time is likely within the first week or two. Instead of focusing on this unspecified window of time, focus on an integration plan that optimizes the time you do have right away.

Methods of Integration

Earlier on, we discussed how critical the dosing variable is when it comes to working with a specific substance. Similarly, "dosing" for integration may be dependent on the substance you used and the overall significance of your experience. Each of these factors plays an important role in determining how long your integration will last. It could be a few hours, a few days—or even years.

A good rule of thumb is that the more powerful the substance or the higher the dose, the more time you should plan to devote to integration. It's not uncommon for someone who has experienced a profound journey with ayahuasca or iboga to later say, "I will be integrating this journey for the rest of my life." Some elements of your experience may immediately settle into your daily patterns and psyche. Other aspects will gradually become a part of your life and continue to unfold for years to come.

How you proceed with integration is a highly individualized process. If you already have experience with more esoteric practices, you may not need a therapist or coach to assist you through this process. But if you're struggling to make sense of your experience, having help from others can be an incredibly beneficial tool in your integration toolbox.

Keep in mind the "favorite restaurant menu" analogy from the chapter on preparation. When exploring all the ways you can integrate your experience, consider each as an item on a menu. Remember that you do not need to eat, or even try, every item at once. Trying to do this will only cause stress and make you feel like there's not enough time in the day to live your life. The whole point of this work is to enjoy your life and relieve suffering, so try ordering one item from the physical, psychological, and spiritual sections of the "menu," then continue adding and subtracting items slowly, in a way that feels supportive to you. If your brain is highly plastic and capable of learning new things, then the feeling of overwhelm during your integration process is exactly the opposite of what you want it to learn. Be gentle and give yourself grace.

RETURN TO YOUR INTENTION

If you have been following the previous steps in the framework, you will have already written an intention to help guide your experience. My first postexperience recommendation is to evaluate your experience through the lens of this intention.

No matter what happened—a beautiful experience, a challenging one, or no experience at all—write your intention at the top of a page in your journal and try freewriting for fifteen to twenty minutes, seeing what kinds of conscious or unconscious connections arise. Discussing these with your facilitator, coach, or therapist can be a helpful exercise, as your mind may want to make literal sense of something that is more metaphorical.

As you write, you may find that words cannot adequately describe some aspects of your experience. There are ineffable moments we can only experience as they happen to us. Don't overexert yourself attempting to document these moments or explain them to anyone else. Applying words to the ineffable will only diminish its potency.

USE PHYSICAL BODY TECHNIQUES

Safe and Supportive Landing

Some people exit a powerful experience feeling energized and ready to tackle the world. Others may feel exhausted, as if they have been wrung out like a wet rag for the past eight hours. Plan to return home to a supportive physical and emotional environment to ensure a soft landing from your elevated state of consciousness. Try to have your friends, family, or your care team standing by to help in the event of a challenging experience, but also let them know you may not want a lot of human contact. In the immediate hours after your experience, stay flexible when making decisions that will best support your healing process. That may mean processing with loved ones, or it could mean curling up alone in bed for deep and nourishing rest. You get to choose what best supports your needs.

Rest

If it's possible, avoid rushing back into your normal routine. Most modern-day cultures make us feel as though our task lists are never-ending, and life frequently makes us feel like we're always behind and running to the next thing. Try using the time directly following your experience to retrain your mind to accept more rest and relaxation.

Nutrition

Eating high-quality foods and drinking lots of fresh water are two wonderful ways to nourish your body after your experience. Stay away from sweets or escapist substances such as cannabis and alcohol. If you are looking to improve your physical health, you need to focus on establishing new, healthy habits that will support your body.

Self-Care

Taking a bath, a nap, or getting a massage are wonderful ways to care for your physical body in the days and weeks following your experience. Incorporating any of your preferred self-care practices into your integration work can help remind you to incorporate compassion and empathy into your process.

Movement and Breath

This is a broad category including anything that involves moving your body and breathing; this could be yoga, tai chi, qigong, going to the gym, or even consciously hiking or walking through the park. Unless you are struggling to come out of your experience, strenuous activity is not required. (If your experience doesn't feel like it is completing in the timeframe expected, see "When Your Experience Won't End" in the following pages.)

USE PSYCHOLOGICAL BODY TECHNIQUES

Document Your Journey

I never recommend seeking out other people's trip reports, but documenting your own should be a top priority. Consider writing an inclusive and emotional account of your experience. Start by establishing the date, substance, and dosage, then include as much subjective detail as you can remember. If it's available, listen to your playlist while you write.

Journaling

In the days and weeks that follow, continue journaling to process and unpack your experience more deeply. Pick up a new journal and try to simply freewrite a few pages per day for a week or two after your experience. Remember, there is no "right answer" or perfect outcome you're trying to achieve. Let go of your craving for understanding and perfection, and simply put pen to paper.

Coaching and Therapy

Working with your facilitator, an integration coach, or a therapist—especially if their cosmology is oriented to the more transpersonal aspects of the psychedelic experience—can help you cement good habits you want to keep after your journey. This type of work can take weeks, months, or even years.

Peer Support Groups

If one-on-one work doesn't feel accessible or necessary, sharing your experience within a psychedelic community or peer group can be a wonderful way to not only integrate your experience, but also help others integrate theirs. Many integration groups are often low or no cost, and available online or in person. For more information or to join an online group, visit PsychedelicIQ.com.

Music

Music can be one of the easiest ways to integrate and return to your experience. I create a custom playlist for each of my clients and encourage them to listen to it the day after their experience—or for longer, if they'd like. Music can reignite memories, insights, or flashbacks of your experience, or even help you recall aspects that were seemingly "forgotten," allowing you greater access to feel or write about them. Many clients have even reported listening to their playlist years after their experience and being instantly transported back into the visions, thoughts, and feelings that came with that day.

Write a Letter to Yourself

In his book *Waking Up*, Sam Harris says, "On one level, wisdom is nothing more profound than an ability to follow one's advice."[81] One of my favorite ways to help my clients follow their own advice is to have them write a letter to themselves immediately following their experience. Then, a year later, I will send them this letter. Often a fantastic surprise and meaningful gift, letters like this can help us see how far we've come and how much we've grown. If your facilitator can't mail your letter at a later date, you can put yours in a sealed envelope and then add a note to your phone's calendar to remind you to open it later.

Art

Incorporating art into your integration practice is a way to bypass verbal and cognitive processing, and allow your unconscious mind to come to the surface. A common art practice in psychedelics and Holotropic breathwork is to create a mandala. To do this, take a blank piece of paper and draw a large circle in the center. Try to draw a visual representation of your journey within this circle—however that might look. Painting, sculpture, collage, and photography are other ways to use art to capture a visual representation of your experience.

Dreamwork

You can tap into your unconscious by paying close attention to your dreams directly following your psychedelic experience. Some experiences may require days and weeks to fully resolve and integrate. During this time, more content could arise in your dream world. Keep a dream journal near your bed and document whatever you can remember first thing upon waking. Finding guidance from a practitioner skilled in dream interpretation may further help integrate your experience.

Singing and Dancing

Step more deeply into music and incorporate song and dance into your integration plan. A BMJ study published in 2024 showed that dancing was the activity most strongly correlated with reducing the symptoms of depression, and at a rate far greater than traditional antidepressants.[82] Incorporating the healing aspects of your experience into verse is a long-practiced tradition of many Indigenous cultures.

Meditation

After a powerful experience, mindfulness meditation can offer much-needed quiet time upon returning to your normal routine. Disconnecting from your thoughts and allowing them to rise and fall from your consciousness can create more space in a busy mind.

Daily Mental Health Support

For less than the price of a therapy session, Cope Notes is a beautiful tool I recommend to many of my clients. This inexpensive service sends you daily text messages to support your healing journey. These are relatable texts from real people with real feelings. You can learn more about this service by visiting the resources section on PsychedelicIQ.com.

USE SPIRITUAL BODY TECHNIQUES

Nature

One of my favorite quotes from Isak Dinesen is "The cure for anything is salt water—tears, sweat, or the sea." Spending time in nature is a beautiful way to ground yourself back into your human experience and connect with the energy of Mother Nature. If you're feeling ungrounded, walking barefoot in the grass can be a remarkable way to settle your energy. Going for a long walk, feeling the sun against your face and the breeze against your hair, or spending time near (or in) water can help soothe your nervous system.

Prayer and Ritual

You may or may not have believed in an Infinite Source before your journey, but if you are open to engaging with a higher power postexperience, now is an excellent time to honor this new connection. Taking the time to speak quietly to this new connection (whatever you'd like to call it) or perform intentional acts of devotion can be an excellent way to deepen your relationship with this new source of love, compassion, and wisdom. These prayers or rituals do not have to be formal or look anything like organized religion. They are 100 percent yours to create and own.

Build an Altar

Altars have been used in spiritual practices for centuries. Traditionally, an altar includes sacred artifacts, candles, or incense. Building your own personal altar with photographs, crystals, leaves, stones, or any other unique elements that signify your devotion to change is a beautiful way to manifest the spiritual universe into the physical world. Our psychedelic work often includes honoring our "inner child" or reencountering supportive figures in our lives. Representing these entities on your altar and spending an intentional moment with them daily is a great reminder to continue deepening your integration practice.

Jim's Story

When I first began my self-help journey, I believed I had to tackle it alone. It felt like a solitary path where I needed to figure everything out for myself. But over time, I've realized how crucial community is to personal growth. Being part of a supportive network has provided me with invaluable wisdom, encouragement, and a sense of belonging.

Now, I wake up each day with an open mind and a commitment to keeping my ego in check. My progress so far is due not only to my own efforts, but also to the shared learning and support within my community. Every member brings unique experiences and insights, creating a collective pool of knowledge that accelerates everyone's growth. Learning from others' successes and mistakes has been unexpectedly enriching.

What stands out most is the feeling of being understood and accepted. In this community, I've found a safe space to share my thoughts, fears, and aspirations, knowing I'm surrounded by people with similar goals and values. This sense of connection has been both healing and motivating.

Reflecting on my journey, it's clear that the community has played a vital role in my progress. Initially, I saw self-help as a solo mission, but now I recognize the power of collective effort. The shared wisdom and diverse perspectives have helped me approach challenges with more creativity and confidence.

Having people to celebrate milestones with, big or small, makes the journey more rewarding. Each success feels like a shared victory that strengthens our bond. The emotional support of my peers is equally important, especially on tough days, when they remind me that setbacks are part of growth.

For anyone starting a self-help journey, I can't stress enough the importance of finding a supportive community. Self-improvement can be challenging, but with the right people by your side, it can become a shared adventure filled with learning, support, and celebration. This sense of community has been a game-changer for me, and it's made all the difference in my personal growth.

Risks of Nonintegration

Maharishi Mahesh Yogi, the founder of Transcendental Meditation, was fond of separating faith from action using the term "mood-making." Unfortunately, many practices in the New Age spiritual movement align more with making you temporarily feel good than they do with creating sustainable change. When mood-making activities dominate your integration plan, or if you have no integration plan at all, the risks of nonintegration surface.

In his book, *Psychedelic Integration: Psychotherapy for Non-Ordinary States of Consciousness,*[83] author Marc Aixalà offers the following four risks of not integrating your experience:

Not Taking Full Advantage of the Experience

Taking a substance for recreational purposes is one thing, but once you direct your attention inward and use psychedelics for healing, it becomes essential to integrate your experiences to receive their true value. Some people have reported "tripping" hundreds of times yet received nothing substantial from their experiences. This is not by happenstance. It is a choice.

Ego Inflation

Psychedelics have the potential to create profound changes in one's self-perception. They dissolve the boundaries of one's ego, allowing the seeker to connect to the Divine or a sense of "oneness." However, after the experience, some individuals might interpret this as evidence of their own specialness or importance, leading to an inflated sense of self. One common way this shows up is when individuals, despite having had only a few powerful experiences themselves, believe they must serve psychedelics to others with no mentorship or training.

Spiritual Bypass

A term coined by John Welwood, a Buddhist psychotherapist and practitioner, "spiritual bypass" refers to using spiritual ideas and practices to avoid dealing with unresolved emotional issues, psychological wounds, and unfinished developmental tasks. Signs of spiritual bypass include running away from one's problems, frequently attending spiritual retreats, and having recurring peak experiences. After returning home, one may feel enlightened for a short time before eventually falling victim to their triggers and returning to a state of dis-ease. When we place an over-abundance of emphasis on our spirit and avoid our human personality, we fall into the trap of bypass.

Psychedelic Bypass

An offshoot of spiritual bypassing is "psychedelic bypassing," explained by author Sean Lawlor as "the many ways the mind can excuse abuse, ignore the darker sides of ourselves, categorize the vast scale of emotions into little boxes of 'good' and 'bad,' and cast aside anything deemed 'lesser than'— all in the pursuit of a more enlightened life."[84] It's not uncommon in psychedelic circles to encounter an avoidance of "low-vibration emotions" such as sadness, fear, or anger. You may also hear recurring phrases like "We're all one" and "I am love." While these phrases are accurate from the perspective of Absolute Reality (i.e., Brahman), we also have a duty to honor our human incarnation and individual responsibility (i.e., Atman). Individuals who focus on and repeat these phrases as a means to escape their humanness may be in the throes of psychedelic bypass.

Attachment and Addiction to Experience

Classical psychedelics are not physically addictive, but they can become psychologically addictive. When one does not integrate and grow from their experiences, it's easy to fall into a pattern of returning to these substances to escape the more challenging aspects of life. When the afterglow of psychedelics fades, rather than dealing with these challenging facets of life and growth, it becomes easier to avoid them by seeking another peak experience.

When Your Experience Won't End

In chapter 7, "Risks," we discussed potential adverse outcomes of a journey. When psychedelics are used safely and with a qualified facilitator, the risks are relatively low compared to the possible rewards. But when things go wrong, they can go *really wrong*, and recovering from the experience can feel really confusing, if not impossible. Unfortunately, some of these adverse outcomes, especially when left untreated or unresolved, can become life-threatening.

Much of what happens in a psychedelic experience is impossible to measure or understand. When an individual has a challenging experience, it all happens within their inner world, unseen and unmeasurable by an outside observer. Repairing these experiences is rarely fast or easy. In most cases, modern medicine or psychiatry does not provide any helpful relief, and time (days, weeks, months, or even years) may be required to achieve complete resolution.

Journeys can often last longer than expected, both physically and psychologically. If you are still feeling the effects of the medicine long after it should have worn off, there are a few simple ways to encourage it to move through (and out of) your system:

Break a Sweat

One way to help move the medicine through your physical body is by sweating. Going for a brisk walk, a jog, or sitting in a sauna can help the body trigger its natural detoxification method.

Swim or Shower

A traditional Indigenous detoxifying practice involves swimming in a natural body of water such as a pond, a lake, or the ocean. Indigenous cultures believe that Mother Earth can help clean and absorb the excess energy from your body. As an alternative, taking a shower can help reduce some physical symptoms and return your body back to baseline.

Increase Electrolytes

Electrolytes are minerals that dissolve in water and carry an electric charge. Since we are all energy and our bodies are the superconductors of this energy, electrolytes help regulate our essential physiological functions. They help us with maintaining fluid balance, transmitting nerve signals, and contracting muscles. If you do not have access to commercial electrolyte products, try drinking a glass of salt water.

Encourage Bowel Movement

While sweating is one way the body releases toxins, the liver and kidneys are the most responsible for detoxifying the body. If you are struggling to have a bowel movement, try ingesting a small amount of caffeine in coffee or black tea to help stimulate your bowels. Caffeine will stimulate your body, and it will also stimulate your mind. The latter is not ideal in this scenario, so try not to consume any more than necessary.

Sleep

If possible, try to sleep. With some substances, especially mescaline and LSD, which have a long half-life, sleep can be difficult postexperience. If sleep doesn't feel possible, melatonin or an herbal tea may be used. This potential challenge is another good reason to consider your psychedelic experience a two-day, rather than a one-day, event.

Return to the Medicine

If your ongoing experience feels less physical and more psychological, potential options for resolution become more complicated. In *LSD Psychotherapy*, Stanislav Grof proposes that if an experience does not resolve, clients should consider breathwork as a means of release. If that doesn't work, going back into the psychedelic session may be required. If you had a challenging experience and are struggling with its aftereffects, going back into an altered state may sound terrifying. However, facing the unresolved content and bringing your process to a successful completion may be your fastest way out. Finding a safe and experienced practitioner to assist you in this process is essential.

If you are struggling to integrate your experience, please visit the resources section on PsychedelicIQ.com for a list of organizations that can help.

On the Day of Completing Your Experience

Our memory is unreliable. In their research, the Innocence Project determined that 69 percent of DNA exonerations occurred due to inaccurate witness testimony, and that states of stress and emotional arousal can further lead to memory loss or alterations.[85] Understanding the inherent fallibility of our minds, the first thing I encourage my clients to do to start their integration process is document as much of their experience as they can remember before leaving the ceremony space.

Here is an example of a process I use with my clients as they are completing their journeys:

- + Describe your experience using three words.
- + Spend about fifteen to thirty minutes coloring a mandala to represent your experience visually.
- + Using only bullet points (no paragraphs, explanation, or understanding required), log everything you can remember from your experience.
- + Answer the following prompts:
  - ◇ How did your experience relate to your intention, and do you feel you made progress?
  - ◇ What did you learn during your experience?
  - ◇ How do those teachings apply to your life?

- ⋄ Based on these lessons, what are one to three things you could immediately do to improve your life?
- ⋄ If you had an experience relating to your "inner child," what would that young part of you want you to remember about your experience?

Not every client does every step. Many times, the more mystical the journey you have, the less objective your answers will be. The lessons for some journeys may not materialize for days, and there may not be an immediate set of steps to take. The point is not about perfection but about pointing you toward integration.

Integration Following Indigenous Traditions

If you're working one-on-one with a facilitator or attending a psychedelic retreat, dedicated time for integration is expected and should be built in to your protocol or agenda. However, if you join the booming psychotourism industry and travel to a foreign country to work with psychedelics, integration experiences will vary dramatically. The same may also be true if you sit with an Indigenous medicine carrier or group ceremony in the Global North.

Most Indigenous practitioners do not recognize integration as a separate step in their process. To them, integration is already seamlessly incorporated into their lives. My teacher often reminds me that "every day is a medicine day," implying that even when you're not ingesting a substance, you should treat every day of your life as an opportunity to learn and grow.

When I take participants on an experience out of the country, we will frequently sit with medicine one day and take the next day off. Rather than scheduling dedicated time to unpack our experiences, integration often comes in casual conversation. It can appear as Indigenous teachings shared during a hike, a chat in the van, a visit to a sacred site, or talk over the dinner table. (This assumes you have access to the curandero or facilitator before and after your experience, so depending on the structure of your trip, your mileage may vary.)

As we have discussed, once you embark on a journey, you must take responsibility for your safety needs. If you're planning a trip to South America, ask questions to see how you will integrate your experience and how much time you will have to speak with the curandero serving the medicine. If you're attending a retreat, inquire about the type of integration opportunities they provide for participants and the ratio of individual to group activities. Both activities are very effective, but having some time dedicated to working one-on-one with someone skilled in integration is helpful.

Please keep one thing in mind: if your experience doesn't include integration, or if you feel you need more integration than what was offered, you should find these resources *before* your experience. Doing so after, with an unstable body, mind, or spirit, can be very challenging. An ounce of preparation is worth a pound of integration. You are ultimately the responsible party, and if you have a tough experience, a safe place to land will be invaluable to your mental and physical health.

Healing Requires Patience

One area where science and spirituality can work together, hand in hand, is with integration. With what we know about how psychedelics open critical brain development periods and boost neurogenesis and neuroplasticity, we should plan to schedule our most potent integration activities during this window. When used effectively, the first couple of weeks after your experience can cement positive changes into your life.

If you don't get the results you want right away, please be gentle with yourself. You didn't create your neuroses in a day, and it's equally unlikely that they'll all disappear in one journey. A single psychedelic experience will not instantly solve all your problems, and healing is a long journey.

I spent the better part of two decades trying to address my unhealthy habits. During my sobriety journey, I realized I was far less addicted to alcohol than I was to sugar. Sugar addiction was my earliest coping mechanism, and it's the first substance I turn to when life gets hard. After ten years of very intentional medicine work and asking the medicine again and again to help me release my sugar addiction, I have finally been able to heal the majority of underlying trauma that caused me to overindulge. While psychedelics never directly changed my behavior, they helped me cleanse and release the memories that were triggering my behavior.

It's important to remember that we're not in charge of the speed of our healing. Love yourself for the work you've already done. Whether or not you fully understand it, whatever happens during your journey is progress. If you didn't make as much progress as you hoped, give yourself some grace, integrate as much as you can, and continue with the next step on your path. More will be revealed in time.

If you decide to incorporate ongoing, intentional use of psychedelics in your healing practice, you may want a more objective way to measure your long-term integration progress. A study published in 2022, titled "The Psychedelic Integration Scales: Tools for Measuring Psychedelic Integration Behaviors and Experiences,"[86] offers two sets of questions to help you track your experiences and integration over time.

The Psychedelic Integration Scales

Please state your level of agreement with the following statements, considering the time period since your most recent psychedelic experience. If you have already filled out this questionnaire, indicate your responses only with respect to the time period since you last filled out the questionnaire. Answer as honestly as possible. There are no right or wrong answers. At any given time your responses will naturally vary between lower and higher scores.

*Scores are measured on a Likert Scale with anchors "Strongly Disagree," "Disagree," "Neither agree nor disagree,""Agree," and "Strongly agree."

Integration Engagement Scale

- I've given myself mental space to reconnect to the experience.
- I've read, viewed, or listened to informative content relevant to my experience.
- I've gained insight on my experience through talking with supportive people.
- I've spent time in silent contemplation of my experience.
- I've spent time in nature to nurture my experience.
- I've followed up on my experience with focused attention practice (meditation, mindfulness, mantra, journaling, visualization, etc.).
- I've applied learnings from my experience to my life.
- I've found ways to carry the intentions I had for my experience into my daily life.
- Because of my experience, I've prioritized my overall wellness.
- I've spent time in environments that help me stay attuned to the lessons following from my experience.
- I've been supportive of others as a result of my experience.
- I've made healthy life choices for myself because of my experience.

Experienced Integration Scale

- I feel at peace with my experience.
- I feel more balanced since my experience.
- I have a continued sense of open-minded curiosity about my experience.
- I feel harmony between the experience and my inner being.
- I feel harmony between my daily life and my experience.
- I feel a sustained connection to my experience.
- I feel more connection in my life because of my experience.
- I have a deep feeling of connection between nature and my experience.
- I feel greater self-awareness since my experience.
- I feel the benefit from my experience expressed in my life.
- I feel the positive effect of the way I interpret my experience.
- I've felt the benefit of my experience extending past myself into my community.

TABLE 7. The Psychedelic Integration Scales

The Japanese concept of *tsundoku* refers to the act buying books and not reading them. If you're anything like me, you probably have a pile of books on your bookshelf, coffee table, or nightstand that are waiting to be read. A psychedelic journey without integration is a lot like *tsundoku*. Your piles of untapped knowledge will grow and eventually topple over unless integration becomes a part of your healing journey. No one will read these books for you, and just like a good novel, integration takes time, attention, and patience.

17

Activation

"Rainbow" by Kacey Musgraves

L ong before I became a transformational coach, and before my career in corporate America, I spent fifteen years as a DJ. I've played over 500 wedding dances, countless proms, homecomings, and class reunions, and I even spent a couple of years working aboard cruise ships. During those years, I was mostly playing music for people partying. Today, I use those same skills to play music for people using psychedelics, many of whom are ready to put down unproductive habits like drinking.

One parallel between playing music and psychedelic work can be found in the transitions from one song—or experience—to another. It's not appealing to the ear when a DJ sharply cuts off one song and starts playing another. The goal of the world's best DJs is to mix their music in such a way that the listener never knows exactly where one song stops and another starts. This crossfading between songs is a skill developed over time. Now it's time for you to develop this same skill of seamless transitions in your life.

Psychedelics often reveal to us how we are living our lives out of alignment with our deepest and most authentic Selves and desires. Maladaptive behaviors we've learned to take care of ourselves and protect ourselves from the world often cause this lack of alignment. Once you know how you're supposed to live, acting out of alignment with your true calling only causes more suffering.

Some Eastern traditions refer to concept of alignment as your *swadharma*. Sri Sri Ravi Shankar said, "*Swadharma* is that action which is in accordance with your nature. It is acting in accordance with your skills and talents, your own nature (*svabhava*), and that which you are responsible for (karma)."[87] To paraphrase: when we know better, we do better.

If, after your psychedelic experience, you *know* better, how will you then start *doing* better? Just like a DJ crossfading a new song into the mix, you must start slowly transitioning out your old, unhealthy ways of being and raising the volume on the new. But remember, you're not instantaneously pressing "stop" on your old life and pressing "play" at full volume on your new life. Slowly fading from one to the other is our goal. It's not about instantly discarding all your old habits. It's about gently integrating new, healthier ones into your life.

I use this metaphor intentionally because, all too often, people will see fantastic visions, have incredibly uncomfortable sensations, or receive profound instructions from their psychedelic experience—and then try to change their lives all at once. Not only is this not sustainable (think of the dismal success rate of New Year's resolutions), but it can also be incredibly destabilizing. Deciding to quit your job, liquidate your 401(k), and sell your house so you can move to the jungle and become an *ayahuascaro* may feel like what you're supposed to do *now*, but it usually turns out to be a poor decision in a few months. Remember, change is a process that requires patience and careful consideration.

What Is Activation?

Activation is where real, lasting change happens in your life. If integration equates to "understanding," activation is the "doing." Many psychedelic users and practitioners mistakenly think that integrating and understanding your journey is all the work that needs to be done. If you understand enough, your life will change all on its own. I'm here to tell you that integration alone will not change your life.

Activation is an essential step if you're looking to get (and stay) "unstuck." As figure 5 in chapter 4, "A New Psychedelic Framework for the Modern Era," shows, healing is never a straight line. There are three primary phases to growth: learning, understanding, and doing—and these align perfectly with the PSW spokes of experience, integration, and activation. If you've already been through a transformational experience and understand what happened and how it relates to your life, you're ready to move past learning and understanding, and start doing.

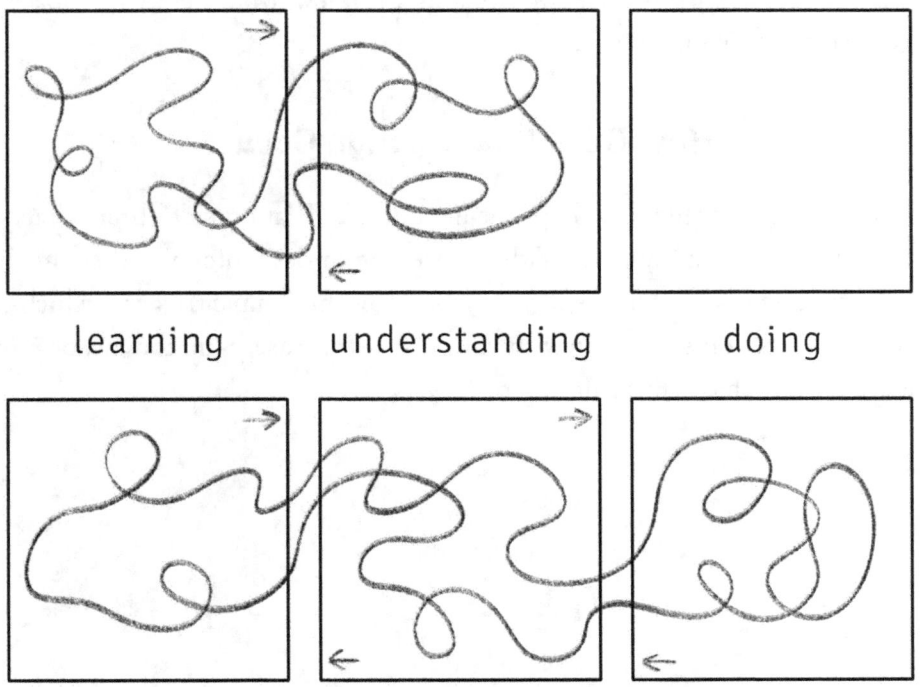

FIGURE 12. Learning, understanding, doing

We often receive so much information and awareness from our psychedelic experiences that we can end up spending a lot of time trying to understand, only to then fail to turn these insights into action. Think of receiving all this new content like reading a self-help book. Thomas Lewis offers wonderful context in his book, *A General Theory of Love*:

> *Self-help books are like car repair manuals: you can read them all day, but doing so doesn't fix a thing. Working on a car means rolling up your sleeves and getting under the hood, and you have to be willing to get dirt on your hands and grease beneath your fingernails. Overhauling emotional knowledge is no spectator sport; it demands the messy experience of yanking and tinkering that comes from a limbic bond. If someone's relationship today bears a troubled imprint, they do so because an influential relationship left its mark on a child's mind. When a limbic connection has established a neural pattern, it takes a limbic connection to revise it.*[88]

Activation is not just about physical action. It is more complicated than waking up at 4:30 a.m., doing twice weekly cold plunges, and starting a meditation practice. Those are all amazing practices and may serve you well on your path, but activation also includes all the thoughts and mental modifications that need to change in your life. The next section of this chapter explains a framework to help you unpack how change occurs within our systems.

How Does Real Change Occur?

Let's say something challenging happens in your life. That outside stimulus acts as a trigger that shocks your system. Without needing to determine whether this heavy energy or trauma is stored in the brain or the body, this simple trigger—which could be any experience you encounter with your eyes, ears, nose, skin, tongue, or mind—initiates a process that is difficult to interrupt:

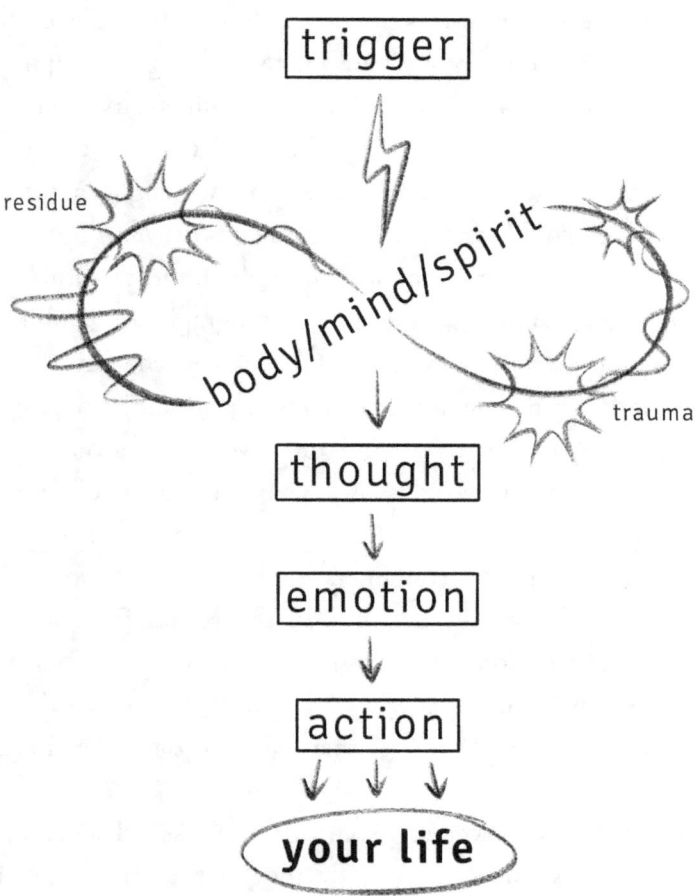

FIGURE 13. Thoughts, emotions, actions, life

1. **You judge the event as positive and/or negative.** If what has happened to you feels good, your thoughts will usually be positive. If you interpret what happens as bad, your thoughts will be negative. It can become even more confusing when something good happens that causes a negative thought. Many call this "waiting for the other shoe to drop," or foreboding joy. The key takeaway here is that the judgment of this (and any) situation is actually the root of *all* your suffering.

2. **You experience emotions.** Emotions can be either conscious or unconscious. After surveying a group of 7,000 people, Brené Brown found that, on average, most people can identify only three emotions as they are actually feeling them: happiness, sadness, and anger. We are most assuredly feeling more than just these three emotions, but our lack of consciousness prevents us from accurately naming or dealing with them. Understanding and managing these emotions is a key part of the journey to change.

3. **Your body processes emotions through action.** Depending on the emotion's type and intensity, your body may want to discharge it as quickly as possible. Without the nervous system strength or mindfulness practices offered by methods like meditation, it may feel excruciating to sit in an emotion, so we take action. If the emotion is challenging, we might engage in addictive behaviors, which could range from seemingly positive things like being productivity or going to the gym, to more compulsive and harmful behaviors such as substance abuse, shopping addiction, pornography, or gambling.

4. **The sum of your actions is your life.** Our lives are the physical and outward representations of the average of our most common thoughts and beliefs. If you constantly think you're unsafe or unworthy of love, your actions will reflect that. Your outside world is always a manifestation of your inner world.

Knowing that our lives are the containers holding all our actions, if we want to change our lives, we must first change our actions. If we're going to change our actions, we must first change our emotions. If we want to change our emotions, we must first change our thoughts. The philosopher René Decartes famously said, "*Cogito, ergo sum*," or "I think, therefore I am." I propose that "*Ego, ergo cogito*," or "I am, therefore I think" is more accurate.

Enter the transformative power of psychedelics. These substances are uniquely capable of many things, but most importantly, they help us recognize and shift the thoughts and actions that no longer align with our authentic Selves. They also act as purification agents (as we discussed in chapter 2), cleansing stored energy and trauma trapped within our bodies, minds, and spirits. Once we remove that debris, the outside triggers that once made us think and behave in ways we didn't like simply become white noise that we can observe with equanimity. If we truly take advantage of the increased neuroplasticity that directly follows our experience, we can use this brief window of time to practice new thoughts and learn new behaviors more easily than ever.

Building an Activation Plan

Just like with integration, it's helpful to think about creating an activation plan. Here are two very easy ways to begin the activation of your experience:

FOCUS ON BUILDING HEALTHY HABITS

You can consciously choose better and healthier thoughts. Mindfulness practices, journaling, coaching, and therapy are a few ways to get started. Microdosing can also offer excellent ongoing support, as it allows you to more easily recognize and healthily engage with your thoughts. You can also incorporate rituals and routines into your life that are designed to develop new, positive habits. After performing these actions enough times, your thinking will begin to fall into alignment with your actions. It is very difficult to *think* your way into right action. It is far easier to *act* your way into right thinking. You can literally change your mind by consistently choosing more positive actions.

ACTIVATION "BULLSEYE" EXERCISE

Grab a blank piece of paper and draw a dartboard with a bullseye in the center and two rings around it. Make sure the circles are large enough to write in. Let this bullseye be a representation of your life. Consider the top three lesson you learned from your psychedelic experience. Summarizing each in a few words, write these lessons inside the rings, putting the most important lesson within the bullseye and working your way outward.

Next, choose one behavior or change in your thinking that would support you in solidifying these teachings into your life. Many psychedelic experiences can feel like drinking awareness from a firehose. You receive so much insight that you don't know what to do with it all. If you try to enact too many changes at once, none of them will hold enough focus to turn into long-term change. Aim for slow and sustainable growth to set yourself up for success. And remember, if you frame your psychedelic work as an ongoing practice, you'll have more neuroplasticity opportunities in the future.

Once you've identified your three lessons, chosen your corresponding behavior, and documented them on your bullseye, stick the image to your refrigerator or bathroom mirror to remind yourself of your goals for change.

When the Afterglow Fades

Many seekers often experience what is referred to as the "afterglow effect." During the days or weeks immediately following your experience, you might feel a boost in mood or energy and enhanced perception, mental clarity, and emotional openness. During these glorious weeks, it's like getting to look at your life from a completely fresh vantage point. You engage in all the healthy habits you've been trying to cultivate for years. You eat healthier, are kind and loving to your spouse and kids, feel extra productive at work, and it seems like you're living the life you've always dreamed of. Then, like Dorthy returning from Oz, you suddenly touch the ground with your ruby-slippered feet. The 220-volt outlet you've been plugged into for the past month gets turned back down to 110 volts. Your old life and habits begin to creep back in. If depression or fear had been removed during your experience, you might notice these feelings reentering your consciousness, or you might develop a new, nagging fear that the original symptoms will return at any moment.

This is a fairly common experience. Unfortunately, most humans are incapable of consistently maintaining the level of energy and consciousness experienced in psychedelic work. Eventually, you have to fully land. Don't waste energy *expecting* this to happen, but if it does, know that you've done nothing wrong. The best thing to do is have a plan ready to address it.

Ideally, you will already be working with a coach, therapist, integration circle, or have developed healthy relationships to keep you accountable to your activation plan. If you've used your postexperience time wisely, you've already started putting positive habits into place. Lean further into these habits and double down on your thought work. Like going to the gym, we often hit plateaus in our growth that require further dedication and hard work.

Uncomfortable aspects of your life that were present before your experience may suddenly become even more uncomfortable. This can occur now that you have a deeper understanding of what you truly need in your life. If you didn't like your job before your journey, and you received information that it's time for a career change, returning to that job may become even more painful. The delta, or change, between your authentic Self and your adapted self has become more prominent, and you will have many choices to make in the coming months or years as you decide which parts of yourself want to nourish. Remember, this isn't about cutting one song and starting another. This process is about learning how to fade one aspect of your life out while gently increasing the volume of a more desirable aspect.

Pause on Making Major Decisions

It's not uncommon to finish a powerful psychedelic experience and feel that the medicine has given you very specific instructions, or even brought repressed memories or difficult bodily sensations to the surface. A paradox of this work is paying attention to these instructions while simultaneously holding them with a light grip. Some of them may require action, but possibly not in the way you think.

The medicine frequently speaks to us in metaphors, and misunderstanding the messages of your psychedelic experience is a widespread occurrence. Acting impatiently or recklessly can cause more problems than it will solve. A month rarely goes by where I don't hear of someone returning from their first ayahuasca retreat who has a story that starts with "the medicine told me to…" I can't stress how important it is to slow down your process and spend more time in the integration phase. Discernment, and the wise counsel of your support team, will help you figure out the difference between metaphor and direct instruction.

In Alcoholics Anonymous, the amends process presented in step nine states, "Make direct amends to such people wherever possible, except when to do so would injure them or others." One thing I can tell you from my work with addicts and psychedelic clients is that reconciliation need only be a one-way street. If you've hurt someone and amends need to be made, by all means, make amends if it does not cause further harm. But if someone has hurt you, and you think you need an apology or validation from them to fully heal, that is 100 percent false. Healing is an inside job, and demanding an apology from those who have hurt you will only prolong your suffering.

Similar to the unfounded "Satanic Panic" the US experienced in the 1980s, the increase in psychedelic use has also shown an increased focus on childhood trauma and sexual abuse. Some facilitators or retreat centers (whether intentionally or not) prime their clients for this type of wounding/healing experience before even ingesting the medicine. While I never want to diminish the real and true harms caused by these abusive acts, if you experienced repressed memories or receive "signals," feelings, messages, or instructions related to severe childhood trauma that you were not aware of before your experience, I strongly advise working with a qualified helping professional for assistance in unravelling these complicated circumstances *before* contacting any family members or potential perpetrators. Sometimes, the damage caused by acting too quickly and calling out possible offenders may do more harm than good.

If you were given specific instructions during your experience, write down everything that the medicine instructed you to do. The small stuff, especially the things that are undoubtedly good for you, like eating more vegetables and exercising, are all engines go! But if Doctor Ayahuasca told you to get a face tattoo, propose to your childhood sweetheart who you haven't seen in two decades, divorce your spouse, or move to the jungle and become a shaman, hit pause. I advise waiting thirty to ninety days after your experience before making any major decisions; sometimes even longer. The bigger the decision, the longer you should wait and the more carefully you should think it through.

Serving Others Requires Training

When it comes to serving psychedelics to others, go slower than you think. Out of all the instructions "given by the medicine," serving others is, without a doubt, the most frequently experienced. Maybe it's the sentience of the medicine attempting to propagate itself and heal more people. Maybe it's your ego trying to convince you that you're the real healer. Either way, if you're a newcomer to this work, sitting with mushrooms, LSD, or DMT a few times does not yet qualify you to support others. Psychedelic substances heal and raise the vibrations of those who use them, often manifesting as strength and confidence. A new or renewed sense of confidence is lovely when dealing with your family, a colleague at work, or singing karaoke. But deciding to serve these substances to others with misplaced confidence, and while lacking proper direction and guidance, is extremely dangerous.

If you genuinely want to work with these substances in a professional capacity, first, do your own work. This will likely include therapy and/or coaching. Next, find a teacher, an apprenticeship, or, at minimum, a reputable training course that can help you understand the complexities of this work and minimize the chances of you hurting someone. Professional therapists spend thousands of hours in supervision before they're licensed, and a maestro spends decades practicing their craft. Getting to meet God during a 5-MeO-DMT journey in no way qualifies you to guide someone else into this experience.

Psychedelic neophytes who take it upon themselves to serve medicine without supervision or training are dangerous and can cause serious harm. Even with the purest of intentions, unintentional harm can manifest out of ignorance. Please do not put yourself (or your potential victims) in this position.

When Should I Do My Next Journey?

Many studies have shown that two to three psilocybin or MDMA experiences spread across weeks or months can be an effective and durable treatment for depression and PTSD. But if you're paying attention to your body and your heart, you may find that you don't feel the need for another session for six months, a year, or maybe ever.

My most straightforward advice is: you're ready for your next journey when you've integrated your last one. Some journeys may take a lifetime to integrate, and each integration experience is unique to the seeker. Returning to the medicine too quickly can turn you into an experiential journeyer who is focused more on escapism than healing.

An Opportunity, Not a Guarantee

There is an old parable often referred to as The Tale of Two Wolves. It goes like this:

One evening, an elder told his grandson about a raging battle happening within each of us.

"My son," he said, "There is a battle between two 'wolves' inside us all. One is Evil and filled with anger, envy, jealousy, sorrow, regret, greed, arrogance, self-pity, guilt, resentment, inferiority, lies, false pride, superiority, and ego. The other is Good and filled with joy, peace, love, hope, serenity, humility, kindness, benevolence, empathy, generosity, truth, compassion, and faith."

The young boy thought in silence for a minute. Finally, he asked, "Which wolf wins?"

The elder simply replied, "The one you feed."

When it comes to activation, the thoughts and habits you feed are the ones that win the battle. With each level we rise through on the Map of Consciousness, our battles diminish, our thoughts become lighter, and our lives become more enjoyable.

During psychedelic journeys, the most amazing things can happen. One moment, you're standing firmly at the top of a mountain, gazing down at your life. The sun is in your face, the moon is at your back, you're bathing in the Divine love of Infinite Source, and you never want the joy of it to end. Then, in the blink of an eye, you find yourself lying on your mat, surrounded by a group of vomiting strangers all having their own experience, and you remember that a few hours ago, you ingested a psychedelic and are now coming down. The feeling that you've just experienced God consciousness is impossible to shake. It may have been the most profound experience of your life, and like a frying pan to the temple, the disorienting realization hits you… it was all just a dream. *Or was it?* Will you ever be able to feel that way again?

Sara's Story

I have sat in ceremony with many different medicines and many different practitioners. I have had powerful experiences, but not all have left a lasting imprint on my life. Is part of that simply the nature of this work? Sure. There are lessons in every journey, and some resonate more deeply than others.

However, regardless of the journey, when integration and activation were emphasized, the experience was more directly connected to my life at large. Once I made this connection, I began thinking, feeling, and acting in ways that aligned with what I was shown during my journey. And that is where the rubber really meets the road.

We need to integrate and understand our experience to see how it fits into the big picture of our healing and growth process. But as we know, awareness is not enough to inspire change. One has to take action, and that's where the crucial step of activation comes in. When I identified what I wanted to change and took specific, tangible steps to make it a part of my daily life, it led to the most effective and efficient change I have ever experienced. I had friends tell me how I was showing up differently, and I could *feel* in my heart and my body that I was operating on a different level.

I felt so much more open, vulnerable, and free. I felt liberated from the confines of my mind, which has been a safe but also limiting place for most of my life. I moved from a cognitive way of navigating the world to a more heartfelt way of being.

One of the most profound ceremonies I've ever had was a one-on-one guided session. At the end of the session, my facilitator said with a shrug, "Well, you moved a lot, for sure, but that wasn't a life-changing journey or anything." But for me, it was! It was the first time I was clearly introduced to activation and given straightforward, direct steps to take. As a diligent student and someone who is very much committed to my own growth and evolution, I took it all to heart. I spent a great deal of time processing my experience, gleaning the gifts and messages I received, and putting them into practice in my life, both personally and professionally.

I want to make sure to say this: it's not all butterflies, rainbows, and magical activation unicorns. We call this "work" because it takes time, intentionality, and effort. Medicine may illuminate our blind spots, but it's not going to do the work for us. It is of paramount importance that we are active participants in our own healing.

I see a lot of people who take a laissez-faire approach to psychedelic work, where the only thing they do is sit with the medicine. After that, they go back to business as usual and are often disappointed when their epiphanies don't merge into the fabric of their life. That's precisely why activation is so important—we must weave those threads into the tapestry of reality that we're creating. Sitting in ceremony and not engaging in integration and activation would be like going to the gym once and expecting your body to change. As we all know, that's not the case. Instead, it takes consistency and intentionality to make any transformation both meaningful and enduring.

Sometimes, if you're really lucky, the medicine does most of the hard work for you. Something inside of you will shift and you will be forever different without having to do a single thing. It's almost unexplainable. But remember that these "silver bullet journeys" are the exception and not the rule. In my experience, these sweet and easy, zero-effort healing sessions represent only around 20 percent of psychedelic journeys.

This is both the magic and the agony of deep, spiritual, mystical work. You may have thought you were home free and would never have to come down from the mountain. You may have believed you would undergo a permanent transformation or total psychic change. But then reality sets in, and you understand just how much work you've got to do to climb back to that peak. It's rarely the psychedelic that changes you, but rather the hours, days, weeks, months, and years of work you put in after your experience.

In many spiritual traditions, being born into a human body is considered a gift, as it allows for the unique experience of living in the physical world, interacting with others, and having the potential to grow, learn, and contribute to society. Your human body provides you with a vessel to experience life in its fullest. It's a unique opportunity to burn off a tremendous amount of karma in a short period of time. Regardless of the path you choose to walk up the mountain, you must develop a deep sense of discernment between your healing process and your human process. No matter how hard you try, you cannot abdicate your human process and rely solely on the medicine to do all the work. You were given this human body for a reason, and you must learn to use it—and the world around you—to achieve even deeper levels of freedom.

Hopefully, you will come to realize that all the challenging parts of your life have been perfectly designed to reveal where your secret stash of reactivity is hiding. That reactivity to people, places, things, and situations is what is keeping you "stuck." Working through and releasing that reactivity sets you free. When you realize this, you will eventually come to understand that all suffering eventually transforms into grace.

Psychedelics are an opportunity, not a guarantee—a catalyst, not a cure-all or a shortcut. Epiphanies rarely generate value without work to catalyze permanent change. It's up to you (and you alone) to bridge the realm of the medicine and your life. As I write these words, a sign hangs above my desk, bearing the words of Ram Dass: "The world is a curriculum for the soul." The longer version of this quote goes on to ask, "Are you willing to accept that you are in school? Are you willing to take the curriculum? I invite you to join me in matriculating."

Conclusion

"You Are My Sunshine" by Morgane & Chris Stapleton

Would you believe me if I told you that your life is a lot like that of a cater-pillar? A caterpillar's life begins when a butterfly lays a tiny, round egg on the leaf of a tree that will eventually serve as an early food source for the caterpillar. After hatching, the caterpillar emerges as a tiny, often translucent version of itself, and begins consuming as much food as it possibly can to fuel its growth. The caterpillar sheds its skin several times time to accommodate its quickly increasing size. To protect itself, a caterpillar may join a small group for protection, and as it grows, it begins to form its distinct colors and markings. It is becoming who it perceives as its true self: a fully formed and beautiful little caterpillar. The caterpillar has no aware-ness that what it is now has almost nothing to do with who it will eventually become.

Once fully grown, the caterpillar begins to spin silk and attach itself to a branch, securing itself for the beginning of a most miraculous transformation. Once ready, it sheds its outer skin one last time and forms a hard protective casing around itself, called a chrysalis. It is inside this shell that that the caterpillar undergoes a process known as metamorphosis.

The caterpillar's body begins breaking down into what I affectionately call "uni-versal goo." During this period, there is no caterpillar and yet also no butterfly. In this liminal state, a specialized group of cells, known as imaginal disks, begins to reorganize into something new. But this is not a simple or easy process. There exists a fascinating interplay between the old caterpillar cells and the new imaginal cells. Conflict arises as these new cells face resistance from the caterpillar's immune system, which treats them as foreign invaders. The old structures resist change and attempt to maintain the status quo. But the imaginal cells band together, fight back, and gradually overpower the old ways of being in an effort that will eventually form the legs, antennae, and wings of a butterfly.

What happens next is very important. Once the butterfly is fully formed within its cocoon, it begins to break free. At this moment, its wings are crumpled and soft, and it's incredibly vulnerable. As blood pumps into its wings, the butterfly remains very still, allowing its body to stabilize and avoiding the attention of predators. But let's say some overly kind human strolls by and says, "Oh, you poor butterfly, I see you trying to get out of that tight cocoon. Here, let me help you," and begins opening the chrysalis. Due to this premature assistance, and as the butterfly's wings are not yet strengthened, the butterfly eventually falls prey to a passing bird.

Yet if that human had simply held space for the butterfly, supporting it from afar by keeping the birds and dragonflies away, the butterfly—all on its own—will build enough strength to emerge from its metamorphosis and fly high into the sky, having no memory that it was once confined to only crawl as a caterpillar.

Psychologist Carl Jung talked about our lives being divided in half. The first half we spend living for others, focused on establishing our external identity, developing our ego, and meeting the expectations of society. In the second half, we begin living for ourselves. Our focus shifts inward, emphasizing self-reflection, personal meaning, and spiritual growth. The term Jung uses for our metamorphosis is "individuation." It refers to the psychological process of becoming a fully integrated and authentic individual (the opposite of the adapted self we created in the first half of our lives). It is the journey of realizing one's true Self by harmonizing the conscious and unconscious aspects of the psyche, and ultimately achieving a sense of wholeness. He did not limit this process to only personal growth but expanded it to include our path of fulfilling a deeper spiritual calling—what the Hindus might call dharma. In the West, we might refer to this as destiny. The process of the butterfly is a wonderful representation of individuation.

Many cultures call this process a rite of passage. Sadly, outside of the Native American tradition, the Global North has lost (or perhaps never possessed) this essential initiation into life. Some may consider graduations, confirmations, bar/bat mitzvahs, quinceañeras, or getting your driver's license a rite of passage. But all those lack the structured, communal, and spiritually significant frameworks experienced in many Indigenous or traditional societies and ceremonies.

I sincerely believe that psychedelics carry with them the potential for a new rite of passage, and an opportunity for many modern cultures to reclaim what has gone missing. One beautiful part of this work is that your age does not matter. Nor does the psychedelic style you choose. Breaking free from your chrysalis and returning to yourself can just as easily happen in a scientific study, on a therapist's couch, while working with an underground guide, or with a South American maestro or shaman.

In each case, this work can initiate a psychic change like you've never before dreamed. It signifies a bell that can never be unrung—a fire that, once touched, can never be forgotten. This is such truly important work that we, as a species, must take it very seriously. When held with the proper intention and energy, I have witnessed countless experiences of sick, depressed, and lost humans returning to wellness despite existing in an incredibly sick world.

While writing this book, I learned of the term "meta crisis," which describes the interconnected and systemic nature of global challenges facing humanity today. Crises that fall under this umbrella include climate change, economic inequality, the mental health epidemic, and the deep polarization of political systems. These problems did not exist before we created them, and as Albert Einstein said, "The problem cannot be solved from the same level of consciousness that created it."

Returning to our earlier discussion of the Map of Consciousness, you'll find many of the emotions that have created this meta crisis all fall within what David Hawkins calls the "Survival Paradigm." These emotions include pride, anger, desire, grief, apathy, guilt, and shame—most often in direct service to money, power, and control. These are the default tools of the human mind when it resides in a persistent state of fear, scarcity, and trauma.

While many activists espouse the need to "save the planet," the reality is that if we were not around, Mother Earth would be just fine. The only way to heal our planet will be to first heal ourselves. Saving ourselves demands an evolution of consciousness far beyond that offered in schools or on therapist couches. After twenty years of doing my own healing work, and having traveled across the globe studying with swamis, shamans, and healers, I truly believe that the intentional use of psychedelics is one of the fastest and most effective solutions (and maybe the only solution left) to increase our level of consciousness and slow down the suffering that humanity faces.

So, rather than trying to "heal the collective," consider first healing yourself. Once we heal ourselves, the people around us begin to heal as well. Jiddu Krishnamurti, an Indian philosopher, speaker, writer, and spiritual figure said, "It is no measure of health to be well adjusted to a profoundly sick society." Let your evolution and growth be the drop of water that ripples throughout your life and eventually the lives of others. Consciously or not, humans are naturally attracted to a higher vibration. Change can occur without uttering a single word. Your efforts are truly that important, because healing yourself can help heal the planet and our profoundly sick society.

Recognizing subtle progress in your growth and healing can be difficult. Pay attention to what your friends and family share with you, and how the world around you starts treating you differently. Your loved ones will almost certainly recognize the changes in you before you recognize them in yourself. Place your trust in the mirror they are holding up for you, because it takes longer than you think to unwind your own self-delusion, doubt, guilt, and shame. If you pay attention to how different your life is becoming and remember that everything on the outside is a reflection of what's happening on the inside, the healing path becomes a lot easier to see.

Before I conclude this book, I would like to offer you a few of the most profound personal lessons I have learned over the past twenty years, which have affected my life in the most positive ways. The first three I will take credit for learning on my own. The others were handed down to me by my maestro and contain some of the simplest, yet most potent healing wisdom I have ever received.

1. **Listen to the wisdom keepers.**

   The sooner you become willing to listen to people who are more familiar with typewriters than they are computers, the sooner your true healing will begin. All the *knowledge* of artificial intelligence will never surpass the *wisdom* held by our elders.

2. **Everyone (including you) is always doing the best they can with what they've got.**

   This one takes effort but has positively impacted my daily life more than any other mantra.

3. **Healing is forgetting so much that we finally remember.**

   Remind yourself that you need nothing new or additional to feel better. You only need to release that which no longer serves you.

4. **Healing can be sweet and easy.**

   "Strong and hard" is the way you've been taught to exist. You can let that go any time you'd like.

5. **Trust in yourself and Infinite Source; they are one and the same.**

   When you embody the paradox that you are both 100 percent human and 100 percent Divine, you can begin trusting your instincts again.

6. **Do your best to receive the best.**

   Every action has a consequence. Be conscious of what you're creating and the energy with which you're creating it. When you act in alignment with your highest good, the Universe will reward you accordingly.

7. **Let go of the outcome.**

   If you've done your best, you are not entitled to the fruits of your actions. Leave the outcome up to Infinite Source.

8. **Enjoy your life.**

   Turn your gaze inward and do what makes your heart sing. Outward pleasures will always be impermanent, but inner fulfillment is free and lasts forever.

Today, after two decades of work, thousands of hours of therapy, hundreds of psychedelic journeys, countless hours on my yoga mat and meditation cushion, and regular contact with mentors and teachers, I now experience a level of peace, joy, and freedom I never dreamed possible. In fact, some of the biggest breakthroughs in my life occurred while writing this book. Only yesterday—two days before submitting this manuscript for a final proofread—I received one of the sweetest and most beautiful gifts I've ever been offered by the medicine: the belief that I, too, deserve *the best*.

That I am worthy of all the gifts the Universe has to offer, and that I no longer have to settle for less.

What's most surprising and beautiful is that all it took was a mini dose of 0.5 grams of mushrooms—no hero's dose, no emotional breakdown, no purge. Just a pure intention and a willingness to ask the doctors for help. Please believe me when I say, "You, too, are deserving of *the best!*" How long it takes to feel this truth is up to you and Infinite Source.

Everything you've read within these pages was written at my current level of consciousness—but who knows what new levels of understanding tomorrow (or my next psychedelic journey) will bring. I rewrote a third of this book after a single ayahuasca ceremony, because the person who wrote the first version of that text was not the person who's writing now. My commitment is to truth rather than consistency, and like you, I'm doing the best I can with what I've got.

Next time you notice a caterpillar sitting on a branch, imagine that fuzzy little creature looking up into the sky, noticing a butterfly, and saying fearfully, "You'll never get me up in one of those things!" Maybe this is how you're feeling right now.

Here me when I say this: You are perfect, and you're right on time, and the path is wiser than the traveler.

Acknowledgments

No one ever told me that writing a book is a lot like raising a child—it truly takes a village. As this is my first published work, I find myself overwhelmed with gratitude for the many souls who have shaped and supported me along this journey of healing, growth, and discovery.

First and foremost, to Roberto and René Flores Solís and the entire Hanaq Pacha team: After nearly two decades of seeking and self-discovery, I finally found the maestros I had been waiting for. Your unwavering love, support, and wisdom have been a light on my path. I am eternally grateful.

To my clients: Your trust, courage, and willingness to embark on your own healing journeys make up the heartbeat of this book. Each of your unique stories and experiences taught me something profound, and I am humbled that this work exists because of you.

Sobriety was the catalyst for my healing journey, beginning in 2007. Along the way, I have been blessed to walk alongside countless extraordinary humans. My first sponsor, Connie Lungrin, often said, "My God has skin." I don't think I fully grasped the depth of that phrase until this very moment. To Connie and Doug Black: May you both rest in peace. You loved me until I could learn to love myself. I was not an easy nut to crack, and I thank you for your patience and grace.

To my teacher, Ram Dass, who illuminated the way forward: Though you've dropped your body, your words continue to fill my heart and guide my steps. In 2018, you gave me the name Govind Dass, and it wasn't until May of 2023 that I finally understood why. Thank you for seeing me before I saw myself.

Kathy Ellis, my first therapist, helped me remember that I had feelings, laying the foundation for the work I do today. Kelly Tadlock, my first coach: Your fingerprints are all over this book in the most beautiful ways. The work I did with you changed my life, and I will never be able to thank you enough. Your intuition and brilliance helped me to truly understand where the sacred meets the secular.

To Saul David Raye, my first "real" yoga teacher: Your words on that first day of teacher training—"I've got bad news for you; once you step onto the path, you can never turn back"—have proven to be the truest of wisdom.

To Jyothi Chalam, may you rest in peace: You introduced me to Advaita Vedanta, opened my eyes, and taught me the distinction between spirituality and religion. Your wisdom and gentle spirit opened doors within me that I didn't even know existed, and I firmly believe you were the first enlightened soul I have ever met.

To my medicine teachers: Max Stein, your trust and guidance planted the seeds for the life I now live. Your integrity continues to be a model for all my work. Elliott Isenberg, my beloved mensch, meeting you truly exemplifies the saying "Coincidence is God's way of remaining anonymous." Your mischievous, loving energy has been a gift. Kristina Hunter, thank you for helping me transition from an enthusiast to a professional. Your wisdom belies your years, and your support has been invaluable.

To three very special people who have supported me and this book from the beginning: JJ Kirkpatrick, your unwavering belief in me and my work has been a cornerstone of this journey. Thank you for reading my words, editing the PsychedelicIQ podcast, and being a steadfast friend. Wilde Lawson King, you entered my life as a "random" breathwork partner, but your support has been anything but random. More times than I can count, your words filled up a tank that was running on empty. And Timothy Cooper, my illustrator and "accidental" partner: Walking this path with you has been a tremendous blessing in my life. Your presence, honesty, and creativity have been both the stimulus and the source of so much healing in my life. I love you all deeply.

To my Conscious Shala, church, and medicine communities: There are too many of you to name, but your collective love, trust, and support over the past decade have transformed me in ways I could never adequately express. I am a better person because of you. Thank you for believing in me when I didn't believe in myself.

To my editor, Ashten Luna Evans: this book is so much better because of your gentle hand and brilliant guidance. To MC Calvi, thank you for sharpening my sword and polishing the mirror. Your proofreading precision and expertise are truly beyond words.

And since this is my first published work, I can't help but honor three of the best English teachers this planet has ever known, who planted the seeds of this book long ago: Shari Hofmann, Sandra Mann, and Gaile Lowenburg—your passion and dedication to your craft left an indelible mark on me.

Finally, to my mom and dad: what a wild journey we've all been on. Without you, this book would never have had a reason to exist. I know my path may not be what you imagined, but life has been full of surprises for all of us. Writing this book has been one of the most challenging and rewarding endeavors of my life, and the strength and determination it took to see it through came from you. The apple, it seems, didn't fall far from the tree. Thank you for your love and support—it means the world to me.

About the Author

Gv Freeman is an opti-mystic, tipper of sacred cows, and dynamic force in the world of human transformation. As a transformational coach and facilitator, he teaches his clients to use centuries-old tools to solve modern-day problems. With one foot in the sacred and the other in the secular, Gv offers a unique blend of coaching and Sacred Medicine work to help individuals "unstuck" themselves in pursuit of purpose, prosperity, happiness, and freedom.

After two decades as a serial entrepreneur, Gv's life now forms a Venn diagram of psychedelics, spirituality, mental health, and entrepreneurship. Having been initiated into an ancient Peruvian medicine lineage, Gv now studies under the direction of maestro Roberto Flores Solís. Gv, short for Govind Dass (a name given to him by his first teacher, Ram Dass), has also been a devoted student of Advaita Vedanta, yoga, and somatic psychotherapy.

He is the visionary behind PsychedelicIQ and the Conscious Shala, and when he's not leading retreats or being a spiritual tourist, Gv is a foodie, lover of all things music, and deeply cherishes his time with friends and soul family. *Healing with Psychedelics* is his first book.

Appendix

One of the primary reasons people are turning to psychedelics for treatment is to improve their mental health. Among those most affected by the current mental health crisis—particularly rising suicide rates—are veterans.

The following article was cowritten by Derek Blumke, Veteran Impact Fellow for the Grunt Style Foundation, a national nonprofit dedicated to providing life-changing resources and support for service members, veterans, and their families. If you are a veteran seeking healing and support, visit www.gruntstylefoundation.org for more information.

While this article focuses on veteran mental health, the overprescription of pharmaceuticals is a widespread issue affecting far more than just the veteran community. The data presented here may reflect broader negative trends in suicide rates and antidepressant prescriptions across larger populations.

Screening + Drug Treatment = Increase in Veteran Suicides

The alarm over suicides of military veterans has been regularly sounded over the past fifteen years, prompting the US Department of Veterans Affairs to declare that "preventing suicide among Veterans is the VA's top clinical priority." The VA's 2019 report on suicide provides reason to sound the alarm again, for it tells of a suicide rate that has continued to climb, particularly for younger veterans who have served since 9/11.

Indeed, a close review of VA data provides reason to conclude that the rise in suicide is being driven, at least in part, by the VA's suicide prevention efforts. Its screening protocols have ushered an ever-greater number of veterans into psychiatric care, where treatment with antidepressants and other psychiatric drugs is regularly prescribed. Suicide rates have increased in lockstep with the increased exposure among veterans to such medications.

According to the 2019 report, the age-adjusted suicide rates for all veterans rose from 25.5 per 100,000 population in 2005 to 35.8 per 100,000 in 2015, a 40% increase. The rate for veterans using Veterans Health Administration (VHA) facilities rose from 29.6 per 100,000 in 2005 to 40.1 in 2017, a 35% increase.

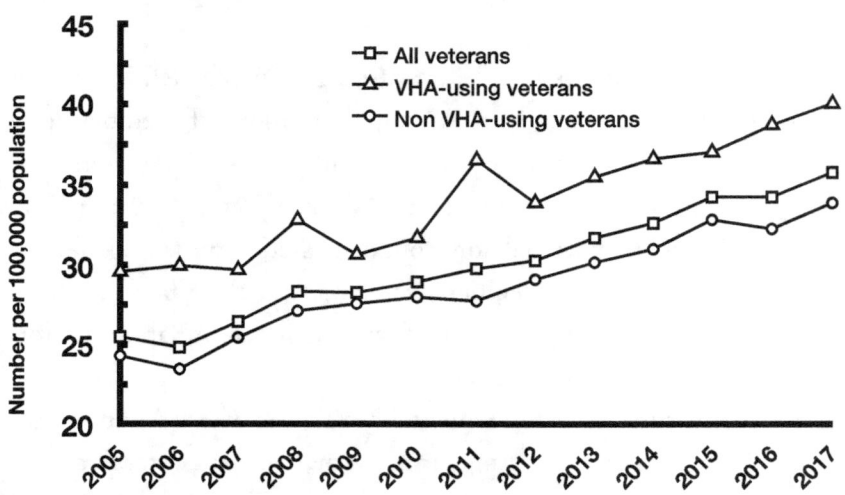

Age-Adjusted Suicide Rates for U.S. Veterans, 2005 to 2017

Source: U.S. Department of Veterans Affairs, 2019 National Veteran Suicide Prevention Annual Report; National Data Appendix.

The increase in suicide was even more pronounced for veterans 18 to 34 years old. The suicide rate for this group increased from 25.3 per 100,000 in 2005 to 44 per 100,000 in 2017, a 74% increase. For this age group using VHA facilities, the suicide rate rose from 20.9 per 100,000 in 2005 to 51 per 100,000 in 2017, a 144% increase.

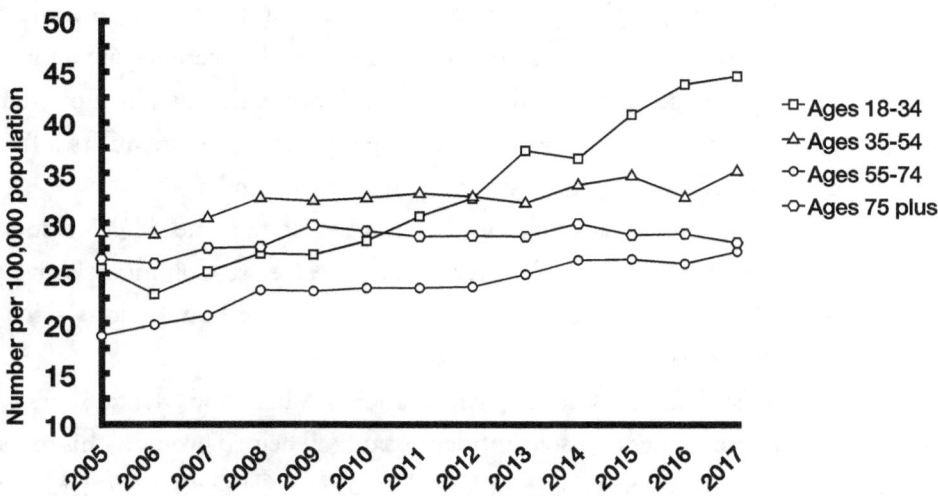

Suicide Rates for Veterans by Age Group, 2005 to 2017

Source: U.S. Department of Veterans Affairs, 2019 National Veteran Suicide Prevention Annual Report; National Data Appendix.

In a previous MIA Report, we made the case that "suicide prevention efforts," which are based on the premise that suicide is a "public health" problem that can best be addressed by getting more people diagnosed and into treatment, have fueled a steady rise in suicide rates in the United States since 2000. An investigation into the rise in suicide among veterans can be seen as a "replication" study. In the VA's data, is it possible to identify the same treatment-related forces at work?

There is, buried in the VA's 2016 suicide report, data on the suicide rates for treated and untreated patients that make this a question of particular urgency.

Suicide in the Civilian Population

The initiation of suicide prevention efforts in the United States began in the late 1980s, shortly after Prozac—the first selective serotonin reuptake inhibitor (SSRI) antidepressant—came to market. The American Foundation for Suicide Prevention was established then, and although it promoted a "public health" message, it was a nonprofit that was funded, to a significant extent, by pharmaceutical companies, which understood that a "suicide prevention" campaign would boost sales of their drugs. Academic psychiatrists with financial ties to the makers of antidepressants led its scientific advisory board and served terms as directors of the foundation.

The American Foundation for Suicide Prevention promoted a very simple message to the American public. Suicide was said to be a "public health" problem that was "underrecognized." Many people with mood disorders went "untreated," and this was the population at particularly high risk of suicide. People who were feeling depressed or suicidal were urged to seek help from mental health professionals. The Foundation pushed screening programs as a way to get more people into treatment. Its advisory board and presidents touted antidepressants as "anti-suicide" pills.

"Use of antidepressants to treat major depressive episode is the single most effective suicide prevention measure in Western Countries," said Columbia University psychiatrist John Mann, who had long been a fixture on the Foundation's scientific advisory board, and served for a time as its president.

The American Psychiatric Association, the National Alliance on Mental Illness, and the pharmaceutical companies that sold antidepressants all helped promote this message to the public. In 1997, their efforts prompted both houses of Congress to declare suicide a "national problem." Two years later, US Surgeon General David Satcher issued a "Call to Action to Prevent Suicide," and the US Department of Health and Human Services formed a task force, composed of individuals and organizations from the private and public sectors, to develop a "National Strategy for Suicide Prevention." The task force published its recommendations in 2001, which doubled down on the "public health" approach that had been promoted by the American Foundation for Suicide Prevention.

Government agencies at all levels—federal, state, and local—launched suicide prevention efforts. Crisis call centers were established, depression screening programs were initiated, checklists for assessing the risk of suicide in depressed patients were developed, and medical professionals were trained to recognize the "warning signs" of suicide. The goal was to get more people struggling with mood disorders into treatment, with antidepressants recommended as a first-line therapy.

These efforts have been successful in that regard: the prescribing of antidepressants has increased steadily since 2000. Yet, since 2000, the age-adjusted suicide rate for the American population, rather than decrease, has risen steadily, from 10.4 per 100,000 to 14.0 per 100,000 in 2017.

U.S. Age-Adjusted Suicide Rates: 2000 to 2017

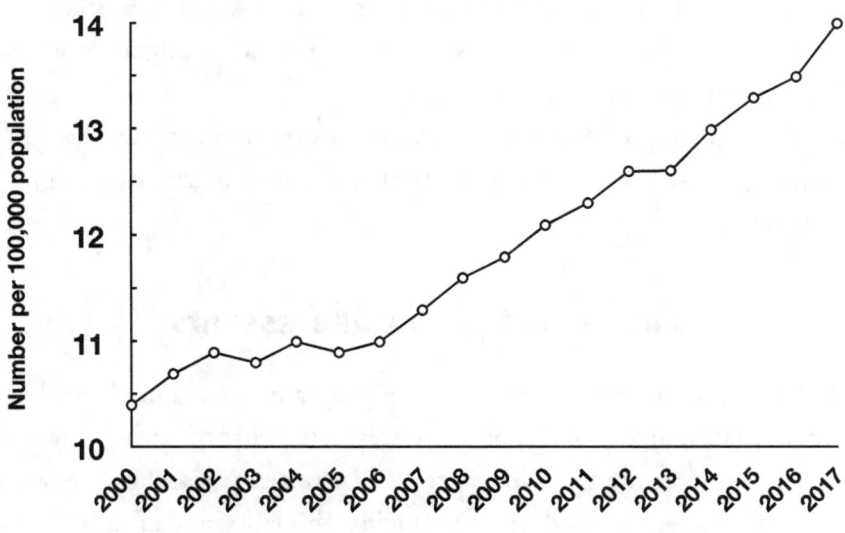

Source: Centers for Disease Control

The failure of this approach to suicide prevention, which emphasizes getting people into treatment, is not a uniquely American phenomenon. In the 1990s, the World Health Organization urged countries around the world to develop national mental health policies and to improve their mental health services, which included providing their citizens with better access to psychiatric medications. The belief was that this would lead to better mental health outcomes, which would become visible in the form of reduced suicide rates.

Researchers from the UK, Denmark, and Australia have now conducted three studies of whether such efforts have affected suicide rates, and all came to the same conclusion: **improved access to psychiatric services and psychiatric drugs was associated with an increase in national suicide rates.**

In a similar vein, a large Danish study of suicides in Denmark from 1996 to 2009 came to the disturbing conclusion that the risk of suicide escalated dramatically upon entry into psychiatric care. They found that, in comparison to a matched control group who hadn't had any involvement with psychiatric care during the previous year, the risk of suicide was:

- 5.8 times higher for people receiving psychiatric medication (but no other care)
- 8.2 times higher for people having outpatient contact with a mental health professional
- 27.9 times higher for people having contact with a psychiatric emergency room
- 44.3 times higher for people admitted to a psychiatric hospital

Although it could be expected that the suicide risk would increase for each step up the "treatment" ladder, what surprised the researchers was that it occurred even in those who were married, and in those with higher incomes or higher levels of education and no prior history of attempted suicide.

In an accompanying editorial, two Australian experts in suicide research wrote that the findings "raise the disturbing possibility that psychiatric care might, at least in part, cause suicide."

The Impact of Antidepressants

Although the promoters of suicide prevention programs have touted antidepressants as a treatment that reduces the risk of suicide, evidence that the drugs might have the opposite effect arose in the first clinical trials of Prozac. A significant percentage of patients given Prozac suddenly developed suicidal thoughts, and after Prozac came to market, there were numerous case reports of patients prescribed the drug committing suicide. By the early 1990s, with Paxil and other SSRIs entering the marketplace, the FDA was forced to convene a public hearing on this concern.

The controversy has circulated within research circles—and in the public mind—ever since.

There is clear evidence that SSRIs and SNRI antidepressants can provoke suicidal impulses and acts in some users, and the reason is well known. SSRIs and other antidepressants can stir extreme restlessness, agitation, insomnia, severe anxiety, mania, and psychotic episodes. The agitation and anxiety, which is clinically described as akathisia, may reach "unbearable" levels, and akathisia is known to be associated with suicide and acts of violence, including homicide.

At the same time, there are many people who tell of how SSRIs or some other antidepressant saved their lives, as their suicidal impulses waned after going on the drugs. Individual responses to antidepressants may vary greatly, and so the public health question is about the net effect of these drugs on suicide rates. On the whole, do they increase or decrease the risk of suicide in people so treated?

There are several types of studies that provide an "evidence base" for answering that question.

RANDOMIZED CLINICAL TRIALS (RCTS)

RCTs are seen as the "gold standard" for assessing the merits of a drug treatment, at least over the short term, as the trials typically last only six weeks or so. Thus, the trials might be expected to identify whether SSRI and SNRI antidepressants trigger any increase in suicidal behavior when patients are first put on the medication.

The FDA, in its review of industry-funded RCTs of SSRIs and other antidepressants, concluded that these drugs increase the risk of suicidal thinking for those under 25 years old; have a neutral effect on those 25 to 64 years old; and are protective against suicidal thinking for those over 64.

However, it is well known that the pharmaceutical companies sought to downplay—or hide—suicidal risks in the trial reports they sent to the FDA. In 2003, UK psychiatrist David Healy and a team of Canadian researchers conducted an exhaustive meta-analysis of all RCTs of SSRIs, which incorporated findings from trials that weren't funded by pharmaceutical companies, and they found that suicide attempts were 2.28 times higher for those treated with an SSRI compared to a placebo.

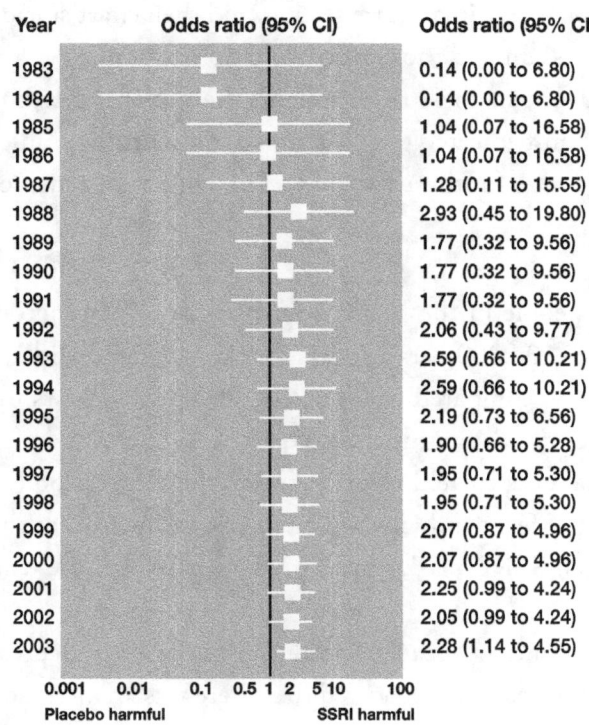

Year	Odds ratio (95% CI)	Odds ratio (95% CI)
1983		0.14 (0.00 to 6.80)
1984		0.14 (0.00 to 6.80)
1985		1.04 (0.07 to 16.58)
1986		1.04 (0.07 to 16.58)
1987		1.28 (0.11 to 15.55)
1988		2.93 (0.45 to 19.80)
1989		1.77 (0.32 to 9.56)
1990		1.77 (0.32 to 9.56)
1991		1.77 (0.32 to 9.56)
1992		2.06 (0.43 to 9.77)
1993		2.59 (0.66 to 10.21)
1994		2.59 (0.66 to 10.21)
1995		2.19 (0.73 to 6.56)
1996		1.90 (0.66 to 5.28)
1997		1.95 (0.71 to 5.30)
1998		1.95 (0.71 to 5.30)
1999		2.07 (0.87 to 4.96)
2000		2.07 (0.87 to 4.96)
2001		2.25 (0.99 to 4.24)
2002		2.05 (0.99 to 4.24)
2003		2.28 (1.14 to 4.55)

0.001   0.01   0.1   0.5 1 2   5 10   100
Placebo harmful   SSRI harmful

All fatal and non-fatal suicide attempts in placebo-controlled trials: double the risk for those on SSRIs

Two recent analyses of clinical trial data have led to similar findings. First, after reviewing 64,381 pages of clinical study reports filed with the European Medicines Agency, Peter Gøtzsche and colleagues concluded that antidepressants doubled the risk that patients would experience akathisia, a known risk factor for suicide.

Second, European researchers Michael Hengartner and Martin Plöderl conducted an exhaustive review of the trial data submitted to the FDA for all antidepressants approved from 1991 to 2013, a database that numbered more than 40,000 patients, and they determined that suicide attempts were 2.5 times higher for those taking antidepressants compared to placebo.

OBSERVATIONAL STUDIES IN PRIMARY CARE PATIENTS

During the past twenty-five years, there have been hundreds of studies of different types—observational studies, epidemiological studies, and so forth—that have sought to assess whether antidepressants are protective against suicide, or conversely increase suicide rates. Those studies have produced a welter of conflicting findings. However, the studies that are of most relevance to suicide prevention efforts are those that look at patients diagnosed with depression in a primary care setting, and then chart suicide rates for those who take an antidepressant and those who avoid doing so.

That initial choice serves as a fork-in-the road moment, the patients heading down either a medicated path or a nonmedicated one. There are at least three studies that provide a comparison of suicide rates for these two paths following a diagnosis of depression in primary care.

+ In a 1998 study of 35,436 people in the Puget Sound area of Washington, the risk of suicide was 43 per 100,000 person years for those treated with an antidepressant in primary care, compared to 0 per 100,000 person years for those treated in primary care without antidepressants.
+ In a 2003 analysis of UK patients treated in primary care for depression (or for other "affective disorder"), Healy and Chris Whitaker concluded that the suicide rate for those taking an SSRI was 3.4 times greater than for those who chose "non-treatment."
+ In a study of 238,963 UK patients who experienced a first episode of depression between 2000 and 2011, researchers reported that there was an increased risk of suicide for those treated with SSRI antidepressants during the first month of treatment, and again in the first month after quitting the drug.

This last study reveals why observational studies that simply assess medication use at the time of a suicide may present skewed results. The high-risk period that occurs when someone is withdrawing from an SSRI antidepressant is a risk that comes from going on the drug in the first place, yet in most observational studies, the suicide is chalked up to the "off medication" column.

There are other classes of drugs that may contribute to an increased suicide risk, most notably benzodiazepines. Polypharmacy does so as well. The focus on antidepressants is because this class of drugs is regularly touted, in suicide prevention programs, as protective against suicide.

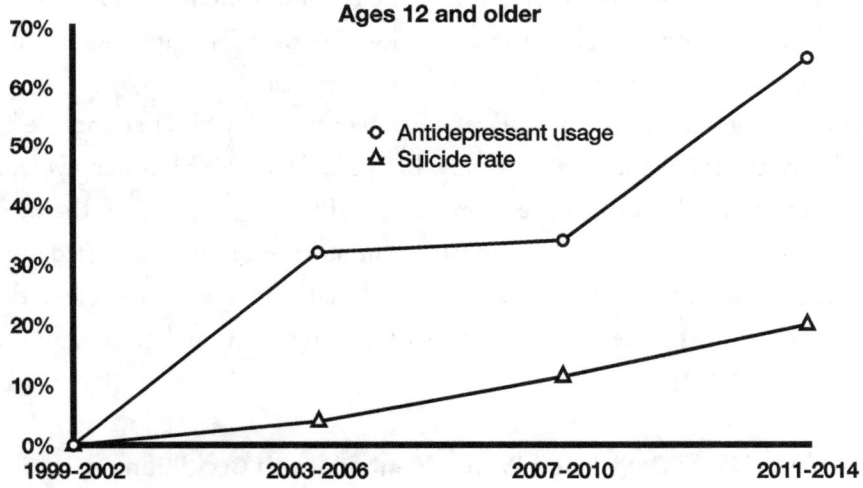

Percentage Increases in Antidepressant Usage and Suicide Rate in the United States, 2000 to 2014

Suicide Prevention at the VA

The VA launched a focused suicide prevention effort in 2006, when it appointed a National Suicide Prevention Coordinator. The following year it established a toll-free Veterans Crisis line, and since then it has steadily increased the resources devoted to this effort. One such effort was its Make the Connection campaign, which spent nearly $20 million to market the Veterans Health Administration's (VHA) services to veterans.

Like the federal government, the VA conceives of "suicide" as a "public health" problem, and thus its bottom-line goal is to increase the identification of mental health problems in the veteran community, and get those who are given a mental health diagnosis into treatment, which is expected to reduce the suicide risk.

About two-thirds of the 20 million veterans in the United States do not use Veterans Health Administration facilities, and the VA, since it launched its toll-free crisis line in 2007, has regularly conducted mental health awareness campaigns to encourage veterans who are not users of VHA care to seek medical help for such problems. In 2018, it partnered with a pharmaceutical company, Johnson & Johnson, to promote a No Veteran Left Behind campaign, which featured Tom Hanks and urged "each and every American" to reach out to veterans in crisis and help get them "mental health services." The communications plan, the VA stated, was "led by Johnson & Johnson."

Within its own VHA facilities, the VA has introduced mandatory screening for all vets. Every vet entering the system is screened for depression, PTSD, and substance abuse, and all those who are diagnosed with a psychiatric disorder are assessed for "suicidal intent." Such screening continues to be a regular feature of VHA care, as screening of some type is part of every patient appointment. Every vet is screened annually for depression, and all of those diagnosed with PTSD upon entry into VHA care are rescreened for this disorder for the next five years.

With this regular screening in place, the percentage of VHA patients with a mental health diagnosis has increased steadily. In 2014, 41% of VHA-using veterans had a mental health or substance abuse diagnosis (SUD), with depression the most common diagnosis.[2] Although the VA's most recent suicide reports haven't detailed this diagnostic information, it can be safely assumed that this steady increase in diagnosis has continued, and that perhaps 44% of VHA-using veterans had a mental health/SUD diagnosis in 2017.

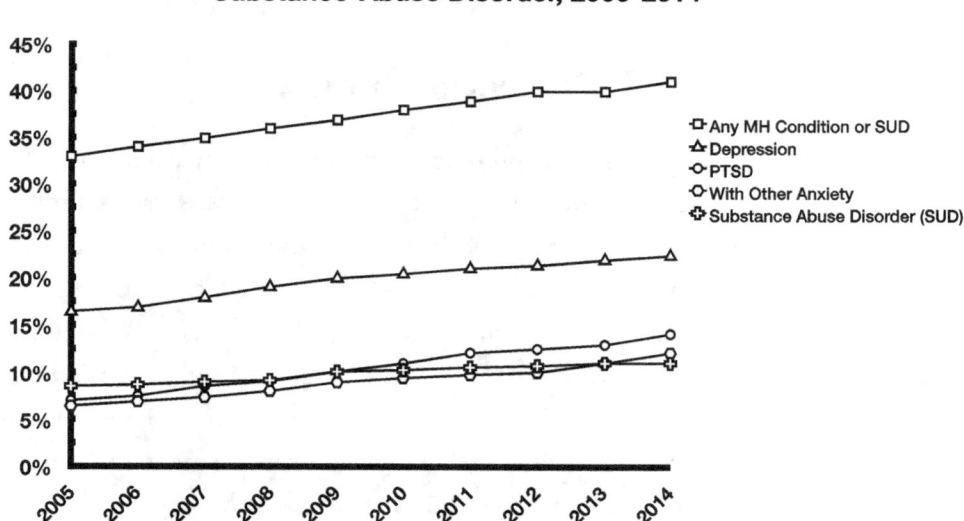

VHA- Users Diagnosed With a Mental Health Condition or Substance-Abuse Disorder, 2005-2014

Source: U.S. Department of Veterans Affairs, "Suicide Among Veterans and Other Americans, 2011-2014. August 3, 2016.

Treatment in the VA

The VA's clinical care guidelines for treating depression and PTSD, which are the two most commonly diagnosed psychiatric disorders, recommend SSRI and SNRI antidepressants as first-line therapies. However, the guidelines also provide recommendations for CBT and other psychotherapies, and particularly in primary care settings, these treatments may be offered as stand-alone therapies.

Even so, the prescribing of antidepressants to those diagnosed with depression or PTSD is routine. According to a 2015 report by the U.S. General Accounting Office (GAO), 94% of all VHA patients diagnosed with depression from 2009 to 2013 were prescribed an antidepressant. Studies of VHA patients diagnosed with PTSD have reported that about 80% are prescribed a psychiatric medication, with antidepressants the drug class of choice.

A 2019 GAO report that sampled prescribing practices at a small number of VHA facilities found that only 15% of diagnosed patients were offered psychotherapy in lieu of drug treatment. Forty-four percent were offered a combination of both, and the remaining 41% drug treatment only.[3]

Polypharmacy is also common in VA settings, particularly since half of those diagnosed are said to be comorbid for two or more mental disorders. The 2019 GAO report found that among those diagnosed with depression who were treated in "primary care and specialty mental health care" settings, 35% percent were taking two classes of psychiatric drugs, and 15% three classes of drugs. The polypharmacy was even more pronounced for those diagnosed with PTSD: 36% were taking two classes of psychiatric drugs and 25% were taking three or more classes.[4]

Suicide Rates for VHA Patients

As noted above, the suicide rate among veterans has been steadily rising since 2005. The VA, in a 2016 report, divided the VHA-using patients into four subgroups:[5]

+ Undiagnosed and untreated (for a mental health or substance abuse disorder)
+ Undiagnosed and treated (with either a psychiatric drug or nonpharmacologic treatment)
+ Diagnosed and untreated
+ Diagnosed and treated

If antidepressants are effective in reducing suicide risk, it is easy to see how the suicide rates for the four groups should stack up.

Given that the VHA regularly screens for mental health disorders, the "undiagnosed" patients apparently do not show the symptoms of depression, PTSD, or any other psychiatric disorder that, during the screening process, would generate a diagnosis. These patients should be at a low risk of suicide, and thus any treatment to patients in this "undiagnosed" category should—at least in theory—further reduce this risk, since it is being prescribed as a balm for whatever ailment is bothering the patients. As such, the undiagnosed/treated patients could be expected to have a lower suicide rate than the undiagnosed/untreated group.

The "diagnosed" patients should be at a higher risk of suicide. Suicide prevention efforts focus on getting these patients into treatment, with antidepressants seen as a first-line therapy that can lower the risk of suicide. Thus, if suicide prevention efforts are helpful, the suicide rate for the diagnosed patients who are treated should be lower than for diagnosed patients who, for whatever reason, shun treatment. The 2019 GAO report found that 18% of diagnosed patients did not get treatment.

Here are the results.

First, those without a diagnosis who got MH treatment were more likely to die by suicide than those without a diagnosis who did not access such treatment. In 2014, those who got treatment died at twice the rate of the "untreated" group.

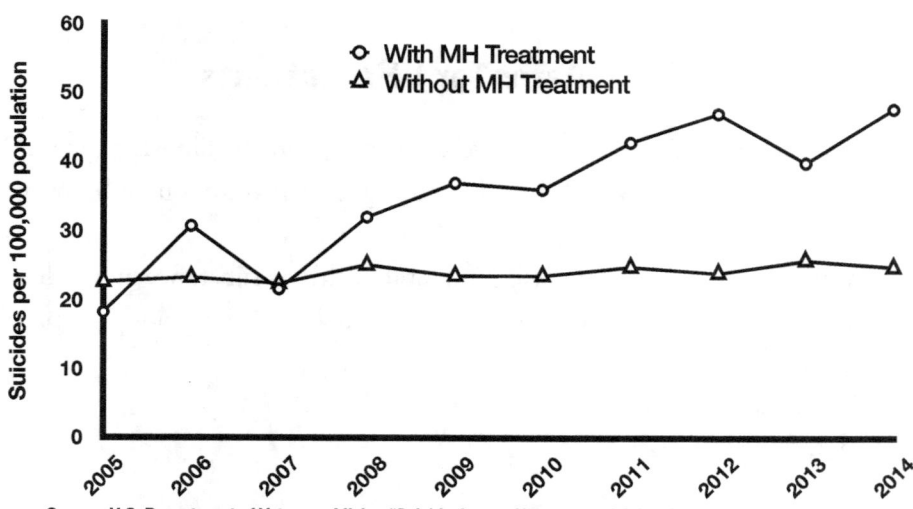

Suicide Rates in VHA-Using Veterans Without a Mental Health/Substance Abuse Diagnosis

Source: U.S. Department of Veterans Affairs, "Suicide Among Veterans and Other Americans, 2011-2014. August 3, 2016.

Second, those with a mental health or substance abuse diagnosis who got mental health treatment were roughly twice as likely to die by suicide as those who had a diagnosis but did not access mental health treatment.

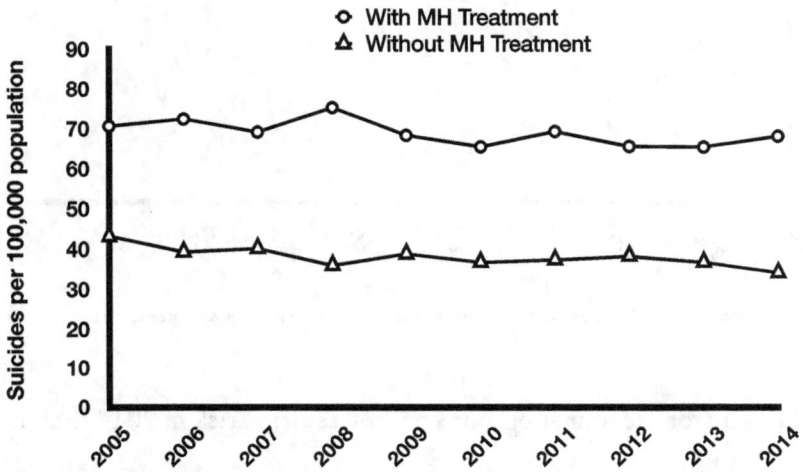

Suicide Rate in Veterans With a Mental Health/ Substance Abuse Diagnosis

Source: U.S. Department of Veterans Affairs, "Suicide Among Veterans and Other Americans, 2011-2014. August 3, 2016.

This difference in suicide rates for the treated and untreated groups is consistent over time, year after year. Moreover, these findings are based on the VA's review of millions of patient records. The VA published them in a 2016 report that it touted as the "most comprehensive analysis of Veteran suicide in our nation's history."

There is a third comparison that can be made that leads to a particularly troubling finding. It could be expected that in any comparison between the less severely ill (the undiagnosed) and the more severely ill (the diagnosed), the less severely ill group would have a lower suicide rate, regardless of any treatment effect. Yet, from 2010 to 2014, those without a diagnosis who got MH treatment were more likely to die by suicide than those with a diagnosis who were "untreated."

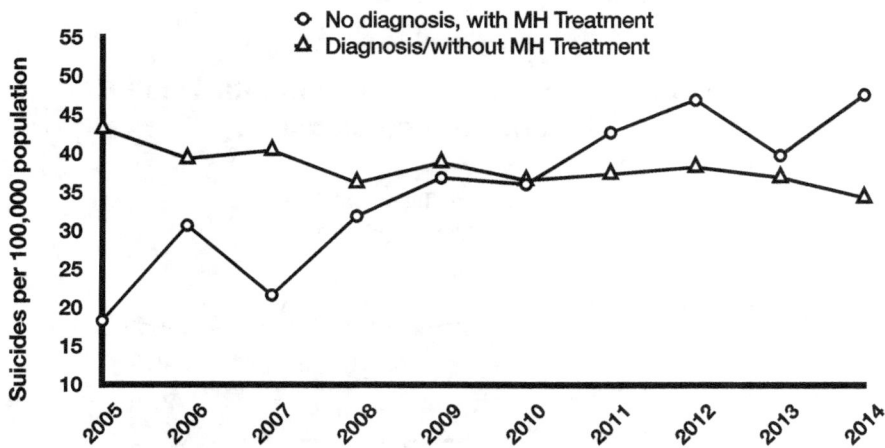

Suicide Rate in Veterans With Less Severe "Treated" Illness Versus More Severe "Untreated" Illness

Source: U.S. Department of Veterans Affairs, "Suicide Among Veterans and Other Americans, 2011-2014. August 3, 2016.

In sum, the data for the four subgroups tells of a suicide risk in 2014 that increased in this steplike fashion:

+ Undiagnosed/untreated: 24.8 per 100,000
+ Diagnosed/untreated: 34.4 per 100,000
+ Undiagnosed/treated: 47.6 per 100,000
+ Diagnosed/treated: 68.2 per 100,000

This is a finding that runs directly counter to the variable suicide rates that would be expected if "treatment" for a mental health condition were effective. However, it is a finding consistent with RCT data showing that antidepressants double the risk of suicide compared to placebo. In the comparison for "diagnosed" patients, that is precisely the increase seen in the treated group.

The Perils of Diagnosis

The suicide rates for those diagnosed with a mental health or substance abuse diagnosis have remained stable since 2005. Year after year they have hovered around 70 per 100,000 population. The reason that the suicide rates for VHA patients have been rising is that the VA's suicide prevention efforts—the outreach campaigns and the mandatory screening—have led to a steady increase in the number of veterans diagnosed and treated for those disorders, and as the VA's subgroup data shows, this moves patients into a category that has the highest suicide rate.

This gets to the mathematical heart of why the VA suicide prevention efforts have failed. The effort is based on the premise that screening will get patients into treatment that will lower their suicide risk, thus lowering the overall suicide rates. But the subgroup data shows that treatment is elevating the risk of suicide, which leads to this tragic equation: screening + drug treatment = increase in veteran suicides.

	Number of Veterans Using VHA Care	% with MH/ SUD Diagnosis	Total Diagnosed	Suicide Rate per 100,000
2005	5,230,872	33%	1,726,188	29.6
2006	5,323,518	34%	1,809,996	30.0
2007	5,378,603	35%	1,882,511	29.7
2008	5,454,501	36%	1,963,620	32.8
2009	5,627,383	37%	2,082,131	30.6
2010	5,837,333	38%	2,218,187	31.7
2011	5,998,133	39%	2,339,271	36.5
2012	6,111,761	40%	2,444,470	33.9
2013	6,211,152	40%	2,599,276	35.5
2014	6,339,698	41%	2,599,276	36.6
2015	6,420,743	42%	2,696,712	37.9
2016	6,467,042	43%	2,780,828	38.7
2017	6,506,469	44%	2,862,846	40.1

Source: U.S. Department of Veterans Affairs, 2019 National Veteran Suicide Prevention Annual Report; U.S Department of Veterans Affairs. "Suicide Among Veterans and Other Americans, 2011-2014." The figures for 2015 to 2017 are projections based on the trends in increase in diagnosis from 2005 to 2014.

The rise in suicide among younger veterans reveals, with great clarity, the perils of screening that leads to treatment with psychiatric drugs.

The VA, as part of its suicide prevention strategy, has sought to bring younger veterans newly discharged from the military into VHA care so that an initial screening for depression, PTSD, and other psychiatric disorders can be done, and their suicide risk assessed. There were 1.2 million veterans who entered VHA care from 2002 to 2015, and 58% of those veterans were given a psychiatric diagnosis.

With this screening protocol and outreach in place, the number of 18-to-34-year-old veterans who received VHA care grew rapidly from 2005 to 2017, from 344,938 to 687,936. Given that 58% of veterans entering care during this period were given a psychiatric diagnosis, it is reasonable to conclude that a high percentage of this population were prescribed antidepressants and other psychiatric medications, which means they were ushered into the "diagnosed and treated" subgroup with the highest risk of suicide.

The suicide numbers tell the tragic result. The suicide rate for VHA-using veterans 18-to-34-years-old rose from 20.9 per 100,000 in 2005 to 51 per 100,000 in 2017, a 144% increase. Moreover, because the number of VHA patients in this age category grew as well, the total number of suicides by younger veterans in VHA care jumped from 68 in 2005 to 351 in 2017, a five-fold increase.

	Number of Veterans Ages 18-34 Using VHA Care	Number of Suicides	Suicide Rate per 100,000
2005	344,938	68	20.9
2006	350,939	73	20.8
2007	384,376	79	20.6
2008	425,730	106	24.9
2009	475,000	114	24.0
2010	526,000	151	28.7
2011	567,481	206	36.3
2012	612,029	204	33.3
2013	648,627	266	41.0
2014	683,549	280	41.0
2015	702,015	304	43.3
2016	702,491	344	49.0
2017	687,936	351	51.0

Source: U.S. Department of Veterans Affairs, 2019 National Veteran Suicide Prevention Annual Report

Veteran Suicides Outside VHA Care

The VHA is understood to provide care to veterans with greater social and medical difficulties than those veterans who receive care outside the VHA. Yet, in non-VHA settings, there are similar pressures to screen for depression and prescribe antidepressants to those who are so diagnosed.

If such pressures are driving up suicide rates for VHA-using veterans, then it could be expected that they would do so in general medical settings as well. The VA's 2019 report documents that this is so. The suicide rate for all non-VHA-using veterans rose from 24.3 per 100,000 in 2005, to 33.9 per 100,000 in 2017, a 40% increase.

Age-Adjusted Suicide Rates for Veterans by VHA Use, 2005 to 2017

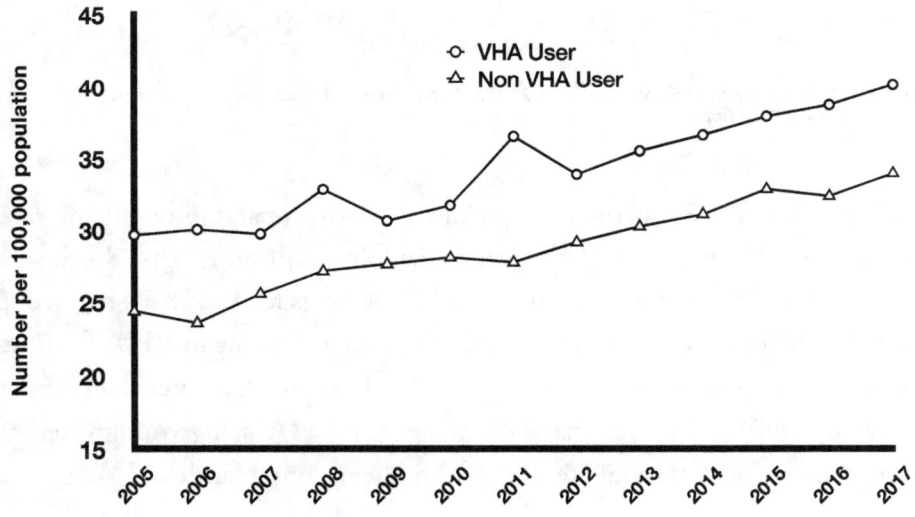

Source: U.S. Department of Veterans Affairs, 2019 National Veteran Suicide Prevention Annual Report

And just like in the case of young VHA-using veterans, the increase in the suicide rate among veterans ages 18 to 34 has been particularly pronounced in non-VHA settings, rising from 26.2 per 100,000 in 2005 to 41.1 per 100,000 in 2017, a 57% increase.

Suicide Rates for Veterans Ages 18-34 by VHA Use, 2005 to 2017

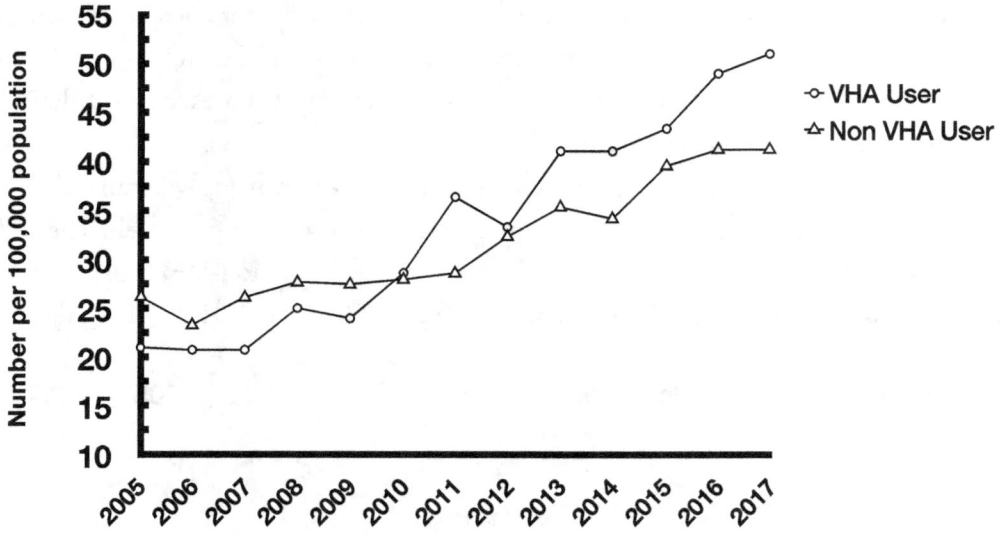

Source: U.S. Department of Veterans Affairs, 2019 National Veteran Suicide Prevention Annual Report, National Data Appendix.

There is one other noteworthy element in this last comparison of suicide rates in the two settings. At the start of the VA's suicide prevention efforts, the suicide rate was lower in VHA settings than in non-VHA settings for the 18-34 age group. Yet, since 2005, the increase in the suicide rate for young veterans in VHA facilities, where screening is imposed with a military rigor, has been much greater than in non-VHA settings. In 2017, the rate was 24% higher for VHA-using young veterans. This may be one more data point telling of the harm done from the VA's suicide prevention efforts.

The Puzzle Pieces Fit Together

The rising suicide rate among veterans since 2005, which is when the VA launched its focused suicide prevention efforts, simply serves as a starting point for an investigation: is there evidence that could explain why such efforts would drive suicide rates upward?

In this case, there is evidence of many types that fit together into a coherent whole. Specifically:

Efforts to improve mental health programs and increase access to psychiatric drugs in global settings have led to increased suicide rates.

+ RCTs have found that antidepressants increase the risk of suicide.
+ Observational studies of depressed patients treated in primary care have found that those who take antidepressants have a higher rate of suicide during follow-up periods.
+ The VA reports tell of an increasing number of veterans exposed to antidepressants and other psychiatric drugs.
+ In the VA's subgroup findings, treated patients in both the diagnosed and undiagnosed comparisons have much higher suicide rates than the untreated patients.
+ In the VA's subgroup findings, from 2010 forward, treated patients without a diagnosis had a higher suicide rate than untreated patients with a diagnosis.

As can be seen, there is in this review a collection of evidence that tells of psychiatric treatment that increases the risk of suicide, with the RCT data for antidepressants at the center of this "evidence base." The VA's suicide reports tell of an increasing number of veterans diagnosed and treated with antidepressants, which could be expected to produce a rising suicide rate, and that is precisely what has occurred since 2005, when the VA initiated its focused suicide prevention efforts.

The VA's Explanations for the Rising Suicide Rates

The VA reports tell of how suicide rates have risen for all veterans, both for those who use VHA care and those who do not. The VA offers several explanations for this rise in suicide in both settings.

First, it notes that this rise has occurred against a backdrop of rising suicide rates in the general public, and thus is not limited to the VA. Second, the VA explains that the suicide rate is higher for VHA-using veterans because, as a group, they suffer from a broader range of ills than the non-VHA-using veterans, such as physical illness, combat injuries, fewer financial resources, and homelessness. Third, the reports cite research comparing the two medical systems that found that "engagement in VHA mental services was associated with decreased rates of suicidal ideation and suicide attempts."

All of that may be true. But none of these explanations address the basic question investigated in this MIA Report: Do suicide prevention efforts that focus on screening for depression and other mental health disorders, with those so diagnosed then regularly treated with antidepressants, increase suicide rates?

If so, they could be expected to increase the suicide rate in the general public, in veterans that use non-VHA medical facilities, and in VHA-using veterans. And that is precisely what has occurred since suicide prevention efforts have been introduced into general medical settings and into VHA care.

Harm Done

There have been more than 70,000 suicides by veterans since 2006, when the VA launched its suicide prevention efforts. It is impossible to calculate the extent of the harm done that is evident in this review of the rising suicide rates in this community of 20 million veterans. However, it is easy to conclude that if suicide rates had remained stable at the rate they were in 2006, there would have been 10,000 to 15,000 fewer suicides among our veterans.

That is a number greater than the total of all combat deaths since 9/11.

All of this begs for further investigation by the U.S. Department of Veterans Affairs.

Reprinted with permission from authors Robert Whitaker and Derek Blumke. The original article was published on November 10, 2019, on the Mad in America website.[89]

About the Authors

Robert Whitaker is a journalist and author of two books about the history of psychiatry, *Mad in America* and *Anatomy of an Epidemic*, and the coauthor, with Lisa Cosgrove, of *Psychiatry Under the Influence*. He is the founder of madinamerica.com.

Derek Blumke is an Air Force veteran; cofounder and past president of Student Veterans of America; former editor of Veterans and Military Families for Mad in America; was the founding director of a national mental health program for the US Department of Veterans Affairs; and was a founding committee member of the National Action Alliance on Suicide Prevention. Derek now chairs the Psychiatric Drug Safety Subgroup of the Michigan Governor's Challenge and leads advocacy efforts for the Grunt Style Foundation to address the role of overprescribing and unsafe prescribing practices of psychiatric medications that has driven a large part of the veteran suicide epidemic.

Notes

1. "Fast Food Worker Salary: Hourly Rate October 2024 USA," ZipRecruiter, n.d., https://www.ziprecruiter.com/Salaries/Fast-Food-Worker-Salary.
2. Sachin R. Pendse, Neha Kumar, and Munmun De Choudhury, "Quantifying the Pollan Effect: Investigating the Impact of Emerging Psychiatric Interventions on Online Mental Health Discourse," *Association for Computing Machinery*, May 11, 2024, https://doi.org/10.1145/3613904.3642477.
3. Sachin R. Pendse, Neha Kumar, and Munmun De Choudhury, "Quantifying the Pollan Effect: Investigating the Impact of Emerging Psychiatric Interventions on Online Mental Health Discourse," *Association for Computing Machinery*, May 11, 2024, https://doi.org/10.1145/3613904.3642477.
4. "The Gut-Brain Connection," Cleveland Clinic, accessed May 1, 2024, https://my.clevelandclinic.org/health/body/the-gut-brain-connection.
5. Stephanie Hollington-Sawyer, "The Wisdom of Trauma," *Dr. Gabor Maté* (blog), May 19, 2024, https://drgabormate.com/the-wisdom-of-trauma/.
6. Nathalie Conrad et al. "Incidence, Prevalence, and Co-occurrence of Autoimmune Disorders Over Time and by Age, Sex, and Socioeconomic Status: A Population-Based Cohort Study of 22 Million Individuals in the UK," *The Lancet* 401, no. 10391 (2023): 1878–90, https://doi.org/10.1016/s0140-6736(23)00457-9.
7. Gabor Maté, *The Myth of Normal: Trauma, Illness, and Healing in a Toxic Culture* (Penguin, 2022).
8. David R. Hawkins, *Power vs. Force*, (Hay House, 2014).
9. Peter A. Levine, *Waking the Tiger: Healing Trauma* (North Atlantic Books, 1997).
10. "The Science of HeartMath," HeartMath, accessed October 4, 2024, https://www.heartmath.com/science/.
11. Rollin McCraty, *Science of the Heart* (HeartMath, 2015), vol. 2, chap. 6, https://www.heartmath.org/research/science-of-the-heart/energetic-communication/.
12. Eduardo E. Schenberg, "Ayahuasca and Cancer Treatment," *SAGE Open Medicine* 1 (2013): 205031211350838, https://doi.org/10.1177/2050312113508389.
13. Ram Dass, "Ram Dass Gives Maharaji the 'Yogi Medicine,'" Love Serve Remember Foundation, 2014, https://www.ramdass.org/ram-dass-gives-maharaji-the-yogi-medicine/.
14. Mary Cronin, "How Does Systems Thinking Enhance Leadership in Sustainability?," *UpThink* (blog), March 28, 2023, https://upthink.works/how-does-systems-thinking-enhance-systems-leadership-in-sustainability/.
15. "Assembly Bill A10375," The New York State Senate, 2023, https://www.nysenate.gov/legislation/bills/2023/A10375.

16. Syed F. Rab, Charles L. Raison, and Elliot Marseille, "An Estimate of the Number of People with Clinical Depression Eligible for Psilocybin-Assisted Therapy in the United States," *Psychedelics* (2024), https://doi.org/10.61373/pp024r.0025.

17. Jennifer M. Mitchell et al., "MDMA-Assisted Therapy for Severe PTSD: A Randomized, Double-Blind, Placebo-Controlled Phase 3 Study," *Nature Medicine* 27, no. 6 (2021): 1025–33, https://doi.org/10.1038/s41591-021-01336-3.

18. "Psychedelic Research," ClusterBusters, n.d., https://clusterbusters.org/pr/psychedelic-research/.

19. SingleCare Team, "Prescription Drug Statistics 2024," The Checkup, January 24, 2024, https://web.archive.org/web/20241230021947/https://www.singlecare.com/blog/news/prescription-drug-statistics/.

20. Brandon Weiss, Victoria Nygart, Lis Marie Pommerencke, Robin L. Carhart-Harris, and David Erritzoe, "Examining Psychedelic-Induced Changes in Social Functioning and Connectedness in a Naturalistic Online Sample Using the Five-Factor Model of Personality," *Frontiers in Psychology* 12 (2021), https://doi.org/10.3389/fpsyg.2021.749788.

21. Max Wolff et al., "Learning to Let Go: A Cognitive-Behavioral Model of How Psychedelic Therapy Promotes Acceptance," *Frontiers in Psychiatry* 11 (2020), https://doi.org/10.3389/fpsyt.2020.00005.

22. Luisa Prochazkova et al., "Microdosing Psychedelics and Its Effect on Creativity: Lessons Learned from Three Double-Blind Placebo Controlled Longitudinal Trials," *PsyArXiv*, June 14, 2021, https://doi.org/10.31234/osf.io/emcxw.

23. Mike Baker, "'Is This Hell?' The Pilot Accused of Trying to Crash a Plane Tells His Story," *The New York Times*, updated November 16, 2023, https://www.nytimes.com/2023/11/10/us/alaska-airlines-pilot-joseph-emerson-mushrooms.html.

24. Mike Baker, "'Is This Hell?' The Pilot Accused of Trying to Crash a Plane Tells His Story," *The New York Times*, updated November 16, 2023, https://www.nytimes.com/2023/11/10/us/alaska-airlines-pilot-joseph-emerson-mushrooms.html.

25. Sandeep M. Nayak et al., "Naturalistic Psilocybin Use Is Associated with Persisting Improvements in Mental Health and Wellbeing: Results From a Prospective, Longitudinal Survey," *Frontiers in Psychiatry* 14 (2023), https://doi.org/10.3389/fpsyt.2023.1199642.

26. Jared T. Hinkle, Mariana Graziosi, Sandeep M. Nayak, and David B. Yaden, "Adverse Events in Studies of Classic Psychedelics: A Systematic Review and Meta-Analysis," *JAMA Psychiatry* 81, no. 12 (2024): 1225–35, https://doi.org/10.1001/jamapsychiatry.2024.2546.

27. "Challenging Psychedelic Experiences Project," Challenging Psychedelic Experiences Project, n.d., https://challengingpsychedelicexperiences.com/.

28. Jules Evans, "Ecstatic Integration," Ecstatic Integration, n.d., https://www.ecstaticintegration.org/.

29. Shariq Mansoor Khan, Gregory T. Carter, Sunil K. Aggarwal, and Julie Holland, "Psychedelics for Brain Injury: A Mini-Review," *Frontiers in Neurology* 12 (2021), https://doi.org/10.3389/fneur.2021.685085.

30. Shariq Mansoor Khan, Gregory T. Carter, Sunil K. Aggarwal, and Julie Holland, "Psychedelics for Brain Injury: A Mini-Review," *Frontiers in Neurology* 12 (2021), https://doi.org/10.3389/fneur.2021.685085.

31. Melissa Suran, "Study Finds Hundreds of Reddit Posts on 'Trip-Killers' for Psychedelic Drugs," *JAMA* 331, no. 8 (2024): 632–34, https://doi.org/10.1001/jama.2023.28257.

32. Otto Simonsson, Peter S. Hendricks, Richard Chambers, Walter Osika, and Simon B. Goldberg, "Prevalence and Associations of Challenging, Difficult or Distressing Experiences Using Classic Psychedelics," *Journal of Affective Disorders* 326 (2023): 105–10, https://doi.org/10.1016/j.jad.2023.01.073.

33. "Mental Illness," National Institute of Mental Health, updated September 2024, https://www.nimh.nih.gov/health/statistics/mental-illness.

34. Alan Watts, *The Wisdom of Insecurity: A Message for an Age of Anxiety* (Vintage, 2011).

35. Leonard Cohen, "Anthem," retrieved from Genius, n.d., https://genius.com/Leonard-cohen-anthem-lyrics.

36. "Plant Dietas," Ayahuasca Foundation, accessed April 24, 2024, https://www.ayahuascafoundation.org/courses/medicinal-plants/plant-dietas/.

37. Ram Jain, "Complete Guide to the 3 Gunas of Nature: Sattva, Rajas and Tamas," *Arhanta Yoga* (blog), accessed May 9, 2024, https://www.arhantayoga.org/blog/sattva-rajas-tamas-gunas/.

38. David Erritzoe, Tommaso Barba, Meg J. Spriggs, Fernando E. Rosas, David J. Nutt, and Robin Carhart-Harris, "Effects of Discontinuation of Serotonergic Antidepressants Prior to Psilocybin Therapy Versus Escitalopram for Major Depression," *Journal of Psychopharmacology* 38, no. 5 (2024): 458–70, https://doi.org/10.1177/02698811241237870.

39. Julia Cameron, *The Artist's Way: 25th Anniversary Edition* (TarcherPerigee, 2016).

40. Belinda Luscombe, "Brené Brown Thinks You Should Talk About These 87 Emotions," *TIME*, November 23, 2021, https://time.com/6122081/brene-brown-atlas-of-the-heart/.

41. Gloria Wilcox, "The Feeling Wheel," Positive Psychology Practitioner's Toolkit, n.d., https://www.gnyha.org/wp-content/uploads/2020/05/The-Feeling-Wheel-Positive-Psycology-Program.pdf.

42. University of Sussex, "It's True: The Sound of Nature Helps Us Relax," ScienceDaily, March 30, 2017, https://www.sciencedaily.com/releases/2017/03/170330132354.htm.

43. "432Hz- Alpha Waves Heal the Whole Body and Spirit, Emotional, Physical, Mental & Spiritual Healing," posted June 10, 2023, by Healing Energy for Soul, YouTube, https://www.youtube.com/watch?v=u3papaX85MA.

44. "All 9 Solfeggio Frequencies - Full Body Aura Cleanse & Cell Regeneration Therapy," posted June 29, 2017, by Meditative Mind, YouTube, https://www.youtube.com/watch?v=goyZbut_KFY.

45. Ally Boothroyd, "Yoga Nidra to Calm the Mind," posted April 30, 2024, by Ally Boothroyd | Sarovara Yoga, YouTube, https://www.youtube.com/watch?v=erPTAbkglE4.

46. Roland R. Griffiths, Ethan S. Hurwitz, Alan K. Davis, Matthew W. Johnson, and Robert Jesse, "Survey of Subjective 'God Encounter Experiences': Comparisons Among Naturally Occurring Experiences and Those Occasioned by the Classic Psychedelics Psilocybin, LSD, Ayahuasca, or DMT," *PLOS ONE* 14, no. 4 (2019): e0214377, https://doi.org/10.1371/journal.pone.0214377.

47. Akemi Furuyashiki, Keiji Tabuchi, Kensuke Norikoshi, Toshio Kobayashi, and Sanae Oriyama, "A Comparative Study of the Physiological and Psychological Effects of Forest Bathing (Shinrin-yoku) on Working Age People With and Without Depressive Tendencies," *Environmental Health and Preventive Medicine* 24 (2019), https://doi.org/10.1186/s12199-019-0800-1.

48. Paulo Coelho, *The Alchemist* (HarperCollins, 2015).

49. Pamela Kryskow, Paul Stamets, Joseph La Torre, Katherine Sattler, Vivian W. L. Tsang, and Monnica Williams, "'The Mushroom Was More Alive and Vibrant': Patient Reports of Synthetic Versus Organic Forms of Psilocybin," *Journal of Psychedelic Studies* 8, no. 3 (2024): 303–12, https://doi.org/10.1556/2054.2024.00379.

50. Jennifer M. Mitchell et al., "MDMA-Assisted Therapy for Moderate to Severe PTSD: A Randomized, Placebo-Controlled Phase 3 Trial," *Nature Medicine* 29 (2023): 2473–80, https://doi.org/10.1038/s41591-023-02565-4.

51. Centers for Disease Control, "Understanding Your Risk for Cannabis Use Disorder," CDC, December 5, 2024, https://www.cdc.gov/cannabis/health-effects/cannabis-use-disorder.html.

52. Fireside Project, Fireside Project, n.d., https://firesideproject.org/.

53. Mollie M. Pleet, Joshua White, Joseph A. Zamaria, and Rachel Yehuda, "Reducing the Harms of Nonclinical Psychedelics Use Through a Peer-Support Telephone Helpline," *Psychedelic Medicine* 1, no. 2 (2023): 69–73, https://doi.org/10.1089/psymed.2022.0017.

54. Scott Jeffrey, "List of Virtues: A Master List from Ancient Traditions," *Scott Jeffrey* (blog), August 17, 2024, https://scottjeffrey.com/list-of-virtues/.

55. Mark Haden and Birgitta Woods, "LSD Overdoses: Three Case Reports," *Journal of Studies on Alcohol and Drugs* 81, no. 1 (2020): 115–18, https://pubmed.ncbi.nlm.nih.gov/32048609/.

56. Erowid, "LSD Dosage," The Vaults of Erowid, n.d., https://erowid.org/chemicals/lsd/lsd_dose.shtml.

57. Rachel Mabe, "Jim Harris Was Paralyzed. Then He Ate Magic Mushrooms.," *Outside*, November 9, 2022, https://www.outsideonline.com/outdoor-adventure/exploration-survival/psychedelics-research-paralysis-treatment-jim-harris/.

58. Ido Hartogsohn, "Constructing Drug Effects: A History of Set and Setting," *Drug Science, Policy and Law* (2017), https://doi.org/10.1177/2050324516683325.

59. Michael James Winkelman, "The Evolved Psychology of Psychedelic Set and Setting: Inferences Regarding the Roles of Shamanism and Entheogenic Ecopsychology," *Frontiers in Pharmacology* 12 (2021), https://doi.org/10.3389/fphar.2021.619890.

60. Otto Simonsson, Peter S. Hendricks, Richard Chambers, Walter Osika, and Simon B. Goldberg, "Prevalence and Associations of Challenging, Difficult or Distressing Experiences Using Classic Psychedelics," *Journal of Affective Disorders* 326 (2023): 105–10, https://doi.org/10.1016/j.jad.2023.01.073.

61. Jules Evans et al., "Extended Difficulties Following the Use of Psychedelic Drugs: A Mixed Methods Study," *PLOS ONE* 18, no. 10 (2023): e0293349, https://doi.org/10.1371/journal.pone.0293349.

62. Logan Neitzke-Spruill, "Race as a Component of Set and Setting: How Experiences of Race Can Influence Psychedelic Experiences," *Journal of Psychedelic Studies* 4, no. 1 (2019): 51–60, https://doi.org/10.1556/2054.2019.022.

63. Ralph Metzner and Timothy Leary, "On Programming Psychedelic Experiences," *Psychedelic Review* 9 (1967): 5–19, https://maps.org/wp-content/uploads/2007/11/n09005met.pdf.

64. William James, "The Varieties of Religious Experience: A Study in Human Nature," (Longmans, Green and Co., 1902), http://dx.doi.org/10.1037/10004-000.

65. Suzanne L. Russ, Robin L. Carhart-Harris, Geoffrey Maruyama, and Melody S. Elliott, "States and Traits Related to the Quality and Consequences of Psychedelic Experiences," *Psychology of Consciousness: Theory Research and Practice* 6, no. 1 (2018): 1–21, https://doi.org/10.1037/cns0000169.

66. Bill Wilson, *Alcoholics Anonymous: The Big Book* (Ixia Press, 2019).

67. Tim Ferriss, "Breathing Techniques to Reduce Stress and Anxiety | Dr. Andrew Huberman on the Physiological Sigh," posted on October 25, 2021, by Tim Ferriss, YouTube, https://www.youtube.com/watch?v=kSZKIupBUuc.

68. Darren M. Slade, Adrianna Smell, Elizabeth Wilson, and Rebekah Drumsta, "Percentage of U.S. Adults Suffering from Religious Trauma: A Sociological Study," *Socio-Historical Examination of Religion and Ministry* 5, no. 1 (2023): 1–28, https://doi.org/10.33929/sherm.2023.vol5.no1.01.

69. Michael Lipka and Claire Gecewicz, "More Americans Now Say They're Spiritual but Not Religious," *Pew Research Center*, September 6, 2017, https://www.pewresearch.org/short-reads/2017/09/06/more-americans-now-say-theyre-spiritual-but-not-religious/.

70. Jeffrey M. Jones, "In U.S., 47% Identify as Religious, 33% as Spiritual," *Gallup*, September 22, 2023, https://news.gallup.com/poll/511133/identify-religious-spiritual.aspx.

71. Roland R. Griffiths, Ethan S. Hurwitz, Alan K. Davis, Matthew W. Johnson, and Robert Jesse, "Survey of Subjective 'God Encounter Experiences': Comparisons Among Naturally Occurring Experiences and Those Occasioned by the Classic Psychedelics Psilocybin, LSD, Ayahuasca, or DMT," *PLOS ONE* 14, no. 4 (2019): e0214377, https://doi.org/10.1371/journal.pone.0214377.

72. Rachael Petersen, "Taking Mushrooms for Depression Cured Me of My Atheism," The Outline, April 29, 2019, https://theoutline.com/post/7367/taking-mushrooms-for-depression-cured-me-of-my-atheism.

73. Erika Perez, "How to Create an Intention for Your Psychedelic Experience," Psychedelic Passage, December 9, 2023, https://www.psychedelicpassage.com/how-to-create-an-intention-for-your-psychedelic-experience/.

74. Christina Grof and Stanislav Grof, *Spiritual Emergency: When Personal Transformation Becomes a Crisis* (Penguin, 1989).

75. Jennifer Cooper et al., "Classification of Patient-Safety Incidents in Primary Care," *Bulletin of the World Health Organization* 96, no. 7 (2018): 498–505, https://pmc.ncbi.nlm.nih.gov/articles/PMC6022620/.

76. Wikipedia contributors, "Overview Effect," Wikipedia, accessed October 5, 2024, https://en.wikipedia.org/wiki/Overview_effect.

77. Stanislav Grof, *LSD Psychotherapy* (Hunter House, 1980).

78. Joshua S. Siegel et al., "Psilocybin Desynchronizes the Human Brain," *Nature* 632 (2024): 131–38, https://doi.org/10.1038/s41586-024-07624-5.

79. Toketemu Ohwovoriole, "Critical Period in Brain Development: Definition, Importance," Verywell Mind, July 25, 2023, https://www.verywellmind.com/critical-period-in-brain-development-definition-importance-7556041.

80. Romain Nardou et al., "Psychedelics Reopen the Social Reward Learning Critical Period," *Nature* 618 (2023): 790–98, https://doi.org/10.1038/s41586-023-06204-3.

81. Sam Harris, *Waking Up: A Guide to Spirituality Without Religion* (Simon and Schuster, 2014).

82. Michael Noetel et al., "Effect of Exercise for Depression: Systematic Review and Network Meta-Analysis of Randomised Controlled Trials," *BMJ* 384 (2024): e075847, https://doi.org/10.1136/bmj-2023-075847.

83. Marc Aixalà, *Psychedelic Integration: Psychotherapy for Non-Ordinary States of Consciousness* (Synergetic Press, 2022).

84. Sean Lawlor, "Psychedelic Bypassing: When Avoidance Is Mistaken for Healing," Psychedelics Today, accessed June 5, 2024, https://psychedelicstoday.com/2024/06/05/psychedelic-bypassing-when-avoidance-is-mistaken-for-healing/.

85. Innocence Staff, "How Eyewitness Misidentification Can Send Innocent People to Prison," Innocence Project, April 15, 2020, https://innocenceproject.org/how-eyewitness-misidentification-can-send-innocent-people-to-prison/.

86. Tomas Frymann, Sophie Whitney, David B. Yaden, and Joshua Lipson, "The Psychedelic Integration Scales: Tools for Measuring Psychedelic Integration Behaviors and Experiences," *Frontiers in Psychology* 13 (2022), https://doi.org/10.3389/fpsyg.2022.863247.

87. "What Is Swadharma?," Art of Living, June 7, 2013, https://www.artofliving.org/what-swadharma.

88. Thomas Lewis, Fari Amini, and Richard Lannon, *A General Theory of Love* (Random House, 2000).

89. Robert Whitaker and Derek Blumke, "Screening + Drug Treatment = Increase in Veteran Suicides," Mad in America, November 10, 2019, https://www.madinamerica.com/2019/11/screening-drug-treatment-increase-veteran-suicides/.

www.ingramcontent.com/pod-product-compliance
Lightning Source LLC
Chambersburg PA
CBHW081653120626
46550CB00010B/2877